A Home for the Homeless

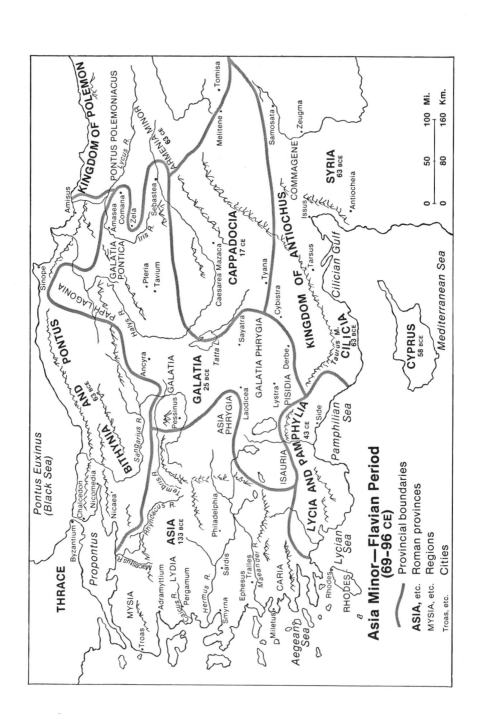

Asia Minor—Flavian Period (69–96 CE)

Provincial boundaries

ASIA, etc.   Roman provinces

MYSIA, etc.   Regions

Troas, etc.   Cities

THRACE

Pontus Euxinus (Black Sea)

KINGDOM OF POLEMON

PONTUS POLEMONIACUS

ARMENIA MINOR

•Tomisa

•Melitene

Samosata

COMMAGENE •Zeugma

SYRIA 63 BCE

•Antiocheia

Mediterranean Sea

KINGDOM OF ANTIOCHUS

Issus•

•Tarsus

Cilician Gulf

CILICIA 63 BCE

CYPRUS 58 BCE

Taurus M.

•Cybistra

•Tyana

CAPPADOCIA 17 CE

Caesarea Mazaca

•Pteria

•Tavium

GALATIA PONTICA

Amisus

Amasea •Comana

Zela•

Sebastea•

Iris R.

Lycus R.

KINGDOM OF POLEMON

Sinope•

PAPHLAGONIA

Halys R.

Ancyra•

GALATIA

GALATIA 25 BCE

Tatta L.

GALATIA PHRYGIA

•Sayatra

Derbe•

PISIDIA

ISAURIA

•Lystra

•Laodicea

ASIA PHRYGIA

Pessinus•

Sangarius R.

BITHYNIA AND PONTUS 63 BCE

Byzantium•

Chalcedon•

Nicomedia•

Nicaea•

Propontis

Rhyndacus R.

Maeesus R.

MYSIA

•Troas

Adramyttium•

Pergamum

Caicus R.

Hermus R.

LYDIA

Sardis•

Philadelphia•

Smyrna•

Ephesus•

Tralles•

Meander R.

Miletus•

CARIA

RHODES Rhodes•

Aegean Sea

ASIA 133 BCE

LYCIA AND PAMPHYLIA 43 CE

•Side

Lycian Sea

Pamphilian Sea

0   50   100 Mi.

0   80   160 Km.

A Sociological Exegesis of
1 Peter, Its Situation and Strategy

A Home for the Homeless

JOHN H. ELLIOTT

FORTRESS PRESS   **PHILADELPHIA**

ACKNOWLEDGMENTS

I am grateful to the following for permission to quote from their publications:

Harper and Row, Publishers, Inc., and Heinemann Educational Books, London, for permission to quote from *Magic and the Millennium* by Bryan R. Wilson. Copyright © 1973.

Harper and Row, Publishers, Inc., (Thomas Y. Crowell), for permission to quote from *The Social Philosophers* by Robert Nisbet. Copyright © 1973.

The American Sociological Association for permission to quote from "An Analysis of Sect Development" by Bryan R. Wilson in the *American Sociological Review*, vol. 24, 1959.

Biblical quotations, unless otherwise noted, are from the Revised Standard Version of the Bible, copyrighted 1946, 1952, © 1971, 1973 by the Division of Christian Education of the National Council of the Churches of Christ in the U.S.A., and are used by permission.

Library of Congress Cataloging in Publication Data

Elliott, John Hall.
A home for the homeless.

Includes bibliographical references and indexes.
1. Bible. N.T. 1 Peter—Criticism, interpretation, etc. 2. Sociology, Biblical. I. Title.
BS2795.2.E42   227'.9206   80–2394
ISBN 0–8006–0659–0   AACR1

8584K80   Printed in the United States of America   1–659

To Greg and Michael

Hört man stille und lange zu, so zeigt auch die Wander-sehnsucht ihren Kern und Sinn. Sie ist nicht Fortlaufen-wollen vor dem Leide, wie es schien. Sie ist Sehnsucht nach Heimat, nach Gedächtnis der Mutter, nach neuen Gleichnissen des Lebens. Sie führt nach Hause. Jeder Weg führt nach Hause, jeder Schritt ist Geburt, jeder Schritt ist Tod, jedes Grab ist Mutter.

—Hermann Hesse, *Wanderungen*

Contents

Abbreviations

The abbreviations of ancient texts, reference works, periodicals and serials are those prescribed in the *Journal of Biblical Literature* 90 (1971) 510–19. The following additional or alternate abbreviations have also been used:

BAGD   W. Bauer, W. F. Arndt, F. W. Gingrich, and F. Danker, *Greek-English Lexicon of the New Testament,* 2d revised and augmented edition, 1979

CIL   *Corpus Inscriptionum Latinarum* 1863–1909

ESAR   T. Frank (ed.), *An Economic Survey of Ancient Rome,* 4 vols.

FGrHist   *Fragmente der Griechischen Historiker,* F. Jacoby (ed.)

FS   Festschrift

IGR   R. Cagnat (ed.), *Inscriptiones Graecae ad Res Romanas pertinentes,* 4 vols., 1911–14

KEK   H. A. W. Meyer, *Kritisch-exegetischer Kommentar über das Neue Testament*

LCL   Loeb Classical Library

LSJ   H. G. Liddell, R. Scott, and H. S. Jones, *A Greek-English Lexicon,* revised and augmented edition, 1940 (including *A Supplement,* 1968)

MM   J. H. Moulton and G. Milligan (eds.), *The Vocabulary of the Greek New Testament*

OGIS   W. Dittenberger (ed.), *Orientis Graeci Inscriptiones Selectae,* 2 vols. 1903–05

SEHHW	M. Rostovtzeff, *The Social and Economic History of the Hellenistic World,* 3 vols., 1941 (corrected impression, 1953)
SEHRE	M. Rostovtzeff, *The Social and Economic History of the Roman Empire,* 2 vols., 2. revised edition, 1957
SIG³	W. Dittenberger (ed.), *Sylloge Inscriptionum Graecarum,* 4 vols., 3. ed., 1915–24 (SIG³ = Dit., *Syll.*)
TBLNT	L. Coenen, E. Beyreuther, and M. Bietenhard (eds.), *Theologisches Begriffslexikon zum Neuen Testament,* 2 vols.
THAT	E. Jenni and C. Westermann (eds.), *Theologisches Handwörterbuch zum Alten Testament,* 2 vols.

Preface

This study of homelessness and strangerhood is itself the product of an odyssey. What began several years ago as an article has, during a sabbatical leave from the University of San Francisco in 1977–1978, become a book. So it is only appropriate for me at this point to express a word of thanks to all the hosts who have sustained and sheltered me during its composition with their fraternal hospitality and words of encouragement and critique.

Colleagues in the Bay Area Seminar for Theology and Related Disciplines provided the first testing ground for the hypotheses set forth here as well as the company for interdisciplinary dialogue and religiously motivated social action. My work with Norman K. Gottwald in particular has been a constant source of sociotheological insight and stimulus for challenging what he has called the "domain assumptions" of historiography and exegesis. During my term as scholar in residence at the Institut zur Erforschung des Urchristentums in Tübingen (fall, 1977), the director, Dr. S. Scott Bartchy, painstakingly scrutinized an original draft of this manuscript and contributed much to its reorganization and clarification. In the spring semester of 1978 writing continued in Rome where, as visiting professor of the Catholic Biblical Association of America, I taught a course on 1 Peter at the Pontifical Biblical Institute. The students there, particularly those from marginally Christian situations in the Third World, gave me valuable feedback as well as illuminating analogies for understanding and describing the situation of the Christians in 1 Peter. In the Institute as well as the Collegio S. Roberto Bellarmino where I lived,

I enjoyed the hospitality of my Jesuit *fratelli* who cordially received this Lutheran *paroikos* of sorts into their *oikos* and broadened my experience of Christian fraternity. To my colleague in the sociology department at USF, Dr. Shirley Cartwright, I am indebted not only for an extensive critique of the sociological orientation of this study but, even more, for her generous mystagogic efforts on behalf of my initiation into the mysteries of the sociological discipline. The staffs of the library of the Pontifical Biblical Institute and of Gleeson Library at USF have taught me anew the extent to which librarians are the right arms of the scholars. A right arm and more is what Joseph A. Romeo has been over the years. To him I am most recently indebted for the careful typing and meticulous proofreading of the entire manuscript, as for aid in the preparation of the indexes.

To one and all I offer my profound gratitude together with the obvious exoneration of complicity in any errors of fact or judgment.

In this International Year of the Child, 1979, I dedicate this study on home and homelessness to my children Greg and Michael. During its composition they have been so patient with their absent father and yet so instrumental in my experience of home.

University of San Francisco   JOHN H. ELLIOTT

Introduction

SOCIOLOGICAL EXEGESIS:
SOME METHODOLOGICAL PROLEGOMENA

This study is an exercise in sociological exegesis—an attempt to articulate a fresh interdisciplinary approach to some unresolved issues. It complements and improves the prevailing method of biblical interpretation through more rigorous attention to the social dimension of the biblical text and to the sociological dimension of the exegetical task. The focus of this sociological exegesis is the first epistle of Peter; more specifically, the focus is on the circumstances of its origin, composition and socioreligious strategy, and its contribution to the consolidation, theology and ideology of the early Christian movement in Asia Minor.

One of the most noteworthy and promising developments in the world of biblical scholarship is the growing interest in the social world of the Bible and the social dimension of its literature. To a great extent this interest is no doubt traceable to the experiences and frustrations produced by the times in which we all live. It is an age of social and political upheaval, a period rife with public and private insecurity, protest and movement against immoral discriminations, undeclared wars, corruption in high places, international conspiracies, technological and multicorporational oppression, underground and aboveground terrorism, and all the other disintegrating inhumanities to which our atomic age flesh has become heir. Small wonder, in the face of such everyday experiences, that exegetes and theologians along with all the rest of Adam's kin should experience a raising of their social consciousness and a growing sensitivity to the social implications of their religious life and loyalties.

For theologians and for those lay people and experts alike who have the desire or the charge to hear the word of God afresh in the present hour, such social sensitization cannot help but stimulate the need for a rigorous social hermeneutic, a more alert and refined socioreligious perspective on the conditions of life under which we live and the visions of hope we entertain. Once venerable traditions and useful or "meaningful" world views have, in times such as these, a proclivity toward instant obsolescence. New categories of thought and fresh models of analysis and critique become necessary in order to comprehend the complexities of the day.

It is not the nature and spirit of our time, however, which alone account for the current social interests of a growing number of exegetes. It is the perceived limitations of the exegetical art itself. John G. Gager, in a groundbreaking study of "the social world of early Christianity,"[1] has enumerated several of these limitations and has thereby articulated a discontent among exegetes that has been brewing for some time. In general this discontent stems from an awareness that "the study of early Christian materials [or of the biblical materials in their totality] has been characterized by an overemphasis on a literary-historical and theological point of view to the detriment of the sociological."[2] For Gager this means that narrowly limited perspectives have obscured the fact that early Christianity was "a social world in the making." It means as well that any attempt to derive insight and inspiration from the biblical witness for the contemporary articulation of a Christian social ethic or a religious response to the social situation today labors under enormous and unnecessary restrictions.

The problem for exegetes has not been the absence of good intentions but the lack of a sociological method adequate for the task. What has failed heretofore is a genuinely sociological perspective and a sociological technique.

To be sure, emphasis upon social context, the social conditioning and the social *Sitz im Leben* of the biblical documents has been a hallmark of modern biblical interpretation. This focus, however, has characterized the spirit more than the letter, the intention more than the praxis, of modern exegesis. Form critics, for instance, from the progenitors Gunkel, Dibelius and Bultmann onward, have attended to the question of the situational context of the biblical documents and their component traditions. Where *explicit evidence* as to social and historical context is contained in the texts themselves, such data have been collected in order to ascertain *what* was going on *when* and *where*. This information, we have assumed, would help us understand the form and content of the oral and written traditions under analysis. The detection of *implicit evidence,* however, is another matter. Such detection requires an ability to "read between the lines," as it were, the exercise of sociological imagination and conceptualization. At this point conventional exegesis has been stymied and generally has resorted to the various situational standbys of conditioning didactic, missionary, cultic or apologetic circumstances. Small wonder that in this dilemma exegetical dissensus runs rampant. Moreover, the terms "social" and "sociological" have generally been used indiscriminately so that mere social description has been equated—erroneously—with sociological explanation. What has been lacking is a process for ascertaining not only *what* the sociohistorical circumstances of given traditions and compositions were but also *how* and *why* these circumstances gave rise to the productions under consideration. That which is needed is a means for conceptualizing and explaining the interrelation of the biblical literature and its social world, the conditions under which specific literary documents were produced and circulated, and the specific socioreligious functions which such products were designed to serve. An urgent desideratum of the exegetical enterprise, in short, is the development of a sociology of the scriptural literature.

Our attention has been directed predominantly to the literary and formal features of a document, its traditional components, its redaction and theological themes and motifs. Social data have been used often merely to "round out the picture," illustrating or clarifying literary or theological conclusions already formulated. What is needed is a procedure for appropriating and applying sociological models and concepts which at each stage of the exegetical analysis could aid our understanding and interpretation of the interrelation of literary, theological and sociological aspects and dimensions of composition.

Moreover, we have generally assumed, perhaps without reflection or intention, that history is basically or essentially the history of *ideas*. In our analysis of the literature and history of the early church we have conceived of the problems facing the early Christians almost exclusively in conceptual terms. Letters, gospels and other documents were composed, we have said, in order to combat wrongheaded ideas, false Christologies, and theological heresies, or to propagate ideas, say, of salvation as history. The significance or influence of specifically social needs, social conflicts, group interests and clashing ideologies has received little attention or mention. Exegetically we have failed to take account of the fact that all ideas, concepts and knowledge are socially determined. And we have lacked the stimulus or the means for analyzing the correlation or reciprocity between social realities and religious symbolizations.

Where and when social factors have been examined, this analysis has regularly been subsumed under the rubric of *"historical criticism,"* Text*geschichte,* Form*geschichte,* Traditions*geschichte,* etc. The predominant, if not exclusive, focus has been upon historical diachronic sequence rather than upon social synchronic interaction as well. The qualifying adjectives "historical" and "social" (or occasionally "sociological") have been used as though they were synonymous. There is, to be sure, an obvious relation between the disciplines of history and sociology. It is equally obvious, however, that each discipline has its specific and indispensable point of reference. Our *Religionsgeschichte* all too often has been a *Theologiegeschichte* lacking a *sozialgeschichtliche* component.

As lively heirs of our nineteenth-century forebears, furthermore, we have continued to nurture the notion that biblical history and biblical texts were the results of *individual* genius. The charismatic character and power of many specific individuals in the undulating course of biblical history are indeed not to be denied. But we have as yet failed to grasp the significance of Max Weber's epoch-making study of charisma which stresses the fact that even charisma is a *social* phenomenon. Charisma is not simply the innate power, genius, and leadership quality of individuals; it is power and authority that are recognized and accepted by others. Charisma applies and pertains to the existence of *groups.* It is such groups and not individuals alone who are the shakers of the established foundations and the movers of history. What has yet to be developed in exegesis is a sophisticated sociological approach to such group phenomena as the stimuli of group formation, the conditions of social organization, the cultivation and expression (including religious expression) of group interests and goals, the conflict of diverse interest groups and their varying ideologies, and the effect of group interaction, both internal and external, upon the composition of the biblical literature as well as upon the direction and success of the movements to which the groups belong. In a word, the task yet before exegetes is the interpretation of the biblical literature as products and reflections of a dynamic social process, of socioreligious movements. We have still to develop a method for perceiving and explaining the interstices of biography, institutions and history and the correlation of "religious worlds of meaning" with the factors and forces of politics, economics, social structures and culture in general.

That which is needed in contemporary exegesis is the cultivation of "sociological imagination" and the development of a sociological-exegetical method. The first phrase is that of the sociologist C. Wright Mills.[3] Sociological imagination, according to Mills, "enables its possessors to understand the larger historical scene in terms of its meaning for the inner life and the external career of a variety of individuals." It is concerned with the *intersections* of biography and history. It attends to such issues as the structures of particular societies and the relation of their essential components, and the meaning of their peculiar features for group continuance and change; the specific place of societies within human history and their characteristic ways of history-making; the varieties of men and women within a society of a given period and the manner in which they are liberated or repressed, alienated or offered fellowship; the distinction and relation of "the personal troubles of milieu" and "the public issues of social structure." "To be aware of the idea of social structure," Mills maintains, "and to use it with sensibility is to be capable of tracing such linkages among a great variety of milieux. To be able to do that is to possess the sociological imagination."[4]

Such a need for sociological imagination has indeed begun to capture the theological imagination of an ever increasing number of the international exegetical guild. Gager himself has listed several "encouraging signs of discontent" with the limitations of our exegetical approaches thus far, including closer scrutiny of the social conditions of oral tradition, of historical and theological "trajectories," and of the conditions and concerns of redactional composition.[5] This interest is further evident in the several national and international professional exegetical societies which have established "task forces" or subgroups whose aim is to analyze "the social world of early Israel" or to produce a "social description of early Christianity."[6] Although still in its infancy, this movement among contemporary exegetes, if we can call it such, has already produced an impressive body of literature.[7] Useful interdisciplinary bibliographies[8] are being assembled, possible methodological correlations between exegesis and the subdisciplines of sociology in particular are being discussed[9] and exegetical studies with a sociological orientation are now beginning to appear in growing number.[10]

In the field of New Testament research the work of an American on one side of the Atlantic, John G. Gager,[11] and that of a German scholar, Gerd Theissen,[12] on the other, deserve particular mention. Both scholars have offered imaginative and innovative interpretations of the social world and social movements of early Christianity which have drawn heavily on the research and perspectives of sociology; and both have succeeded in kindling curiosity, stimulating ire, and in any case provoking wide and lively reactions throughout the international exegetical world.

To this current interest in the social world of early Christianity could be added still further exhibits of international research including Fernando Belo's *Lecture matérialiste de l'évangile de Marc* (2. rev. ed., 1975),[13] Robert McQueen Grant's *Early Christianity and Society* (1977),[14] Abraham J. Malherbe's *Social Aspects of Early Christianity* (1977),[15] and the publications of a team of scholars in Germany: *Jesus von Nazareth— Hoffnung der Armen* by Luise Schottroff and Wolfgang Stegemann (1978)[16] and the two-volume work *Der Gott der kleinen Leute: Sozialgeschichtliche Auslegungen,* a collection of Old and New Testament studies edited by Willy Schottroff and Wolfgang Stegemann (1979).[17]

Most of these studies illustrate one or more of the methodological approaches enumerated in a survey article by Jonathan Z. Smith under the title "The Social Description of Early Christianity."[18] Such approaches may have as their goals either: (1) "a description of the *social facts* given in early Christian materials, i.e., the *realia* which they contain"; or (2) "the achievement of a genuine *social history* of early Christianity" or of specific phases of the Christian movement; or (3) an analysis of "the *social organization* of early Christianity in terms of both the *social forces* which led to the rise of Christianity and the *social institutions* of early Christianity"; or (4) an interpretation of "early Christianity as a *social world,* as the creation of a world of meaning which provided a plausibility structure for those who chose to inhabit it." The main focus of current research has been on the social features, processes and developments of early Christianity. Exegetical data are employed and correlated with historical and social data in order to arrive at fresh understandings and interpretations of early Christian organization, internal and external social interaction, and phases of early Christian social history. The differences in the approaches taken often reflect the degree to which actual sociological theory and method are involved in the analysis, the degree to which sociology is seen as a necessary instrument of social-historical description and interpretation.

In combination with such socially oriented research, I would suggest, however, there is also need for a sociologically oriented exegesis of individual texts. The biblical documents themselves are already the products and instruments of social forces and social interaction. In addition to the need for a comprehensive social description of early Christianity on a broad scale, there is a need for a social understanding of the texts which are employed to construct that larger description. This would serve the purposes of mutual corroboration and critique. Heretofore we have described exegesis as a historical-critical enterprise: the analysis of texts as determined by their historical contexts. The results of such exegesis were used along with other relevant data to reconstruct the history of early Christianity. To this procedure we now need to add the sociological ingredient. Exegesis is also a social-critical enterprise: the analysis of texts as determined by their social as well as historical contexts. From such social-critical exegesis come the building blocks for the reconstruction of the social world and social history of early Christianity. As this interpretation of the social world provides the contours within which the documents are interpreted, so a sociological exegesis of the documents provides the data by which the larger delineations of social history are corroborated and critiqued.

Among biblical scholars currently interested in the social world of the Bible and the social dimensions of its literature, various labels have been given to the varying approaches taken. Some describe their work as "social description," others as "biblical sociology," or "sociology of the Bible," "a materialist reading of the Scriptures," "social history," "social hermeneutic," or as a specific branch of the "sociology of literature." Since the primary concern of the following study is with the social dimension and interpretation of a specific biblical *text,* namely 1 Peter, rather than with the general social world of early Christianity, I describe the approach which I have taken as *sociological exegesis.* This phrase or methodological label succinctly designates the two main features of the method of interpretation which has been employed.

As applied in the study of 1 Peter in particular and of biblical documents in general, sociological exegesis is the analytic and synthetic interpretation

7

of a text through the combined exercise of the exegetical and sociological disciplines, their principles, theories and techniques. The method is *sociological* in that it involves the employment of the perspectives, presuppositions, modes of analysis, comparative models, theories and research of the discipline of sociology. It is *exegetical* in that it focuses centrally upon a biblical document and through the employment of all the subdisciplines of exegesis attempts to determine the meaning and impact of that text within its various contexts. For such a sociological exegesis, in distinction from other socially oriented study of Scripture, the literary text serves as the primary focus, starting point, and empirical control of sociological analysis. Its primary goal is the interpretation of the text as it has been designed to serve as a vehicle of socioreligious interaction. Sociological exegesis asks not only what a text said "then and there" but also how and why that text was designed to function, and what its impact upon the life and activity of its recipients and formulators was intended to be. A more comprehensive designation of the method would be a "literary-historical-sociological-theological analysis" with each aspect of the exegesis understood as interrelated with the other. The *textual* focus of the analysis distinguishes it from the wider diachronic scope of social history and from the synchronic analysis of an entire society at a given period. At the same time the relation of the text to both synchronic and diachronic factors remains an important issue for purposes of mutual exegetical, historical and sociological corroboration and critique.

The general objective of our sociological exegesis is the analysis, interpretation, and synthesis (correlation) of (1) the literary, sociological and theological features and dimensions of the text (1 Peter) and (2) this text's relation to and impact upon its narrower and wider social contexts. More specifically, the objective of our sociological exegesis is the determination of the social as well as literary and theological conditions, content and intended consequences of our text; that is, the determination of the sum of its features which make it a vehicle of social interaction and an instrument of social as well as literary and theological consequence. The immediate field of interaction to be interpreted comprises the author(s) and intended recipients, their respective situations (political, historical, social, economic, cultural and religious), the nature of their relationship, and the manner in which the text is designed through the literary, sociological and theological strategy of its author(s) to be a specific response to the specific situation of the intended audience as perceived by the author(s). The wider field of interaction to be interpreted comprises the intended and/or actual effect of the document upon the social condition, constitution, and interests of both author(s) and recipients within their larger social and historical contexts.

Such an interdisciplinary approach to a biblical text involves a plethora of presuppositions. In general it may be said that a sociological exegesis operates comprehensively and yet critically with the received presuppositions and methodological principles of both sociological and exegetical disciplines. This requires as wide an acquaintance with, and as critical an acceptance of, the assumptions, procedures and "assured results" of each discipline as is possible. In addition, however, the fusion of the perspectives and procedures of both disciplines may well be expected to generate new methodological insights and cast unidisciplinary presuppositions and techniques into critical light. The following presuppositions, however, seem to me especially worthy of note.

1. To commence with the obvious, a sociologically oriented exegesis assumes that biblical documents and the traditions which they receive and redact are the products and vehicles of ongoing social interaction. They reflect not isolated or static moments in history but rather transindividual and often recurrent and comparable actions and movements in an ongoing social-historical process.

2. A sociological exegesis of a biblical text therefore attempts to discover and explain the interpersonal or social *trans*actions and relationships to which a text points either explicitly or implicitly. Moreover, such analysis is directed beyond the aspects of individuality and peculiarity to the aspects of the typical, the recurrent, and the general. Beyond a singular conditioning factor of a specific situation it is concerned with the structure of social relationships which characterize many and repeated situations.

3. A further assumption, derived from the sociology of knowledge, is that biblical texts and the perspectives which they represent are conditioned socially as well historically and religiously. The ideas which the texts formulate, most often in theological symbolical form, stand in a reciprocal relationship with the social experience, the class position and status, the activities and interests of their formulators. "Theories and ideas," as Peter Berger has put it,

> continually interact with the human activity from which they spring. . . . The relationship between consciousness and activity is a dialectical one— activity produces ideas, which in turn produce new forms of activity. The

9

more or less permanent constellations of activity we know as "societies" are, therefore, in an ongoing dialectical relationship with the "worlds" that form the cognitive and normative meaning coordinates of individual existence. Religious worlds, as much as any others, are thus produced by an infrastructure of social activity and, in turn, act back upon this infrastructure.[19]

Sociological exegesis attempts to discover and explain this dialectical interaction of theory and praxis, of theological literary expression and social experience.

4. The social factors that condition a biblical text are often more implicit than explicit or are mentioned selectively. Therefore a sociological exegesis must employ not only what Theissen[20] calls a "constructive procedure" in assessing the explicit social *realia* mentioned in a given text. It must also employ analytic and comparative methods which operate by inference or *Rückschlussverfahren*. It attempts social reconstruction through inferences drawn from historical occurrences, evident social norms and religious symbols. It examines the affinity between the social world and the semantic, structural and paradigmatic aspects of the text and its religious myths. And it seeks supplementary information on social structures, activities and modes of interaction through the comparative use of analogous explicit social data and sociological models. Through such analysis the exegete attempts, as in form criticism and yet beyond its restricted interest in the correlation of literary *form* and *Sitz im Leben,* to infer from the sum features of a given document's genre, structure and content the *function* or social impact (*Wirkung*)[21] that a text was designed to have in the realm of social interaction.

5. Sociological exegesis thus operates less with the conventional correlation of form and *Sitz im Leben* or of "occasion and purpose," often conceived in purely theological terms (e.g., "heresies" which necessitated gospels), than with the *correlation of situation and strategy.*[22] I use the term "situation" to designate what Klaus Berger[23] refers to as the various typical fields of interpersonal or social interaction which have shaped the composition of a text (such as the need for group self-clarification, demarcation from other groups, social competition and conflict, group consolidation, legitimation of authority and the like). I prefer the term "strategy" rather than "purpose" or "intention" because, as in the strategy of a game plan or the tactics of military warfare, strategy implies not simply the commu-

nication of ideas but the deliberate design of a document calculated to have a specific social effect on its intended hearers or readers. Sociological exegesis thus seeks to discover the manner in which a given document has been designed as a response to a given situation, and how it has been composed to elicit a social response on the part of its audience.

6. Concern with strategy involves concern with the self-interests that motivated the composition and transmission of a text. Although self-interests are among the most notoriously difficult factors of human activity to detect (who of us is always willing or even able to "lay his cards out on the table"?), from the standpoint of sociology self-interests constitute an essential component of human interaction. The matter of self-interest, furthermore, is to be seen not simply in an individual but also in a collective light. Some biblical texts may have been the products of individual authors rather than composite in nature or the work of a group or the results of the gradual accretion of tradition. Yet even in the rarer cases of individual authorship, the author speaks not only for himself but reflects as well the interests and perspectives of a particular group. In the New Testament this would be true not simply of the anonymous writings but of the epistolary literature as well. Beyond the issues of individual authorship and anonymity or pseudonymity, a sociological exegesis is concerned with the extent to which a biblical document reflects the social interests, class positions, organizational structures, geographical locations, and modes of authority of diverse groups within a given socioreligious movement. It inquires as to the social as well as historical and theological factors which have conditioned the writings and outlook of the Pauline circle, the Petrine circle, the Johannine and Matthean "schools" and the similarities and differences among these respective groups.

7. Furthermore, a *sociological* exegesis attempts to be sensitive to the manner in which group interests and the documents expressing such interests reflect or have led to the formulation of a collective early Christian *ideology* or perhaps of contrasting ideologies. I am using the term "ideology" to embrace, but also to encompass more than, what is customarily referred to as the "theological" interests or goals of a biblical document and its authors. Whereas the theology of a given author usually implies, or can be taken to imply, a conceptual framework separable or even isolated from the social reality in which he is writing, the term "ideology" does not al-

low this separation and in its sociological usage cannot be so understood. Although its definition and the history of its usage are indeed problematic, its use here implies the assumption of an interrelation and inseparability of social and religious meanings, functions, and frames of reference. Ideology is used here not in the reductionist Marxian sense of false consciousness nor as a reference to unrealized situationally transcendent ideas (Karl Mannheim). It is rather employed in a more neutral sense akin to the description given by the social historian David Brion Davis. Thus ideology is intended to refer to:

> an integrated system of beliefs, assumptions and values, not necessarily true or false, which reflects the needs and interests of a group or class at a particular time in history. Because ideologies are modes of consciousness, containing the criteria for interpreting social reality, they help to define as well as to legitimate collective needs and interests. Hence there is a continuous interaction between ideology and material forces of history.[24]

Attention to the ideological content and character of a biblical document involves not only an assessment of the manner in which the document attempts an integration of religious beliefs, traditions, values and goals, i.e., the construction of a "symbolic universe."[25] It also involves an analysis of the *social* function which this integration was intended to have in the social world of the document's authors and addressees.

8. Finally, in this by no means complete list of assumptions, it is taken for granted that the exegete himself or herself, no less than the biblical authors, is conditioned by his or her own social and psychological experience. We bring to the text questions that we have been conditioned to ask, not only theologically but also socially. As the biblical writers wrote, so we exegetes interpret out of self-interest. Our method and presuppositions are also *seins-* and *ortgebunden*. What we see in the text, especially its implications, is what our experience, our gender, our social position, and our political affiliations have prepared us to see. This crucial insight of the sociology of knowledge means that our sociological imagination, however to be nurtured, is seriously limited, as is our ability to sympathize with and intuit the situation of the *Anawim,* the Jewish converts to Christianity, and the struggles of a sectarian Christian community to define and consolidate itself. It also implies that an interclass reading of the Bible is impossible, that Nicaraguan Sandanistas or Mexican farmers are liable to dis-

cover social implications in the Scriptures which we middle-class North Americans never would have dreamed of seeing. Hence a genuinely sociological exegesis of the Scriptures would seem to require not only the ongoing dialogue of exegetes and sociologists but also necessary involvement and teamwork of persons from different cultures and strata of society. Such an exegesis then can never pronounce *das letzte Wort* over a text but will always attempt to be critical of its own perspectives and constantly attentive to the perspectives of others. To this extent exegesis itself becomes a social enterprise. The interpretation of the text, like the original composition and transmission of the text, becomes part of an ongoing social interaction.

There are several reasons for my choice of 1 Peter as the object of such a sociological-exegetical analysis. In the first place, the document admirably lends itself to the exploration of social issues. As Leonhard Goppelt, author of a recent commentary of 1 Peter, has observed,[26] this is the only New Testament writing which systematically and thematically has addressed the issue of Christian alien residence within the structures of society. At the same time there exists at present such lack of exegetical consensus concerning virtually every aspect of the document that the time seems ripe for taking a fresh, more sociologically oriented approach to its problems in the hope of moving beyond old exegetical cul-de-sacs. Finally, I regard this study as a necessary expansion upon my earlier research on 1 Peter, beginning with the publication of *The Elect and the Holy* in 1966.[27] The necessity for further research and the direction which this work should take has become clear to me not only as a result of the broadening of my own social perspective but also through the helpful criticism of Professor Nils A. Dahl. In an unpublished review of *The Elect and the Holy* which he has kindly shared with me, Professor Dahl has strengthened my growing personal conviction that the lack of attention there to the social context and issues of 1 Peter was a serious lacuna which had to be remedied. The present study is an attempt to meet that need while at the same time serving as an exemplification of sociological exegesis.

THE APPROACH OF THIS STUDY

The starting point and primary focal point of this exercise in sociological exegesis is a hitherto unexamined correlation of two terms which, it is hypothesized, provide the key to determining both the situation and strategy of 1 Peter. These are the two terms by which the intended audience is chiefly characterized: *paroikoi* and *oikos tou theou*. The study shall therefore revolve around an examination of these terms and their related word fields, the social realities to which they point, and the indications they provide of the integrated conception of 1 Peter and its intended socioreligious function. It begins in chapter 1 with an examination of the meaning and use of the word *paroikos* (and related terms) in 1 Peter and its social world as a first step toward determining the social situation of the letter and its audience. Chapter 2 extends the study of the social situation through a consideration of the various geographical, legal, economic, social and religious factors that bear on the audience of 1 Peter and the conditions of the document's composition. Here and in the following chapter a comparative typology will be employed in order to explore the sectarian character and problems of the communities addressed. Chapter 3 examines the variety of elements—literary, theological and sociological—that constitute the general strategy underlying the response of 1 Peter to the situation as described in the preceding chapters. This strategy is linked to the identification of the addressees as members of a conversionist sect and the specific problems encountered by this sect in its alien environment. Chapter 4 in turn focuses upon the central organizing concept of 1 Peter, namely, the identification and exhortation of the audience as the household of God and the literary-theological-sociological function of the *oikos-paroikos* correlation. Finally, chapter 5 explores questions concerning the group within which 1 Peter originated, the interests which conceivably motivated the letter's composition and dispatch, and the role which the household ideology developed in 1 Peter played in the wider context and subsequent course of early Christian social history.

NOTES

1. J. G. Gager, *Kingdom and Community: The Social World of Early Christianity* (Englewood Cliffs, N. J.: Prentice-Hall, 1975).

2. Ibid., p. 3, quoting from a paper of Jonathan Z. Smith, "The Social Description of Early Christianity," which was subsequently published in *Religious Studies Review* 1 (1975): 19–25; quotation from p. 19.

3. C. Wright Mills, "The Sociological Imagination," in *The Sociological Perspective,* ed. S. G. McNall (Boston: Little, Brown and Co., 1968), pp. 21–28.

4. Ibid., p. 27.

5. *Kingdom and Community*, pp. 7–9.

6. Such groups have been initiated in both the Old and New Testament areas of the Society of Biblical Literature and in the Studiorum Novi Testamenti Societas; a task force of the Catholic Biblical Association of America has studied the subject of early Christian ministry and church order with a similar objective in mind. The work of the Bay Area Seminar for Theology and Related Disciplines in California and the productive efforts of the Philadelphia Seminar for Christian Origins (PSCO) could also be mentioned. Some work of the SBL groups is available in the published papers of the annual SBL meetings. See *Society of Biblical Literature Seminar Papers*, 1974 ff. See also Wayne Meeks, "The Social World of Early Christianity," *Bulletin of the Council on the Study of Religion* 6 (1975): 1, 4–5. One product of the PSCO collaborations is the important collection of essays in *The Catacombs and the Colosseum: The Roman Empire as the Setting of Primitive Christianity*, ed. S. Benko and J. J. O'Rourke (Valley Forge, Pa.: Judson Press, 1971).

7. The literature listed in these notes can only be representative rather than exhaustive. Further references, especially to older literature, are to be found in the rich bibliographies contained in several of the works mentioned here, as well as in the footnotes of the chapters that follow. For the most recent surveys of research involving a social-scientific approach to the NT, see Daniel J. Harrington, "Sociological Concepts and the Early Church: A Decade of Research," *TS* 41 (1980): 181–190; Robin Scroggs, "The Sociological Interpretation of the New Testament: The Present State of Research," *NTS* 26 (1980): 164–179; and Howard Clark Kee, *Christian Origins in Sociological Perspective* (Philadelphia: Westminster Press, 1980).

8. See, e.g., Hans G. Kippenberg, "Wege zu einer historischen Religionssoziologie: Ein Literaturbericht," *VF* 16 (1971): 54–82; also his "Religion und Interaktion in traditionalen Gesellschaften: Ein Forschungsbericht zu neuen Theorien der Religionsgeschichte," *VF* 19 (1974): 2–24; Willy Schottroff, "Soziologie und Altes Testament," *VF* 19 (1974): 46–66; Smith, "Social Description," pp. 21–25; Sheldon R. Isenberg and Dennis E. Owen, "Bodies, Natural and Contrived: The Work of Mary Douglas," *RSR* 3 (1977): 1–17. For earlier research see also the several publications of Robert North, esp. *Sociology of the Biblical Jubilee*, Analecta Biblica 4 (Rome: Pontifical Biblical Institute, 1954) and the literature on "Biblical Sociology" listed on pp. xi–xxv of his bibliography.

9. See Robert North, "Sociologia," in *Enciclopedia de la Biblia*, vol. 6 (Barcelona: Garriga, 1963), cols. 773–78; Erhardt Güttgemanns, "Die Soziologie als methodologische Grundlage der Formgeschichte und der allgemeinen Sprach- und Literaturwissenschaft," in *Offene Fragen zu Formgeschichte des*

Evangeliums: Eine methodische Skizze der Grundlagenproblematik der Form-und Redaktionsgeschichte, Beiträge zur evangelischen Theologie 54 (Munich: Kaiser, 1970), pp. 44–68; see also pp. 167–88; Hans G. Kippenberg, "Versuch einer soziologischen Verortung des antiken Gnostizismus," *Numen* 17 (1970): 211–31; Dietfried Gewalt, "Neutestamentliche Exegese und Soziologie," *EvTh* 31 (1971): 87–99; Gerd Theissen, "Theoretische Probleme religionssoziologischer Forschung und die Analyse des Urchristentums," *Neue Zeitschrift für systematische Theologie und Religionsphilosophie* 16 (1974): 35–56; also his "Die soziologische Auswertung religiöser Überlieferungen," *Kairos* 17 (1975): 284–99; Norman K. Gottwald and Frank S. Frick, "The Social World of Ancient Israel: An Orientation Paper for the Consultation," *Society of Biblical Literature Seminar Papers,* vol. 1 (Missoula, Mont.: Scholars Press, 1975), pp. 165–78; also Gottwald, "Biblical Theology or Biblical Sociology?" *Radical Religion* 2 (1975): 42–57; Sheldon R. Isenberg, "Mary Douglas and Hellenistic Religions: The Case of Qumran," *Society of Biblical Literature Seminar Papers,* vol. 1 (1975), pp. 179–185; also Isenberg and Owen, "Bodies, Natural and Contrived"; Brian W. Kovacs, "Contributions of Sociology to the Study of the Development of Apocalypticism: A Theoretical Survey," an unpublished paper delivered to the Consultation on the Social World of Ancient Israel at the annual meeting of the Society of Biblical Literature, St. Louis, 1976 (32 pages); Henry A Green, "Gnosis and Gnosticism: A Study in Methodology," *Numen* 24 (1977): 95–134; Kurt Rudolf, "Das Problem einer Soziologie und 'sozialer Verortung' der Gnosis," *Kairos* 19 (1977): 35–44; Klaus Berger, "Wissenssoziologie und Exegese des Neuen Testaments," *Kairos* 19 (1977): 124–33; also the chapter on "Soziologische Fragen," in his *Exegese des Neuen Testaments: Neue Wege vom Text zur Auslegung* (Heidelberg: Quelle & Meyer, 1977), pp. 218–41; Hans G. Kippenberg, *Religion und Klassenbildung im antiken Judäa: Eine religionssoziologische Studie zum Verhältnis von Tradition und gesellschaftlicher Entwicklung,* SUNT 14 (Göttingen: Vandenhoeck und Ruprecht, 1978); J. W. Rogerson, *Anthropology and the Old Testament* (Atlanta: John Knox, 1979); Norman K. Gottwald, "Sociological Method in the Study of Ancient Israel," in *Encounter with the Text: Form and History in the Hebrew Bible,* ed. Martin J. Buss, SBL Semeia Supplements (Missoula, Mont.: Scholars Press and Philadelphia: Fortress Press, 1979), pp. 69–81; Walter Brueggemann, "Trajectories in OT Literature and the Sociology of Ancient Israel," *JBL* 98 (1979): 161–85; and *Zur Soziologie des Urchristentums: Ausgewählte Beiträge zum frühchristlichen Gemeinschaftsleben in seiner gesellschaftlichen Umwelt,* ed. Wayne A. Meeks, trans. G. Memmert, Theologische Bücherei 62 (Munich: Kaiser, forthcoming).

10. In addition to the works already mentioned see, e.g., James Alan Wilde,

A Social Description of the Community Reflected in the Gospel of Mark (Ann Arbor, Mich.: Xerox University Microfilms, 1974); John Howard Schütz, *Paul and the Anatomy of Apostolic Authority,* SNTSMS 26 (Cambridge, University Press, 1975); the essays in *The Bible and Liberation: Political and Social Hermeneutics, A Radical Religion* Reader, ed. Norman K. Gottwald and Antoinette C. Wire (Berkeley: Community for Religious Research and Education, 1976); Walter Brueggemann, *The Land,* Overtures to Biblical Theology (Philadelphia: Fortress Press, 1977); Alfred Schreiber, *Die Gemeinde in Korinth: Versuch einer gruppendynamischen Betrachtung der Entwicklung der Gemeinde von Korinth auf der Basis des ersten Korintherbriefes,* NTAbh 12 (Münster: Aschendorff, 1977); Ronald F. Hock, "Paul's Tentmaking and the Problem of His Social Class," *JBL* 97 (1978): 555–64; Bengt Holmberg, *Paul and Power: The Structure of Authority in the Primitive Church as Reflected in the Pauline Epistles* (Lund: CWK Gleerup, 1978; Philadelphia: Fortress Press, 1980); Bruce J. Malina, "The Social World Implied in the Letters of the Christian Bishop-Martyr (Named Ignatius of Antioch)," *SBL Seminar Papers,* ed. Paul J. Achtemeier, vol. 2 (Missoula, Mont.: Scholars Press, 1978), pp. 71–119; Norman K. Gottwald, *The Tribes of Israel: A Sociology of the Religion of Liberated Israel, 1250–1050* (Maryknoll, N. Y.: Orbis, 1979); Wayne A. Meeks, " 'Since then you would need to go out of the world': Group boundaries in Pauline Christianity," in *Critical History and Biblical Faith: New Testament Perspectives,* ed. Thomas Ryan (Villanova, Pa.: College Theology Society, 1979) pp. 4–29, and his forthcoming study, "The Social World of Pauline Christianity," in *Aufstieg und Niedergang der Römischen Welt,* ed. Hildegard Temporini and Wolfgang Haase (Berlin: de Gruyter).

11. *Kingdom and Community.* See also Gager's "The Gospels and Jesus: Some Doubts About Method," *JR* 54 (1974): 244–72. For a critique of Gager's work see Brian W. Kovacs, "A Methodological and Theoretical Interpretation of John G. Gager's *Kingdom and Community: The Social World of Early Christianity,*" an unpublished paper delivered at the Consultation of the Social World of Early Christianity, at the annual meeting of the Society of Biblical Literature, San Francisco, 1977 (12 pages) and the three essays in *Zygon* 13 (1978): 109–35.

12. G. Theissen, "Wanderradikalismus: Literatursoziologische Aspekte der Überlieferungsform von Worten Jesu in Urchristentum," *ZThK* 70 (1973): 245–71 (E.T.: "Itinerant Radicalism: The Tradition of Jesus Sayings from the Perspective of the Sociology of Literature," trans. A. C. Wire, with abridged notes, in *The Bible and Liberation,* pp. 84–93); "Theoretische Probleme" (see above, n. 9); "Soteriologische Symbolik in den paulinischen Schriften," *KD* 20 (1974): 282–304; "Soziale Integration und sakramentales Handeln: Eine

Analyse von I Cor. XI 17–34," *NovT* 16 (1974): 179–206; "Soziale Schichtung in der korinthischen Gemeinde: Ein Beitrag zur Soziologie des hellenistischen Christentums," *ZNW* 65 (1974): 232–72; *Urchristliche Wundergeschichten: Ein Beitrag zur formgeschichtlichen Erforschung der synoptischen Evangelien,* SNT 8 (Gütersloh: Gütersloher Verlagshaus—Gerd Mohn, 1974); "Soziologische Auswertung" (see above, n. 9); "Die Starken und Schwachen in Korinth: Soziologische Analyse eines theologischen Streites," *EvTh* 35 (1975): 155–72; "Legitimation und Lebensunterhalt: Ein Beitrag zur Soziologie urchristlicher Missionäre," *NTS* 21 (1975): 192–221; "Die Tempelweissagung Jesu: Prophetie im Spannungsfeld von Stadt und Land," *ThZ* 32 (1976): 144–58; " 'Wir haben alles Verlassen' (Mc. X 28): Nachfolge und soziale Entwurzelung in der jüdisch-palästinischen Gesellschaft des I. Jahrhunderts n. Ch.," *NovT* 19 (1977): 161–96; *Soziologie der Jesusbewegung: Ein Beitrag zur Entstehungsgeschichte des Urchristentums,* ThExHeute 194 (Munich: Kaiser, 1977) (E.T.: *The First Followers of Jesus* [London: SCM, 1978] and *Sociology of Early Palestinian Christianity,* trans. John Bowden [Philadelphia: Fortress Press, 1978]). For a critique of Theissen's work see John H. Schütz, "Steps Toward a Sociology of Primitive Christianity: A Critique of the Work of Gerd Theissen," an unpublished paper delivered at the Consultation on the Social World of Early Christianity at the annual meeting of the Society of Biblical Literature, San Francisco, 1977 (16 pages). See also Hendrikus Boers, "Sisyphus and His Rock: Concerning Gerd Theissen, *Urchristliche Wundergeschichten,*" *Semeia* 11 (1978): 1–48 and Paul J. Achtemeier, "An Imperfect Union: Reflections on Gerd Theissen, *Urchristliche Wundergeschichten,*" ibid., pp. 49–68.

13. F. Belo, *Lecture matérialiste de l'évangile de Marc: Récit-Pratique-Idéologie,* 2. rev. ed. (Paris: Cerf, 1975). See also the work of his student Michel Clévenot, *Approches matérialiste de la Bible* (Paris: Cerf, 1976) and the collection of essays edited by George Casalis, *Introduction à la lecture matérialiste de la Bible* (Geneva: World Student Christian Federation, 1978).

14. R. M. Grant, *Early Christianity and Society: Seven Studies* (New York: Harper & Row, 1977).

15. A. J. Malherbe, *Social Aspects of Early Christianity* (Baton Rouge/London: Louisiana State University, 1977).

16. L. Schottroff and W. Stegemann, *Jesus von Nazareth—Hoffnung der Armen* (Stuttgart: Kohlhammer, 1978).

17. W. Schottroff and W. Stegemann, eds., *Der Gott der kleinen Leute: Sozialgeschichtliche Auslegungen,* 2 vols. (Munich: Kaiser and Gelnhausen: Burckhardthaus, 1979).

18. See above, n. 2.

19. P. Berger, "A Sociological View of the Secularization of Theology," *JSSR* 6 (1967): 3–16; quotation from p. 10.

20. Theissen, "Soziologische Auswertung."

21. K. Berger, *Exegese des Neuen Testaments,* pp. 111–27; see also pp. 242–69 on his proposed "wirkungsgeschichtliche Hermeneutik."

22. The choice of the term "strategy" and its correlation with "situation" in the subtitle of the present study was made without awareness of its proposed use elsewhere. I am grateful to my colleague Hugh Dawson of the English department at the University of San Francisco, however, for pointing out to me that the literary critic Kenneth Burke in several publications has stressed the relationship between "literary 'strategies' and extra-literary 'situations' " (Foreword to *The Philosophy of Literary Form: Studies in Symbolic Action,* 2. ed. [Baton Rouge: Louisiana State University Press, 1967], p. ix). Concerning situations and strategies Burke, for instance, has observed:

> Let us suppose that I ask you: "What did the man say?" And that you answer: "He said 'Yes.' " You still do not know what the man said. You would not know unless you knew more about the situation, and about the remarks that preceded his answer.
>
> Critical and imaginative works are answers to questions posed by the situation in which they arose. They are not merely answers, they are *strategic* answers, stylized answers. For there is a difference in style or strategy, if one says "yes" in tonalities that imply "thank God" or in tonalities that imply "alas!" So I should propose an initial working distinction between "strategies" and "situation," whereby we think of poetry (I here use the term to include any work of critical or imaginative cast) as the adopting of various strategies for the encompassing of situations. These strategies size up the situations, name their structure and outstanding ingredients, and name them in a way that contains an attitude toward them. (p. 1)

See also pp. 293–304 ("Literature as Equipment for Living") where Burke outlines features of a "sociological criticism" of the situations and strategies of literature.

23. K. Berger, *Exegese des Neuen Testaments,* pp. 117–26.

24. D. B. Davis, *The Problem of Slavery in the Age of Revolution 1770–1823* (Ithaca/London: Cornell University Press, 1975), p. 14.

25. The expression "symbolic universe" is taken from Peter L. Berger and Thomas Luckmann, *The Social Construction of Reality: A Treatise in the Sociology of Knowledge* (Garden City, N.Y.: Doubleday, 1967); see esp. pp. 42–128.

The aspect of ideology as involving conceptual integration is born of the general need to "make sense of things," especially of perplexing or incongruous circumstances. It reflects the desire to know how things really are (cognitive need), why things are the way they are (explanatory need), and whether things ought or ought not to be the way they are (need for norms). One of the key functions of ideology is to legitimate: to clarify but also to justify and to validate. Standards of value and behavior as well as accepted assumptions and goals fall within the purview of ideological reflection.

Berger and Luckmann describe legitimation as a " 'second-order' objectivation of meaning" whose function is to integrate and "make objectively available and subjectively plausible the 'first-order' objectivations that have been institutionalized." This process, according to the authors, can encompass various levels of complexity and scope from the initial use of any meaningful vocabulary or systems of signs (e.g., "family," "brotherhood"), to the development of explanatory "theoretical propositions in rudimentary form" (proverbs, maxims, legends, folktales), to explicit theories propounded and transmitted by the "leaders or experts," and finally to the construction of "symbolic universes" of theoretical tradition that integrate the provinces of, for instance, collective identity, group cohesion, personal and societal behavior and goals—all aspects of the institutional order—into a symbolic (i.e., referring to realities beyond everyday experience) totality.

26. L. Goppelt, *Der erste Petrusbrief*, KEK 12/1, ed. Ferdinand Hahn, 1. ed. (Göttingen: Vandenhoeck und Ruprecht, 1978), p. 41. The still more recent commentary of Norbert Brox (*Der erste Petrusbrief*, Evangelisch-Katholischer Kommentar zum Neuen Testament 21 [Zurich: Benziger and Neukirchen-Vluyn: Neukirchener Verlag, 1979]) unfortunately appeared after the completion of the present study and therefore could not be taken into consideration. The social orientation of Brox's analysis, like that of Goppelt's, deserves close attention.

27. J. H. Elliott, *The Elect and the Holy: An Exegetical Examination of 1 Peter 2:4–10 and the Phrase* Basileion Hierateuma, NovT Supplements 12 (Leiden: E. J. Brill, 1966).

The Homeless Strangers
of 1 Peter

A STARTING POINT

First Peter, like all documents of the early Christian movement, is a product of and a contribution toward a "social world in the making."[1] The overarching purpose of this study is to examine how this particular document, in its literary, social and religious dimensions, is both a reflection of and a response to the interaction of the early Christian movement and its social environment. In order to achieve this objective, it appears advisable, if not necessary, to attempt a fresh approach to the interpretation of 1 Peter. The approach includes both a sociologically oriented type of analysis and a new point of exegetical departure from which to investigate the interrelation of text and context, social situation and literary-sociological-theological strategy.

From the words of the text itself it appears that 1 Peter is a letter sent from the apostle Peter (1:1) and his associates in Babylon (5:12-13) which contains words of exhortation and confirmation (5:12) intended for fellow Christian visitors and resident aliens (1:1, 2:11) dispersed among four or five Roman provinces or regions of Asia Minor (1:1) who are currently suffering from various types of hostility, conflict and trials of faith (1:6; 2:12, 19-20; 3:14-16; 4:1, 4, 12-16, 19; 5:9). Or at least so it seems to be on an initial reading of the text. In the course of modern exegetical research on the New Testament and on this document in particular, however, serious questions have been raised concerning such initial impressions. Is the document, for instance, indeed a genuine integral letter or do not the presence

21

of liturgical and creedal formulas, along with possible interruptions and repetitions in the text, point to its being a combination of letters or a baptismal homily or even liturgy encased in epistolary form? Is the apostle Peter its real author or do not its literary style, its destination, its content and time of composition suggest pseudonymous authorship, perhaps by a Paulinist long after the death of the apostle? Is a locality with the actual name of Babylon its place of origin or is this term rather a cryptic code name for Rome and hence a covert indication of the need for secrecy required by the open hostility between empire and church? If so, would this not also make the Petrine authorship and early date of the document (before Peter's death ca. 67 c.e.) even more unlikely? If, moreover, the document is pseudonymous and late, would this not indicate its lack of originality and theological significance and limit its canonical importance relative to what are considered by many to be the main New Testament writings?

Such questions when compounded by further problems concerning the precise nature and cause of the anti-Christian accusations and sufferings mentioned, their interpretation as either indications of official Roman persecution or occasional trials of faith, the lack of clarity regarding the general legal and social status of the addressees at the time, and differing opinions about the overall message or purpose of the document have resulted in making 1 Peter one of the most disputed writings of the New Testament. Yet, despite this lack of scholarly consensus concerning its genre, content and historical situation, its testimony to the early church's coming to grips with its situation and stance within secular society make 1 Peter one of the most important and intriguing contributions to the history, theology and sociology of the early Christian movement.

The various problems associated with virtually every aspect of 1 Peter are amply enumerated in the introductions and commentaries treating this text. It is not the intention of this study to review such research but rather to examine the text and its problems from a fresh perspective.[2] Earlier interpretations will be mentioned and evaluated to the point that they are germane to issues under investigation here or to illustrate positions which require reconsideration. Here an attempt will be made to "reach beyond old conclusions, set categories, and conventional methods" with the aim of transcending old impasses to understanding and thus breaking new ground.

As a starting point proper to a sociological-exegetical analysis, I wish to focus attention on a hitherto overlooked correlation in 1 Peter which will serve as a basis for an expanding examination of the setting and strategy of the document. This correlation involves the terms *paroikos(-oi)* and *oikos (tou theou)*, "resident aliens" and "household (of God)," words which together with associated imagery in 1 Peter point to broader details concerning social condition and socioreligious response. The importance of these terms within 1 Peter is evident from their recurrence at key points in the structure of the document. In the first major unit of exhortation concerning the interaction of the readers within their social environment (2:11 ff.), the recipients are designated *paroikous kai parepidēmous* ("resident aliens and visiting strangers," 2:11). The latter of these two related words, *parepidēmoi*, repeats and reemphasizes the initial designation of the addressees in the letter's opening salutation: "Peter, an apostle of Jesus Christ, to the elect *visiting strangers* of the diaspora of (i.e., located in) Pontus, Galatia, Cappadocia, Asia and Bithynia" (1:1 author's translation, hereafter au.). The noun *paroikia*, "alien residence (in a foreign land)," furthermore, describes the social condition of the readers again in 1:17: "And if you invoke as Father him who judges each one according to his deeds, conduct yourselves with awe and reverence throughout the time of your *alien residence"* (au.).

On the other hand, the linguistic paronym[3] of *paroikos, oikos,* also occurs in 2:5 and 4:17 in sections of the text which contain key statements regarding the identity of the addressees and their relation to society at large (2:4–10 and 4:12–17, respectively). Since, as will be discussed below, both *paroikos* and *oikos* are linked with other terms and thus form wider semantic fields, and since these words figure so significantly in the construction and development of the document's message, there is reason to suspect that the structural position, conceptual associations, and rhetorical function of these words call for close scrutiny. Since, moreover, these related terms are used in the hellenistic environment of 1 Peter to depict specific modes of social condition and organization, there is likewise reason to suspect that in 1 Peter they constitute important indicators of the social as well as religious circumstances concerning the document and its purpose. Such factors, in other words, suggest that *paroikos* and *oikos* are not merely linguistic but also sociological and theological correlates.

What do these terms mean and imply? To what social circumstances do they point? How do these terms and their correlation in 1 Peter provide clues to the social condition of the addressees as well as to the socioreligious response offered by the document itself? If the recipients are indeed "strangers in a strange land," then in what sense are they simultaneously and paradoxically "at home with" or "the household of" God? To consider these questions in sequence let us first turn to an analysis of the meaning and use of the term *paroikos* and related terms in 1 Peter and its secular and religious environment.

THE MEANING AND USE OF THE TERM *PAROIKOS* IN THE SECULAR AND RELIGIOUS ENVIRONMENT OF THE GRECO-ROMAN WORLD

Lexical studies are virtually unanimous regarding the general and technical meaning and use of *paroikos* in the ancient world. The LSJ definition of both the adjective and the substantive is representative: adj.: "dwelling beside or near, neighboring"; subst.: "neighbor, sojourner in another's house"; generally, "alien, stranger."[4] In this general sense *paroikoi* are strangers, foreigners, aliens, people who are not at home, or who lack native roots, in the language, customs, culture, or political, social, and religious allegiances of the people among whom they dwell. The composite substantive *par-oikos* derives its meaning from the denotations and connotations of the *oik-* root and such terms as *oikos, oikia, oikeō,* and *oikeios. Oikos* circumscribes one of the most fundamental social, economic, political and personal realities of the ancient world. *Oikos* (less frequently, *oikia*) is my house and home with all its personnel and property, my family and lineage, my "given identity," the place where I "belong" and exercise my personal and communal rights and responsibilities, my moral obligations. The verb *oikein* means "to inhabit, permanently reside, to be at home." The adjective *oikeios* denotes domestic affairs, kinship bonds, and that which is personal, private, or proper to oneself. As these and many related *oik-* terms refer to kith and kin, friend and brother, the familiar and the familial, so, contrariwise, *paroikos (paroikein, paroikia* etc.) denotes the strange, the alien, the foreign, the "other." Whereas *oikos* connotes associations and impressions of home, belongingness, and one's proper place, *paroikos* depicts the "DP," the displaced and dislocated person, the curious or suspicious-looking alien or stranger. Distinguished from *oik-* terms and combined in both secular and biblical literature with such words as *allos, allotrios, xenos* and *parepidēmos*—all of which variously denote the stranger, foreigner or transient visitor—*paroikos* in a general sense implies social separation, cultural alienation and a certain degree of personal deprivation.

More specifically and much more frequently, however, *paroikos (-oi)* is found to have been used with a technical, political-legal meaning to denote "the state, position or fate of a resident alien, 'dwelling abroad' without civil or native rights."[5] Similar to the use of *oikos* and its paronyms in conjunction with terms such as *dēmos* ("district, country"), *polis* ("city"), and *patris* ("fatherland") to supply the vocabulary and models for broader political functions and social institutions, *paroikos* and its paronyms eventually were used in a technical sociopolitical sense. Such use is documented not only in the Old Testament (LXX)[6] but also generally in the literature and particularly in the inscriptions of the Greco-Roman world. Hans Schaefer in his Pauly-Wissowa article[7] has assembled all available occurrences of the term, noting their frequent appearance in lists of city residents (where *paroikoi* are ranked below full citizens [*politai*] and above strangers [*xenoi*], freedmen and slaves) as well as the virtual identity of the institution of *paroikoi* (*paroikia*) with that of *metoikoi* which it eventually replaced, especially in Asia Minor in the hellenistic period.[8] *Paroikoi,* Schaefer summarizes, constituted a politically recognized institution of the state and a registered stratum of the population which was distinguished legally and socially from the superior full citizens, on the one hand, and the inferior transient strangers, on the other.[9] Inclusion of strangers among the *paroikoi* was possible on the basis of a sufficient length of local residence or when the state granted such status to slaves, freedmen and other classes with lesser rights in order to obligate them and secure their loyalty.[10] Classification among the *paroikoi* involved both advantages and disadvantages. For the "fluctuating stratum of the declassed, homeless and foreign element of even barbaric origin in part,"[11] admission to *paroikos* status offered some modicum of political-legal advance and upward social mobility. The fundamental distinction, however, between the rights, privileges and rewards of full citizenship and those of all others remained clear and binding. In social intercourse the differentiating features of origin, language, custom and religion continued to brand the "nouveau *paroikos*" as a quasi outsider. Nor was he allowed to forget that his advancement to *paroikos* status came with strings attached: political and economic exploitation, continued disdain and suspicion by the citizenry, and competition and envy from those below him. For some, inclusion among the *paroikoi* could also amount to a reduction of rights or political-social position. This would be true of those who were required to reside permanently away from their homeland without the full protection and rights they once enjoyed, as in the case of Abraham among the Hittites,[12] Moses in Midian[13] and the Israelites in Egypt,[14] to take but the most ready examples. Of course this would obtain all the more in the instance of alien residence abroad due to forced deportation. For this the Jews in Babylonian captivity ("the sons of *paroikia*," 2 Esd. [Ezra] 8:35; also 1 Esd. 5:7) and the transfer by Antiochus III of 2,000 Jewish families from Mesopotamia and Babylonia to Phrygia are well-known examples.[15] For the Jews in Egypt during the reign of Claudius (ca. 39/40 c.e.), on the other hand, classification among the "aliens and foreigners" (*xenous kai epēludas*) constituted a demotion in political-legal status which they were most anxious to avoid.[16]

Insufficient data exist for determining the actual number of *paroikoi* in relation to the full citizenry in various localities during the hellenistic and early imperial age. Schaefer, however, advises that the figure should not be underestimated. The situation at Rhodes (305 b.c.e.)[17] indicates, for example, that the proportion was 1,000 *paroikoi* to 6,000 full citizens. In the subsequent period in Asia Minor the number of *paroikoi* generally increased. While most of the pertinent data attest to circumstances in the cities, where the *paroikoi* labored as merchants, traders and artisans,[18] they were also numerous in the rural areas, especially among the villages gradually annexed by the city territories. In his discussion of various types of land tenure in Asia Minor, Michael Rostovtzeff observes:

> Besides the land which was divided among the citizens (*klēroi*), many of the ancient Greek cities possessed extensive tracts which were cultivated and inhabited by natives. From the Roman point of view these villages were "attached" or "attributed" to the city; from the Greek point of view the villages were inhabited by "by-dwellers" (*paroikoi* or *katoikoi*) who never had had and never were destined to have the full rights of municipal citizenship. How to deal with these large numbers of peasants was a serious problem for the city aristocracy as was the problem of the city proletariat.[19]

"Juridically and politically they, as well as the inhabitants of the cities, were subjects of the Roman state."[20] Of their economic condition little is known, though Rostovtzeff finds it

> difficult to accept that the *paroikoi* and *katoikoi* of the Roman period were landowners. They were probably still, as they had been in the Hellenistic age, tenants of the cities or the landowners, perhaps better defended against the abuses of the landlords by the Roman government than they had been in the Hellenistic age.[21]

Inscriptional evidence from Pamphilia about Sillyum (ca. second century c.e.) shows that "in a public distribution the *paroikoi* received the same sum or the same amount of corn as the freedmen and the *vindictarii*, while members of the senate, those of the *gerousia*, the members of the public assembly (*ekklēsiastai*), and the common citizens received much more."[22]

Shifting our attention from Asia Minor and extrabiblical evidence to the Old Testament, we find that in the LXX the meaning and use of *paroikos* is consistent with that of its secular environment. Here too *paroikos* (thirty-three occurrences), *paroikeō* (sixty-nine occurrences) and related terms[23] designate the situation and the political, legal, and social and religious conditions of living abroad as resident aliens.[24] The term refers to Israelites residing away from home as well as to resident aliens in Israel's midst or living elsewhere: e.g., Abraham and his seed in the land of Egypt (Gen. 12:10; 15:13),[25] among the Hittites (Gen. 23:4) or in Canaan (Gen. 17:8; Ps. 104 [105]:12);[26] Lot in Sodom (Gen. 19:9); a Levite from Bethlehem-Judah in Ephraim (Judg. 17:7-9); Elimelech and his family in Moab (Ruth 1:1); Moses and his family in Midian (Exod. 2:22);[27] the patriarchs residing in Mesopotamia (Jth. 5:7,8,10); or generally of Israelites as resident aliens in a land left unnamed (1 Chron. 29:15; Pss. 38[39]: 12; 118[119]:19). Less frequently the terms designate resident aliens among the Israelites (e.g., Exod. 12:45; Lev. 22:10; Num. 35:15)[28] or others such as the Beerothites (2 Kgdm. [2 Sam.] 4:3), the outcasts of Moab (Isa. 16:4) or Cretans (Zeph. 2:5).[29] Characteristic of the perspective on *paroikoi* in the Old Testament is the manner in which the *paroikos* and *paroikia* existence is used as a basis for inculcating moral and religious attitudes. Resident aliens among the Israelites, while restricted from participation in certain cultic rights and duties, still enjoyed certain rights of legal protection and social acceptance.[30] This treatment serves as an example for the support to be accorded to the brother Israelite who has been reduced to poverty: "you shall maintain him; as a stranger and a resident alien he shall live with you" (Lev. 25:35 au.) . . . "you shall not make him serve as a slave: he shall be with you as a wage earner and resident alien" (25:39–40a au.). "You shall not abhor an Egyptian, because you were a resident alien in his land" (Deut. 23:8 LXX, au.). This recollection of Israel's history as *paroikoi* in alien territories also serves as a symbol of its enduring divine calling typified in the patriarch Abraham "in whom the people of Israel sees its own true nature. . . . Throughout his wanderings Abraham accepted his alien status as a sign of faith and obedience towards God, as an example of the modesty which people must always observe in face of God when it asks concerning its being under His promise."[31] Thus King David prays: "For we are *paroikoi* before you and live as resident aliens (*paroikountes*) like all our fathers" (1 Chron. 29:15 au.), remembering that "all things come from you and of your own have we given you" (v. 14). Similarly, in seeking relief from his illness the psalmist prays: "Hear my prayer, O Lord, and give ear to my cry; hold not your peace at my tears. For I am a *paroikos* before you, like all my fathers" (Ps. 38[39]: 12 au.).

Moreover, Israel's condition as *paroikoi* in foreign lands makes the maintenance of its purity and its fidelity to the Law a crucial issue. Thus the psalmist observes: "How can a young man keep his way pure? By guarding it according to your word. . . . I am a *paroikos* in the land; hide not your commandments from me!" (Ps. 118[119]:9, 19 au.). Since both of these Psalms texts are frequently cited as illustrative of a purely "spiritual" or cosmological meaning of *paroikos* in 1 Peter, these passages deserve an additional word of comment. First, use of the term *paroikos* to portray in a figurative religious sense the relation of believer to God (as in the prayer of Psalm 38[39] and that of David) in no way precludes the actual social experience from which this metaphorical usage derives and receives its symbolic force.[32] Secondly, although some translations (e.g., RSV, JB) and interpreters render the text of Ps. 118(119):19 "sojourner (exile) *on earth*,"[33] the Septuagintal occurrences of *en tē gē*, particularly when in conjunction with *paroikos,* mean not "on earth" but "in the land."[34] The contrast is not cosmological but socioreligious, as is clear in the context of Psalm 118[119] and vv. 53–54 (au.) in particular: "Hot indignation seizes me because of the wicked who forsake your law. Your statutes have been [for me, in contrast to the wicked] my songs in the place of my *paroikia*" (i.e., surrounded by his enemies[35]). In the following psalm, *paroikia* again involves social conflict and frustration: "Woe is me, that my *paroikia* is prolonged; I have dwelled among the tents of Kedar. I have long been a resident alien. I have been peaceable among those who hated peace; when I spoke to them, they warred against me without cause!" (Ps. 119[120]: 5–7 au.).

Dislocation from home, dispossession of the land of promise, life under the conditions of political, and social and religious estrangement were the trying experiences of Israel which shaped the language and symbolism of religious despair and hope. To isolate these formulations of faith from the experience of life whence they were derived is unwarranted and unnecessary. For in none of the occurrences of *paroikos* and related terms in the LXX is a purely "spiritual" sense or a cosmological distinction (between heaven and earth) required or even likely.

In the later, postexilic writings there are retrospective references to the patriarchs as resident aliens in Mesopotamia (Jth. 5:7, 8, 9) and Egypt (Jth. 5:10; Wisd. of Sol. 19:10), in Sodom (Lot, Ecclus. 16:7[8]), to the Jews in Babylonian captivity (1 Esd. 5:7; 2 Esd. [Ezra] 8:35) and to the Jews in Egypt under the reign of Ptolemy Philopater (3 Macc. 6:36; 7:19). Still later during the reign of Ptolemy Euergetes, according to its prologue, the book of Jesus ben Sirach was published (ca. 132 B.C.E.) for the benefit of the Jews residing as aliens (*en tē paroikia*) in Egypt (Ecclus. Prologue 34). At one point the author elaborates on *paroikia* conditions by giving a moving description of the socioeconomic plight and degrading experiences of the *paroikos*:

> The essentials for life are water and bread and clothing and a house (*oikos*) to cover one's nakedness. Better is the life of a beggar (*ptōchos*) under the shelter of his roof than sumptuous food in another man's house (*en allotriois*). Be content with little or much and you will not hear reproach of your alien residence (*oneidismon paroikias*). It is a miserable life to go from house to house (*oikia*); and where you reside as an alien (*paroikēseis*) you may not open your mouth. You will play the host and provide drink without being thanked, and besides this you will hear bitter words: "Come here, alien (*paroike*), prepare the table, and if you have anything at hand, let me have it to eat." "Give place, alien (*paroike*), to an honored person; my brother has come to stay with me; I need my house." These things are hard to bear for a man who has feeling: scolding about

lodging (*oikias*) and the reproach (*oneidismon*) of the moneylender (Ecclus. 29:21–28 au.).[36]

Also noteworthy in this passage is the contrast between home and homelessness expressed through the correlation of *oikos* (*oikia*) and *paroikos* (*paroikeō*).

In the Psalms of Solomon a reference to the Jewish *paroikia* of the diaspora occurs in a passage which seems to suggest a solidarity between them and the pious Hasidim who fled Jerusalem and eventually constituted the communities of Damascus and Qumran:

> And the children of the covenant in the midst of the mingled peoples surpassed them [in wickedness];[37] there was not among them one that wrought in the midst of Jerusalem mercy and truth. They that loved the synagogues of the pious fled from them, as sparrows that fly from their nest. They wandered in the deserts that their lives may be safe from harm, and precious in the eyes of them that lived abroad (*paroikias*) was any that escaped alive from them. Over the whole earth were they scattered (*ho skorpismos autōn*) by lawless men (Ps. Sol. 17:15–18).

Occasionally in this LXX literature we meet the combination of *paroikos* and *parepidēmos* (Gen. 23:4;[38] Ps. 38[39]:12[39]) as well as evidence suggesting that in certain cases "*paroikia* might simply be taken as an equivalent of *diaspora,* with the same implied questions and ideas."[40] There is thus precedence for such associations in the latter text of 1 Peter (1:1; 2:11). In the combination of *paroikos* and *parepidēmos,* however, the first term has technical political-legal implications which are not associated with the second. Whereas *paroikos* specifically designates the "resident alien" (with his attendant, though restricted, rights and civil status), the rarer *parepidēmos* refers more generally to the transient visitor who is temporarily residing as a foreigner in a given locality.[41] Thus Edward Gordon Selwyn correctly notes that "*parepidēmos* emphasized the transitoriness of the sojourner's stay in a place, *paroikos,* his legal status as a non-citizen."[42] In the light of more general social and cultural attitudes of the natives toward all classifications of foreigners, of course, both terms approximate one another in their depiction of the suspected, disdained and vulnerable "outsider."

In contrast to the wide use of *paroikos* in the technical sense in the secular as well as religious literature surveyed, *diaspora* as a technical reference to "the dispersion of the Jews among the Gentiles" or "the Jews as thus scattered" and living beyond the limits of the land of Israel appears to be a specific LXX coinage representative of the perspective of the Greek Jewish "dispersion."[43] *Diaspora* in the LXX (12 occurrences) lacks a technical equivalent in the Hebrew text but the term to which it most frequently corresponds is *golah* or *galuth*.[44] The proximity of *diaspora* and *paroikia* or related terms is reflected in the fact that on at least one occasion *paroikia* also translates the Hebrew *golah* (2 Esd. [Ezra] 8:35) and that other Greek equivalents of the *oik-* root (e.g., *apoikia, apoikismos, metoikesia*) are also used to render *golah* and *galuth*.[45] According to Karl Ludwig Schmidt who has carefully analyzed the linguistic evidence, adoption of the term *diaspora* in a technical sense may reflect a more positive reassessment of the conditions and cause of life abroad. "Voluntary emigration contributed to the extension of the *diaspora* as well as deportation."[46] Gradually the prophetic version of the dispersement of God's people as an act of divine judgment and curse (Isa. 35:8, Hebrew: "it and he is for them a wayfarer," Jer. 3:24, Ezek. 22:15) is mitigated by a sense of "hellenistic optimism." Thus in the LXX the term *diaspora* veils "the stark severity of the Hebrew expressions which piteously describe the judgment of scattering which God executed on Israel."[47] Whereas, then, *diaspora* points to the *geographical* division and separation of Judaism (with diminishing religious implications of divine punishment), *paroikia* and related terms again refer to the political, legal and social dimensions of Jewish residence in lands beyond Palestine.

In moving closer to the period of the New Testament, Schmidt notes that:

> as later more and more Jews came to live in the diaspora, this was bound to affect Israel's consciousness of its alien status, on the one side by enhancing it, on the other by diminishing it. Whereas eschatological and apocalyptic Judaism, followed by primitive Christianity, brought the dispersion into connection with recollection of the Babylonian captivity and therefore directly with the land of Palestine, Hellenistic Judaism went its own way and increasingly weakened the historical bond.[48]

The chief example of this countertrend is the Alexandrian Jewish philosopher Philo (fl. 39/40 c.e.) who uses *paroikos* and related terms to depict the righteous man as a stranger on earth separated from his heavenly

home.[49] "The contemporary background of this psychological interpretation of man's alien status in the world," as Schmidt has observed, "is the
Cynic-Stoic diatribe, e.g., in Muson[ius] and Epictet[us], and Platonising
Stoicism in general."[50] This interpretation of *paroikia* is a far cry from the
social consciousness of apocalyptic Judaism and Christianity, however, and
finds its only early Christian counterpart in the similar cosmological and
theological perspective of the Epistle to the Hebrews.

In the literature of rabbinic Judaism and Josephus, on the other hand,
the predominant political, legal, social and religious implications of *paroikos* continue to prevail. Thus the rabbis distinguish aliens who stand in
religious and social relation to Israel into three classes: the full proselyte,
the half-proselyte or godfearer, and the resident alien. The last is "an immigrant who has settled in Israel and works there while remaining a non-
Jew. If the Rabb[is] demand certain concessions from the resident alien,
this is because as *paroikos* he is economically and socially dependent on his
Jewish environment and is thus a kind of client."[51] Josephus likewise uses
paroikos in its prevailing political-legal sense, referring, for instance, on
one occasion, to "certain of the Jewish resident aliens *(paroikōn)*" at
Parium on the European coast of the Hellespont *(Ant.* 14.10.8).[52]

The classic sociological study of Judaism as a "pariah people" is that of
Max Weber.[53] In his treatment of Judaism's alien and marginal political,
legal and social status since the exile he takes full account of the technical
implications of the terms related to *paroikia*. The term "pariah people,"
also employed by Weber in a technical sense, was intended to describe
Judaism as more than merely a "guest people."

> Guest people, guest artisans, and similar terms refer to groups or indi-
> viduals who as a result of invasion or conquest have been expropriated
> from their lands by immigrant groups and have been reduced to economic
> dependence on the conquerors. These may reduce the native population to
> the "guest status" regardless of residential seniority. Similarly, migrations
> of groups or individuals may result in guest-host relationships. The status
> relationship between the guest and host groups may vary, the guests may
> be legally and conventionally privileged or underprivileged. Where the
> status relationship is implemented by ritual barriers [established by the
> guest group] Weber proposes the term "pariah people."[54]

Whatever its shortcomings might have been judged to be in the light of
over fifty years of research since its first appearance (1917–19), this early
work of one of the fathers of modern sociology is a masterful demonstra-

tion of the compatibility and complementarity of sociology and exegetical research, particularly in regard to the study of social and religious alienation.

This brings us, finally, to the occurrences of *paroikos* and related terms in the New Testament and 1 Peter in particular. An important point which I wish to stress at the outset is that in this body of literature also the meaning and use of this terminology is best determined in the light of its prevalent meaning and use in the materials already discussed, as well as in light of its immediate literary contexts. This seemingly self-evident point requires emphasis for at least two main reasons. Exegetical decisions concerning these terms in 1 Peter in particular frequently ignore, or at least fail to mention, their political, legal and social import. This is the case when discussion is restricted exclusively to the "religious" or "figurative" use of the terms. Moreover, such procedure is assumed to be warranted by a series of further assumptions: e.g., that other vocabulary with which these terms occur indicate a figurative sense to all terms; or that a rare form of usage in one document should take precedence over the predominant use in many. Or, as an even more comprehensive theological assumption, it has been suggested that terms such as *paroikos* have undergone a sudden and fundamental transformation of meaning due to a belief in the advent of the kingdom of God[55] or some related form of *Jenseitsgläubigkeit:* "the Christian considers himself as a *paroikos* on this earth in view of the hereafter."[56]

Reasoning, often circular reasoning, and assumptions such as these require close scrutiny and advise caution. The problems which emerge here are numerous and positions taken at this point have serious implications not only for the interpretation of 1 Peter but for a sociohistorical understanding of the early Christian movement as a whole.

In the New Testament the substantive *paroikos,* the verb *paroikeō* and the noun *paroikia* occur a total of eight times in five documents (*paroikos:* Acts 7:6, 29; Eph. 2:19; 1 Pet. 2:11; *paroikeō:* Luke 24:18; Heb. 11:9; *paroikia:* Acts 13:17; 1 Pet. 1:17). With the possible exception of Ephesians, all documents are characterized by a keen awareness of and interest in the social circumstances and history of the Christian groups which they describe. And in several instances where the terms are used, the historical precedent of Israel's *paroikia* experiences figures significantly in Christian proclamation and exhortation.

In his self-defense before the Jewish council in Jerusalem (Acts 7:2–53),

Stephen, according to Luke, recalls that alien residence in foreign territories was the historical course and destiny of God's people from the very
beginning. Thus the grand patriarch Abraham was called by God to "de-
part from your land and your kinfolk and go into the land which I shall
show you" (7:3 au., citing Gen. 12:1). From this land, Haran, God again
removed Abraham and "settled him as a resident alien (*metōikisen*)" in
the land of Canaan (Acts 7:4 au.). "And God spoke to this effect, that his
posterity would be aliens (*sperma . . . paroikon*) in a land belonging to
others [the Egyptians], who would enslave them and ill-treat[57] them four
hundred years" (7:6, citing Gen. 15:13)

Later in this same speech Stephen notes the experience of Moses also,
who, in fear for his life in Egypt, "fled and became a resident alien
(*paroikos*) in the land of Midian where he became the father of two sons"
(7:29 au., alluding to Exod. 2:11–22).[58] Then, recalling Israel's succumbing
to the idolatrous ways of its neighbors and God's punishment thereof,
Stephen cites the words of the prophet: "Did you offer to me slain beasts
and sacrifices, forty years in the wilderness, O house of Israel (*oikos
Israel*)? And you took up the tent of Moloch, the star of the god Rephan,
and the figures which you made to worship; and I will settle you as aliens
(*metoikiō*) beyond Babylon" (7:42–43 au., citing Amos 5:25–27).[59]

In his sermon[60] at Pisidian Antioch in Asia Minor, the apostle Paul also
recalls the *paroikia* of the patriarchs: "The God of this people Israel chose
our fathers and made them great during their *paroikia* in the land of
Egypt and with uplifted arm he led them out of it" (Acts 13:17 au.).

Acceptance of *paroikia* as an act of faith is stressed by the author of the
Epistle to the Hebrews who, in his list of the heroes of faith, also cites the
example of Abraham: "By faith Abraham obeyed when he was called to
go out. . . . By faith he lived as a resident alien (*parōikēsen*) in the land of
promise as in a foreign land, living in tents with Isaac and Jacob . . . "
(Heb. 11:8–9 au.).

According to the Lucan narrative of the postresurrection appearance of
Jesus on the way to Emmaus, Jesus himself was (mis)taken for a *paroikos*
unaware of recent local events. Cleopas, one of the two to encounter Jesus,
exclaims: "Are you only a resident alien (*paroikeis*) in Jerusalem and do
not know the things that have happened in these days?" (Luke 24:18 au.).

Finally, aside from 1 Peter 1:17 and 2:11, the only other New Testament
occurrence of the *paroik-* root is in Eph. 2:19 where, in a context replete

with political terminology (2:11–22 au.), the Gentile Christian addressees are declared to be "no longer strangers and resident aliens (*xenoi kai paroikoi*)" to the people of God but "fellow citizens (*sympolitai*) with the saints and members of the household of God (*oikeioi tou theou*)."

In all instances of their occurrence, we note, these terms convey the conventional sense of "being or living as a resident alien in a foreign environment or away from home." It is also clear that the political, legal and social limitations of *paroikos* status were understood to constitute the conditions according to which union with and fidelity toward God were tested, relinquished or affirmed.[61]

This is precisely the sense in which the meaning and use of these terms in 1 Peter are best understood. In 1:17 as in 2:11 the political-legal and social condition of the addressees' situation as resident aliens in Asia Minor is acknowledged and its acceptance in faith and obedience to God's will is encouraged. In 1:17 the addressees are told to use the time of their alien residence as an occasion to renounce former ignorant and futile ways of behavior (1:14, 18) and opt instead for exclusive reverence and obedience of God: "And if you invoke as Father him who judges each one according to his deeds, conduct yourselves with awe and reverence during the time of your alien residence (*tēs paroikias*)" (au.). The social situation in which you exist, in other words, with all its implications of limitation and estrangement, is an opportunity and a challenge for you to manifest your holiness and allegiance to God alone. The same refrain is sounded in 1 Peter 2:11. The addressees, who are classed among their neighbors as resident aliens and transient strangers (*paroikous kai parepidēmous*), are to use this to their advantage in establishing their distinctive religious identity as well. Thus, directly following an elaborate description of the readers as the elect and holy people of God (2:4–10), the author exhorts them once again to manifest also the religious dimension of their social strangerhood: "Beloved, I exhort you as resident aliens and visiting strangers to keep apart from the fleshly passions [of their Gentile background and environment] which wage war against you" (2:11 au.). This negative warning is followed by the positive encouragement: "Maintain good conduct among the Gentiles [as in 1:17], so that although they speak against you as evildoers, they may see your good deeds [again, as in 1:17] and glorify God on the day of visitation" (2:12 au.).

In both these passages the actual political and social condition of the addressees as *paròikoi* is used as an occasion to encourage their religious peculiarity and strangeness as well. In both, an exhortation to social nonconformity is coupled with a call for conformity to the will of God. In both, *paroikia* in a strange and hostile environment is portrayed not simply as a regrettable social condition but as the Christian community's divine vocation. With this observation we have touched upon a key element in the strategy of the letter which will occupy our full attention later on. For the moment let us look briefly at two other terms with which *paroikos* and *paroikia* are closely related in 1 Peter; namely, *parepidēmos* and *diaspora*.

In regard to their place of origin, familial and friendship ties, language, social customs, opinions, *Weltanschauung,* and object of their religious devotion,[62] *parepidēmoi* and *paroikoi* identify the addressees of 1 Peter in general terms as strangers and aliens in the territories where they dwell. In this sense each term occurs elsewhere in the New Testament joined with the general word for "stranger," *xenos,*[63] or paronyms of *allos* and *allotrios* ("the other," the opposite of *oikeios* which denotes the familial and familiar).[64] And in addition to 1 Pet. 2:11 they are combined in Gen. 23:4 and associated in the *parallelismus membrorum* of Ps. 38(39):12. In their indication of specific political-legal realities, however, we have already noted that these two terms function somewhat differently. Whereas *paroikoi* denotes a class of the population juridically defined as "resident aliens with specified limited rights and status," *parepidēmoi* refers more generally to the "temporary visitors, transients, immigrants or wanderers" who have no intention or opportunity to establish permanent residence where they currently live. Although persons who were either *paroikoi* or *parepidēmoi* were both subject to juridical and social restrictions, since impermanent residence also affected political status, the Greek *paroikos* and its Latin equivalent *peregrinus* were the conventional terms used to designate the rank and class of the noncitizen (the non*polites* or non*civis*). As in Greek and hellenistic time, shown by the material discussed above, so in Roman law the position and rights of the *paroikoi/peregrini* were carefully defined. Adolf Berger, in his *Encyclopedic Dictionary of Roman Law,* describes the situation as follows:

> [The peregrinus is] a foreigner, a stranger, a citizen of a state other than Rome. A great majority of the population of Rome were peregrines, subjects of Rome after the conquest of their country by Rome. With the in-

crease of the Roman state the number of peregrines grew constantly without being compensated by the number of new citizens to whom Roman citizenship was granted. Within Roman territory the peregrines enjoyed the rights of free persons unless a treaty between Rome and their native country granted them specific rights. Generally, the legislation under the Republic, both statutes and *senatusconsulta,* applied to peregrines only when a particular provision extended their validity to them. Peregrines had no political rights, they could not participate in the popular assemblies, and were excluded from military service. A *peregrinus* might conclude a valid marriage (*iustae nuptiae*) only when he had the *ius conubii* . . . either granted to him personally or acquired through his citizenship in a *civitas* which obtained this right from Rome. A peregrine could not make a testament in the forms reserved for Roman citizens nor act as a witness thereto. He could not be instituted an heir of a Roman citizen nor receive a legacy (*legatum*) except in a testament of a soldier. He was able to conclude a commercial transaction with a Roman citizen if he had the *ius commercii,* which was granted in the same ways as *ius conubii.* Though excluded from the proceedings by *legis actio,* a peregrine had the benefit of protection in Roman courts, in particular before the praetor who had jurisdiction *inter peregrinos* . . . from the middle of the third century B.C. . . . Foreigners from the same state concluded transactions in accordance with the laws of that state and litigations among them were settled according to their own laws.[65]

THE MEANING AND USE OF *PAROIKOS* AND RELATED TERMS IN 1 PETER

The information quoted above allows us not only to trace the social position of *paroikoi* from hellenistic through Roman periods; it also enables us to envision more concretely the social situation of the addressees of 1 Peter. As resident aliens and transient strangers they shared the same vulnerable condition of the many thousands of Jewish and other ethnic *paroikoi* of Asia Minor and throughout the Roman empire. Legally their status within the empire, according to both local and Roman law, involved restrictions concerning intermarriage and commerce (*connubium et commercium*), succession of property and land tenure, participation in public assembly and voting, taxes and tribute, the founding of associations (*koina, collegia*), and susceptibility to severer forms of civil and criminal punishment.

On the other side of the coin, elevation to the ranks of the *paroikoi,* especially at the local level, with its conferral of albeit limited rights was far superior to that of *xenos* status with no legal protection whatsoever. Thus issues and struggles revolving around the *paroikoi* were significant factors contributing toward the political and social tensions which characterized the history of the eastern provinces since the advent of Roman rule. For the Christian *paroikoi* of Asia Minor, like their Jewish counterparts in Alexandria,[66] tenuous existence as resident aliens was fraught with profound and far-reaching political and socioeconomic as well as religious consequences. It is such implications that will be helpful later on for our understanding of the aspects of social tension and suffering which the addressees of 1 Peter are said to be experiencing.

If the denotation of the addressees as *paroikoi* and *parepidēmoi* speaks of their *social* strangeness, the word *diaspora* with which *parepidēmoi* is associated in 1 Pet. 1:1 suggests a further historical and religious aspect of their situation. In each of its three New Testament occurrences (John 7:35; Jas. 1:1; 1 Pet. 1:1) the term *diaspora* circumscribes geographically and socially, as it did in its technical LXX usage, a body of people living beyond the limits of Eretz Israel (Palestine). In John 7:35, consistent with Jewish usage, it identifies either "Greeks in whose territories the Jews live," or more likely, "hellenistic Jews from abroad currently in Jerusalem."[67] On the other hand, in Jas. 1:1 and 1 Pet. 1:1, contrary to conventional Jewish usage, *diaspora* is used for the first time as a designation for *Christians* (most probably an admixture of both Jewish and Gentile converts) who, like their former Jewish counterparts, now also live beyond the borders of Palestine. Whereas in James the exact geographic locality is left unspecified (" . . . to the twelve tribes which are in the *diaspora/* dispersion"), in 1 Peter this detail is explicit: ". . . to the elect visiting strangers of (the) *diaspora/*dispersion in (or of) Pontus, Galatia, Cappadocia, Asia and Bithynia" (au.). The noteworthy aspect of both these instances is that this novel usage reflects a stage in the Christian movement in which epithets once proper to Judaism alone ("diaspora," "the twelve tribes," "elect") are expropriated and now are used to designate the Christian community as coheirs or perhaps sole heirs of the legacy of Israel. Thus this designation of Christians as the "dispersed people (of God)" or "the people (of God) in the dispersion" indicates their religious identity and roots as well as their social condition of displacement and estrangement. As the heirs of Abraham,[68] Christians now share in the fateful history but also unique honor of the people of God.

In 1 Peter, moreover, the designation of the addressees as "of (the) diaspora" at the beginning of the letter is paralleled by the term *Babylōn* as the location of the authors at the letter's conclusion (5:13). The motivation for this thematic association, which also forms a literary inclusion of the whole document, may well have been the traditional apocalyptic association of the diaspora with Babylon,[69] that notorious place which most poignantly epitomized the trials and tribulations of Israel's diaspora existence and separation from home.

All these words which we have examined thus far—*paroikia, paroikoi, parepidēmoi, diaspora* and *Babylōn*—constitute in 1 Peter a constellation of terms or word field which points with varying nuances to the political-legal, social and religious identity and situation of the addressees and authors of 1 Peter. In the modern translations and interpretations of 1 Peter, however, the linguistic nuances and particularly the political, social and historical overtones of these terms are frequently overlooked or ignored. This failure needs to be examined and challenged, for it manifests itself in several different ways and appears to involve unfounded assumptions and circular modes of reasoning.

First of all, in some cases inappropriate words are chosen to translate the Greek terms of 1 Peter and frequently there is a lack of consistency within translations as well as among different versions. As a sample we might compare the following:[70]

1 PET. 1:1

KJV:	" . . . to the strangers scattered throughout Pontus . . . "
RSV:	" . . . to the exiles of the dispersion in Pontus . . . "
NEB:	" . . . to those of God's scattered people who lodge for a while in Pontus . . . "
JB:	" . . . to all those living among foreigners in the Dispersion of Pontus . . . " Cf. the equivalent French text: " . . . aux étrangers de la Dispersion: du Pont . . . "
NAB:	" . . . to those who live as strangers scattered throughout Pontus . . . "
TEV:	" . . . to God's chosen people who live as refugees scattered throughout the provinces of Pontus . . . "
Vulgate:	" . . . electis advenis dispersionis Ponti . . . "
Luther:	" . . . den erwählten Fremdlingen hin und her in Pontus . . . "
Zürcher:	" . . . an die Fremdlinge in der Zerstreuung in Pontus . . . "

Goodspeed: " . . . to those who are scattered as foreigners over Pontus . . . "

Phillips: " . . . to God's people now dispersed in Pontus . . . "

Reicke: " . . . to chosen immigrants of the dispersion in Pontus . . . "

Beare: " . . . to the chosen sojourners of the Dispersion in Pontus . . . "

Kelly: " . . . to God's scattered people settled temporarily in Pontus . . . "

Goppelt: " . . . an die erwählten Fremden in der Diaspora von Pontus . . . "

1 PET. 1:17

KJV: " . . . pass the time of your sojourning *here* in fear:"

RSV: " . . . conduct yourselves with fear throughout the time of your exile."

NEB: " . . . you must stand in awe of him while you live out your time *on earth.*" (Emphasis added.)

JB: " . . . you must be scrupulously careful as long as you are living away from your home." Cf. the equivalent French text:
" . . . conduisez-vous avec crainte pendent le temps de votre exil."

NAB: " . . . conduct yourselves reverently during your sojourn in a strange land."

TEV: " . . . you must, therefore, spend the rest of your lives *here on earth* in reverence for him." (Emphasis added.)

Vulgate: " . . . in timore incolatus vestri tempore conversamini . . . "

Luther: " . . . so führet euren Wandel, solange ihr *hier* wallet mit Furcht . . . "

Zürcher: " . . . so wandelt in Furcht während der Zeit eurer Pilgerschaft."

Goodspeed: " . . . you must live reverently all the time you stay *here* . . . " (Emphasis added.)

Phillips: " . . . you should spend the time of your stay *here on earth* with reverent fear." (Emphasis added.)

Reicke: " . . . then live out the time of your sojourn [*here*] in fear." (Emphasis added.)

Beare: " . . . conduct yourselves with reverent fear during your *earthly* pilgrimage . . . " (Emphasis added.)

Kelly: " . . . conduct yourselves with fear for the duration of your temporary stay."

Goppelt: " . . . so wandelt in Furcht während der Zeit eurer Fremd-
lingschaft."

1 PET. 2:11

KJV: "Dearly beloved, I beseech *you* as strangers and pilgrims
. . . "

RSV: "Beloved, I beseech you as aliens and exiles . . . "

NEB: "Dear friends, I beg you, as aliens in a foreign land . . . "

JB: "I urge you, my dear people, while you are *visitors and pilgrims* . . . " (Emphasis in original.) Cf. the equivalent
French text: "Très chers, je vous exhorte, comme *étrangers
et voyageurs* . . . " (Emphasis in original.)

NAB: "Beloved, you are strangers and in exile; hence I urge you
. . . "

TEV: "I appeal to you, my friends, as strangers and refugees *in
this world!* . . . " (Emphasis added.)

Vulgate: "Carissimi, obsecro vos tanquam advenas et peregrinos . . . "

Luther: "Liebe Brüder, ich ermahne euch als die Fremdlinge und
Pilgrime: . . . "

Zürcher: "Ihr Geliebten, ich ermahne euch als Pilger und Fremdlinge: . . . "

Goodspeed: "Dear friends, I beg you, as aliens and exiles *here* . . . "
(Emphasis added.)

Phillips: "I beg you, as those whom I love, to live *in this world* as
strangers and 'temporary residents' . . . " (Emphasis added.)

Reicke: "Beloved, I exhort you as pilgrims and immigrants . . . "

Beare: "Beloved, I beseech you as foreigners and sojourners . . . "

Kelly: "I appeal to you, dear friends, as aliens and temporary sojourners . . . "

Goppelt: "Geliebte, ich ermahne (euch), dass ihr euch als Fremde
und Beisassen . . . "

This selection of translations from older and more recent versions and
commentaries illustrates a lack of unanimity concerning the original denotations and connotations of the terms *paroikia, paroikoi,* and *parepidēmoi,*
and hence a lack of consensus with regard to their most appropriate contemporary rendition. It demonstrates as well the translational inconsistencies within a single translation. Still another problem comes to the surface
when words are added to the text which have no equivalent in the original Greek; namely, the modifiers "on earth" (*NEB, TEV,* and Phillips

at 1:17), "earthly" (Beare at 1:17) and "in this world" (*TEV* and Phillips at 2:11). Thus, especially in the case of the layperson without the benefit of the original Greek text, the specific social aspects of this language fail to be communicated. Imprecise terms such as "exile" and "pilgrims" are employed which could, and often do, conjure false associations. And, perhaps most serious of all, the impression is not infrequently given that 1 Peter represents a theological message for "pilgrims and exiles in this world" based on a contrast between present life on earth and a future life in the heavenly home.

Among those who share this impression, the comment of Francis Wright Beare is typical. In regard to *paroikous kai parepidēmous* in 2:11 he writes:

> The words differ little in meaning . . . he applies [them] in a spiritual sense to the earthly life of all Christians. (Cf. his use of *paroikia*, in 1:17, and of *parepidēmoi* in the salutation.) The thought that the true homeland of Christians is in heaven and that on earth they are in a foreign territory, is now made the basis of a moral appeal. The indulgence of the "fleshy desires" belongs to the order of earthly existence, now alien to them, and must be given no place in their new, heaven-centered life.[71]

But this is surely not the case for several reasons. First, such an interpretation of these terms completely ignores or at least minimizes their vital political and social currency in both the secular and religious literature (including the New Testament) before, during, and after the composition of 1 Peter. Secondly, this position involves the dubious assumption that these terms are used in an exclusively figurative or "spiritual" sense. Apart from the fact that such a "spiritual" sense exclusive of social or historical points of reference is most difficult to imagine, let alone document, the assumption is gratuitous and unnecessary. There is neither need nor reason to postulate mutually exclusive literal/figurative options here. As we have already seen, these words in 1 Peter are used to describe religious *as well as* social circumstances. In 1 Peter the actual social condition of the addressees as resident aliens and strangers is the stimulus for the encouragement that they remain so for religious and moral reasons. Third, the details of social alienation, confrontation and conflict recorded in 1 Peter are fully consonant with and illustrative of the recipients' position as actual resident aliens and visiting strangers within their Asia Minor society. Fourth, this means that the fundamental contrast in 1 Peter is not a cosmological but a sociological one: the Christian community set apart from and in tension with its social neighbors. To be sure, in the benediction with which the letter commences (1:3–12), the readers are reminded that they, along with the authors, have been reborn to a living hope (v. 3), a salvation ready to be revealed (v. 5), and "an inheritance which is imperishable, undefiled, and unfading, kept in heaven" (v. 4). This functions, however, as the first of several statements emphasizing the distinctive quality of the Christian addressees in contrast to the nonbelievers, Jews and Gentiles alike. The contrast here is not primarily spatial but *temporal*. As converts to Christianity the addressees have died to old associations and have been reborn to a living hope regarding their future prospects and present responsibilities (as, for example, in 1:13–21; 2:2, 10, 25). As 4:1–5 makes especially clear, such temporal contrasts are used to underline the social and religious distinctions between the believers and their hostile neighbors.

Fifth and finally, the immediate contexts of the terms under discussion also indicate not their figurative but rather their concrete socioreligious dimensions. In 2:11–12 and following verses, the "selfish desires" (*tōn sarkikōn epithymiōn*) from which the Christian resident aliens and visiting strangers are to separate themselves are not, as Beare suggests, an indulgence which "belongs to the order of earthly existence" but those cravings which typify the lives of the Gentiles (i.e., nonbelievers). The exhortation concerns a social and religious contrast, not a cosmological one. This is confirmed by a related passage in 4:1–6 which also refers to "selfish desires" and contains the only other occurrence in 1 Peter of the term "Gentiles" (*ethnē*). Here too a contrast is drawn between Christian conduct in accord with the will of God and living by "selfish desires" which characterized the addressees' former pre-Christian behavior. They are to "let the time that is past suffice for doing what the Gentiles like to do, living in licentiousness, selfish desires" (au.). Such isolation may be met with blasphemous slander on the part of former cronies who are now alienated (*xenizontai*) by this social breach (as indicated also in 2:12), but they will be called to account by God.

The negative admonition of 2:11 is explained and balanced by the positive thrust of 2:12. The Christians are to abstain from Gentile vices because they inhibit an exemplary and distinguished kind of conduct among the Gentiles, who despite their slanderous accusations should be led by

Christian good works to the glorification of God. Together vv. 11 and 12 reflect not a cosmological but a sociological distinction. They state thematically, first negatively and then positively, the socioreligious stance of Christian strangers toward their unbelieving social environment.

The context of 1:17 where *paroikia* occurs also shows affinity with the passage just cited, 4:1–6. Many commentators suggest that here also an "earthly pilgrimage" is implied in contrast to the heavenly home of Christians.[72] The actual contrast, however, is not between a "time of pilgrimage on earth" and a future "abode in heaven" but rather between the different types of behavior and associations which characterize the present and past stages of the readers' lives. As converts to Christianity the readers have been "reborn" (1:3; cf. v. 23 and 2:2), "called," "elected," and "sanctified" by God (1:1, 14–16; 2:4–10 etc.). *At present* they have been redeemed by God "from the futile ways inherited from your fathers" (1:18) and for these reasons must cease conformity "to the selfish desires of your *former* ignorance" (1:14 au.; cf. 2:15). The duration of their time of alien residence among the Gentiles is to involve, as 4:2–4 reiterates, a clean break from the sinful ways of these Gentiles which they previously had shared *prior* to their conversion. *Now* they are to obey God rather than the counsels of sinful men (4:2–3) and to conduct themselves as *paroikoi* who show fear (*phobos*, "awe and reverence") to God alone (see the same distinction made in 2:17 between honor due to the emperor and reverent awe due God). Thus the comment of Selwyn correctly captures the meaning and function of 1:17:

> "The time of your sojourning" takes up the description of the readers in the address as *parepidēmoi* (i. 1), and it prepares the way for its reiteration in ii. 11. Their lack of real place in the society of Asia Minor is not allowed to be forgotten, and conditions of their life. The "time" alluded to corresponds to *ton epiloipon en sarki . . . chronon* of iv. 2, in contrast with *ho parelēlythōs chronos* of the pre-Christian estate.[73]

In 1:17 and its context, as elsewhere in 1 Peter, temporal contrasts are used not to distinguish earthly from heavenly life but present holy from past unholy phases of the Christian's life. The purpose of this distinction is to underline the actuality of and necessity for continued Christian social and religious distinctiveness within society.

Discussions of 1 Pet. 1:1 also show how unfounded assumptions and circular argumentation can run rampant. Here the statement of Werner Georg Kümmel is typical:

> Since the letter is addressed to Gentile Christians, their designation as "the elect exiles of the Dispersion" in the regions mentioned is not to be understood literally. What is in view is Christians as members of the true people of God, who live scattered throughout *the earth* [emphasis added] as strangers, since their true home is in heaven (cf. Gal. 6:16; Phil. 3:20; Heb. 13:16; also 1 Pet. 1:17; 2:11).[74]

First of all, in regard to the New Testament passages which are so frequently cited to illustrate the supposed widespread Christian notion of a "heavenly home," it should finally be acknowledged that of all the New Testament documents only the Epistle to the Hebrews makes this a major and consistent theme.[75] Gal. 6:16 is not at all illustrative of this notion. And Paul's reference to a Christian "commonwealth" (*politeuma*) in heaven (Phil. 3:20), like the reference to the "heavenly inheritance" in 1 Pet. 1:4, is intended to depict the location of the Savior whom the Christians await and to underline the distinction between the godly Christians and the ungodly "enemies of the cross of Christ" (Phil. 3:18). In neither Philippians nor 1 Peter is an embracing theology of "Christian pilgrimage on earth" to be discerned. The same is true of Ephesians and James from which passages containing *paroikoi* (Eph. 2:19) and *diaspora* (Jas. 1:1) are frequently used to further support this idea.

In addition, it should at long last be recognized that such efforts at biblical harmonization—even among critical scholars—only enhance the obscurity of specific linguistic usage and of the specific content and perspective of specific documents.

Secondly, the position represented by Kümmel is based on questionable assumptions and circular argumentation. For one thing, the internal evidence of 1 Peter indicates that a mixed audience composed of both former Gentiles[76] *and Jews*[77] has been addressed. This is all the more likely in view of the mixed population of Asia Minor which included, according to one recent estimate,[78] about 250,000–280,000 Jews as well as 5,000 Christians in a total population of about four million prior to 67 c.e. The rapid advance of Christianity, especially on Asia Minor soil in the subsequent period,[79] could undoubtedly be attributed to the fact that there, as elsewhere, Christianity made its earliest and most extensive gains among Jewish converts and former Gentile proselytes to Judaism.[80] Sociologically and historically viewed, the assumption of exclusively Gentile-Christian or, for that matter, exclusively Jewish-Christian communities throughout Asia Minor in the time of 1 Peter is preposterous.

Even the likely preponderance of ex-Gentiles in the audience of 1 Peter, however, does not require, no less prove, that *diaspora* was used as a figure of speech for an earthly sojourn. In its New Testament usage the term can always be taken to connote geographical, social and religious distinction rather than cosmological separation from heaven. Furthermore, the Jewish roots of the senders of 1 Peter, Peter, Silvanus and Mark, could account for the conventional Jewish sense of diaspora in 1:1. Even apart from this possibility, addressees who could be taught and motivated by frequent reference to the Jewish Scriptures could certainly be expected to conceive of their place of *paroikia* as the diaspora with its religious as well as geographical and social connotations.[81]

The use of the term *diaspora* therefore proves neither that the addressees were exclusively Jews, as held earlier,[82] nor that, as applied to Gentiles, it is purely figurative and implies a transitory abode here on earth or "in the world." It indicates, as Leonard Goppelt has observed, the "sociological component" of the recipients' situation.[83] *Diaspora* here is a term with which the Christians "characterize their position *in society*" (emphasis added).[84]

Before we summarize the foregoing analysis, a final clarification of the most appropriate English equivalents for the terms under discussion is in order. This appears necessary in view of the confusion caused by the plethora of variant and often misleading translations. None of these terms employed by 1 Peter (*diaspora, paroikia, paroikoi, parepidēmoi*) specifically means "exiles" or "exiled persons." Nor does the conventional Greek term *phygē* (cf. also *phygas* and the Latin equivalents *exsilium* and *deportatio, relegatio*) ever occur in 1 Peter. The addressees cannot be considered "exiles" in the conventional and then contemporary sense of that word. Aside from rarer instances of voluntary self-removal, exile or banishment "was a compulsory departure from the country if given as a punishment. Voluntary exile was tolerated in the case of a person sentenced to death in a criminal act, but in such cases there followed an administrative decree which outlawed the fugitive" and "deprived him of

Roman citizenship (*captis deminutio media*) and his property."[85] Exile was a habitual tool of the Roman emperors for ridding the city of Rome, the senate, or simply the air, of troublemakers, undesirables, contenders for power, and overzealous critics. There is no indication in 1 Peter that its addressees were exiles in this sense or the victims of such political or legal actions. To be sure, *diaspora* and *Babylōn,* when applied to a Christian situation, imply that the Christians view their condition as analogous to that of Israel of old. But the limitations of that analogy are obscured when the word *exile* or *exiles* is used as though it were clearly employed in the original text of 1 Peter. Exiled persons might have been living as *paroikoi* and *parepidēmoi* in foreign territories, but not all strangers and resident aliens were exiles.

Pilgrims is likewise an inappropriate rendition of *paroikoi* or *parepidēmoi.* Indeed the English word derives from the Latin *peregrinator* (*peregrinus*)[86] but in modern times it has lost the specific legal nuances involved in the original Latin and is associated with religious observances, visits to shrines and even special Holy Year charter rates which are too far removed from the world of the first century to accurately reflect the specific social situation of the Christians in Asia Minor. Furthermore, it is too often understood in the light of a Christian spirituality which sings "I am but a pilgrim here, heaven is my home," a perspective which has led translators to even "improve" on the original text by adding such qualifying words as *earthly* pilgrimage and pilgrims *in this world.*

Finally, if "exile" and "pilgrims" and "pilgrimage" should be eliminated for reasons of imprecision, "sojourn" and "sojourners" should be dropped today because of their obsolescence.

For these reasons, in addition to the linguistic evidence given above, I suggest that the term *paroikia* be consistently rendered "alien residence" or "residence as aliens"; that *paroikoi* be translated "resident aliens" and *parepidēmoi* as "visiting strangers." These terms depict the addressees of 1 Peter as an admixture of permanent and temporary strangers and aliens, some of whom are residing permanently and others of whom are living temporarily in the five regions or four provinces of Asia Minor. Living under conditions of estrangement and socioreligious alienation in the "diaspora" and "Babylon" analogous to their Israelite forebears, the addressees and authors share in a certain sense the predicament as well as the hope of God's special elect and holy people. The social details of that situation and the novel social and religious concretizations of that hope will be the issues which will occupy our attention in the following chapters.

SUMMARY

In 1 Peter the terms *paroikia, paroikoi* and *parepidēmoi* identify the addressees as a combination of displaced persons who are currently *aliens permanently residing in (paroikia, paroikoi)* or *strangers temporarily visiting or passing through (parepidēmoi)* the four provinces of Asia Minor named in the salutation (1:1). These terms, as their conventional and widespread usage in contemporary secular and religious texts demonstrates, indicate not only the geographical dislocation of the recipients but also the political, legal, social and religious limitations and estrangement which such displacement entails. As *paroikoi* they may well have been numbered among the rural population and villagers who had been relocated to city territories and assigned inferior status to the citizenry. And as both *paroikoi* and *parepidēmoi* they may have been included among the numerous immigrant artisans, craftsmen, traders, merchants residing permanently in or temporarily traveling through the villages, towns and cities of the eastern provinces. The terms *diaspora* (1:1) and *Babylōn* (5:13) indicate the similar condition of both Christian addressees and authors. They also express an additional religious-historical dimension of the condition of Christian estrangement in society. Like the words "elect (visitors of the diaspora in . . . , " 1:1) and "coelect (of Babylon . . . , " 5:13) they recall, from a religious-historical perspective, the link of the Christian strangers and aliens with both the alienated predicament and the exalted status of God's unique redeemed community. The religious implications of the terms *diaspora* and *Babylōn* in no way vitiate the social conditions of the strangers and aliens to whom they are applied. Nor do they suggest or, even less, require that *paroikia, paroikoi* and *parepidēmoi* be taken in an exclusively figurative or "spiritual" sense. To the contrary, their evocative power derives from the fact that now Christians, like God's Israel of old, find themselves in an analogous situation of actual social and religious estrangement and alienation. As little as Israel's alien residence in Egypt or Babylon was figurative, so little is that of the Christians in Asia Minor. On the other hand, the Christian expropriation of epithets which were once exclusive attributes of Israel indicates a stage of development in which Jews as well as pagans are now regarded as "outsiders" and opponents of the Christian movement. All these terms point to various aspects of the political, legal, social and religious situation of the addressees and authors of 1 Peter.[87] They have not been used to compose a "theology of Christian exile or pilgrimage on earth," for the consistent contrast in this letter of abundant contrasts is sociological, not cosmological. As at least a few commentators have recognized,[88] the central focus of 1 Peter concerns the interaction of Christians and society, the social contrasts and conflicts which have created a crisis for the Christian movement in Asia Minor. 1 Peter is a letter addressed to resident aliens and visiting strangers who, since their conversion to Christianity, still find themselves estranged from any place of belonging. They are still displaced *paroikoi* seeking an *oikos*.

The role which social and religious estrangement played in both the crisis to which 1 Peter was a response and the strategy of that response itself will become clearer when we next consider further aspects of the geographical, social and historical circumstances of the addressees.

NOTES

1. The phrase is John Gager's (*Kingdom and Community: The Social World of Early Christianity* [Englewood Cliffs, N.J.: Prentice-Hall, 1975] p. 2), following Peter L. Berger and Thomas Luckmann, *The Social Construction of Reality: A Treatise in the Sociology of Knowledge* (Garden City, N.Y.: Doubleday, 1967).

2. For surveys of recent research on 1 Peter see John H. Elliott, "The Rehabilitation of an Exegetical Step-child: 1 Peter in Recent Research," *JBL* 95 (1976): 243–54; F. J. Schierse, "Ein Hirtenbrief und viele Bücher," *Bibel und Kirche* 31 (1976): 86–88. Throughout the present study reference will be made to the "letter" (of 1 Peter). The evidence for, and implications of, its epistolary genre will be discussed in due course. A periphrastic outline of the letter is given below on p. 234.

3. Paronym: "a word from the same root as another" (J. T. Shipley, ed., *Dictionary of World Literary Terms, Forms, Techniques, Criticisms,* rev. ed. [London: George Allen and Unwin, 1970 (1943)], p. 232 s.v.).

4. LSJ, s.v. Similarly, e.g., MM, BAGD, s.v.; Karl Ludwig Schmidt and Martin A. Schmidt, Rudolf Meyer, *"Paroikos"* etc., *TDNT* 5 (1967/1954):

841–53, esp. 842; Hans Schaefer, *"Paroikoi,"* PW 18/4 (1949) cols. 1695–1707, esp. 1695.

5. Schmidt, *"Paroikos,"* p. 842.

6. Ibid., pp. 842–48.

7. See above, n. 4.

8. Schaefer, *"Paroikoi,"* cols. 1695–99; for agreement on this latter point see also H. Hommel, *"Metoikoi,"* PW 15/2 (1932) cols. 1413–58, esp. 1420; for the related term *katoikoi* see F. Oertel, *"Katoikoi,"* PW 11/1 (1921) cols. 1–26.

9. MM, s.v. and Adolf Deissmann, *Bible Studies,* trans. A. Grieve (Edinburgh: T. & T. Clark, 1901) pp. 227–28 offer evidence of this same political-legal usage which, however, is not mentioned in BAGD or most commentaries.

10. So Schaefer, *"Paroikoi,"* col. 1698. Inscriptions from Pergamon (*OGIS,* p. 338; ca. 132 B.C.E.) and Ephesus (*SIG³,* 742; ca. 85 B.C.E.) offer good examples of the latter. For a discussion of these inscriptions and of the political, legal, economic and social standing of the *paroikoi* in Asia Minor see also S. Dickey, "Some Economic and Social Conditions of Asia Minor Affecting the Expansion of Christianity," in *Studies in Early Christianity,* Frank Chamberlin Porter and Benjamin Wisner Bacon FS, ed. Shirley Jackson Case (New York/London: The Century Co., 1928) pp. 393–416, esp. 398–99; T. R. S. Broughton, "Roman Asia Minor," in *An Economic Survey of Ancient Rome,* ed. Tenney Frank (Baltimore: The Johns Hopkins Press, 1938), 4:499–918, esp. pp. 637–45; David Magie, *Roman Rule in Asia Minor to the End of the Third Century after Christ,* 2 vol. (Princeton: Princeton University Press, 1950), pp. 149, 225, 1036–37, n. 8; and Michael Rostovtzeff, *The Social and Economic History of the Roman Empire (SEHRE),* 2. ed. rev. by P. M. Fraser (Oxford: Clarendon Press, 1957), vol. 2, Index, s.v. "By-dwellers."

11. Schaefer, *"Paroikoi,"* col. 1701.

12. Gen. 23:4; also Ps. 104 [105] :12.

13. Exod. 2:22; see also 18:3.

14. Deut. 23:7.

15. Josephus, *Ant.* 12.3.4. See also the deportation of 100,000 Jewish captives from Syria-Palestine to Egypt by the victorious Ptolemy I ca. 312 B.C.E. (*Ep. Arist.* 12, 35, 37).

16. See the comments of E. Mary Smallwood, *Philonis Alexandrini: Legatio ad Gaium,* 2. ed. (Leiden: E. J. Brill, 1970), pp. 3–31, esp. p. 20: "Flaccus attacked the rights of the Jewish *politeuma* by issuing a proclamation in which he declared that the Jews were 'aliens and foreigners' in Alexandria" (Fl [accum] 53–54). "By this measure he apparently degraded them from their legal position of *katoikoi* (resident aliens [= *paroikoi*]) to that of *xenoi.* Presumably this constituted an attack on the Jews' *politeuma* in that its develop-

ment had depended on the Jews' status as *katoikoi* and that its existence was consequently jeopardized when that status was lost."

17. Diodorus 20.84; Schaefer, *"Paroikoi,"* 1701

18. See Broughton, "Roman Asia Minor," ESAR, 4: 544.

19. Rostovtzeff, SEHRE 1: 255–57. For similar descriptions of the village *paroikoi* see also Dickey, "Economic and Social Conditions," p. 406, and Broughton, "Roman Asia Minor," pp. 628–48. On the sociopolitical status of the *paroikoi* through the second and third centuries in Bithynia and elsewhere in Asia Minor see Magie, *Roman Rule,* 1: 639–40; 2: 1503, n. 26.

20. Rostovtzeff, *SEHRE* 2: 655, n. 4.

21. Ibid.

22. Ibid., p. 654, n. 4.

23. *Paroikesia* (2 times), *paroikēsis* (4 times), *paroikia* (16 times), *paroikizō* (1 time).

24. For a discussion of these details see Schmidt, *"Paroikos,"* pp. 842–48; also Karl Ludwig Schmidt, "Israels Stellung zu den Fremdlingen und Beisassen und Israels Wissen um seine Fremdling- und Beisassenschaft," *Judaica* 1 (1945–46): 269–96 where Greek and Hebrew equivalents are also treated. *Paroikos, paroikeō* refer to the *permanently* resident alien and generally translate the Hebrew *ger, gur, magor* except for Exod. 12:45; Lev. 22:10; 25:6, 23, 35, 40, 45, 47 (2 times); Num. 35:15 where *toshav* occurs (in the P redaction, according to Schmidt, "Israels Stellung," p. 279, n. 15).

25. See also Gen. 47:4; Deut. 23:8 (LXX) and 1 Chron. 29:15 (no specific location named).

26. See also Gen. 20:1 (Gerar); 21:34 (land of the Philistines); 26:3 (Canaan); 35:27 (Hebron); Exod. 6:4 (Canaan).

27. See also Exod. 18:3; note in both texts the explanation of the naming of Moses' son, Gershom: "I have been a resident alien in a foreign land" (au.).

28. See also Lev. 25:6, 45, 47; Deut. 14:21; Jth. 4:10.

29. See also the Amalekite messenger to David (2 Kgdm. [2 Sam.] 1:13); the Hagrites (MT; *paroikoi,* LXX) in the region around Gilead (1 Chron. 5:10); nonexistence of resident aliens in Edom following its devastation (Jer. 30:12 [MT 49:18], hereafter [ ] = Masoretic Text); resident aliens living around the Ammonites (Jer. 30:21 [49:5]); resident aliens who were "neighbors of Zion" (RSV) (Bar. 4:9, 14, 24).

30. See Schmidt, *"Paroikos,"* pp. 844–46.

31. Ibid., p. 846.

32. This is true also in one instance where God is compared to a *paroikos*: "(You are) Israel's hope, Lord, and you save in time of troubles; why have you become like a resident alien in the land . . . ?" (Jer. 14:8 au.).

33. *NEB* notes "Or *in the land*."

34. See, e.g., Exod. 2:22; 18:3; Deut. 23:8 (LXX); Jer. 14:8.

35. See vv. 21–24, 43, 51, 53, 69–70, 78–79, 84–87, 95, 115, 118, 121, 134, 150, 157, 161.

36. For *paroikos,* etc., see further 21:28; 41:5; 44:6. For similar sentiments concerning the plight of *paroikia* see also Pseudo-Phocylides 39–41.

37. Following the suggestion of G. Buchanan Grey in *APOT,* 2:649, note on v. 17(15); translation according to Grey. For *paroikia* see also 12:3.

38. *Paroikos kai parepidēmos egō eimi meth' hymōn.*

39. . . . *Paroikos egō eimi para soi* (A, S; *en tē gē,* B) *kai parepidēmos kathōs pantes hoi pateres mou.*

40. Schmidt, *"Paroikos,"* p. 842, n. 6.

41. So Schmidt, *"Paroikos,"* p. 842; W. Grundmann, *"Dēmos,"* etc., *TDNT* 2 (1964/1935): 63–65, on *parepidēmos,* 64–65; Hommel, *"Metoikoi,"* cols. 1414–15; MM, s.v. *paroikos* and *parepidēmos;* see also Deissmann, *Bible Studies,* p. 149 (on *parepidēmos*). The participle *parepidemountes* thus is joined with and modifies *xenoi* to denote the temporary strangers in contrast to the *katoikoi* (*paroikoi*), e.g., *OGIS* 339.29 (Sestos, ca. 125 B.C.E.); see Oertel, *"Katoikoi,"* col. 1 for further examples.

42. E. G. Selwyn, *The First Epistle of St. Peter,* 2. ed. (London: Macmillan, 1955) p. 118 (on 1 Pet. 1:1), following Theodor Zahn.

43. See Karl Ludwig Schmidt, "Diaspora," *TDNT* 2 (1964/1935): 98–104; also A. Stuiber, "Diaspora," *RAC* 3 (1957): 972–82.

44. Ibid., p. 99.

45. *Apoikia* for *golah*: e.g., Jer. 30(49):3; 36(29):1; 2 Esd. [Ezra] 1:11; 2:1; 4:1 etc.; for *galuth*: e.g., Jer. 35(28):4; 36(29):22; 47(40):1, etc. *Apoikesia* for *golah*: 4 Kgdm. [2 Kings] 24:15; 2 Esd. [Ezra] 6:19, 20, 21; 9:4; 10:6; for *galuth*: 2 Esd. [Ezra] 6:16; see also *apoikizō. Metoikesia* for *golah*: 4 Kgdm. [2 Kings] 24:16; 1 Chron. 5:22; Nah. 3:10; Ezek. 12:11; for *galuth*: 4 Kgdm. [2 Kings] 25:27; Obadiah 20; see also *metoikizō.* Literary associations between *diaspora, diaspeirō* etc. and *apoik-* terms also deserve mention; e.g., Bar. 2:13–14; 3:7–8; Ps. Sol. 9:1 and in 17:17–18 the juxtaposition of *paroikia* and *ho skorpismos.*

46. Schmidt, *"Diaspora,"* p. 100.

47. Ibid.

48. Schmidt, *"Paroikos,"* p. 848.

49. E.g., *Cher.* 120, 121; *Conf. Ling.* 77–78.

50. Schmidt, *"Paroikos,"* p. 849.

51. R. Meyer, in Schmidt, *"Paroikos,"* p. 850; see pp. 850–51.

52. In an appended note to the analysis of Josephus (Schmidt, *"Paroikos,"* p. 850, n. 48), G. Bertram adds: "On the whole one finds more secular modes

of expression in Joseph[us]. He speaks of emigration and immigration, but the religious concept of the alien does not occur to him."

53. Max Weber, *Ancient Judaism,* trans. and ed. Hans H. Gerth and Don Martindale (Glencoe, Ill.: Free Press, 1952) from *Das Antike Judentum,* Gesammelte Aufsätze zur Religionssoziologie, vol. 3 (Tübingen: J. C. B. Mohr, 1921). See especially ch. 13, "The Pariah Community" (pp. 336–55) but also chs. 14–16 (pp. 356–424) for the social history of Judaism from the exile to its confrontation with early Christianity.

54. This is the explanation given by the translator-editors (preface, p. xxiii). On the sociological implications of alien residence and marginality see also pp. xxiii–xxvi.

55. Hommel, *"Metoikoi,"* col. 1457 (citing Heb. 11:13; 1 Pet. 2:11; 1:17 and 1:1; Diognetus 5:5).

56. Schaefer, *"Paroikoi,"* col. 1707 (citing no New Testament evidence).

57. *Kakōsousin;* note its occurrence in a similar sense in 1 Pet. 3:13.

58. See especially v. 22 (and 18:3) where the naming of his one son Gershom is explained to signify that "I have become a resident alien in a foreign land."

59. The LXX and Hebrew texts read "Damascus" where Acts 7:43 has "Babylon."

60. Here, as in Acts 7, questions of Lucan redaction are left aside.

61. New Testament usage indicates that whereas *katoik-* terms generally denote "inhabitants" and "habitation" (e.g., Matt. 2:23; Mark 5:3; Acts 1:19; Acts 17:26) in general, and *perioik-* terms denote "neighbor, neighboring" (Luke 1:58, 65), the root *metoik-* is most proximate to *paroikos* etc. in the implication of dislocation and resident alien status. Acts 7 (vv. 4, 6, 29) however suggests the near synonymity of *katoikizō, metoikizō* and *paroikos.* Noteworthy is the absence of all *apoik-* terms in the New Testament in contrast to the LXX. Also noteworthy is the correlation and contrast of *paroikos* and *oikos* in the passages of Acts and Ephesians cited above.

62. On aspects of strangerhood in antiquity and the pertinent Greek and Latin equivalent terms see Erich Fascher, "Zum Begriff des Fremden," *ThLZ* 96/3 (1971): 161–68.

63. See Eph. 2:19 (*xenoi kai paroikoi*) and Heb. 11:13 (*xenoi kai parepidēmoi,* a probable allusion to Ps. 38[39]:12). See also Acts 17:21 (*hoi epidēmountes xenoi*) and, for a secular occurrence, *OGIS* 339.29 (Sestos, ca. 125 B.C.E.: *tōn ʾparepidēmountōn xenōn*). On *xenos* and paronyms see Gustav Stählin, *TDNT* 5 (1967/1954): 1–36.

64. See, e.g., Acts 7:6 (*paroiken en gē allotria*), alluding to Gen. 15:13; cf. Gen. 23:4; also Heb. 11:9. On *allos* and paronyms see Friedrich Büchsel, *TDNT* 1 (1964/1933): 264–67.

65. Adolf Berger, *Encyclopedic Dictionary of Roman Law,* Transactions of the American Philosophical Society, new series, vol. 43, part 2 (Philadelphia: American Philosophical Society, 1953), s.v. *Peregrinus,* pp. 626–27. See further, M. Clerc, *De la condition des étrangers domiciliés dans les différentes cités grecques* (Bordeaux: Feret & Fils, 1898) and H. Francotte, "De la condition des étrangers dans les cités grecques," *Musée* 7 (1903): 350–88.

66. See above, p. 24 and n. 16.

67. See Schmidt, *"Diaspora,"* pp. 101–02 and on James and 1 Peter, pp. 102–04.

68. For references to Abraham see Jas. 2:21–23 and 1 Pet. 3:6.

69. See., e.g., Isa. 39:6; Jer. 13–14; 15:7; 41(34):17; Dan. 2:12; Jth. 5:19. Note also the occurrence of "Babylon" with terms of the *metoik-* root: Matt. 1:11, 12, 17 (*metoikesia Babylōnos*) and Acts 7:43.

70. Abbreviations of the following translations/versions are as follows:

KJV—The Holy Bible, King James Version (1611).

RSV—The Holy Bible, Revised Standard Version (New York: World Publishing Co., 1946, 1952/© 1971, 1973).

NEB—The New English Bible: The New Testament, 2. ed. (New York: Oxford University Press, 1970/1961).

JB—The Jerusalem Bible; Reader's Edition (Garden City, N.Y.: Doubleday, 1966); translated from La Sainte Bible traduite en français sous la direction de l'Ecole Biblique de Jerusalem (Paris: Cerf, 1956/©1955).

NAB—The New American Bible, 1. ed. (Cleveland and New York: The Catholic Press; distributed by the World Publishing Co. 1971/©1970).

TEV—Today's English Version of the New Testament (New York: Macmillan, 1966); originally published as Good News for Modern Man.

Vulgate—Biblia Sacra. Vulgatae Editionis Sixti V Pontificis Maximi iussu recognita et Clementis VIII auctoritate edita (Rome: Editiones Paulinae, 1957/1592).

Luther—Die Heilige Schrift nach der deutschen Übersetzung D. Martin Luthers. Neu durchgesehen (1914) nach dem vom Deutschen Evangelischen Kirchenausschuss genehmigten Text (London: Britische und Ausländische Bibelgesellschaft, 1954/1522).

Zürcher—Die Heilige Schrift des Alten und Neuen Testaments (Zürich: Zwingli-Verlag, 1957).

Goodspeed—The Complete Bible, an American translation. The Old Testament translated by J. M. Powis Smith and a group of scholars. The Apocrypha and the New Testament translated by Edgar J. Goodspeed (Chicago: The University of Chicago Press, 1948).

Phillips—J. B. Phillips, The New Testament in Modern English, rev. ed. (London: Collins, 1972).

Reicke—Bo Reicke, ed. and trans. *The Epistles of James, Peter, and Jude,* 2. ed., The Anchor Bible 37 (Garden City, N.Y.: Doubleday, 1964).

Beare—F. W. Beare, ed., *The First Epistle of Peter,* 3d. rev. ed. (Oxford: Basil Blackwell, 1970).

Kelly—J. N. D. Kelly, *A Commentary on the Epistles of Peter and of Jude,* Harper's New Testament Commentaries (New York: Harper & Row, 1969).

Goppelt—Leonhard Goppelt, *Der erste Petrusbrief,* KEK 12/1; ed. Ferdinand Hahn (Göttingen: Vandenhoeck und Ruprecht, 1978).

71. Beare, *First Epistle of Peter,* p. 135 (on 1 Pet. 2:11). For similar recent views see, e.g., Reicke, *Epistles of James, Peter, and Jude,* p. 93; Karl Hermann Schelkle, *Die Petrusbriefe, der Judasbrief,* HTKNT 13/2 (Freiburg-Basel-Wien: Herder, 1961), pp. 19, 47–48; Kelly, *Epistles of Peter and of Jude,* pp. 41, 72, 103; Wolfgang Schrage, *Die "Katholischen" Briefe: Die Briefe des Jacobus, Petrus, Johannes und Judas,* 11. aufl., with Horst Baltz, NTD 10 (Göttingen: Vandenhoeck und Ruprecht, 1973), pp. 66, 76, 85.

Below I shall discuss three further studies which also represent this position; the articles, namely, of Max-Alain Chevallier, "Condition et vocation des Chrétiens en diaspora. Remarques exégétiques sur la 1re Epître de Pierre," *RSR* 48 (1974): 387–98; Christian Wolff, "Christ und Welt im 1. Petrusbrief," *TLZ* 100 (1975): 334–42; and Victor Paul Furnish, "Elect Sojourners in Christ: An Approach to the Theology of 1 Peter," *Perkins Journal* 28 (1975): 1–11.

72. See note 71 above.

73. E. G. Selwyn, *The First Epistle of St. Peter,* p. 144. Compare the phrase *ton tēs paroikias hymōn chronon* in 1 Pet. 1:17 with the virtually identical phrase in 3 Macc. 7:19 (*ton tēs paroikias autōn chronon*) where it is narrated that the Jews in Ptolemais celebrated a feast of thanksgiving for their return home by king Ptolemy Philopater "and they determined to keep *this time of their alien residence* as days of joyfulness." Here, as in 1 Pet. 1:17, the social rather than a figurative "earthly" character of the *paroikia* is clearly meant.

74. W. G. Kümmel, *Introduction to the New Testament,* trans. Howard Clark Kee, rev. English ed. (Nashville: Abingdon, 1975), p. 418.

75. Concerning the fundamental significance of this theme in Hebrews there is exegetical unanimity. All too often, however, on the basis of terms commonly used in both Hebrews and 1 Peter (esp. *paroikoi, paroikeō* and *parepidēmoi;* cf. Heb. 11:9; 11:13 and 1 Pet. 1:1, 17; 2:11) the false assumption is made that 1 Peter shares the same Platonic cosmological perspective as Hebrews and that therefore the former document should be read in the light of the latter.

76. See 1 Pet. 1:14, 18; 2:10(?); 4:2–4 where former Gentile ignorance (of God), isolation from Israel and sinful behavior are involved.

77. See the use of and appeal to the Jewish Scriptures (1 Pet. 1:16, 24; 2:3,

4–10; 2:22–25; 3:10–12, 14; 4:18; 5:5c), to venerated Hebrew persons (Abraham and Sarah, 3:6; the prophets, 1:10–12), cardinal events in Hebrew-Jewish history (the Passover, 1:13; exodus, 1:18–19; exile, "Babylon" in 5:13) and honorific predicates of the ancient people of God ("holy," 1:14–16; 3:5, 15; and "elect," 1:1; 5:13 and esp. 2:4–10) which suggest readers of Jewish origin or with previous Jewish background, for whom such tradition would have the most meaning and weight.

78. See Bo Reicke, *The New Testament Era, The World of the Bible from 500* B.C. *to* A.D. *100,* trans. David E. Green (Philadelphia: Fortress Press, 1968), pp. 302–04.

79. Reicke, ibid., estimates that by the turn of the first century the total population figure as well as the Jewish population had remained the same. On the basis of Pliny's description of Christianity's growth and influence in the cities and the countryside (*Epistles* 10.96), however, he posits an increase of the Christian population to about 80,000. Certain demographic data from this period are notoriously scarce and all estimations run the risk of either understatement or exaggeration. Whatever the actual amount of Christianity's growth during this initial period, it is quite reasonable to conclude that adherents to the new movement continued to be drawn from both Jewish and pagan sectors of the population.

80. This is obvious from the Pauline letters and Acts. Details on the Jewish diaspora, including Asia Minor, and its political, legal, social and religious status are available in a host of literature. See especially: 1 Macc. 15:16–24; Philo, *Flacc.* 7; *Leg.* 33, 36, 281–82; Josephus, *Ant.* 12.3.4; 14.7.2; *War* 2.16.4; 7.3.3; *Sib. Or.* 3.271; Jean Juster, *Les Juifs dans l'Empire romain: leur condition juridique, economique et sociale,* 2 vols. (Paris: Geuthner, 1914), esp. 1: 180–209 and 2: 1–27; Salo Wittmayer Baron, *A Social and Religious History of the Jews,* 2. rev. ed., vol. 1 (New York: Columbia University Press, 1952/ 1937); Nils Alstrup Dahl, *Das Volk Gottes: Eine Untersuchung zum Kirchenbewusstsein des Urchristentums* (Darmstadt: Wissenschaftliche Buchgesellschaft, 1963), esp. pp. 92–104; Emil Schürer, *Geschichte des Jüdischen Volkes im Zeitalter Jesu Christi,* 3 vols. (Leipzig: J. C. Hinrichs, 1901–11[4] and reprint of Hildesheim, New York: Georg Olms Verlag, 1970), esp. 3: 1–188; Victor Tcherikover, *Hellenistic Civilization and the Jews,* trans. S. Applebaum (New York: Atheneum, 1974/1959), esp. pp. 269–377; and *The Jewish People in the First Century: Historical Geography, Political History, Social, Cultural and Religious Life and Institutions,* vol. 1 of *Compendia Rerum Iudaicarum ad Novum Testamentum,* ed. S. Safrai and M. Stern (Philadelphia: Fortress Press, 1974).

81. Perhaps it is also unnecessary to add that if diaspora is to be taken fig-

uratively, then why not the following place references "Pontus, Galatia," etc.? Of course neither Kümmel nor anyone else has proposed this but we might wonder why the qualification of diaspora by these actual localities did not move proponents of a figurative sense to less theological imagination and more sociological sobriety.

82. See Schmidt, "*Diaspora,*" pp. 102–04, for literature.

83. Goppelt, *Der erste Petrusbrief,* p. 79.

84. L. Goppelt, "Prinzipien neutestamentlicher Socialethik nach dem 1. Petrusbrief," in *Neues Testament und Geschichte,* Oscar Cullmann FS, ed. H. Baltensweiler and B. Reicke (Zürich: Theologischer Verlag and Tübingen: J. C. B. Mohr, 1972), pp. 285–96; quotation from p. 286.

85. A. Berger, *Encylopedic Dictionary of Roman Law,* p. 463, s.v. *exilium.* Notable exiles or banishments in the first century of the Roman Empire include, among others, those of Julia (daughter of Augustus), the philosophers Seneca, Epictetus, and Dio Chrysostom, the Jewish ethnarchs Archelaus and Herod Antipas (and wife), and quite probably the author of the Christian apocalypse, the prophet John who was relegated to the island of Patmos (Rev. 1:9). For contemporary views on the subject of exile see Epictetus, *Discourses* 1.4.24; 24.4; 2.1.10, and Dio Chrysostom, *Orations* 8.16; 12.1 and *Orat.* 13. On the attitudes and measures of Rome see Ramsay MacMullen, *Enemies of the Roman Order: Treason, Unrest, and Alienation in the Empire* (Cambridge, Mass.: Harvard University Press, 1966) passim.

86. "Pilgrim" is actually a cognate derivative of *peregrinator/peregrinus* in which the liquids r/l and n/m are exchanged; see the Italian *peregrino, pellegrino.* For this observation I am grateful to my wife, Dietlinde Elliott. See further, F. Kluge and W. Mitzka, *Etymologisches Wörterbuch der deutschen Sprache,* 19. ed. (Berlin: de Gruyter, 1963), s.v. "Pilger."

87. The complementarity rather than exclusivity of these aspects has been stressed by at least one earlier scholar; see Marco Adinolfi, "Stato civile dei Cristiani 'Forestieri e Pellegrini' (1 Pt. 2,11)," *Antonianum* 42 (1967): 420–34. *Paroikoi (forestieri)* and *parepidēmoi (pellegrini)* not only echo Israel's religious history, they "riflette anche la situazione concreta del mondo greco-romano nella seconda metà del primo secolo alludendo al particolare stato civile dei cristiani dell'epoca" (p. 420). After discussing the constituencies of the ancient city and the status of the Jews in particular, he notes the similarities of Christians and Jews in political as well as religious aspects: "Privi la maggior parte del diretto di cittadinanza, cosi difficile da ottenere, vivevano ai margini della vita civica come semplici residenti nelle città del Ponto, della Galazia, della Cappadocia, dell'Asia e della Bitinia" (p. 434).

88. See Karl Philipps, *Kirche in der Gesellschaft nach dem 1. Petrusbrief*

(Gütersloh: Gütersloher Verlagshaus-Gerd Mohn, 1971): "Das Ineinander von Kirche und Gesellschaft kommt im 1. Petrusbrief besonders prägnant zum Ausdruck" (p. 55). See, earlier, Theophil Spörri, *Der Gemeindegedanke im ersten Petrusbrief: Ein Beitrag zur Struktur des urchristlichen Kirchenbegriffs,* Neutestamentliche Forschungen, 2. Reihe (Gütersloh: C. Bertelsmann, 1925) and, above all, the recent commentary of Leonhard Goppelt, *Der erste Petrusbrief,* passim.

The Addressees of 1 Peter
and Their Situation:
A Social Profile

In the foregoing chapter we have seen that the identification and accentuation of the addressees in 1 Peter as "visiting strangers" and "resident aliens" is a significant indication of both the situation which prompted this communication and the strategy according to which it was composed. In order to gain as broad a perspective as possible on this key factor of socioreligious estrangement and the total social context to which it is related, it is now necessary to consider further features of the addressees and their situation in general. On the basis of data drawn from 1 Peter and supplementary external sources,[1] a "social profile" of the recipients[2] and implications for the concrete setting of the letter on the whole can be outlined through attention to the following factors: (1) the geographical location of the addressees; (2) their ethnic composition; (3) their legal, economic and social status; (4) their religious allegiance and the social form which such religious affiliation assumed; and (5) the nature and historical circumstances of the conflict in which they were involved.

THE GEOGRAPHICAL LOCATION OF THE ADDRESSEES

The *geographical location*[3] of the intended recipients is indicated in the letter's address: " . . . to the elect visiting strangers dispersed through (in the diaspora of) Pontus, Galatia, Cappadocia, Asia and Bithynia" (1:1). These names refer to five areas of Anatolia which, in the process of Roman eastward military expansion and conquest, since 133/31 B.C.E. onward, had gradually come under Roman control. By 17 C.E. this vast amount of territory comprising an area of some 128,889 square miles and a population of approximately 8,500,000 according to the estimates of T. R. S. Broughton,[4] had been organized into four Roman provinces with Bithynia and Pontus united as a single provincial unit since 65/63 B.C.E.

The separate mention of Pontus and Bithynia in 1:1 could suggest that the names in this verse referred to native regions rather than Roman provinces. Such an inference, however, is unlikely. On this possibility it would be difficult to explain why the regions of Paphlagonia, Phrygia, Pisidia and Lycaonia had been omitted since they too fall within the area circumscribed by the terms of 1:1 and, in the case of the latter three regions, were areas of Christian activity since the missions of Paul. Furthermore, inscriptional evidence also attests to the occasional independent or separate mention of Bithynia and Pontus in references to groups of Asia Minor provinces.[5] From Strabo's description of the geography and history of Asia Minor[6] it is clear that the Taurus mountain range extending from east to west across the southern expanse of Asia Minor was one of the determinate factors of geographical and political boundaries. From the names included in the address of 1 Pet. 1:1 and from the omission of the provinces of Lycia and Pamphilia which lay south of this mountain range we may conclude that the letter was intended for the sum of the Christian communities residing in the whole of Roman Asia Minor north and west of the Taurus.

Its address makes it clear that 1 Peter was designed as a general letter to be circulated throughout these four provinces. A theory which makes plausible the order of names in 1:1 is one which takes this process of circulation into account. The sequence of the provinces listed in 1:1 may correspond to the route according to which the letter was to be circulated. Pontus and Bithynia could have been mentioned separately because they were meant to designate the more specific parts of the united province at which the bearer of the letter would commence and conclude his journey.[7] Such a theory would be compatible with, but not proof of, a western origin of the letter, such as Rome. On the other hand, the commencement of the letter's address with Pontus, followed by Galatia and Cappadocia, might also reflect an awareness of the reorganization of these eastern provinces undertaken by Vespasian in the year 72 C.E.[8] If so, this would supply a useful anchor point for the dating of the letter. In any case the data remain circumstantial rather than conclusive. Nevertheless, analyses of the geographical particularities of 1 Peter along these lines seem far more substantive and promising than neglect of these issues altogether on the unfounded assumption that 1 Peter is simply addressed to the Pauline communities and mission field of Asia Minor. Before dealing with this assumption directly, however, there are further geographical factors to be considered.

One outstanding feature of the geographical location of the addressees is the enormous *diversity* of the land, peoples and cultures. The terrain, which varied from the coastal sections of Asia, Bithynia and Pontus to the mountain ranges traversing the northern and southern extremities of the territory and to the lakes and central plateau of the interior, established, along with the river systems, the natural boundaries of the area. This diverse topography reinforced and was paralleled by a diversity of peoples and cultures marked by different origins, ethnic roots, languages, customs, religions, and political histories. What David Magie said of the province of Galatia is, in general, applicable to all these provinces taken together: it is "a fantastic conglomeration of territories" whose inhabitants "were as varied as the districts of which the province was composed.[9]

By the advent of the Imperial Age older and more recently founded cities were numerous in Asia and dotted the coast of Bithynia-Pontus. Inland, however, urbanization and the process of hellenization and romanization which accompanied it had made little headway. Among the Galatian tribesmen at this time, writes Broughton,

> no cities existed. In spite of the unification of the royal power, the tribal organization remained, and the population continued to live in their villages, forts, and strongholds. Ancyra was still only a fort when Strabo wrote, and Pessinus, a temple and a market, their nearest analogue to a city.[10]

The picture is the same for Bithynia-Pontus and Cappadocia and altered little from the first to the third centuries. In Galatia, as elsewhere, a few city territories eventually replaced the tribes but in general urbanization and even military colonization were remarkably minimal.[11] Even at the end of this period tribal territories and villages predominated in the provinces of Asia Minor.

> In much of Inner Bithynia and Paphlagonia the artificial character of the cities is evident. In Galatia the numerous villages flourished upon the large

city territories. In eastern Pontus the same remained true of the city territories, and several tribes remained uncivilized and were left under the rule of chieftains. In several regions of Cappadocia the cities never occupied as much as one-third of the area; the strength of the people remained in the villages. . . . The process of hellenization proceeded no farther than that of urbanization. National characteristics and native languages took long to disappear. The Greek of the sequestered valleys of Phrygia is barbarous, and Latin anywhere exotic indeed. . . . Gallic was still spoken in Galatia in the fourth [century]. It is unlikely that Lycaonian speech ceased soon after St. Paul's visit, and in Cappadocia bad Greek and the native speech persisted together in the fourth century.[12]

The limited "urbanizing" of Asia Minor demonstrates, for one thing, the remarkable strength and tenacity of the many different native groups and institutions within its borders. Thus for the audience of 1 Peter there is no reason to expect any previous or current group loyalties which transcended local and regional differences and on which an appeal to a common Christian allegiance might build. For the advance and consolidation of the Christian movement here this diversity constituted an acute problem which had to be addressed and overcome. The underlying purpose and strategy of any circular letter such as 1 Peter surely have to be analyzed with this in mind.

At the same time the limited success of Rome's urbanization program—one of its chief strategies for the peaceful extension of Roman control and influence in the provinces—in unifying the various peoples of this area and securing their common allegiance suggests that great caution should be exercised against overestimating the role of Rome in the conflict in which the Christians throughout these provinces were engaged. The direct confrontation with the imperial cult in the cities of Asia (see the Apocalypse of John) can by no means be assumed as the situation underlying the social problems of the Christians in the hinterlands of Bithynia, Pontus, Galatia and Cappadocia. 1 Peter is a circular letter and speaks of a social conflict common to the Christian movement "throughout the world" (5:9). Accordingly, the causes and features of this conflict must be sought in the social conditions which characterized the interaction of Christians and the society of Asia Minor as a whole. In this case it is more likely that the conflict had been locally and socially determined rather than that it was due to direct confrontation with Rome.

Furthermore this evidence underlines the extent to which the population

of Asia Minor was and remained a predominantly *rural* population. This
is an additional significant element in the social description of the Christians of Asia Minor. Unfortunately it is one which is regularly overlooked
in the conventional descriptions of the Christian movement which represent it primarily, or even exclusively, as an urban phenomenon.[13] The
Pauline letters and mission, along with the Acts and the Johannine Apocalypse, indeed demonstrate the urban roots and orientation of one element
of the Christian movement. This is by no means the case, on the other
hand, for such writings as James, Hebrews, the Johannine and Petrine
literature, Jude and even the Gospels. In the case of 1 Peter in particular, both the external evidence of the predominantly rural environment of
its addressees and the internal evidence of the text itself suggest that the
letter is directed to a predominantly rural audience. Thus the *paroikoi* who
are addressed can be associated with the tenant farmers who worked the
land and were organized in manorial households, whose social centers
were villages and whose lands were gradually annexed to larger trade centers and city territories where they were then classified explicitly as "resident aliens." This of course does not exclude the probability that 1 Peter
reached the cities as well where merchants, traders and artisans had also
espoused Christianity in the status of resident aliens. On the whole, however, the content of 1 Peter supports the likelihood that the audience envisaged was rural as well as urban based. This is indicated by the sweeping
address of the letter itself, the use of agrarian (1:22–24), herding (2:25;
5:2–4) and domestic (the abundant recurrence of household imagery)
metaphors, the allusions to the rural environment of Asia Minor (the
graphic term *phrouroumenos* of 1:5 recalling the many forts and strongholds [*phrouria*] of the provincial interior; the term *klēroi* in 5:3 reminiscent of the apportioned sections of land given to clients of the king or to
Roman military veterans; the obviously rural metaphor of the ravenous
lion in 5:8) and the striking absence of *polis*-related terminology for Christian community such as Paul's preferred term *ekklesia* or the *politeuma*
image of Phil. 3:20. For the situation in Pontus a few decades later than
1 Peter, in fact, we have the explicit testimony of the provincial governor
Pliny contained in his letter to the emperor Trajan (ca. 111/112 c.e.). Concerning the location and expansion of the Christian movement he notes:
"This contagious superstition has spread not only through the cities, but
also throughout the villages and rural areas" (*vicos etiam atque agros;
Epistles* 10.96.9). Of the 80,000 or more Christians who have been esti-

mated to have resided in Asia Minor as a whole by the turn of the century,[14] it may be reasonably assumed that a rural population constituted the majority.

From this evidence concerning the geographical location of the addressees, certain implications concerning the letter in general can also be drawn. First, the vast amount of territory inhabited by the intended recipients of 1 Peter—some 129,000 square miles—presupposes an extensive and intensive Christian mission here prior to the composition of 1 Peter. The only such missionizing in Asia Minor for which there is any clear New Testament evidence is that undertaken by Paul, and this encompassed only Galatia and Asia. The only other New Testament reference to two further provinces, Pontus and Cappadocia, occurs in an enumeration of Jewish pilgrims (Acts 2:9–11) present at a speech of Peter (2:14–36) on the occasion of the church's first Pentecost festival in Jerusalem. It is conceivable that, upon their return home, these Jewish converts, under the impulse of Peter and the Jerusalemite believers, initiated the Christian movement in these areas. This would account for the early conversion of such provincials as Aquila of Pontus (Acts 18:2). In any event, two facts seem likely: (1) Bithynia-Pontus and Cappadocia were evangelized by persons other than Paul and his immediate associates; and (2) sufficient time beyond the campaigns of Paul must be allowed for Christianity to have spread throughout all the provinces named in 1 Pet. 1:1. The date of this letter, therefore, can reasonably be set no earlier than two to three decades after the conclusion of Paul's activity in this area.

The predominantly rural composition of the provinces and people addressed, and the absence of evidence for the existence of city churches in all areas except Asia, also suggest that 1 Peter was addressed to *household communities*, domestic pockets of Christians dispersed across the landscape of Asia Minor. This would be supported, as already noted, not only by the absence of the term *ekklesia* so basic to Paul's urban propaganda but also by the central role that household terminology and imagery play in the consolation and exhortation of 1 Peter.

In the light of these observations the significant differences between 1 Peter and the correspondence and activity of Paul deserve stress. 1 Peter was addressed to Christians who were located beyond the borders of the Pauline mission and who were living not only in the cities but also in the wide rural areas. The letter's geographical destination offers neither evidence nor reason for regarding 1 Peter as intended for Pauline churches or for areas of the Pauline mission field. To the contrary, these geographical considerations alone, quite apart from additional factors to be examined later, provide cogent grounds for dissociating 1 Peter, its origin, destination and intent, from the influence of Paul and the Pauline circle.[15] 1 Peter is best read on its own terms, as an independent though complementary witness to the diversified growth of early Christianity in Asia Minor.

A related point should also be made in regard to the *situation* that the letter envisions. The problems that Christian converts confronted in the cities and hellenized province of Asia, as reflected in Acts and the Apocalypse as well as in the correspondence of Paul, cannot be assumed to be those of the Christians in the interior of Asia Minor. Typical, recurrent causes of social and local tensions between natives and displaced aliens and outsiders in their midst must be considered in the case of the situation presented in 1 Peter. In the rural interiors the role of Rome in such conflicts will have been negligible. On the other hand, the social tension and prejudice which, as Ramsay MacMullen has described them, regularly marked the interaction of urban and rural elements of the population, suggest that their "rusticity" was a further factor that contributed to the alienation of the addressees living in the cities. *"Urbanitas* opposed not only *rusticitas* but *peregrinitas* as well."[16]

Finally, the numerous aspects of diversity that characterize this conglomeration of provinces historically, politically, culturally and religiously posed a critical problem for the Christians here and one which 1 Peter may well have been designed to meet. A movement composed of converts from diverse regions, cultures and religious backgrounds, a "dispersion of strangers," presents the practical problem of social coordination and unification. Hostility within their environment and pressures for conformity would have made the problem even more critical. This remains an important point to consider in our further examination of the issues of situation and strategy.

THEIR ETHNIC COMPOSITION

The ethnic composition of the communities addressed in 1 Peter, as discussed earlier, was mixed, consisting of both former Jews and non-Jews with a preponderance of the latter. This is consistent with the general heterogeneity of the Asia Minor population, the mixed composition of all the early Christian communities described in the New Testament,[17] and the content of 1 Peter in particular.[18] Evidence for the spread of the Jewish diaspora throughout all the regions and provinces of Asia Minor in both its cities and rural areas is abundant.[19] The exact numerical size of the Jewish diaspora here, however, is difficult to pinpoint; Reicke's figure of 250,000[20] represents a conservative estimate. It is this extensive dispersion of Jews which provided not only the starting point and communication network of the Christian mission here, thereby enabling its rapid advance, but also the occasion of the eventual tensions between both groups. Parallel to the campaigns of Paul initiated among the Jewish communities in Galatia and Asia, it may have been Cappadocian and Pontic Jews returning from their Pentecost pilgrimage (Acts 2) who first brought the messianic message to their compatriots in the more northerly territories. "An excellent road," Selwyn notes,

> ran from the Cilican Gates northwards through Cappadocia and Galatia to Amisus [of Pontus] on the Euxine, probably the first city on that coast to receive the Gospel; and at Mazaca (Caesarea [in Cappadocia]) it crossed another fine route which the enterprise of Ephesian traders had utilized so effectively as to direct the commerce of Cappadocia from Sinope [also on the Black Sea coast] to their own Levantine seaboard. Syrian Antioch occupied a key position in relation to both routes; and we can be sure that the Christian Church there would lose little time in following up with a more thorough evangelization the trail of the Gospel first blazed by the returning pilgrims.[21]

By the time of 1 Peter, however, recruits from among the Gentiles probably outnumbered their Jewish counterparts. In the letter more is said about the past history of the former and it is upon the difficulties which these former pagans were having in the termination of previous associations that the letter particularly focuses.[22] It is likely that among their number were those pagans whose contact with Christianity was mediated through an earlier association with the synagogue as proselytes to Judaism. This is suggested by the attraction which the Christian movement had for such Gentile proselytes to Judaism in general,[23] the knowledge and persuasive force of the Old Testament which 1 Peter assumes, the Greek version of the Old Testament which the letter quotes, and the use of metaphors for conversion[24] which were common to Jewish as well as Christian missionary propaganda.

The mixed composition of the Christian communities addressed in 1 Peter, in sum, reflects the mixed character of the provincial population as a whole.[25] The vigorous flow of human traffic to and from Asia Minor was a further factor sustaining such heterogeneity. Commerce and trade by land and sea, entrepreneurial activities among the resident aliens from abroad, the attraction of educational opportunities (such as at the university at Tarsus) and health spas (at the renowned Asclepian spring shrines) and athletic and dramatic festivals, religious pilgrimages, mass movements of deported groups,[26] the banishment of individuals,[27] and the peregrinations of assorted itinerant philosophers and religious missionaries—all such occasions of movement to and from Asia Minor contributed toward the ethnic diversity of the peoples to whom and by whom the Christian gospel might be proclaimed. The mixture of nationalities, cultures, religions and social classes resulting from such movement would not only imply a diversity among these recruited to Christianity. It would also account for the number of strangers and resident aliens living here and for the social tensions resulting from the conflicting interests of the many different and often competing groups within the general population.

THEIR LEGAL, ECONOMIC AND SOCIAL STATUS

The legal, economic and social status of the Christians of Asia Minor in the first century c.e. is a complex and as yet unsettled issue. Without attempting either a survey or a resolution of the problem here, it will be helpful to view it from the vantage point of the *paroikos* status of those addressed in 1 Peter. In chapter 1 we have already seen that *paroikos* and its related terms were used with both general and, more often, specific denotations. Denoting the "stranger" or the "alien" in a general way, these terms applied to persons who were differentiated from the natives among whom they lived in respect to their land of origin, ethnic or familial roots, their different views and opinions, and their language, property and religion.[28] In general, furthermore, such distinctions inevitably involved political, legal, economic and social restrictions and disadvantages for those so identified as "strangers" and "foreigners." More often, however, the *paroikos* was viewed as a member of a distinct legal-social class within the general native population. Occurring in inscriptions and literature from predominantly eastern Greek regions including Asia Minor from the hellenistic period onward, the term was applied to "a stratum of the population which is reckoned neither to the full citizen nor to the [complete] strangers [*xenoi*] but which stands in the middle of these two extremes."[29] "The most significant feature of the *paroikia*," it was noted, "is that it is recognized by the individual state as an institution" to which both individuals and underprivileged groups could be admitted with official consent.[30] Included among the *paroikoi* were slaves, serfs and those constituting the multitude of the déclassé and homeless strangers who lacked citizenship either in their previous homeland or where they currently resided. Although the cities had their share of such *paroikoi*, the far greater number were found among the rural populace of tenants, farmers, slaves and local artisans. In the hellenistic and Roman periods the *paroikoi* of Asia Minor were comparable to the earlier institution of the *metoikoi* of Greece. There, in contrast to the "homo politicus" or full citizen, the metic or "homo oeconomicus" provided the work force and economic basis of the Athenian economy.[31] The *paroikoi* served a similar function in the later periods. The country people in the provinces who belonged to the class of *peregrini* and *paroikoi*, in Rostovtzeff's words, formed the economic backbone of the empire. "Together with the slaves and artisans of the cities they constituted the working-class of the Roman Empire, the class which, under the direction of the city *bourgeoisie*, produced the goods required by the cities and by their imperial army, which were the chief consumers."[32] Excluded from voting and land-holding privileges as well as from the chief civic offices and honors, they enjoyed only limited legal protection, were restricted in regard to intermarriage and the transfer of property, could be pressed into military service, were free to engage in cultic rites but were excluded from priestly offices, and yet shared full responsibility with the citizenry for all financial burdens such as a tribute, taxes and production quotas. "Only the citizens enjoyed full civic rights, while the [alien] residents [known as *metoikoi, paroikoi, katoikoi, synoikoi*] were regarded as foreign-born natives, although they might have been born in the city and have grown up there."[33]

The economic role of the *paroikoi* was determined by their legal and social status. Since only full citizens were permitted to own land, the opportunities for support and survival were restricted to the tilling rather than the owning of the soil, and to local crafts, commerce and trade. Restricted from the main source of wealth and profit, the limitation of their economic status and power within society was assured. Although in everyday life there was little apparent difference between the *paroikoi* and the full citizens, in times of political turmoil or economic adversity these "outsiders" were the first targets and scapegoats of social suspicion, censure and animosity,[34] a point of paramount significance for assessing the situation of the *paroikoi* of 1 Peter.

Such is a description of the legal, economic and social condition of the addressees based on their identification as *paroikoi*. To this description derived from external sources may be added further correlative detail from the letter itself. The "in-between" legal and social situation of the recipients is indicated not only by their designation as *paroikoi* but also in the encouragement of their social distinctiveness on the one hand (e.g., 1:3, 14–16, 18–19; 2:11; 4:2–4) and their civic responsibility on the other (2:12, 13–17; 3:15–16; 4:15–16). It is further likely that, while a predominant number of the addressees are rurally located, the letter is intended for Christians in the cities also. The predominantly rural character of the provinces addressed and the rural metaphors employed in 1 Peter suggest the former; the reference to slaves as *oiketai* ("household servants") in 2:18–20 would suggest the latter. For, as Broughton has noted,[35] "slaves were little used either in agriculture or in industry, the large number attested for Pergamum and probably existent in many other cities must have been used chiefly for household service; it is true that the great majority of the slaves and freedmen that are mentioned in the inscriptions did belong to this class." Such domestic servants, however, also formed part of the personnel of the manors or estates of the countryside[36] and in both rural and urban areas contributed to the most basic and extensive mode of ancient economic organization known as "house economy" or "oikos management."[37] In any case, the specific appeal to *household* servants (rather than the more general "slaves") in 1 Peter and the paradigmatic function that their instruction serves in the letter support the likelihood that the communities addressed were those of households for whom a reminder of household responsibilities would have been most appropriate.

Explicitly mentioned among the recipients, in addition to the household servants, are free men (2:16), wives of non-Christian husbands (3:1–6) for whom the question of Christian relationships with non-Christians would be particularly acute, Christian husbands of Christian wives (3:7), the leaders of these Christian communities (*presbyteroi*; 5:1–4) and recent converts (*neōteroi;* 5:5).[38] Little can be deduced here concerning their economic condition. The admonition of the wives, "Let not yours be the outward adorning with braiding of hair, decoration of gold and wearing of robes" (3:3), might indicate a modicum of wealth. On the other hand, the reference to slaves but omission of a reciprocal exhortation to owners in 2:18–20 seems to point to a generally inferior economic position of the addressees as was characteristic of *paroikoi* on the whole.

The *occupations* of the addressees may be surmised from those of the *paroikoi* of Asia Minor in general and from what is known of the land's natural resources and related industries.[39] *Paroikoi* were involved, above all else, in Asia Minor's chief industry, namely, agriculture. Abundant grazing land and other natural resources such as timber, gold, silver, iron, emeralds and marble made possible the production of textiles (wool, linen and dyeing), leather goods and parchment, fishing, baking, metallurgy, gem and glass making, stone cutting, pottery and terra-cotta production, shipbuilding and building in general in which Christians may also have been employed. Their labor, prior to their conversion, may also have involved them in the industrial guilds and associations of traders so numerous in Asia Minor.[40] This is suggested by the kinds of activity decried in 1 Pet. 4:3. "Drunkenness, revels and carousing" were typical of guild celebrations. But for converts to Christianity such behavior constituted "lawless idolatry" and wild excess from which the believers were to dissociate themselves, even in the face of abuse from their former cronies. Such guilds and associations, including those with Jewish membership,[41] were sources of social and political ferment in this period.[42] Previous membership in such guilds[43] could have been a further factor in the tensions which existed between the Christians and their neighbors, particularly their employers (see the charges leveled against them in 4:15 and the law-abiding admonition of 2:13–17).

Information from 1 Peter on the economic condition of the addressees is, at best, inferential. The vast majority, it may be assumed at any rate, were from the working proletariat of the urban and rural areas. Further inferences may be drawn from what is known generally about the depressed economic circumstances of this class of the Asia Minor populace during this period. Moreover, if the theory of Samuel Dickey may be followed, these circumstances may also have been an important factor in the rapid spread of Christianity which the letter of 1 Peter presupposes. In his study, "Some Economic and Social Conditions Affecting the Expansion of Christianity,"[44] Dickey has described the plundering and exploitation of much of Asia Minor as a result of Greek and Roman expansionist policies. Territorial confiscations, war indemnities, exorbitant tribute and taxation, slavery and the reduced economic level of the free laborers had been the brutal price which the provinces paid for the *pax romana.* Not only was slavery the lot of much of the laboring masses: "More numerous and not less wretched were the free or semi-free agricultural laborers of the country and the poverty-stricken proletariat of the cities."[45] Compulsory services required of individuals and cities by the state, periods of famine and exorbitant prices due to the monopolization of the corn for the city of Rome and the army, the uncertainty of rainfall in a dry country like Asia Minor, and the difficulties of transportation especially by land contributed to the situation of the poor of both city and country.[46] "Proletarian labor in Asia Minor in the first centuries of our era was restive, ... its economic condition justified this unrest, and ... it had no opportunity for redress through either political or economic action."[47] Such conditions, according to Dickey, provoked an "apocalyptic mood" which won for the Christian movement an eager hearing among the laboring proletariat in particular.

> During the first three centuries the general economic status of the laboring classes went from bad to worse. There was no permanent alleviation, and there seemed no hope of it by ordinary processes. Therefore when Christianity entered with its promises of a "new age" of righteousness inaugurated by divine power, which included "feeding the hungry with good things," and "exalting those of low degree," it could not help get a hearing.[48]

Such an apocalyptic mood is clearly echoed in 1 Peter and later Christian literature associated with Asia Minor, especially the Apocalypse of John, the Chiliastic movement to which Papias attests and Montanism.[49] The vision of the black horse of the Apocalypse, furthermore, points to the kind of concrete economic conditions which fanned its fires: "A quart of wheat for a denarius and three quarts of barley for a denarius ... " (Rev. 6:6).

"The amazing rapidity and completeness of the conversion of Asia Minor to Christianity," to which 1 Peter is an early witness, according to Dickey, is in no small measure due to both the material and the religious hope which it proffered.

> . . . [T]he profoundly religious inheritance of the Oriental native stock was here [in Asia Minor] softened, disintegrated, and rendered plastic, to an unusual degree, by the dissolving influence of centuries of Hellenic culture. The most of it was destined to reappear again under new forms in Christianity [which] was religious and concrete, and therefore appealed especially to the ignorant and exploited masses. It made its way with amazing rapidity, for it satisfied in experience and anticipation a multiplicity of their deepest and most universal needs.[50]

On this theory, then, the wide circle of Christians addressed in 1 Peter may imply debilitating economic circumstances in Asia Minor which had led to a fervid interest in Christianity, particularly in view of the unique hope and experience of salvation which it promised (cf. 1 Pet. 1:3, 9, 13, 21; 3:15, 21). Or, as Max Weber, commenting on the religion of nonprivileged classes, has put it: "Since every need for salvation is an expression of some distress, social or economic oppression is an effective source of salvation beliefs, though by no means the exclusive source."[51]

One final factor affecting the legal and social condition of the Christians of Asia Minor was the eventual separation of the Christian sect from its Jewish parent. As long as the Christian movement remained an inner-Jewish phenomenon, adherents to the messianic sect would continue to enjoy the privileges and protection which Rome had long guaranteed Judaism as a special type of *paroikia*.[52] Even subsequent to the gradual separation of the sect from Jewish political, social and religious structures, the *paroikia* style of Jewish life in the diaspora would continue to provide a model for and influence upon Christian communal life as well as a reservoir for its social and religious vocabulary.[53] The Jewish converts to Christianity themselves would assure this continuity. Such a separation, which had become more pronounced from the period of the first Jewish-Roman war (66–70 c.e.) onward, however, involved an important alteration in the legal status of the Christian sectarians. The Jewish diaspora retained its privileged political, legal and religious status in the empire, even despite the Palestinian revolt. The more the messianic movement around Jesus distinguished and separated itself from Judaism, howver, the more it sacrificed the protective cloak of its favored parent. The fact that the persons addressed in 1 Peter had become known to their neighbors by the distinctive name "Christian" (4:16) rather than simply as Jews (of a particular persuasion) implies that such a separation had already become recognizable. This, in turn, would have raised the question of their legal status and invited suspicion of the novel worship which they practiced. The break with all previous alliances necessitated by their conversion had thrown them into a kind of double jeopardy. Already "outsiders" by virtue of their status as strangers and aliens, they had increased the measure of their vulnerability among Jewish and pagan elements of the society alike by becoming "fanatics" (3:13) of a new religious cult as well. Now it remains to examine this religious factor in greater detail.

THEIR RELIGIOUS IDENTITY AND
SECTARIAN COMPOSITION

The religious identity and sectarian composition of the communities addressed in 1 Peter, although inseparably linked to the factors already discussed, played a central role in the situation of the addressees as described in 1 Peter. In addition to their condition as strangers and social "outsiders," it was their religious allegiance, with the exclusiveness that such allegiance required, which had incited the suspicion and hostility of their neighbors. This latter point requires special stress in view of frequent efforts to trace the hostility experienced by the believers to implications regarding their name only. On the basis of what is said in 1 Peter regarding the reproach that the name "Christian" had earned the believers, it has been argued that simply bearing the name "Christian" had already been declared a crime by official Roman policy. "If you are reproached for the name of Christ, you are blessed because the spirit of glory and of God rests upon you. But let none of you suffer as a murderer, or a thief, or a wrongdoer, or a mischief-maker; yet if one suffers as a Christian, let him not be ashamed, but under that name let him glorify God" (4:14–16). For the period of the early Principate, however, there is no clear evidence of such an official imperial policy outlawing Christianity. The correspondence between Pliny and the emperor Trajan (Pliny, *Epistles* 10.96–97) makes it clear that this was still the case at the beginning of the second century.[54] Attribution of the peculiar name "Christian" to the persons addressed in

1 Peter does, however, indicate that they were perceived by others[55] to constitute a specific religious group or sect born within but now distinct from its parent body, Judaism. Given what is known from sociological research about the tension which typifies the relation of sects to society, it is necessary to look no further than the sectarian composition of the communities addressed to account for the conflict that characterizes their situation. To appreciate the religious identity of the addressees and its bearing on their condition in society, I am suggesting, it is essential to consider the social form which their religious allegiance assumed.

Reference to early Christianity as a sectarian movement is, of course, commonplace today. Careful examination of the implications of this fact for the social history of the movement is far less common. Stimulated by the observation that the model of the religious sect "has never been applied in any detail to the emergence of Christianity," an exegete, Robin Scroggs, has undertaken a study to show "that the community called into existence by Jesus fulfills the essential characteristics of the religious sect, as defined by recent sociological analysis."[56] Seven typical sectarian characteristics are used as a basis for comparison: like the sect, the earliest Christian community (1) emerges out of protest; (2) it rejects the view of reality claimed or taken for granted by the establishment; (3) it is egalitarian; (4) it offers its adherents love and acceptance within the community; (5) it is a voluntary organization; (6) it commands and demands total commitment from its members; and (7) like some sects it is adventist (apocalyptic) in its temporal orientation. By measuring the data of the New Testament against the sociological model or "ideal type" of the sect, Scroggs has been able to construct a more concrete social picture of the early Palestinian Christian community. The utility of such a procedure is that once certain social contours of the community are established, fresh perspectives are gained for detecting and interpreting other relevant evidence in the texts and arriving at as comprehensive a social analysis of a community as possible.

Scrogg's attention was restricted to the earliest Christian communities of Palestine. From the evidence provided by 1 Peter, it is clear, however, that the sectarian features of the movement continued to characterize the Christian communities of Asia Minor and determine the nature of their interaction with society.

For a more complete definition of a typical sect we may turn to one of the authorities in the sociological study of sectarian phenomena, Bryan R. Wilson. According to Wilson,

> The sect is a clearly defined community; it is of a size which permits only a minimal range of diversity of conduct; it seeks itself to rigidify a pattern of behaviour and to make coherent its structure of values; it contends actively against every other organization of values and ideals, and against every other social context possible for its adherents, offering itself as an all-embracing, divinely prescribed society. The sect is not only an ideological unit, seeking to enforce behaviour on those who accept belief, and seeking every occasion to draw the faithful apart from the rest of society and into the company of each other. . . . The sect, as a protest group, has always developed its own distinctive ethic, belief and practices, against the background of the wider society; its own protest is conditioned by the economic, social, ideological and religious circumstances prevailing at the time of its emergence and development.[57]

The comparison of the data of 1 Peter with this model leaves no doubt about the sectarian character of its intended recipients. The letter speaks of the recipients as members of a clearly defined, divinely prescribed community: the elect and holy people of God (1:3–2:10) brought into being by the activity of God the Father, the Holy Spirit and Jesus Christ (1:1–2). To the public they were known as the "Christians" (4:16). Separated from the rest of society through a voluntary termination of, and conversion from, past familial, social and religious ties (1:3–5, 10–12, 18–21; 2:4–10; etc.), theirs was a familial-like community or brotherhood (1:22; 2:5, 17; 5:9) defined by a unique faith in Jesus as the Christ, as the agent of the salvation for which they hope (1:2, 3, 6–8, 13, 18–21; 2:3, 4–10) and an ethic which prescribes religious allegiance, "fear" (1:17; 2:17; cf. 3:6, 14) and "obedience" (cf. 2:8; 3:20; 4:17) to the will of God alone (2:15; 3:17; 4:2, 19). The salvation (1:5, 9, 10; 2:2; 3:21; 4:18) or divine grace (1:2, 10, 13) in which all members share equally (3:7; 4:10; 5:5, 10, 12) is anticipated in full measure at the final advent of Jesus Christ soon to take place (1:5, 7, 13; 4:13; 5:1). Until this time the sect is to maintain strict internal discipline (1:22; 2:1; 3:8; 4:7–11; 5:1–5) and to contend vigorously against any encroachment from, or assimilation to, outside pressures (1:14–16, 18–21; 2:11; 3:9, 13–17; 4:1–6, 12–19; 5:8–9).

The more specific subtype of sect to which this Christian community might belong is determined by analyzing the kind of "response to the world" which it represents. Such a response to the world, Wilson points out, is manifested not only in particular doctrines and a sense of mission but also in "many relatively unfocused, unpurposive activities, . . . lifestyle, association and ideology."[58] Basic to the implications of a "response to the world" is the fact that *the sectarian movement always manifests some degree of tension with the world, and it is the type of tension and the ways in which it is contained or maintained* (emphasis added) which are of particular importance."[59] Wilson describes seven distinctive ways in which sects deviate from and reject the prevailing values of society and its cultural arrangements.[60] His characterization of a "conversionist response to the world" and its comprehension of evil and of salvation is that to which the community of 1 Peter most closely conforms. Wilson describes this response as follows:

> The world is corrupt because men are corrupt; if men can be changed then the world will be changed. Salvation is seen not as available through objective agencies but only by a profoundly felt, supernaturally wrought transformation of the self. The objective world will not change but the acquisition of a new subjective orientation to it will itself be salvation.
>
> Clearly this subjective conversion will be possible only on the promise of a change in external reality at some future time, or the prospect of the individual's transfer to another sphere. This is the ideological or doctrinal aspect of the matter, but the essential sociological fact is that what men must do to be saved is to undergo emotional transformation—a conversion experience. This is the proof of having transcended the evil of the world. Since it is a permanent and timelessly valid transcendence, some future condition of salvation is often posited in which objective circumstances come to correspond to the subjective sense of salvation, but the believer also knows, from the subjective change, that he is saved *now*. Thus he can face the evil of the world, the processes of change that threaten men with decay and death, because he is assured of an unchanging condition *and feels this*. This response is the *conversionist* response to the world.[61]

This type of response, which so closely matches the position advocated in 1 Peter, is to be distinguished from others according to which salvation, or, in Wilson's terms, the "overcoming of evil," is sought in the destruction (revolutionist response), manipulation (manipulationist response), reformation (reformist response) of, or withdrawal (introversionist response) from, the natural and social order. For conversionist sects it is the "supernaturally wrought transformation of the self" which enables the believer to apprehend the objective future change of all things as a present reality and as the basis of a confident engagement with the world.

If it is clear that the communities addressed in 1 Peter most closely resemble sects which promote a conversionist type of sectarian response to the world, then we may go on to consider the social conditions which typify the emergence and development of such sects. According to Wilson,

> Conversionist sects appear to arise most readily in circumstances in which a high degree of individuation occurs. Such a condition may occur through the atomization of social groups in a process of profound social upheaval in which more stable social structures are impaired or destroyed, communities are disrupted, and individuals are forcibly detached from their kinsfolk in enforced or induced migration by conquerors or invaders. Thus, many individuals may find need of spiritual and social accommodation in an alien social context. Likeness of circumstances—as with slaves, displaced people, foreigners—may be sufficient to overcome differences of cultural background and ethnicity in the welding of new religiously based communities. Such may have been the condition of the early spread of Christianity. This, then, is a socially enforced process of individuation of social circumstance: it may not go deep into human consciousness, but it is a situation in which the individual is separated from his home culture and must make some new accommodation for himself. The obvious accommodation is to reunite himself with a group—a group which cannot be a natural grouping, but must be one which capitalizes the commonality of circumstance of detached individuals and which draws them into a new synthetic community of love.[62]

Once again we may note how closely this description coincides with our analysis of the displaced aliens addressed in 1 Peter, the unstable social conditions which marked their age, their need for community in an alien social context, and the prospect for a communal experience of salvation in a brotherhood of love which, as 1 Peter indicates, the Christian sectarian movement offered.

Considering in this fashion the features which characterize the Christian movement in Asia Minor as a sect enables us to view not only their religious allegiance but also their relation to their environment in broader and clearer sociological perspective. Christianity as a sect was not just a religious but also a social phenomenon. To its members it represented a place of belonging for the displaced and the disenfranchised. It was an alternate and self-sufficient society where people could cultivate in common the values and ideals which were at variance with those of the society at large. As a sect, Christianity appealed to persons already in tension with the world. Upon their conversion the sect provided them the means for enduring and even accepting that tension. The transformation which was sought concerned not the structures of society but the attitude of heart and conscience (2:19–20; 3:3–4, 15–16, 21) of persons desiring the experience of true brotherhood. The community formed by persons willing to undergo such a conversion, however, constituted an implicit form of organized social protest.

Such protest, even if left unspoken, invited counterprotest. Voluntary termination of social bonds implied repudiation of public responsibilities, civic disloyalty, and personal rejection of those left behind. This interest in complete conversion, symbolized in 1 Peter as "rebirth" (1:3, 22–23; 2:2), "sanctification" (1:2, 14–16) or "purification" (1:22), clearly distinguished the Christian sect from the achievement-oriented, cosmopolitan and secular mystery cults of the empire.[63] Thus it was the conversionist sect of Christianity rather than the mystery cults against which public hostility and resentment were directed. The conflict and suffering which the addressees of 1 Peter were experiencing, in other words, can be seen as a concomitant factor of their organization as such a religious sect. Keeping in mind the sectarian character of the Petrine communities will not only provide a fresh perspective for determining the situation of the addressees; it will also enable us to detect and evaluate aspects of the strategy employed in 1 Peter to confront this situation.

This brings us to the last element of our "social profile," namely, the social conflict in which the addressees of 1 Peter were engaged.

THEIR INTERACTION
WITH NON-CHRISTIAN OUTSIDERS

The most immediate factor in the situation of the addressees which prompted the composition and dispatch of 1 Peter was the interaction of the Christian sectarians with the non-Christian "outsiders": its nature, historical circumstances and impact upon the Christian movement in Asia Minor.

As a religious sect the Christian movement had spread through the urban and rural areas of four or more provinces of Asia Minor. The vision of universal salvation which it embraced and attempted to actualize in its communal life had been found attractive particularly by those estranged from the sources of political power, economic security and social mobility. While describing themselves in terms of the sacred traditions of Judaism, its members professed a distinctive allegiance or faith in one rejected by the Jews (1 Pet. 2:4–7), whom they reverenced as "Christ" or the "Lord." In the eyes of the pagans this made them, in effect, "Christ-devotees," "Christ-sycophants," that is, "Christians." Like the Jews from which this sect once originated, it drew firm social and religious boundaries between its members and all "outsiders." It formed a community set apart and disengaged from the routine affairs of civic and social life. Such would have been the general impression of the sect gained by outside observers—as reconstructed from 1 Peter.

From 1 Peter, however, it is also clear that these outsiders hardly remained neutral in their attitude or behavior toward the Christian sectarians. From the vantage point of the general populace it was the Christians, in fact, who were the outsiders, strangers both socially and religiously. As such they constituted a potential danger to the public order and social weal. Falling under the shadow of suspicion is forever the stranger's lot. Although Rome had taken no official position against these Christians, its execution of their purported Lord in Judea and its indictment of Christians in Rome on the charge of arson (following the great fire of 64 C.E.) suggested that this sect was vulnerable to the charge of evildoing and perhaps of even more specific offenses.

In regard to the nature of the popular reaction against the Christians in Asia Minor, 1 Peter indicates that it was novelty and exclusiveness, far more than familiarity, which had "bred contempt." Ignorance (2:15), curiosity (3:15), suspicion of wrongdoing (2:12; 4:14–16) and aggressive hostility (3:13–14, 16; 4:4) were the public reactions which the Christians had encountered and under which they suffered. Although informed enough of the sect to brand its members collectively as "Christ-sycophants," the outsiders appear to have little specific or accurate knowledge concerning the religion or morality of these strangers. Out of curious ignorance they inquired concerning the strange "hope that is within you" (3:15). Such ignorance on the part of the public, coupled with the standoffishness of the Christians, had also bred suspicion and contempt. Even where the good conduct of the sectarians was evident (2:12; 3:16), the deliberate "ignorance of foolish men" (2:15) had led to the suspicion of immorality, including civic disloyalty (2:13–17). The relationships covered in 2:18–3:7 and 5:1–5 suggest further customary areas where strangers were under suspicion: the continued submission of slaves to the authority of their masters (2:18–20) and of wives to husbands who did not share their religious devotion (3:1–6), husbands who may be mistreating their wives (3:7) or religious leaders who may have been "in the business" for material and personal gain (5:2).

As ignorance bred suspicion, so suspicion engendered slander and reproach. (All the pertinent terms refer to verbal rather than physical abuse or legal action: *katalaloun*, 2:12; 3:16; *epērazein*, 3:16; *oneidizein*, 4:14; and similarly, *kakoun*, 3:3.) The breaking of social bonds, and the cultic ties which they entailed, had prompted not only a sense of estrangement (*xenizontai*, 4:4) on the part of the deserted cronies but also their angry denunciation of the Christians as well as their God (*blasphēmountes*, 4:4). For bearing the name and professing faith in Jesus as the Christ, the outsiders had found them worthy only of reproach (4:14).

Such ignorance, suspicion, slander and reproach had engendered sorrow (*lypēthentes*, potential in 1:6; *lypas*, 2:19), fear (*phobos*, 3:14) and suffering (*paschein*, 2:19, 20; 3:14, 17; 4:1, 15, 19; 5:10; *pathēmata*, 5:9; cf. 4:14) on the part of the Christians.

This completes the inventory of all explicit references in 1 Peter to the attitudes and actions of the outsiders and the resultant experiences of the Christians. Neither the specific terminology of these references nor the contexts[64] in which they occur refer to anything other than the social pressure, religious discrimination and local hostility which customarily were directed by natives against inferior aliens and exotic religious sects. Furthermore, as Ernest Cadman Colwell has noted,[65] such incidents were typical of the popular reactions against Christianity in the early Roman empire. These reactions were prompted not because of any official proscription of Christianity by Rome but by the sectarian exclusiveness of Christianity itself.

> That there was before Decius [249–51 c.e.] no empire-wide rigorous attempt to crush the Christian religion is generally admitted today. Before

Decius strong popular opposition preceded governmental opposition and was in most cases the reason for it. . . . However questionable may be the accusation of Christian apologetics that the Roman courts condemned the Christians merely for the name, there can be no doubt that the mob condemned the Christians as Christians. It was not only the existence in Christianity of disturbing elements, peculiar practices, and peculiar beliefs but the more general matter of Christianity's conception of itself as distinctive that led to opposition. . . . Out of this Christian conception arose the practices and attitudes which alienated the people of the empire. Foremost in the list of alienating products comes the Christian attitude of aloofness and separation.[66]

In regard to the situation described in 1 Peter, C. F. D. Moule has summarized the matter quite adequately:

All the requirements of these passages are equally met by postulating "unofficial" persecution—harrying by Jews and pagans. The fact that [in 4:15, 16] *hōs christianos* is parallel to *hōs phoneus ē kleptēs* (whatever the other words in that list may mean—which is obscure) does not in the least compel the conclusion that to be a Christian was officially a crime in the same category as the indictable offenses. Even if all the other words mean indubitable crimes, all that the Greek says is, If you have to suffer, suffer as a Christian, not as a criminal. . . . It was possible to suffer *hōs christianos* from the moment that that name was given (Acts xi. 26): the Christians did not escape that sort of suffering even before it was an officially recognized offense. And it seems as natural to postulate "private" persecutions here ("pogroms", so to speak) as it is in I Thess. ii. 14–6, Heb. x. 32–9, xiii. 7. . . . In I Pet. iv. 4 there is reference to precisely such social ostracism and unpopularity as might lead to open persecution of this sort, without any state intervention.[67]

Such harrassment of Christians by local opponents seems to have been the rule rather than the exception. The New Testament abounds with examples which parallel the situation described in 1 Peter.[68] If the reports of Acts can be taken as historically reliable, already by the time of Paul's arrival in Rome (ca. 58–60 c.e.) Jews there could say: "With regard to this sect we know that everywhere it is spoken against" (Acts 28:22).

In the case of 1 Peter the identity of the opponents is left unspecified. For ideological purposes all inimical outsiders were reduced to one common social ("Gentiles," 2:12; 4:3) and demonic (5:8–9) denominator. However, there are at least two conceivable groups of agitators, Jews and non-Jews. As the tradition which is cited in 1 Pet. 2:4, 7–8 affirms,[69] opposition to the sect and rejection of its Lord first began with the Jews. Opposition from this quarter, as Acts and the letters of Paul attest, also accompanied every subsequent stage of the sect's expansion in the diaspora. Not only did the sect's missionary zeal (1 Pet. 2:12; 3:1–2) constitute a serious source of competition to Judaism's quest for proselytes;[70] the movement was also perceived as a dangerous threat to the already tenuous social and political relations between Jews and the powers that be. As Jewish leaders from the outset worried about Jesus, that "If we let him go on thus, every one will believe in him, and the Romans will come and destroy both our holy place and our nation" (John 11:48), so in the diaspora they attempted to convince the local authorities that these followers of his were not simply religious but social miscreants who "have turned the world upside down" (Acts 17:6). To add insult to possible injury, these heretical sectarians were claiming to be the exclusive representatives of the true Israel.[71]

On the other hand, a comparison of 1 Peter with the recurrent expressions of pagan contempt for Judaism indicates that non-Jews opposed the *Christiani* for virtually the same reasons that they opposed the people from which this sect emerged. In the latest survey of Antisemitism in the hellenistic Roman period,[72] Jerry L. Daniel has documented and discussed the major areas of Jewish life against which pagan resentment was directed: its ignoble origins, it cultural and religious strangeness, and its exclusiveness and proselytizing. Pagan contempt and distrust of the Jews, Daniel summarizes,

> was bolstered by a feeling that Jews were strange and inferior. It was a protest against religious customs which seemed primitive and superstitious. It was a reaction against the apparent snobbery of a race which insisted on maintaining its exclusiveness, especially in regard to the one God. It was also a reaction against Jewish success in converting others to their strange religion.[73]

To judge from the response given in 1 Peter, similar pagan attacks had been made on similar aspects of Christian sectarian life.[74] For the Christians of 1 Peter, as for the Jews,[75] this pagan opposition amounted not so much to violent persecution as to continuous social polarization.

Polarization with outsiders, furthermore, seems to have been accompanied by polarization and lack of unity within the sect. In regard to the admonitions of 1 Peter we may assume that what is *proscribed* in the letter was possibly current practice in the audience, and that what is *prescribed* had not yet been fully realized. Thus the repeated stress on separation from all pre-Christian associations and types of behavior (1:14, 18; 2:11; 4:1-4) suggests disagreement among the converts concerning their appropriate relation to outsiders. Need membership in the Christian community be so exclusive? In view of the suffering this entails would not moderation and conformity present a more prudent alternative? On the other hand, the injunction to civic obedience (2:13-17) suggests that there may have been some converts more prone to a course of resistance[76] or perhaps total civic withdrawal. The warnings against "malice, guile, insincerity, envy and slander" (2:1) and preoccupation with superficial externals (3:3-4) likewise hint at a certain lack of consensus regarding common group values. In the same vein behavior detrimental to internal unity could have prompted the positive encouragement of brotherly love, mutual affection and concord (1:22; 3:7, 8-9; 4:8; 5:14), ungrudging hospitality (4:9), respect for internal order and authority (the subordination theme of 2:18-3:7; 5:1-5a) and mutual humility (3:8; 5:5b-7). The suffering caused by outside hostility no doubt took its toll on internal solidarity. This indicates that the problem facing the Christians of Asia Minor was a double one. Not only were they suffering at the hands of outsiders; this suffering posed a threat to their internal cohesion as well.

The situation, in summary, was one of internal as well as external tension and conflict which had developed within a configuration of interrelated factors which were geographical, ethnic, social, economic and religious in character. It was a time when the expansion of the Christian movement in Asia Minor and its growing visibility as a distinct socioreligious entity was being encountered and challenged with suspicion, fear and animosity. Spread throughout all the provinces north of the Taurus, the sect had attracted rural as well as urban elements of the population, former Jews as well as a predominant number of pagans. Living on the margin of political and social life, these *paroikoi* no doubt had seen in this new salvation movement new opportunity for social acceptance and improvement of their economic lot. Coming from the already suspect ranks of strangers, resident aliens and lower classes, however, these "Christ-lackeys" gained only further disdain for the exotic religion they embraced.

Sporadic local outbreaks of slander and abuse had led to the suffering of these Christians here as elsewhere throughout the Mediterranean world. In view of the immense territory and diverse cultures through which the sect had spread here in Asia Minor, consolidation of the membership posed an urgent goal. Yet opposition from outside the sect seems to have created tension and discord within. Continued suffering would not only have exacerbated internal tensions and threatened group solidarity but would also have led to disillusionment, despair and defection. Suffering and the opprobrium of "strangeness" could have been minimized or eliminated through the simple step of social conformity or assimilation. But this would have only resulted in the loss of the distinctiveness and exclusiveness to which the sect owed its existence. At stake was not only the future growth but also the very existence of the Christian movement in these eastern provinces. The crisis the Christians faced was not simply coping with suffering in itself but with the elements of their communal life which such suffering threatened to undermine: the necessity of their social distinctiveness and group cohesion and the maintenance of faith and hope in a salvation which seemed to be eluding them.

THE DATE OF 1 PETER

One final aspect of the situation remains to be considered. This concerns the date of 1 Peter and the period within which these developments most likely took place. Any reflections on this problematic subject, however, must remain cautious, provisional and subordinate to other more assured exegetical results. As yet there is little scholarly consensus regarding either the external data which are relevant or the relation of the letter's date of composition to other issues such as its authorship, integrity, literary affinities and place of composition.[77] An independent and comprehensive investigation of the dating of 1 Peter is obviously in order. Provisionally, however, I would cite three points which deserve special attention: (1) the social situation and composition of the recipients as has been examined above; (2) the relation of 1 Peter and its addressees to the larger stream of early Christian literature and social developments, and the location of both documents and recipients on the historical, social and theological "trajectory" of early Christianity; and (3) the political and social conditions generally prevailing in the early Roman empire (including but not restricted to explicit documentation of imperial reaction to Christianity). While this study has concentrated on the first of these points,[78] a preliminary consideration of all three factors leads me to suggest a date for 1 Peter within the middle years of the Flavian age (69–96 C.E.).

This is the period when, in the aftermath of the first Jewish revolt (66–70 C.E.), the Christians of Asia Minor, as elsewhere, were emerging as a peculiar sect distinctive from their Jewish parent body as well as from pagan types of associations and cults. By this time some of the earliest witnesses, authorities and propagators of the Christian movement had died (James of Zebedee in 44; James, brother of the Lord in 62; Peter and Paul, ca. 65–67). Their work was being carried on by circles of their associates who, in their correspondence, wrote in the names of their former inspiring leaders. It was a period of vigorous geographical expansion for the Christian mission and widening social concerns in which larger audiences were addressed (as in James, Hebrews, and the Gospels). The theological concerns reflected the altered social situation. No longer were Mosaic law, temple and circumcision the *predominant* points of socioreligious tension as they were earlier for Paul. At issue was the sect's distinction from, and yet openness to, both Jews and Gentiles alike. Theological legitimation of the break from Judaism and of the mixed ethnic character of its constituency had become a chief concern. Thus the ecclesiastical situation reflected in 1 Peter coincides with that of the Gospels and Acts where double social and ethnic fronts and issues of distinctive Christian identity, integration and legitimation are also in focus. Proximity in time and similarity in situation would also account for the affinities of 1 Peter to other New Testament documents such as James, Hebrews and Ephesians: the wider circle of intended recipients; the less personal relationship of author(s) and addressees; the social distinction or separation of Christian from Jewish communal life and yet the retention and reinterpretation of Jewish tradition, exemplary figures, institutions and events; the ethnic coalescence of both former Jews and Gentiles in the new community of faith; the concern for social cohesion and the development of a theological rationale for suffering. According to both James and Hebrews, as in 1 Peter, suffering is a test of faith (Jas. 1:2–3, 12; 1 Pet. 1:6–7; 4:12) or a means of discipline (Heb. 12:3–11), an experience common to the Christian "dispersion" (Jas. 1:1; 1 Pet. 1:1) or to those strangers and visitors without a natural homeland (Heb. 10:32–34; cf. 11:13–16; 12:18–24; 13:13–14).[79] Like James and

Hebrews (10:32–36; 12:4), and in clear contrast to the later bloody martyrdoms attested in John's Apocalypse,[80] the hour of testing and tribulation envisioned in 1 Peter had not yet been brought about by any direct confrontation with Rome. In 1 Peter the Roman government is viewed neither as a "servant of God" (Rom. 13:1–7) nor as a henchman of Satan (Apocalypse) but simply as a human institution designed to administer justice (1 Pet. 2:13–14) and worthy of respect (2:17).

The period in which such Christian activities of expansion and consolidation were most probably taking place, therefore, was the era of Flavian rule up to about 92 c.e. The last years of Domitian's reign (93–96 c.e.) were marked by the opposition of the senatorial aristocracy, philosophers and religious groups alike. The reign of terror which the suspicious emperor instigated against all of his enemies, real and imagined, was punctuated with his own assassination in 96 c.e.[81] Except for this regrettable finale, the Flavian house had brought to the empire an era of tranquillity, stability and prosperity. Following the Jewish revolt in the east and the year of the four emperors and civil war at Rome (69 c.e.), there emerged with Vespasian a second Augustus, a *restitutor orbis,* who introduced a new dynasty, a consolidation of authority and a gradual return of popular confidence. Organization and unification among the Christians paralleled a reorganization and consolidation of the empire in general. The absence of any evidence of Roman antagonism toward the Christians from 69–92 c.e., correlated with the positive or at least neutral attitude toward the empire manifested in the Christian literature of this period including 1 Peter, indicates a time of toleration and peaceful coexistence. Under Flavian rule the provinces of Asia Minor, Magie has observed, enjoyed unusually favorable Roman provincial administrators and benefactions. Despite the failure of, and resistance to, Domitian in Rome, "in these provinces there is little evidence of cruelty on the part of Domitian or even of exaggerated pretensions to grandeur. . . . In fact, in his administration of the provinces Domitian seems to have shown both vigour and intelligence."[82] His biographer, Suetonius, has recorded: "He took such care to exercise restraint over the city officials and governors of the provinces, that *at no time were they more honest or just,* whereas after his time we have seen many of them charged with all manner of offences" (*Domitian* 8.2, LCL; emphasis added). Thus "it is easy to see," as Reicke notes, "why Christian writers during the first twelve years of his reign considered the existing form of government and society as offering for the most part positive advantages for missionary work, and only afterward condemned it in apocalyptic terms (i.e., as in Revelation)."[83] It is not easy to concur, however, with Reicke's early dating of 1 Peter "before the Neronian catastrophe."[84] The excellent description he provides of the Roman empire in the subapostolic period,[85] and of the situation of Jews and Christians under the Flavians[86] which he illustrates with several references to 1 Peter,[87] points rather to a composition of 1 Peter within the Flavian period.

The social situation and concerns addressed in 1 Peter, when correlated with similar developments within the Christian movement and conditions tolerant of such effort within the empire, suggest for 1 Peter a date between the accession of Vespasian (69 c.e.) and the demise of Domitian (93–96 c.e.). Additional factors might suggest an even more specific time frame. For a *terminus a quo* sufficient time must be allowed for the development of Christian communities throughout the provinces addressed in 1 Pet. 1:1. Time must also be allowed for the popularization and spread of the nomenclature "Christian" from Antioch (Acts 11:26), Caesarea (Acts 26:28) and Rome (Tacitus, *Annals* 15.44; Suetonius, *Nero* 16) to the interior of Asia Minor. In addition there is the possibility, as mentioned above, that the sequence of provincial names in 1 Pet. 1:1 may reflect the administrative reorganization of some of these provinces by Vespasian in 72 c.e. On the other hand, the oppressive measures undertaken by Domitian from 93 c.e. onward would suggest a likely *terminus ad quem* for 1 Peter. In addition to the change of Christian attitude toward Rome reflected in the Apocalypse of John (final stage of composition ca. 96 c.e.), there was about this same time in Pontus a cause for public Christian defection. In his letter to Trajan (*Epistles* 10.96.6) Pliny, writing ca. 112 c.e., mentions that this defection of Pontic Christians occurred some twenty years earlier. The date of these Christian renunciations of the faith would then coincide almost exactly with the inauguration of the Domitian reign of terror. For lack of further information it is impossible to establish a definite relation between the two events. Together, however, they point to circumstances beyond the immediate horizon of 1 Peter. Provisionally, then, this allows us to locate 1 Peter and the situation it describes within the period of time bounded by 73 and 92 c.e.

NOTES

1. Contextual factors have not been totally ignored in the research of 1 Peter; see, e.g., E. G. Selwyn, *The First Epistle of St. Peter*, 2. ed. (London: Macmillan, 1955), pp. 42–52; F. W. Beare, ed., *The First Epistle of Peter*, 3. ed. (Oxford: Basil Blackwell, 1970), pp. 38–43; and especially the earlier remarks of F. J. A. Hort on "The Provinces of Asia Minor included in St. Peter's Address" which is Additional Note III in his *The First Epistle of St. Peter I.1–II.17* (London: Macmillan, 1898), pp. 157–84. However, an extensive analysis of the complementary internal and external evidence has yet to be undertaken. From the abundant secondary literature which has provided a basis for the observations to follow, I would make special note of the following:

A. Studies on Asia Minor and Related Matters in General

Yohanan Aharoni and Michael Avi-Yonah, *The Macmillan Bible Atlas* (New York: Macmillan, 1968), maps 183, 238, 263, 264; George Bean, *Aegean Turkey, An Archeological Guide* (New York: Praeger, 1966); George Bean, *Turkey beyond the Maeander, An Archeological Guide* (Totowa, New Jersey: Rowman and Littlefield, and London: Ernest Benn, 1971); George Bean, *Turkey's Southern Shore, An Archeological Guide* (New York: Praeger, 1968); T. R. S. Broughton, "Roman Asia Minor," in *An Economic Survey of Ancient Rome*, ed. Tenney Frank (Baltimore: The Johns Hopkins Press, 1938), 4: 499–918; W. M. Calder and Josef Keil, eds., *Anatolian Studies Presented to William Hepburn Buckler* (Manchester: Manchester University Press, 1939); John C. Dewdney, *Turkey, An Introductory Geography* (New York: Praeger, 1971); Michael Grant, *Ancient History Atlas*, Cartography by Arthur Banks (New York: Macmillan, 1971); Fritz M. Heichelheim, *An Ancient Economic History from the Paleolithic Age to the Migrations of the Germanic, Slavic and Arabic Nations*, rev. English ed., vols. 1–3 (Leiden: A. W. Sijthoff, 1964–1970), esp. vol. 3, 1970 (ET of *Wirtschaftsgeschichte des Altertums*, 2. aufl., 1938); A. H. M. Jones, *The Cities of the Eastern Roman Provinces*, 2. ed. (Oxford: Clarendon Press, 1971 [1937]); Johannes Leipoldt, "Aus Kleinasien," *Umwelt des Urchristentums*, ed. J. Leipoldt and W. Grundmann, vol. 3, Bilder zum neutestamentlichen Zeitalter (Berlin: Evangelische Verlagsanstalt, 1966), pp. 26–31, plates 80–104; also 1: 101–26 and 2: 81–98; David Magie, *Roman Rule in Asia Minor to the End of the Third Century after Christ*, 2 vols. (Princeton: Princeton University Press, 1950); C. McEvedy, *The Penguin Atlas of Ancient History* (Baltimore: Penguin Books, 1967); Theodor Mommsen, *The Provinces of the Roman Empire from Caesar to Diocletian*, trans. W. P. Dickson, 2 vols. (London: Macmillan, 1909 [1886]); *Monumenta Asiae*

Minoris Antiqua, Publications of the American Society for Archeological Research in Asia Minor, 5 vols. (Manchester: Manchester University Press, 1928–1937); M. P. Nilsson, *Geschichte der griechischen Religion,* 2. ed., vol. 2 (München: Beck, 1961 [for pagan religions of Asia Minor]): Robert North, "Anatolia," *Enciclopedia de la Biblia* (Barcelona: Garriga, 1963), cols. 472–483; Francis E. Peters, *The Harvest of Hellenism: A History of the Near East from Alexander the Great to the Triumph of Christianity* (New York: Simon and Schuster, 1970); F. W. Putzger, *Historischer Weltatlas,* 85. ed. (Bielefeld: Velhagen & Klasing, 1961), maps 16, 26–27, 28; William M. Ramsay, *The Historical Geography of Asia Minor* (Amsterdam: Adolf M. Hakkart, 1962 and Totowa, N.J.: Cooper Sq., 1972; reprint of London: Murray, 1890); Bo Reicke, *The New Testament Era, the World of the Bible from 500 B.C. to A.D. 100,* Trans. David E. Green (Philadelphia: Fortress Press, 1968 [further bibliography, pp. 319–330]); Michael Ivanovich Rostovtzeff, *The Social and Economic History of the Hellenistic World,* 3 vols. (Oxford: Clarendon Press, 1953); Michael Ivanovich Rostovtzeff, *The Social and Economic History of the Roman Empire,* 2 vols., 2. ed. rev. by P. M. Fraser (Oxford: Clarendon Press, 1957 [1926]); A. N. Sherwin-White, *The Letters of Pliny: A Historical and Social Commentary* (Oxford: Clarendon Press, 1966); Johannes Weiss, "Kleinasien," *Realencyclopedie für Protestantische Theologie und Kirche,* 3 aufl., vol. 10 (1901), pp. 535–563.

B. Studies on Early Christianity in Asia Minor

Walter Bauer, *Rechtgläubigkeit und Ketzerei im Ältesten Christentum,* Beiträge zur Historischen Theologie, 10, 2. aufl., ed. von Georg Strecker (Tübingen: J. C. B. Mohr, 1964 [1934]), pp. 71–73, 74–75, 81–98; ET: *Orthodoxy and Heresy in Earliest Christianity,* ed. Robert A. Kraft and Gerhard Krodel, from the 2. German ed. (Philadelphia: Fortress Press, 1971), ch. 3–4; Samuel Dickey, "Some Economic and Social Conditions of Asia Minor Affecting the Expansion of Christianity," *Studies in Early Christianity,* Frank Chamberlin Porter and Benjamin Wisner Bacon FS, ed. Shirley Jackson Case (New York/London: The Century Co., 1928), pp. 393–416; Adolf von Harnack, *Die Mission und Ausbreitung des Christentums in den ersten drei Jahrhunderten,* 3. aufl. (Leipzig: J. C. Hinrichsische Buchhandlung, 1915; ET: *The Mission and Expansion of Christianity in the First Three Centuries,* trans. and ed. James Moffat, 2 vols. [New York: Harper & Row, 1962 (reprint of 1908 ed.)]); F. J. Foakes-Jackson and Kirsopp Lake, eds., *The Beginnings of Christianity,* Part 1. *The Acts of the Apostles,* vol. 5, ed. K. Lake and H. J. Cadbury (London: Macmillan, 1933); Sherman E. Johnson, "Asia Minor and Early Christianity," *Christianity, Judaism, and Other Greco-Roman Cults,* Morton

Smith FS, ed. Jacob Neusner, *Part Two: Early Christianity* (Leiden: E. J. Brill, 1975), pp. 77–145; Sherman E. Johnson, "Early Christianity in Asia Minor," *JBL* 77 (1958): 1–17; Sherman E. Johnson, "Unsolved Questions about Early Christianity in Anatolia," *Studies in New Testament and Early Christian Literature,* Allen P. Wilgren FS, ed. David Edward Aune (Leiden: E. J. Brill, 1972), pp. 181–93; Helmut Koester, " 'Gnomai Diaphorai,' the Origin and Nature of Diversification in the History of Early Christianity," *Trajectories through Early Christianity,* by Helmut Koester and James M. Robinson (Philadelphia: Fortress Press, 1971), pp. 114–157, esp. 143–157; Helmut Koester, "The Origin and Nature of Diversification in the History of Early Christianity," *Harvard Theological Review* 58 (1965): 279–318; William M. Ramsay, *The Church in the Roman Empire before* A.D. *170,* 5. ed. (London/New York: Hodder and Stoughton, 1897); William M. Ramsay, *Cities and Bishoprics of Phrygia,* 2 vols. (Oxford: Clarendon Press, 1897); William M. Ramsay, *The Cities of St. Paul, Their Influence on His Life and Thought: The Cities of Eastern Asia Minor* (Grand Rapids, Mich.: Baker, 1960 [reprint of 1907 ed.]); William M. Ramsay, *The Letters to the Seven Churches of Asia and Their Place in the Plan of the Apocalypse,* 2. ed. (London: Hodder and Stoughton, 1906 [1896]); William M. Ramsay, *St. Paul the Traveller and the Roman Citizen* (Grand Rapids, Mich.: Baker, 1949 [reprint of the 3. ed.; 1. ed., 1895]).

2. For a similar concern regarding the interrelation of what he calls the "socioecological, socioeconomic, sociopolitical and sociocultural factors" bearing on the history and literature of the early Christian movement see the several works of G. Theissen (see above, Introduction, p. 17, n. 12).

3. As an illustration of analyses of the relation of geography in particular to the development of specific religious systems and organizations see David E. Sopher, *Geography of Religions,* Foundations of Cultural Geography Series (Englewood Cliffs, N.J.: Prentice-Hall, 1967).

4. Broughton, "Roman Asia Minor," pp. 812–16; table on p. 815.

5. For example, an inscription (*CIL* 3.318) on a milestone of the road from Ancyra to Doryleum, dated July 80 (–June 81 C.E.) refers to roads built by Titus and Domitian: " . . . vias provinciarum Galatiae, Cappadociae, Ponti, Pisidiae, Paphlagoniae, Lycaoniae, Armenia Minoris staverunt." For the separate mention of Bithynia and Pontus see an inscription of Ancyra (*CIL* 3.249): " . . . proc. fam. glad. per Asiam, Bithyn. Galat. Cappadoc. Lyciam. Pamphl. Cil. Cyrum. Pontum. Paphlag."

6. Strabo, *Geography, Books* 12–14 (*The Geography of Strabo,* trans. Horace Leonard Jones, vols. 5 and 6 of 8 vols., LCL [New York: G. P. Putnam's Sons, 1928–29]).

7. First advanced in detail by Hort (see n. 1, above) and generally admitted as possible by the commentators, this theory has recently received strong sup-

port (with minor additions) in the article of C. J. Hemer, "The Address of 1 Peter," *ExpTim* 89 (1978): 239–43.

8. With Pompey's defeat of Mithridates VI in 63 B.C.E., a series of divisions of the former Pontic kingdom was begun. The western section was joined to Bithynia to form the province of Bithynia-Pontus. Other parts of Pontus were annexed to Galatia (Pontus Galaticus) or given to local rulers under Roman control. In 37 B.C.E. much of eastern Pontus was given to Polemon as puppet king. In 64 C.E. the Romans assumed direct rule of this eastern territory and united it with Galatia (Pontus Polemoniacus) or Cappadocia (Pontus Cappadociacus). Under Vespasian (ca. 72 C.E.) Galatia and Cappadocia were united as one province to which was joined all of Pontus not in the province of Bithynia-Pontus. Later under Trajan (ca. 107/113 C.E.) Galatia and Cappadocia were separated once again and Cappadocia was expanded through the addition of the three former parts of Pontus (P. Galaticus, P. Polemoniacus and P. Cappadociacus). See Magie, *Roman Rule,* 1: 491–96, 574–75; 2: 1349–56, 1435–39, and Broughton, "Roman Asia Minor," p. 597.

9. Magie, *Roman Rule,* 1: 458, echoing R. Syme.

10. Broughton, "Roman Asia Minor," p. 698.

11. Ibid., p. 734.

12. Ibid., p. 738.

13. For the classic sociological expression of this view see Max Weber, *The Sociology of Religion,* trans. Ephraim Fischoff (Boston: Beacon, 1964 [1922]), pp. 96–100. Weber, of course, is intentionally generalizing, and for documentation of the early Christian situation makes no difference between the urban missions of Paul and the rural destination of other branches of the movement.

14. Reicke, *New Testament Era,* p. 303. Reicke reckons that "If local pagans considered the Christians so ominous a factor, they can hardly have numbered less than a fiftieth of the total population of Asia Minor" (ibid.). His estimation of that total population is less than half that of Broughton (4,000,000 vs. 8,500,000) and may therefore represent a very conservative estimate of the Christian inhabitants.

15. Against the prevailing view of the Pauline ambience of 1 Peter of which Horst Goldstein's study (*Paulinische Gemeinde im Ersten Petrusbrief,* Stuttgarter Bibelstudien 80 [Stuttgart: Katholische Bibelwerk, 1975]) is representative.

16. Ramsay MacMullen, *Roman Social Relations 50 B.C. to A.D. 284* (New Haven: Yale University Press, 1974), pp. 28–56 (quote from p. 31); see also pp. 1–27 and 57–87 on "rural" and "urban" areas, respectively.

17. I. Howard Marshall ("Palestinian and Hellenistic Christianity: Some Critical Comments," *NTS* 19 [1973]: 271–87) correctly observes: " . . . a differentiation between Hellenistic Jewish and Hellenistic Gentile churches in

the early period is entirely without foundation. . . . There is thus no specifically Hellenistic Gentile Christianity to be found in the New Testament. No single New Testament document can be labelled as basically Gentile, but for almost every document it is possible to demonstrate its mixed Jewish-Gentile character" (p. 283).

18. See above, ch. 1, pp. 55–56, notes 76 and 77.

19. See, e.g., Philo, *Legatio* 245, 281–82, 314–15; Josephus, *Ant.* 12.125ff., 147–53; 14.213–64; 16.6; *Sib. Or.* 3.271; 1 Macc. 15:22–23; Acts 2:8–11 and Acts, the Pauline letters and the Apocalypse in general. For standard treatments of the Jewish diaspora, including specific reference to Asia Minor, see: Emil Schürer, *Geschichte des Jüdischen Volkes im Zeitalter Jesu Christi*, 3 vols. (Leipzig: J. C. Hinrichs, 1901–11⁴ and reprint of Hildesheim, New York: Georg Olms Verlag, 1970) 3: 12–24 for Asia Minor; von Harnack, 1: 1–18 [including population estimates]); Jean Juster, *Les Juifs dans l'Empire romain: Leur condition juridique, economique et sociale*, vols. 1–2 (Paris: Geuthner, 1914) 1: 188–94 for Asia Minor; Victor Tcherikover, *Hellenistic Civilization and the Jews*, trans. S. Applebaum (New York: Atheneum, 1974); pp. 269–377, pp. 287–89 on Asia Minor; M. Stern, "The Jewish Diaspora," in *The Jewish People in the First Century*, section 1, vol. 1 of *Compendia Rerum Iudaicarum ad Novum Testamentum: Historical Geography, Political History, Social, Cultural and Religious Life and Institutions*, ed. S. Safrai and M. Stern (Philadelphia: Fortress Press, 1974) pp. 117–83, pp. 143–55 on Asia Minor; S. Applebaum, "The Legal Status of the Jewish Communities in the Diaspora," ibid., pp. 420–463.

20. Reicke, *New Testament Era*, pp. 302–13. For implied higher estimates see Harnack and Juster (above note) who assume that Jews throughout the empire in the first century constituted one-seventh of the total population. If, as Broughton suggests ("Roman Asia Minor," p. 815), the total population of the provinces mentioned in 1 Peter was ca. 8,000,000 (i.e., double that proposed by Reicke), the ratio of 1:7 would suggest a Jewish population of some 1,142,000.

21. Selwyn, *First Epistle of St. Peter*, p. 48.

22. See 1:14–16, 18–19; 2:10, 11–12; 4:1–6, 12–19.

23. See the *sebomenoi* or "God-fearers" in Acts 13:16, 26, 43, 50; 16:14; 17:4, 17; 18:7. On the *sebomenoi* as proselytes to Judaism see Kirsopp Lake, "Note VIII. Proselytes and God-Fearers," in *The Beginnings of Christianity*, part 1, vol. 5, K. Lake and H. J. Cadbury, eds. (Grand Rapids, Mich.: Baker, 1966 [1933]), pp. 74–96.

24. For example, conversion as "rebirth" (1:3, 23; 2:2) or as "ransom redemption" (1:18–19). For discussion of the former metaphor see Erik Sjöberg,

"Weidergeburt und Neuschöpfung in palästinischen Judentum," *Studia Theologica* 4 (1951): 44–85 and, more recently, Samuel Parsons, "We Have Been Born Anew: The New Birth of the Christian in the First Epistle of St. Peter (I Petr. 1:3, 23)" (Doctoral diss., St. Thomas Aquinas Pontifical University, Rome, 1978). On the latter passage and the issue in general see Walter Cornelius Van Unnik, *De verlossing I Petrus 1:18–19 en het probleem van den eersten Petrusbrief,* Mededeelingen der Nederlandsche Akademie van Wetenschappen, Afdeeling Letterkunde, N.R. 5/1 (Amsterdam, 1942); "Christianity According to I Peter," *ExpTim* 68 (1956): 79–83; and "Peter, First Letter of," *IDB* 3: 758–66, esp. p. 764.

25. On the mixed population in general see Broughton, "Roman Asia Minor," pp. 872–77; on travel and communications, pp. 857–68.

26. Such as the deportation of 2,000 Jewish families from Mesopotamia and Babylonia to Lydia and Phrygia as military *katoikoi* by Antiochus III (ca. 210–205 B.C.E.).

27. The prophet who authored the Apocalypse while relegated to the island of Patmos is the most notable Christian example.

28. On the phenomenon of strangerhood in antiquity in general see Erich Fascher, "Zum Begriff des Fremden," *ThLZ* 96/3 (1971): 161–68, and J. Gaudemet and E. Fascher, "Fremder," *RAC* 9 (1969): 306–47.

29. Hans Schaefer, *"Paroikoi,"* PW 18/4 (1949), col. 1698.

30. Ibid.

31. H. Hommel, *"Metoikoi,"* PW 15/2 (1932), cols. 1449–50.

32. Rostovtzeff, *SEHRE*, 1: 345–46.

33. Tcherikover, *Hellenistic Civilization and the Jews,* p. 27. According to F. E. Peters ("Hellenism," *IDBSup* [1976]: 395–401), such alienation was the price for the process of hellenization which "was paid by those of the inhabitants who by reason of inferior social and economic status could never aspire to be enrolled as members of the *dēmos*. In a sense, Hellenism institutionalized class differences, where the poor and disenfranchised peasantry were precisely the native population of the area. The fellahin of Egypt, Palestine, and Syria were aliens in their own land" (p. 397).

34. See Hommel's discussion (*"Metoikoi,"* cols. 1451–54).

35. Broughton, "Roman Asia Minor," p. 840; see pp. 839–41.

36. Broughton ("Roman Asia Minor," pp. 631–32) illustrates with an inscription from Sardis the vast divisions of such estates as that of Mnesimachus which include, inter alia, several villages (*kōmē*), "allotments" (*klēroi*), the dwelling plots appertaining thereto, as well as the serfs (*laoi*), slaves (*oiketai*) and their houses.

37. See Rostovtzeff, *SEHRE* 2, Index, s.v. "house economy," "house-indus-

try," "home production." For a general description of *oikos* management of preindustrial societies see Max Weber, *General Economic History,* trans. F. H. Knight (Glencoe, Ill.: Free Press, 1927), pp. 48, 58, 124–131, 146, 162.

38. On the *neōteroi* as recent converts see John H. Elliott, "Ministry and Church Order in the NT: A Traditio-Historical Analysis (1 Pet. 5,1–5 and plls.)," *CBQ* 32 (1970): 367–91, esp. pp. 379–86.

39. Broughton ("Roman Asia Minor") gives a detailed description of the land (pp. 599–695), industry, labor and commerce (pp. 817–81). See also map 60 "Trading Products in the Roman Empire" in Michael Grant's graphic aid, *Ancient History Atlas* (see above, n. 1).

40. Broughton ("Roman Asia Minor," pp. 841–49) gives a list of such Asia Minor guilds; see also Magie, *Roman Rule in Asia Minor,* 2: 1029–32 and Index, s.v. "guilds," "collegia," "gerousia," "neoi," "commonality"; Jean-Pierre Waltzing, *Etude historique sur les corporations professionnelles chez les Romains,* 4 vols. (Hildesheim and New York: Georg Olms, 1970 [= reprint of the original ed., Louvain, 1895–1900]), 3: 24–65 (specifically on Asia Minor). Among the standard works on the associations and guilds in general are: W. Liebenam, *Zur Geschichte und Organization des römischen Vereinswesens* (Leipzig: B. G. Teubner 1890); Erich Ziebarth, *Das Griechische Vereinswesens* (Leipzig: S. Hirzel), 1896); Franz Poland, *Geschichte des griechischen Vereinswesens* (Leipzig: B. G. Teubner, 1909); Francesco de Robertis, *Il fenomeno associativo nel mondo romano dai collegi della repubblica alle corporazioni del basso impero* (Napoli: Libreria scientifica editrice, 1955).

41. See Schürer, *Geschichte des Jüdischen Volkes* 3: 97–105; 2: 501–06; Applebaum, "The Organization of the Jewish Communities," in *The Jewish People in the First Century,* pp. 476, 480–83.

42. See, e.g., Bo Reicke, "Exkurs über die Agitation in den hellenistischen Korporationen," in *Diakonie, Festfreude und Zelos in Verbindung mit der altchristlichen Agapenfeier,* Uppsala Universitets Aarskrift, 1951:5 (Uppsala: A. B. Lundeqvists, 1951), pp. 320–38 (older literature, pp. 320–21); Ramsay MacMullen, *Enemies of the Roman Order: Treason, Unrest, and Alienation in the Empire* (Cambridge, Mass.: Harvard University Press, 1966), pp. 173–79, 341–44, 347, n. 24.

43. For further affinities of 1 Peter with the associations, see Ceslas Spicq, "La Iᵉ Petri et le témoinage évangélique de Saint Pierre," *Vigiliae Christianae* 29 (1966): 137–145; id., "La place ou le rôle des Jeunes dans certaines communautés néotestamentaires," *Revue Biblique* 76 (1969): 508–27. On the popular perception of Christianity as a kind of collegium or association see Robert L. Wilken, "Collegia, Philosophical Schools, and Theology," *The Catacombs and the Colosseum: The Roman Empire as the Setting of Primitive Christian-*

ity, ed. Stephen Benko and John J. O'Rourke (Valley Forge, Pa.: Judson Press, 1971), pp. 268–91.

44. S. Dickey, "Some Economic and Social Conditions," pp. 393–416.

45. Ibid., p. 402.

46. Ibid., p. 410.

47: Ibid., p. 406.

48. Ibid., p. 411.

49. Ibid., pp. 412–14.

50. Ibid., pp. 415–16.

51. Max Weber, "Religion of Non-privileged Classes," in *The Sociology of Religion,* trans. E. Fischoff (Boston: Beacon, 1964), pp. 95–117; quotation from p. 107.

52. See the literature cited above in n. 19.

53. The Epistles of James and Hebrews, as well as 1 Peter, illustrate this point.

54. In the eyes of the Romans, the *Christiani* represented, at worst, "a class of men given to a new and mischievous superstition" (genus hominum superstitionis novae ac maleficae, Suetonius, *Nero* 16.2; see also Tacitus, *Annals* 15.44 and Pliny, *Epistles* 96.8). Thus, in the passage cited, Suetonius refers to Nero's punishment of the Christians in conjunction with his regulation of other, relatively minor, abuses (*animadversa*): the conduct of public banquets, the sale of cooked foods in taverns, the misconduct of chariot-drivers and of pantomimic actors and their partisans (who were banished from the city). The term used by these authors to describe the Christians, *superstitio,* was "regularly used at this time for private and foreign cults" (A. N. Sherwin-White, *The Letters of Pliny,* p. 708). For a detailed discussion of the Pliny-Trajan exchange regarding the Christians see pp. 691–712; and on the broader issue of "The Early Persecutions and Roman Law," Appendix 5, pp. 772–87.

55. Harold B. Mattingly ("The Origin of the Name Christiani," *Journal of Theological Studies* 9 [1958]: 26–37) has presented the most convincing theory concerning the circumstances of the term's origin. About 60 c.e. the Greco-Syrians of Antioch invented the nickname *Christiani* as an opprobrious label by which to ridicule those who in their hymns and professions of faith had allied themselves to one called the Christ. Fashioned after the term *Augustiani,* the label was meant to imply that the followers of Christ behaved in as ludicrous a fashion as the partisans of Nero. The *Augustiani* consisted of that military corps of Roman knights who devoted themselves to the praise of Nero who saw himself as Augustus' spiritual heir. At the hearing of Paul in Caesarea, King Agrippa used the term in a similar mocking manner (Acts 26: 28; cf. 11:26). From the east the label soon followed the believers across Asia

Minor and Greece to Rome. The term represents one not chosen by believers themselves but applied to them for ridiculing effect by others.

56. R. Scroggs, "The Earliest Christian Communities as Sectarian Movement," in *Christianity, Judaism and Other Greco-Roman Cults,* Morton Smith FS, ed. Jacob Neusner; Part Two, *Early Christianity* (Leiden: E. J. Brill, 1975), pp. 1–23. For a less sociological approach see, e.g., Jean Daniélou, "Christianity as a Jewish Sect," in *The Crucible of Christianity: Judaism, Hellenism and the Historical Background to the Christian Faith,* ed. Arnold Toynbee (London: Thames and Hudson, 1969), pp. 275–82.

57. B. R. Wilson, *Sects and Society: A Sociological Study of the Elim Tabernacle, Christian Science, and Christadelphians* (Berkeley: University of California Press, 1961), p. 1. Although the seminal work of Ernst Troeltsch (*The Social Teaching of the Christian Churches,* trans. O. Wyon [New York: Macmillan, 1931]) continues to serve exegesis as a useful guide, particularly because of its specific references to the early Christian source material, Wilson's sociological definition of sect is preferable to the methodologically limited and predominantly theological typology of Troeltsch. For a critique of Troeltsch and similar typologies see Wilson's later work, *Magic and the Millenium: A Sociological Study of Religious Movements of Protest among Tribal and Third-World Peoples* (New York: Harper & Row, 1973), pp. 9–30. A summary of Troeltsch's definition is presented on p. 11, n. 3. For further material on sectarianism see *Patterns of Sectarianism: Organization and Ideology in Social and Religious Movements,* ed. B. R. Wilson (London: Heinemann, 1967) and by the same author, *Religious Sects: A Sociological Study,* World University Library, (London: Weidenfeld & Nicolson, 1970); also Werner Stark, *The Sociology of Religion, A Study of Christendom,* vol. 2, *Sectarian Religion* (London: Routledge & Kegan Paul, 1967).

58. Wilson, *Magic and the Millenium,* p. 20.

59. Ibid., p. 19.

60. Ibid., pp. 22–26.

61. Ibid., p. 22.

62. Ibid., pp. 38–39.

63. Ibid., pp. 41–42. For the centrality of conversion in early Christianity and its distinction from the pagan cults see the classic study of Arthur Darby Nock, *Conversion: The Old and the New in Religion from Alexander the Great to Augustine of Hippo* (New York: Oxford University Press, 1961 [1933]), esp. pp. 134–37, 207–11, 227–29.

64. The conditional particle *ei* in 1:6 and 2:19–20 indicates a potential, rather than actual, situation. Even so, in 1:6 *deon* (divine will) and *peirasmois* (cf. 4:12) show that God, rather than human agents, is the one who allows the

believers to grieve (*lypēthentes*) for the purpose of *testing* them (as explicit in 1:7). The contrast to such sorrow is joy (*aggaliasthe*), not release from pain. In 2:19–20 the domestic servants may experience *lypas*, "grief, sorrow, pain *of mind or spirit*" (BAG, s.v., emphasis added) because of unjustly (*adikōs*) merited harsh treatment. This is a private and not a political matter which probably exemplifies the suspicion of *kakopoiia* in 2.12. In 3:13 *ei* and the optative *paschoite* envision potential suffering. The parallelism of vv. 13–14 implies that the cause for suffering (*dia dikaiosynēn*) is the suspicion that they are excessive moral "fanatics" (*tou agathou zelōtai*). Their break from sin (2:24) and the involvements sin included (4:1–5) and their new preference for righteousness (2:24; 3:13) would also entail a social break and arouse suspicions (3:15–16). In 3:17 *agathopoiountes* is synonymous with *tēn agathēn en Christō anastrophēn* in the previous verse. Thus the suffering is the result of "revilement" (*epēreazontes;* see BAG s.v.) and slander (*katalaleisthe*). Similarly in the parallelism of 4:14–15(16), *paschetō* is used synonymously with *oneidizesthe* ("reproach, revile, be insulted"; see BAG s.v.) although in content 4:15 (negative) is contrasted with 4:14a (cf. 3:14) and 4:16 (positive). Note also again the conditional *ei* framing the unit in vv. 14 and 16. 4:19 concludes the section 4:12–19 and summarizes the basic principle underlying its exhortation. Insult again is the cause of the suffering. God, the "faithful creator" of the sufferers (4:19), will spare them from shame (4:15) but will punish their unbelieving insulters (4:17). In 5:9 the sufferings common to the entire brotherhood throughout the world are attributed appropriately to one common source: not the Roman empire but the devil, the "godless one" (*asebēs*, 4:18) par excellence, the common enemy of God and his people.

65. E. C. Colwell, "Popular Reactions against Christianity in the Roman Empire," in *Environmental Factors in Christian History,* Shirley Jackson Case FS, ed. J. T. McNeill, M. Spinka, H. R. Willoughby (Chicago: University of Chicago Press, 1939; New York: Kennikat Press, 1970), pp. 53–71. For an instructive summary of the issue see Gerhard Krodel, "Persecution and Toleration of Christianity until Hadrian," in *The Catacombs and the Colosseum,* pp. 255–67. See also the more extensive surveys of J. Vogt, "Christenverfolgung I (historisch, Bewertung durch Heiden u[nd] Christen)," *RAC* 2 (1954): 1159–1208, and H. Last, "Christenverfolgung II (juristisch)," *RAC* 2 (1954): 1208–28.

66. Ibid., pp. 53, 57–58.

67. Charles Francis Digby Moule, "The Nature and Purpose of I Peter," *NTS* 3 (1956): 1–11; quote from p. 8. For the same view see the literature cited on p. 8; also Moule's *Birth of the New Testament* (New York: Harper & Row, 1962), pp. 105–24, esp. pp. 112–14; more recently, J. N. D. Kelly, *A Commentary on the Epistles of Peter and of Jude,* Harper's New Testament

Commentaries (New York: Harper & Row, 1969), pp. 5–11; E. Best, *I Peter,* New Century Bible (London: Oliphants, 1971), pp. 36–42; L. Goppelt, *Der erste Petrusbrief,* KEK 12/1, ed. Ferdinand Hahn; 1. aufl. (Göttingen: Vandenhoeck und Ruprecht, 1978), pp. 56–64. On 3:13–17 see especially J. Ramsey Michaels, "Eschatology in I Peter iii. 17," *NTS* 13 (1966–67): 394–401.

68. Moule (ibid., p. 9) presents a list of thirteen such parallels.

69. See Mark 12:10–12/Matt. 21:42–46/Luke 20:17–19; Acts 4:8–12; Rom. 9:30–33 and for a discussion of the tradition, J. H. Elliott, *The Elect and the Holy: An Exegetical Examination of 1 Peter 2:4–10 and the Phrase* Basileion Hierateuma, *NovT Supplements* 12 (Leiden: E. J. Brill, 1966), pp. 26–33.

70. See, e.g., Matt. 23:15 and Jewish "jealousy" over or competition with Christian success in southeast Asia Minor (Acts 13:44–45; 14:1–7, 19), Thessalonica (Acts 17:1–9), Corinth (Acts 18:1–11) and especially western Asia (Ephesus: Acts 19:11–20; 20:19; 21:21–28).

71. On the early opposition of Judaism and Christianity see especially James Parkes, *Conflict of the Church and the Synagogue: A Study in the Origins of Antisemitism* (Cleveland/New York: World Publishing Co. and Philadelphia: Jewish Publication Society of America, 1961), pp. 71–147; Leonhard Goppelt, *Christentum und Judentum im ersten und zweiten Jahrhundert: Ein Aufriss der Urgeschichte der Kirche,* Beiträge zur Forderung christlicher Theologie, 2. reihe, Band 55 (Gütersloh: C. Bertelsmann, 1954); I. Abrahams, *Studies in Pharisaism and the Gospels* (Cambridge: University Press, 1924), pp. 56–71; Robert L. Wilken, "Judaism in Roman and Christian Society," *Journal of Religion* 47 (1967): 313–30; and M. Simon and A. Benoit, *Le Judaisme et le Christianisme antique, Nouvelle Clio. L'histoire et ses problémes,* 10 (Paris: Presses Universitaires de France, 1968).

72. Jerry L. Daniel, "Anti-semitism in the Hellenistic-Roman Period," *JBL* 98 (1979): 45–65.

73. Ibid., p. 65.

74. On the origins of the Christian addressees see 1 Pet. 1:2, 3, 18–19, 23–25; 2:9–10; on their strangeness see 1:1, 17; 2:11; 4:16 (the name and all passages referring to their distinctive faith in Jesus as the Christ); on their exclusiveness see 1:14–16, 17–18; 2:11; 4:1–4; and on their proselytizing see 2:12; 3:1–2.

75. Daniel ("Anti-semitism," pp. 47 and 65, respectively) states that the evidence of pagan opposition to Judaism reflects "a benign dislike rather than an active hatred of the sort that leads to persecution. . . . It was not necessarily a virulent anti-semitism; certainly not (except of occasion) persecution, but rather an enduring concept, coupled with distrust."

76. In 1 Peter, however, the predominant danger to the sect is the attraction

of social conformity, not political resistance. Bo Reicke (*The Epistles of James, Peter and Jude,* 2. ed., The Anchor Bible 37 [Garden City, N.Y.: Doubleday & Co., 1964], pp. xv-xxxviii, 73, 89, 95–96, 99–100, 107–08, 119, 125) goes too far in his contention that 1 Peter was written to quell Christian zealotic opposition to the Neronian regime. In a convincing critique C. Freeman Sleeper ("Political Responsibility According to I Peter," *NovT* 10 [1968]: 270–86) has questioned the exaggerated *political* implications which Reicke has attempted to find in such terms as *zelōtai* (3:13), *kakopoios* (2:12, 14; 3:17; 4:15) and *hypotassesthai* (2:13–25). The "eschatological impatience" to which Reicke finds allusion in 1 Peter suggests dissatisfaction with an alienated social condition on the part of the addressees but not necessarily social revolt. The terms cited by Reicke are best seen within the context of the letter's social and theological strategy rather than as part of a general New Testament "tradition of opposition to social agitation" (Reicke, ibid., p. xxiv; cf. Sleeper, ibid., pp. 284–85).

77. Compare, e.g., the variety of positions represented in the literature cited in the Introductions of Werner Georg Kümmel (*Introduction to the New Testament,* trans. Howard Clark Kee, rev. English ed. [Nashville: Abingdon, 1975], pp. 416–25) and Donald Guthrie (*New Testament Introduction,* 3. rev. ed. [Downers Grove, Ill.: InterVarsity Press, 1970], pp. 771–813); see also J. H. Elliott, "The Rehabilitation of an Exegetical Step-child: 1 Peter in Recent Research," *JBL* 95 (1976): 243–54, esp. pp. 251–53.

78. For a similar approach to the problem see Goppelt (*Der erste Petrusbrief,* pp. 56–65) who favors a date "between 65 and 80" (pp. 64, 65).

79. These passages from Hebrews, however, also illustrate how different its response to the problem of social alienation was from that of 1 Peter. According to 1 Peter, the hostility which the Christian *paroikoi* experienced was a result of their estrangement from the society in which they lived. According to Hebrews, on the other hand, estrangement is to be viewed not simply as a social but ultimately as a cosmological phenomenon. God's faithful people are not simply aliens in society but strangers "on earth" (Heb. 11:13) where they have "no lasting city" but seek the heavenly (11:16) city "which is to come" (13:14). Whereas 1 Peter stresses the need for Christian community here and now as the answer to social alienation, Hebrews directs attention away from the hopeless earthly scene to the heavenly home which awaits those who remain steadfast in faith. The similar problems they address and the similar vocabulary they employ should not be allowed to obscure the fundamental difference in the social and theological perspective of these documents.

80. See Rev. 2:13; 6:9–11; 7:9–17; 14:13, 20; 16:6; 20:4.

81. On these years see Suetonius, *Domitian* 10–17.

82. Magie, *Roman Rule in Asia Minor,* 1: 577; pp. 566–92 on the Flavian period in general. For a more positive assessment of Domitian in particular, see Brian W. Jones, *Domitian and the Senatorial Order.* A Prosopographical Study of Domitian's Relationship with the Senate, A.D. 81–96; American Philosophical Society, vol. 132 (Philadelphia: American Philosophical Society, 1979).

83. Reicke, *New Testament Era,* p. 272.

84. Ibid., p. 248. More recently John A. T. Robinson (*Redating the New Testament* [London: SCM Press, 1976], pp. 150–69) has argued for a similar early dating. To be sure, his critique of supposed evidence for the date of 1 Peter is effective and refreshing (e.g., "Babylon" [5:13] as a veiled reference to Rome; imagined imperial persecution; suffering for "the name" as comparable with the crime of murder [4:14–16]). The major weakness of his argument, however, lies in the assumption that the situation described in 1 Peter is that "of Rome rather than the obscurer parts of Asia Minor" (p. 158). As the present study attempts to show, precisely the opposite is the case. If this were not so, then it would have been the Christians at Rome rather than those in the provinces to whom the letter's message of comfort and exhortation (5:12) should have been directed.

85. Ibid., pp. 253–317.

86. Ibid., pp. 283–314.

87. Ibid., pp. 305, 307, 309, 313.

The Socioreligious Strategy
of 1 Peter

As members of a socially defined and "disprivileged"[1] status group known
as *paroikoi*, the addressees of 1 Peter, we noted in chapter 1, stood in an
estranged legal and social relation to their environment. In chapter 2 we
explored further geographical, economic, and religious aspects of their
social condition which, in various ways, contributed toward and heightened the degree of their alienation. The geographical and cultural diversity
of the lands through which the Christian movement had spread, the social
inferiority of the converts it had attracted, their possible economic deprivation, and the exclusivism required by the sectarian character of the
movement of which they were a part were all contributing factors toward
the predicament in which the addressees found themselves immediately
prior to the composition of 1 Peter. Conversion to Christianity at first appeared to offer a "place of belonging,"[2] fraternal assistance, and participation in a community of equals—benefits which were denied these strangers
in the larger society indifferent to their needs and suspicious of their presence. The vehemence, however, with which the local communities had re-
acted to the Christian sect had made increased suffering rather than security the lot of these believers.

This suffering meant not only hardship on individuals; it posed a threat
to the sect as a whole. The severity of the polarization with outsiders was
endangering the sect's social cohesion, the self-esteem of its members, their
conviction that they possessed a new status conferred by God, their common commitment to the unique religious values, social values, ideals and
goals of the group, and their vision of a common salvation to which even
current anti-Christian opponents would one day be won.

1 Peter, to be sure, does not spell out the problems in these terms. The above description of the situation is rather an attempt to state in more sociological terms what is brought to the surface by exegetical analysis. By comparing the addressees and their situation as described in 1 Peter with the closest sociological analogue, that of a conversionist sect, I am attempting to "read between the lines" of the letter, so to speak, in order to gain a broader and yet more specifically social picture of the issues involved.

This procedure is useful for assessing not only the situation of 1 Peter but also the strategy underlying the letter's response. 1 Peter, I propose, represents a response to those problems with which conversionist sects in general must struggle. Such a sect pursues recruitment of new members on the basis of a thoroughgoing conversion which requires separation from former associations and allegiances. At the same time the conversionist sect must be equipped to deal with the problems which openness to, and yet distinction from, outsiders involve: resistance and hostility from such outsiders, threats to internal social cohesion and member self-esteem, and challenges to the plausibility of the means by which both negative experience and positive hope are explained, legitimated and integrated into a total world of meaning.[3] 1 Peter was a letter to and from members of a sect under such threats. Exhortation and consolation of its addressees is the letter's stated objective (2:11; 5:1, 12). The strategy underlying this generally stated aim and the intended effect of the letter's content will become clearer if we first consider the importance of these features of sectarian life in general and then examine the manner in which these terms are taken up in the response of 1 Peter in particular.

SECT DEVELOPMENT IN SOCIOLOGICAL PERSPECTIVE

Bryan Wilson's analysis of sect development[4] indicates various points which deserve consideration as a basis of comparison with the situation and response of 1 Peter. "Sects proliferate," he notes, "in periods of social unrest."[5] The formation of sects is an indication of, and response to, a variety of factors:

> change in the economic position of a particular group . . . disturbance of normal social relations . . . the failure of the social system to accommodate particular age, sex and status groups. . . . Particular groups [compare the strangers and aliens of 1 Peter] are rendered marginal by some process of social change; there is a sudden need for a new interpretation of their

social position or for a transvaluation of their experience. Insecurity, differential status anxiety, cultural neglect prompt a need for readjustment which sects may, for some, provide. The maladjusted may be communities, or occupational groups, or dispersed individuals [compare again the "dispersed" addressees of 1 Peter] in similar marginal positions.[6]

To such marginal peoples sects extend the promise of salvation within a self-sustaining community or within a community which claims that its support, like its origin, derives from a power greater than that of the given social system.

Sects attempt to promote a high degree of group consciousness and solidarity among their members. In this effort maintenance of the sect's distinctiveness and its separation from the world is of vital importance. "In some measure and by some methods," Wilson observes, "the sect is committed to keeping itself 'unspotted from the world': its distinctiveness must be evident both to its members and to others."[7] These methods can involve injunctions to maintain social separateness ("isolation") as well as insulation through the development of behavioral rules calculated to protect sect values by reducing the influence of the external world when contact is necessary.[8] On the one hand, if a conversionist sect, such as early Christianity, is to be effective in its missionary enterprise, it must present itself as an attractive and distinctive alternative to other groups vying for peoples' allegiance. On the other hand,

> if the sect is to persist as an organization it must not only separate its members from the world, but must also maintain the dissimilarity of its own values from those of the secular society. Its members must not normally be allowed to accept the values of the status system of the external world. The sect must see itself as marginal to the wider society. . . . Status must be status within the sect, and this should be the only group to which the status-conscious individual makes reference.[9]

Again for the conversionist or proselytizing sect, such as early Christianity, "this is often accomplished only with difficulty since the social status of its members may radically affect its prospect of winning recruits."[10] For the purpose of both group cohesion and effective missionizing, therefore, the superior status of the sect established by superior or supernatural agency requires constant emphasis.

Related to this is also a sense of exclusiveness which is vital for sect development. "The more fully the sect sees itself as a chosen remnant, the more fully will it offer resistance to [the forces of social accommodation]. Such resistance is more likely to be successful, however, if the sect has an aristocratic ethic concerning salvation—if it sees itself as a chosen elect."[11]

For the conversionist sect in particular such stress upon separateness, distinctiveness and exclusiveness

> results in certain distinct tensions for the organization and for its members. For each sect there must be a position of optimal tension, where any greater degree of hostility against the world portends direct conflict, and any less suggests accommodation to worldly values.[12]

The principal tension for the conversionist sect arises from its simultaneous interests in both avoiding and yet evangelizing outsiders.

> Evangelism means exposure to the world and the risk of alienation of the evangelized agents. It means also the willingness to accept into the sect new members. This throws a particular weight on the standards of admission if, through the impact of recruitment, the sect itself is not to feel the effect of members who are incompletely socialized from the sect's point of view. The more distinctive are the sect doctrines and the more emphatic the insistence on strict standards of doctrinal understanding [and we might add, internal group discipline], the less likely it is that the sect will suffer from its evangelism.[13]

Sects, finally, develop a characteristic ideology. This refers to the conceptual means by which a sect seeks to explain and legitimate, for members and nonmembers alike, its opposition to society, its distinctive features, the basis of its claimed status, the criteria of its ethic, the "appropriateness" of suffering when it is necessary, and the transcendent, ultimate power and authority by which the life and salvation of all its members are determined. Thus sects are one type of an "ideological primary group." Concerning such groups Edward Shils writes:

> The bond which unites the members of the ideological primary group to each other is the attachment to each other as sharers in the ideological system of beliefs; the members perceive each other as being in possession of, or being possessed by, the sacredness inherent in the acceptance of the ideology. Personal, primordial, and civil qualities are attenuated or suppressed in favor of the quality of "ideological possession." A comrade is a comrade by virtue of his beliefs, which are perceived as his most signifi-

cant qualities. A fully developed ideological primary group is separated by sharply defined boundaries from the "world" from which it seeks to protect itself or over which it seeks to triumph. Stringent discipline over conduct and belief is a feature of ideological primary groups; intense solidarity and unwavering loyalty are demanded (as in revolutionary cells and in separatist religious sects).[14]

The function of such ideology is not only to interpret but to motivate. Sectarian ideology is designed to assure members of their contact with the ultimate power(s) of existence and thereby reinforce their motivation to act. Members "will gain courage from perceiving themselves as part of a cosmic scheme" and undertake actions that "now have the legitimacy which proximity to the sacred provides."[15]

These factors involving sect development which sociological analysis has identified provide an instructive analogue for assessing the content and strategy of 1 Peter. As I shall attempt to show, it was to issues such as these that the letter's message of exhortation and consolation was specifically, if implicitly, directed. The social conflict in which the addressees were engaged had raised basic questions concerning the identity, the integrity and the ideology of the Christian sect. If we might imagine these harassed believers to speak for themselves, their questions would reflect such concerns. Has our conversion to this peculiar religious movement and its "new" vision of salvation brought about any actual improvement of our circumstances? How and where are we experiencing this transformation in our everyday life? Are we not the same isolated and inferior aliens which people claimed us to be prior to our conversion? Are we not as homeless and rootless as ever before? Where is the fraternity and community for which we have yearned? How shall we contend with adamant unbelieving husbands, wives claiming equality, self-serving leaders or insubordinate and disrespectful newcomers? In what sense does faith in Jesus Christ alter our position before God or man? Are we really a distinctive people? Why should we separate ourselves from former associations which are so venerable and so necessary for our workaday life, especially when such isolation prompts such hostile public reaction? Why can we not conform as others do? Why are we so slandered and oppressed? Is not our suffering a sign of our alienation even from the power and presence of God? Why are we the only ones who suffer so? Where indeed is the grace of God and the certainty of our salvation?

Plagued by fears and uncertainty concerning their isolation and suffering, the actuality of any communal existence "in Christ," the hand of God in their lives, and the certainty of their salvation, the addressees of 1 Peter were becoming disillusioned in their hope and discouraged in their faith and commitment. For this wing of the Christian movement to advance, the author(s) of 1 Peter saw it essential to console and exhort the Christian brothers and sisters in Asia Minor in terms that could effectively reinforce a sense of distinctive Christian identity and solidarity and provide a sustaining rationale for their experience and faith.

The manner in which the response of 1 Peter focuses upon the issues of sect life discussed above will become clearer when we turn next to an analysis of the letter's socioreligious strategy.

STRATEGY AND IDEOLOGY IN 1 PETER

1 Peter, like all biblical documents, is predominantly a theological statement. Yet, again like all biblical writings, it is also conditioned by, and the reflection of, a certain set of social circumstances. In the case of 1 Peter these circumstances involved not only the immediate predicament of its addressees in Asia Minor or the affiliation of senders and recipients but also the questions which alienation and suffering raised concerning the continued existence of the sect in its interaction with a hostile non-Christian society. Institutions such as those of the *paroikoi* and the *oikos;* organizational developments such as imperial bureaucratization and diverse, competing sectarian formations within Judaism; tensions between classes, in-groups and out-groups; pressures of social and religious alienation; and problems concerning Christian organizational identity, integrity and ideology—all are factors which combine to shape the situation which 1 Peter describes.

At the same time 1 Peter is a response to that situation which it describes. On the surface that response appears to be formulated in predominantly theological terms. Below the surface and implied in those terms, however, we have reason to suspect social as well as religious concerns, a sociological as well as theological plan which has shaped the letter's composition. As the problems which the letter addressed were not merely religious but also social, so the response which the letter makes may be assumed to have been designed for social as well as religious effect.

To inquire concerning the total effect which the letter was designed to have on its audience is to seek more than is conventionally implied in the quest for its "intention" or "purpose." In order to explore the possible social as well as religious aim of the document, I therefore propose to probe its *socioreligious strategy and ideology*. My concern here is not only with the theology or theological intention of 1 Peter but with its socio-logical design as well, and with the manner in which the latter is implied in the former. The letter, I assume—as I do of all the writings of the New Testament—has a sociological as well as a literary and theological dimension. Examination of the genre, structure, content, adaptation of sources and traditions, and thematic emphases yields conclusions not only regarding its literary composition and theological redaction but also its socio-logical aims.

"Strategy" implies more than an intention to present ideas. As in the interaction of game playing or battle tactics, strategy involves a plan cal-culated to have a specific effect. In the case of 1 Peter this effect would not merely be that the addressees, by reading this letter, feel exhorted and comforted. The problems which we have already identified lead us to sus-pect that 1 Peter represents a calculated attempt by its author(s) to rein-force the group consciousness, cohesion and commitment of the Christian sect in Asia Minor. The strategy of the letter would amount to the man-ner in which it was designed to achieve this goal.

Attention to such a strategy also encourages consideration of the sec-tarian ideology which the letter represents. In 1 Peter appeal is made to sacred Scripture, common religious traditions, established rites and prac-tices, divine norms and sanctions, and distinctive features of Christian faith and fraternity in order to motivate Christian segregation from the "sinners" and solidarity among the faithful. In order to analyze such social aspects of the document and their reflection in the theological language of the text, we shall focus attention therefore on the letter's socioreligious strategy and ideology.

CHRISTIAN RELATIONS WITH OUTSIDERS

One feature of 1 Peter has prompted such divergent conclusions concern-ing the letter's general purpose or aim that it deserves to be considered at the outset. This involves what appears to be a certain tension or discrepancy between ways in which the addressees are encouraged to relate to the Gentiles or outsiders.

On the one hand, 1 Peter presents the relation between the believers and nonbelievers as one of alienation and hostility. The former are being demeaned and abused by the latter as inferior "strangers" and "aliens" (1:1, 17; 2:11), fanatical zealots (3:13), and ridiculous "Christ-lackeys" (4:14, 16). There is friction between slaves and their (possibly non-Christian) owners, wives and their non-Christian husbands (2:18–20; 3:1–6). The public suspects the Christians of immorality and disregard for civic order (2:12, 15; 3:16; 4:4, 15). The readers, moreover, are reminded that they are in a state of war (2:11; 4:1) which implies a radical distinction between themselves the righteous and the impious sinners (4:17–18). They are the brotherhood faithful to God, whereas the Gentiles are in league with the devil (5:8–9). Hence Christians are encouraged to "resist" these opposing forces (5:9) and to separate themselves thoroughly from all the ungodly ways of the Gentiles (1:14, 17; 2:11; 4:1–4).

On the other hand, this same document speaks in positive, optimistic terms concerning the eventual conversion of these outsiders (2:12; 3:1–2), supports a neutral, if not favorable, view of civil government (2:13–17), and utilizes the secularly popular model of the household to discuss the roles and relationships of distinctive Christian behavior (2:18–3:7; 5:1–5a).

One graphic example of this tension between negative and positive aspects of Christian/Gentile interaction and the centripetal and centrifugal directions of the letter's admonitions is present in 2:11–12. Abstinence from Gentile-like modes of behavior (motivated by "selfish desires," 2:11; cf. 4:2) and references to outsider hostility, on the one hand, are immediately followed by an expression of hope for the conversion of these same Gentiles on the other hand (2:12). This tension between the simultaneous centripetal and centrifugal thrusts of the letter's encouragement poses a difficult question concerning its basic aim, or better, its strategy. Some interpreters have perceived this tension but have resorted to exclusively theological solutions, thereby failing to account for the social aspects of the problem in satisfactory sociological terms. Others focus on only one of the two thrusts of the letter and thereby give an unbalanced explanation of its overall orientation. Many overlook or ignore the problem altogether.

To illustrate two characteristic approaches to the problem we may compare the observations of Theophil Spörri with those of a more recent study undertaken by David Balch. Over fifty years ago Spörri noted in 1 Peter the presence of what he called "positive and negative antitheses" which involved, among other things, the relation of the addressees to Israel and to the world.[16] On the one hand 1 Peter encouraged a "solidarity with the world through unshakable *agathopoiein kai paschein* ['the doing of good and suffering'] with the goal of winning people for God" (author's translation, hereafter au.). At the same time identification with the will of Christ is presented as the "norm for [the readers] total separation from the essence and behavior of the world" (au.).[17] For Spörri this represents "a tension for which the author of 1 Peter knows no conclusive solution" (au.).[18]

To account for this tension, therefore, Spörri resorted to the assumption of an integrative *"Grundanschauung,"* a unique theological concept of community (a *"Gemeindegedanke"*), which underlay 1 Peter's composition. Although he realized the importance of assessing the "sociological structure of the community"[19] and its need for social cohesion, he a priori disclaimed any interest of its members in the fulfillment of personal or communal needs.[20] This community was rather a divinely inspired "organism" and *"Wesenseinheit"* which was formed, according to Spörri,[21] exclusively by God through the death and resurrection of the Christ. It was this death and resurrection event, he maintained, which was the basis of the conflict between the believers, Israel and the rest of the world. Outside resistance to the acceptance of this salvific event could only result in continued conflict.

Such an analysis moves too exclusively on an ideational plane and fails to perceive or account for the social factors involved in the Christian/Gentile conflict. The tension in the letter's social perspectives, centripetal and centrifugal, is not explained by merely postulating a theological paradox involving divine judgment and grace. What appears with Spörri to be a promising utilization of the organizational typology of Ernst Troeltsch[22] results not in the identification and interpretation of the sectarian dilemmas of the Petrine community but rather in the confusing conclusion that this community represents and yet transcends the characteristics of church, sect, and mysticism altogether. "The uniqueness of the sociological structure of the community in 1 Peter," Spörri maintains, "consists in the fact that this concept of community represents none of the three types (church, sect, mysticism) exclusively or also only one-sidedly, *but all of them simultaneously* [emphasis added]; at the same time it [the concept of community] is *prior to a differentiation of types* [original emphasis] into extreme constructions and exclusive alternatives" (au.).[23] Spörri's error here lies not only in his failure to consider the different social implications of the three comparative models which he has employed. More seriously, although perhaps inadvertently, he has shifted attention from the actual social structure of the Petrine community to the religious ideology found in the letter, confusing the latter with the former. His comments thus pertain not to the social form of the community but to the *idea* (*Gemeindegedanke*) of that community presented in 1 Peter.

Spörri thus employs a quasi-sociological approach to the issue only to reject it in the end as irrelevant. In the final analysis his persistent dichotomy of theological and sociological frames of reference, his ideational concept of the concrete community and its concerns, and his resort to exclusively theological *interpretamenta* fail to produce a satisfactory *sociological* as well as theological explanation of the tension which he so clearly delineates.

Despite its methodological weaknesses, nevertheless, the merit of Spörri's approach involves its identification of the tensions inherent in the exhortation of the letter and at least its attempt to analyze them sociologically as well as exegetically. Unfortunately much of the subsequent interpretation of 1 Peter failed to follow this promising course. A more recent analysis of 1 Peter illustrates the kind of conclusions which are drawn when this tension between the centripetal and centrifugal thrusts of the letter's exhortation is overlooked and when the sectarian concerns of the community are given inadequate consideration.

David L. Balch's 1974 Yale dissertation on " . . . The Origin, Form and Apologetic Function of the Household Duty Code in 1 Peter,"[24] came to my attention during the writing of this present study. His thesis in general is a welcome attempt to understand the domestic code of 1 Peter in relation to the political and social implications of the household in the Greco-Roman world. Balch has pursued a line of inquiry similar to that adopted in chapter 4 below and has assembled abundant evidence which supports the interpretation of *oikos* in 1 Peter that is given there. Specific reference will be made to his work when we take up the question of the function of the *oikos* theme within the overall strategy of 1 Peter.

A fundamental limitation of his study in regard to 1 Peter in general, however, is his failure to consider the problems related to the sectarian character of the community addressed in the letter and his underestimation of the tension inherent in the response of 1 Peter. Balch disputes the fact that 1 Peter shows any substantive interest in Gentile conversion.[25] For a conversionist sect such as the Petrine community this is sociologically as well as exegetically an unrealistic proposition.[26] Nonetheless Balch maintains that the prime aim of 1 Peter was to foster an attitude of conformity as a remedy for overcoming the conflict between the addressees and their neighbors. Society, he suggests, was hostile toward this new foreign religious sect "because it was understood to be disturbing proper rule and harmony in house and state."[27]

> The purpose [of the letter] is *to reduce tension* [emphasis added] between society and church, to stop the slander. Christians must *conform* [emphasis added] to the expectations of Hellenistic society, so that society will cease criticizing the new cult. The author of I P[eter] writes to advise the Christians who are being persecuted about how they may become socially-politically acceptable to their society. The *Haustafel* describes the behavior *demanded* [original emphasis] by the governor (2:14), even of "aliens."[28]

The exhortation to internal harmony (3:8-9), like the apologetic function of the household code, according to Balch, has as its purpose not the strengthening of group cohesion but rather the fostering of accommodation to "desirable" forms of social behavior. Avoidance of social conflict through social conformity is, in Balch's view, the sole concern and recipe of 1 Peter.

Such an interpretation, however, suffers on several counts. First, it fails to take into account that for its continued existence as a sect this Christian community must maintain a *distinctive* identity. Internal order and discipline are not simply demanded by outsiders but necessitated internally for the sake of group solidarity and cohesion. Social conformity is, as Goppelt has also noted,[29] precisely the trend which 1 Peter was designed to counteract. Secondly, this interpretation ignores or minimizes the tension which Spörri so clearly noted between the centripetal and centrifugal orientations encouraged by 1 Peter. In particular it fails to account for the letter's repeated call for Christian separation from the world and it understates its missionary interests as well. Finally, as shall be discussed further below, it fails to see the relation of the household code in 1 Peter to the

111

larger ecclesiological concept of the household which the letter develops. The use of the code is presented as chief proof of a Petrine desire for conformity without consideration of alternative possibilities.

The studies of Spörri and Balch exemplify two divergent and equally unsatisfactory interpretations of the paradoxical manner in which 1 Peter addresses the problem of Christian/Gentile interaction. While the former acknowledges the tension in the perspectives of openness and isolation, the latter denies it. Both authors fail to consider the role which the sectarian character of the community played in the conflict and the manner in which 1 Peter reflects a sectarian perspective. As a result Spörri attributes hostility and conflict solely to religious differences and Balch to social contrasts which need not be maintained. For Spörri only the conversion of the Gentiles to Christianity will bring an end to the conflict in the view of 1 Peter. For Balch 1 Peter urges not conversion as a resolution of the problem but social conformity.

Both these studies are significant contributions to various aspects of the letter of 1 Peter. The problem which they illustrate, nevertheless, is the difficulty in arriving at a comprehensive sociological-exegetical analysis, in detecting the interrelations of sociological and theological data and perspectives. The problem posed by 1 Peter remains. If the goal of the Christian community is ultimately inclusive, then why should Christians remain so exclusive? If there is hope that even hostile outsiders might one day join Christians in the common glorification of God (2:12), then why does 1 Peter urge continued social separation? To put it another way, how does conflict figure in the strategy of a missionizing conversionist sect?

The Functions of Social Conflict in 1 Peter

Scholars of 1 Peter are in general agreement that conflict of some sort, be it the result of imperially instigated persecution or, as is more likely, the manifestation of local and social animosity, is a major issue with which 1 Peter is dealing. It is likewise generally assumed that the intention of 1 Peter is either to suggest means for eliminating or minimizing such conflict or for accepting it as an inevitable concomitant of Christian faith and obedience. In any case, conflict is viewed in *negative* terms as an evil or regrettable occurrence which theatened the faith and steadfastness of the Christians in Asia Minor and prompted the consoling response of 1 Peter.

The stress upon conflict, contention and contrast which pervades 1

Peter, however, can also be seen in another, more constructive light. The manner in which the social conflict is described, emphasized and interpreted in this document can also be seen, along with its double accent on isolation and openness, as an interesting example of the strategy of the author(s) for addressing a sect under hostile external pressures. In this case conflict might be viewed not simply as a "trouble" which the sect is enjoined to avoid but as a "tool" which the author(s) used in order to achieve a specific social effect.

The basis for this theory lies in the observation of social theorists that conflict in society, although generally viewed as a destructive force, actually has a variety of *constructive* effects. Georg Simmel[30] and, more recently, Lewis Coser [31] have both made significant contributions toward such an appreciation of the positive values of social conflict. Simmel (1858–1918), for instance, had noted in his classic study that conflict plays a substantive role in the establishment of different social groups and in clarification of specific group identities and relationships, as well as in the reinforcement of group cohesion. The major points of Simmel's analysis are summarized by Theodore Caplow:

> It is partly by means of conflict that many individuals are welded together into organized groups. Conflict plays a large part in fixing group boundaries, building status orders, codifying values, and establishing the points of reference that give continuity to the life of an individual and meaning and identity to an organization. In a general way, cooperation *within* groups results from conflict *between* groups. . . . The approach of an enemy forces an organized group to tighten its structures and mobilize its resources. Internal interaction increases, the status order is strengthened, deviance ceases to be tolerated. . . . *Within* a going organization, conflict continues to figure in two important ways. First, the willingness of members to accept internal discipline fluctuates with external threats. In general, internal authority is enhanced by the presence of an enemy who threatens the organizational boundary, and it may be undermined whether by the defeat of the enemy, which removes the apparent need for internal discipline, or by the defeat of one's own organization, which weakens its hold on members. . . . Second [Simmel] sees conflict as a means of adjustment and distribution, the indispensable instrument for ascertaining the relative strength of two organizations and allocating scarce resources between them. These functions of conflict explain why organizations often seek out new enemies, and even invent imaginary enemies when real ones are scarce.[32]

113

Expanding on the observations of Simmel, Coser developed a series of propositions which formulate various constructive functions of social conflict. Several of these propositions are suggestive for assessing the emphasis which conflict is given in 1 Peter.

For one thing, conflict has a group-binding effect. "Conflict with other groups contributes to the establishment and reaffirmation of the identity of the group and maintains its boundaries against the surrounding social world."[33] In the case of the Petrine situation this suggests here also that conflict could be seen in a positive light. Conflict could indeed be detrimental to the sect's stability. On the other hand it also reinforces the boundaries between the sect and its opponents and motivates the Christians to reconsider the advantageous features of their own peculiar community. The response to suffering need not be conformity; it could also be intensified commitment to being different. Awareness of the "war" in which they were engaged (note the metaphorical language in 2:11; 4:1 and 5:8–9) would be an effective stimulus in the resistance of the temptation to accommodate to Gentile modes of behavior. Harnack had a sense for this when, after detailing Jewish hostility to the Christian sect, he perceptively described the *positive* aspects of its internal and external effects:

> . . . [T]here was something satisfactory about the Jewish opposition. It helped both religions to make the mutual breach complete, whilst it also deepened in the minds of Gentile Christians—at a time when this still needed to be deepened—the assurance that their religion did represent a new creation, and that they were no mere class of people admitted into some lower rank, but were themselves the new People of God, who had succeeded the old.[34]

In addition to making group members more conscious of their specific identity and of the factors which differentiated them from others, external conflict can also promote internal cohesion. "Conflict with another group leads to the mobilization of the energies of group members and hence to increased cohesion of the group."[35] Harvé Carrier has put it similarly:

> A group which is considered a minority can quite easily disappear by simple assimilation just as it can become more tightly knit and indefinitely resist majority pressure. Persecution will at times weaken affiliation to a religious group, but it can also confirm and reinforce the bonds between the persecuted faithful. Furthermore, the conflict between religious and

secular values can be a cause of internal disintegration for a community of believers, but it can also provoke a redefinition and deepening of religious loyalties.[36]

1 Peter is clearly concerned with such cohesion and redefinition of loyalties as we shall note later. The stress upon Gentile/Christian contention may be seen as one of the ways in which the letter was designed to effect Christian solidarity. In this connection Coser also calls attention to how " 'searching for the outside enemy' (or exaggeration of the danger which an actual enemy represents) serves not only to maintain the structure of the group, but also to strengthen its cohesion when threatened by a relaxation of energies or by internal dissension."[37] Is it conceivable that in the interest of enhancing Christian solidarity the author(s) of 1 Peter exaggerated the conflict and that less conflict had actually existed? In any case the letter reduces all the opposing forces to a common denominator: "Gentiles" (2:12; 4:3), "sinner(s)" (4:18), "your adversary, the devil" (5:8). Struggle with one common enemy implies the need for a united front.

In a conflict situation the outside antagonists, in addition to being viewed as a threat (and hence an impetus) to internal unity, can also be seen as a "negative reference group."[38] In 1 Peter Christian behavior is depicted with reference not only to those whom the believers were to emulate (preeminently Jesus Christ [2:21–24; 3:18; 4:1–2, 12–16; also the "holy women" and Sarah, 3:5–6], namely a "positive reference group"), but also with reference to the Gentiles whose ungodly ways the believers were to shun (2:11–12; 3:9; 4:2–4, 15). This may suggest a purpose for the use of the household code material in 1 Peter other than a desire to promote social conformity of Christians to established and acceptable patterns of secular moral behavior. It is equally possible, and in the case of 1 Peter more likely, that such a pattern of communal behavior was employed in order to encourage the consolidation of a counter Christian group which was similar to and yet separate from its "negative reference group," the Gentiles.

Social conflict puts the ideology of contending groups to the test.[39] *Within* groups the degree of collective group consciousness, of commitment to shared standards and values and of consensus concerning the transpersonal goals of the group is challenged. *Between* groups, including Christians and their opponents, conflict involves what the authors of *The*

Crucible of Christianity have called "a clash of ideologies."[40] Conflict presents an opportunity and a reason for the clarification and reaffirmation of those features of the group which make it distinctive, superior and motivated by a common "cause." In 1 Peter focus upon the Christian/Gentile struggle is accompanied by reaffirmation of just these features of distinctive Christian community. It is a unique and exalted ("elect") status group chosen by and filled with the Spirit of God (1:1–2; 1:3–2:10). It is distinguished from a common foe; through its suffering it is united with its Lord Jesus Christ; and it has a collective, transpersonal goal: doing the will of God with good conscience (2:19; 3:16, 21)[41] so that ultimately the chief purpose of human existence will be revealed, namely the universal glorification of God (2:12; 4:11).

> A struggle for a superindividual cause, being stripped of all individual (and hence differing) interests and desires, forces attention upon the one immediate purpose, thus concentrating all forces for concerted action in one direction. Individuals imbued with the feeling that they "represent" the group's purposes, that they *embody* it, will be all the more ready to respond to impersonal appeals.[42]

The challenges faced by the early Christian movement make it obvious why such ideological appeal to transpersonal interests was so frequent. Individuals conceiving of themselves as representatives of the group as a whole will not only identify with, and derive strength from, the divine power they ascribe to the collectivity; they will also be more intransigent vis-à-vis outside groups in their representative role because they see themselves as bearers of a group mission. "Accommodation, which is permissible or even desirable on the level of personal behavior, is no longer permissible for the representative of group interests which transcend the 'merely' personal."[43]

In relation to a conflict situation one important function of ideology is to give the struggle transcendent legitimation and cosmic scope. In this process, according to Coser, intellectuals or leaders such as the circle from which the letter of 1 Peter emanated, have always played a significant role. They are the ones who perpetually transform conflicts of material interest into conflicts of ideas. "Intellectuals have contributed to the deepening and intensification of struggles by stripping them of their personal motivations and transforming them into struggles over 'eternal truths.' "[44]

One final aspect of conflict which helps to clarify the apparently para-doxical centripetal and centrifugal thrusts of 1 Peter is the fact that "con-flict binds antagonists."[45] Conflict is a form in which contending groups *interact* rather than withdraw from one another. From 1 Peter's perspec-tive, maintenance of the struggle of Christians with Gentiles is preferable to complete Christian withdrawal from society, a course pursued, for in-stance, by the Qumran community. Conflict, Coser points out, joins the contending parties in a common struggle and thereby affords an oppor-tunity for each to acquire knowledge about the other. Conflict is "a means to 'test' and 'know' the previously unknown. The stranger may be-come familiar through one's struggle with him."[46] In the Asia Minor con-flict Christians are encouraged to set the record straight. They are to cor-rect Gentile misconceptions of their morality (2:12, 15), to clarify the mo-tives and norms of their behavior (4:12-16), and to give "an account of the hope that is within you" (3:15). In their struggle with the Gentiles, Christians can thereby set the stage for a more positive form of interac-tion. By preserving and clarifying the distinctive features of their commu-nity in their struggle with their detractors, the Christians may create a possibility for the eventual "winning" (2:12; 3:1-2) of erstwhile outsiders. This suggests that the strategy of 1 Peter was to encourage struggle and resistance as a necessary prerequisite for an effective missionary enterprise. The Christian's role in the conflict should not be one, however, of "meet-ing violence with violence." To the contrary, the Christian conflict is an opportunity for confronting evil with good (2:18-20; 3:9, 13-17; 4:12-19) and recalcitrance with patience, humility and a "good conscience" (2:15; 3:1-4, 15-16, 21) in emulation of the Lord (2:21-24; 3:18; 4:1-3, 12-16).

In summary, a consideration of the various constructive effects of social conflict offers considerable assistance in the exegetical and sociological in-terpretation of 1 Peter and its strategy.[47] Outsider hostility directed against the Christians could have debilitating effects and prompt conformity as a way of escape. On the other hand, conflict and suffering could also be interpreted as a divine "testing" of the Christian faith (1:6; 4:12) whose effect was to stimulate awareness of distinctive group identity and status in the sight of God, and to show the necessity of the maintenance of group boundaries and group cohesion. Gentile hostility presented a challenge which could be met through steadfast obedience to the truth (1:22), im-peccable behavior, the maintenance of the boundaries of holiness and the enforcement of internal solidarity. Conflict created the occasion for a recollection of the "ultimate" implications of the struggle beyond that of individual self-interest and was an impetus for the unification of the Christians in a holy cause. It motivated the revitalization of old rules and norms of behavior and the creation of new rules for new circumstances. It not only separated contestants but also bound them together in a struggle for self-definition and thus set the stage for other forms of social interaction.

Such functions of conflict suggest that the strategy of 1 Peter was not to provide ways of eliminating or avoiding social tension but of accentuating the struggle and presenting it as something which could bring about positive results. This strategy was not to encourage withdrawal or escape of "world-alienated pilgrims" from society or, even less, from the earth. Nor was it to urge cultural assimilation or accommodation. It was rather to encourage the recipients to hold their ground, stand fast, and resist, and to equip them for that task by reassuring them of their distinctive union with God, with Jesus Christ, and with each other. From a position of collective strength the addressees not only could effectively resist outside pressures but even could win outsiders to their cause.

From a consideration of the role that conflict plays in the perspective of the letter we may now turn to further related features of its strategy. In what other ways is 1 Peter designed as a response to the situation of the addressees and the problems they faced?

DISTINCTIVE COMMUNAL IDENTITY AND STATUS

1 Peter, we recall, is a response to sagging morale, to relaxation of commitment to group-distinguishing and group-binding values and norms, and to confusion concerning the seeming incompatibility of suffering and salvation. One of the features of the sect thrown into question by the intensity of the conflict between the sectarians and the outsiders concerned the nature of their *distinctive communal identity*. In 1 Peter various aspects of this issue are given particular attention: (1) the *distinctiveness* of the Christians; (2) their *communal structure* and *common commitments;* and (3) the *status* of these strangers in respect to society on the one hand and God on the other. All three aspects of the issue of identity are related. We may begin with a consideration of the manner in which the letter treats the questions pertaining to distinctiveness and status.

Was it necessary for the sect to maintain its distinctiveness? If so, why?

Of what did this distinctiveness consist? Was the maintenance of distinctiveness of any practical advantage or was it not their very strangeness which invited or caused hostile reaction and the suffering of these Christians? Did conversion to the Christian sect bring about any change in the lowly status of these strangers? Was not association with the ridiculed group of "Christ-lackeys" more of a bane than a blessing? How, if at all, did membership in the Christian community provide a solution to the experience of displacement, deprivation and social disadvantage?

A response to these questions concerning separateness and status, like the response to the issues of solidarity and suffering, had to be formulated in both practical and religiously meaningful terms. At stake were issues concerning a common salvation and the dignity of a new organization of peoples, of transindividual interests and hopes and not just matters of personal survival.

One feature of the response which we have already analyzed involved the emphasis of the letter upon the conflict between the addressees and their neighbors as a means for encouraging Christians to separate from the conventional morality of surrounding society. Distinction and separation from Gentile life-styles were necessary for both the maintenance of Christian community and the effectiveness of its missionary witness. Implicitly the social cohesion, stability and viability of the Christian movement were at stake. Explicitly, the letter treats the problem in more religious, ideological terms. The Gentile way of life was a futile (i.e., not leading to salvation, 1:18), self-destructive (2:11), sinful and idolatrous mode of life (4:1–3) ignorant of (1:14; 2:15) and opposed to (4:2) the will of God the creator (4:19). Such a mode of living shall surely be punished by God (4:6, 17–18) who condemns those who cause innocent suffering and vindicates the innocent (2:20, 21–25; 3:14, 18–22; 4:6, 13, 17–19; 5:6–11).

Further means for encouraging separation of believers from nonbelievers may be seen in the various images that are used and in the numerous antitheses which are drawn. The image of birth (rebirth, 1:3, 23; cf. 2:2), for example, and the associated contrast of death/new life[48] symbolize not only an event of religious conversion but also the termination of previous social ties and the commencement of new associations (1:14–16, 17–18; 4:1–6). The imagery of "holiness,"[49] "election,"[50] and "purification"[51] imply similar social as well as religious distinctions and contrasts. Sanctified, elected and purified by God, Christians constitute a new people (2:9–10) "called" by God[52] and distinguished from the unbelieving Gentiles. The imagery of ransom (1:18–19), warfare (2:11; 4:1) and conflict with the demonic (5:8–9) are similarly used to speak of liberation from enslavement to past traditions (read: cultural and religious bonds) and to promote resistance to Gentile influence or pressure.

Among the numerous contrasts or antitheses which fill the letter,[53] it is particularly those drawn between the (ancient Jewish) prophets and "you" (the believers, 1:10–13), the disbelievers and the faithful (2:7), the disobedient and the obedient (2:7–8 or "us," 4:17), the sinners and the rightous (2:24; 3:18; 4:18; cf. 3:12), the evildoers and the Christians (4:15–16) which express the actual social distinction between the addressees and their opponents, Jews and pagans alike. The other antitheses, including the temporal contrasts (1:14–15, 18; 2:10; 4:1–3) reinforce these social distinctions and support the incompatibility of Christian and Gentile styles of life. In the four pithy imperatives arranged chiasmatically in 2:17,[54] a clear distinction of allegiances is affirmed. The honor which is due all men (v. 17a = A) is that which is also deserved by the emperor (v. 17d = A'); love, on the other hand, is reserved for the brotherhood (v. 17b = B) as reverence is reserved for God alone (v. 17c = B'; cf. 3:14–15).

The language used to assert the distinctiveness of the Christian addressees also affirms their new and peculiar *status* as the "elect and holy people of God" (2:4–10). By virtue of the good news which they have received and believed, these Christians are superior to the Jewish prophets who sought but did not experience the Christ and salvation (1:10–12). They have been reborn through an incorruptible rather than a corruptible seed, namely, through the hearing of the word of God as good news (1:23–25). Their inheritance likewise is "imperishable, undefiled and unfading" (1:4) in contrast to the corrupted and devastated land of Israel. In contrast to rejecting Jews and pagans, their faith in Jesus Christ has brought them "honor" (2:7; cf. 1:7) and the peculiar distinction of being God's special people (2:9–10). Their faith and conduct are superior to the "futile ways inherited from your fathers" (1:18; cf. 4:3). They shall experience divine grace and blessing whereas the unbelievers can anticipate only divine condemnation.

Election and Eliteness

The clearest expression of the unique status of the addressees is to be found in the emphasis which is placed on their divine "election." The process of election involves selection, separation and choice. It likewise implies preference, elevation and superiority. From a sociological point of view, the characterization of the readers as *"elect* visiting strangers of (in) the diaspora" (1:1) is a strategic way of both legitimating their distinction from the Jews and pagans while simultaneously attributing to these lowly *paroikoi* special elite status in the economy of God.

In an earlier study, *The Elect and the Holy,* I examined the literary and theological significance of the election theme in 1 Peter and the foregoing tradition upon which it was dependent. Subsequent studies have generally agreed that the concept of election (and holiness) was of fundamental importance to the meaning and message of the document as a whole.[55] In 2:4–10, the most comprehensive statement of the letter on the nature of the readers as the eschatological community of God, the election theme occupies center stage both structurally and thematically. This theme is extended throughout the letter through the related notion of God's "calling" of the believers (1:15; 2:9, 21; 3:9; 5:10) and the further related accent upon holiness. In fact, the description of both recipients and senders as the "elect" (1:1) or "coelect" (5:13) provides a comprehensive inclusion for the entire letter.

At this point I wish to expand on these previous observations by discussing an important sociological aspect of the occasion and use of this concept and its implications of status. An observation by the social historian Ramsay MacMullen concerning the preoccupation with prestige which characterized hellenistic Roman society may serve as a useful point of departure. In considering the question of why people (rich and poor alike) were willing to support the grandeur of Rome, he cites the allure of exclusiveness and status:

> People used the first to emphasize the second. They competitively asserted their status [the fame of their city or native land] against the patriots of neighboring cities through the acknowledged claims of material amenities —a grander temple, a grander amphitheater.[56]

Pride in city and homeland had a transclass effect:

> The masses who heard [such praise] were uplifted from their penurious anonymity to a proud height, while the rich credited themselves with the splendor of thronged streets and marble buildings. Rich and poor alike loved the object which gave them standing in the world.[57]

It is in connection with this universal interest in status, I suggest, that the stress on the election and eliteness of the Christian *paroikoi* of 1 Peter should be viewed.[58] Christianity, according to 1 Peter, was offering to its converts a special, even unique, kind of honor and status (*timē,* 1:7; 2:7; 3:7) within a society obsessed with *philotimia,* the love of prestige.[59] For unenfranchised people some of whom (e.g., the slaves) failed the three or four standard tests of prestige (noble origins, wealth, proximity to Rome and Roman power, culture),[60] the Christian sect promised elevation to equality with all members of the community (3:7; 4:10; N.B.: mutual humility, 3:8; 5:5b) within a community especially singled out for divine favor (2:9). For Jewish converts here was the full experience of the messianic hope (1:10–12, 25); for pagans, an elite status before God to which they previously had had no access (2:10).

The acquisition of status through participation in an elite and egalitarian community would be all the more attractive to *paroikoi* in particular. If, as initially stated, *paroikia* and *oikos* are sociological correlates, so are the phenomena of *paroikia* and election. In the situation of social estrangement and "relative deprivation,"[61] the stranger is forced to come to grips with his strangeness. The predicament of estrangement involves, among other things, diminished access to the generally recognized means for acquiring security, social acceptance and prestige. Membership in an elite community would hold the promise of the realization of some of these goals. Stress upon the group as "elected by God" would also serve subsequently to reinforce the self-esteem of the group when challenged by outsiders as well as to provide a rationale for continued separation from the "less honored." To describe a minority and marginal group as an "elect and holy possession of God" is to claim a divine *incipit, placet* and *vult* for this group's separateness as well as for its exalted position. The idea of election thus can serve as a key factor in an ideology of status whose design is to legitimate new group formation and motivate group maintenance (and recruitment).

For this reason the idea of election plays an important role in sectarian ideology, as we noted earlier. "The more fully the sect sees itself as a chosen remnant," Wilson observed, "the more fully will it offer resistance to [the forces of social accommodation]. Such resistance is more likely to be successful, however, if the sect has an aristocratic ethic concerning salvation—if it sees itself as a chosen elect."[62] Election by God implies or confers status and a shared sense of status is vital to a sect or other minority group especially when its existence is threatened. Assertion of a group's election represents the substitution of a divine for a human standard of estimation.

The social function of a stress upon a community's election (and holiness) when it is estranged from its social environment (i.e., is living in *paroikia*) can be seen not only in 1 Peter but also in three of the Old Testament texts or traditions from which the vocabulary and imagery of 1 Peter have been drawn. In the literary and social contexts of Exodus 19 (1 Pet. 2:4–10), Leviticus 19 (1 Pet. 1:14–16) and Isaiah 43 (1 Pet. 2:4–10)[63] it was the images of election, covenant, holiness and strangerhood which were key features of a theological (and ideological) response to problems concerning Israel's collective identity, solidarity and security.[64]

At critical historical junctures of Israel's formation as one people (Egyptian exodus), reformation under Josiah, and immanent restoration (Babylonian exile), stress was placed on the privileged and unique status of the elect and holy people of God.

> You have seen what I did to the Egyptians, and how I bore you on eagles' wings and brought you to myself. Now therefore, if you will obey my voice and keep my covenant, you shall be my own possession among all peoples; for all the earth is mine, and you shall be to me a kingdom of priests and a holy nation (Exod. 19:4–6).

In the Holiness Code of Leviticus, reflecting on the time of the exodus and settlement in Canaan but representing in its redactional form the separatistic concerns of postexilic priestly circles, we read:

> You shall be holy; for I the Lord your God am holy (19:2). You shall not do as they do in the land of Egypt . . . and the land of Canaan. . . . You shall not walk in their statutes. You shall do my ordinances, and keep my statutes and walk in them. I am the Lord your God (18:3–4). When a stranger sojourns with you in your land, you shall not do him wrong . . . for you were strangers in the land of Egypt: I am the Lord your God (19: 33–34). I am the Lord your God, who have separated you from the peoples. You shall therefore make a distinction between the clean beast and the unclean. . . . You shall be holy to me; for I the Lord am holy, and have separated you from the peoples, that you should be mine (20:24–26). If you walk in my statutes and observe my commandments and do them, then . . . I will make my abode among you, and my soul shall not abhor

you. And I will walk among you, and will be your God, and you shall be my people. I am the Lord your God, who brought you forth out of the land of Egypt, that you should not be their slaves; and I have broken the bars of your yoke and made you walk erect (26:3, 11–13). Yet for all that, when they are in the land of their enemies, I will not spurn them, neither will I abhor them so as to destroy them utterly and break my covenant with them; for I am the Lord their God; but I will for their sake remember the covenant with their forefathers, whom I brought forth out of the land of Egypt in the sight of the nations, that I might be their God: I am the Lord (26:44–45).

These themes of strangerhood, separation, election and covenant resound again in the theological tradition concerning the deuteronomic reform.[65] Here the reactualization of previous experience and tradition and the use of earlier socioreligious paradigms in the reinforcement of current social behavior is particularly evident:

The Lord our God made a covenant with us in Horeb. Not with our fathers did the Lord make this covenant, but with us, who are all of us here alive this day (Deut. 5:2–3). We were Pharoah's slaves in Egypt; and the Lord brought us out of Egypt with a mighty hand . . . and he brought us out from there, that he might bring us in and give us the land which he swore to give to our fathers (6:21, 23). [T]hen take heed lest you forget the Lord, who brought you out of the land of Egypt, out of the house of bondage. You shall fear the Lord your God; you shall serve him, and swear by his name. You shall not go after other gods, of the gods of the people who are round about you . . . (6:12–14). [Y]ou shall make no covenant with them (7:2).

Social disintegration and displacement from the elect land, i.e., divine punishment (6:15), was the inevitable result of cultural amalgamation and sacrifice of exclusive allegiance to Yahweh. "For you are a people holy to the Lord your God; the Lord your God has chosen you to be a people for his own possession, out of all the peoples that are on the face of the earth" (7:6). Yahweh's electing love and liberation require of his chosen people the maintenance of a distinctive social identity, cultic allegiance and social behavior (7:7–11). "Love the sojourner therefore; for you were sojourners in the land of Egypt" (10:9; cf. 23:7).

The deuteronomic historian offers not only a rationale for Israel's disintegration and collapse but also a program for its political, social and religious reintegration. The consolation of Deutero-Isaiah which also stressed the election, covenant and holiness of God's special people was a response to the needs of the Judaean *paroikoi* in Babylon. Traditional examples of *paroikia* existence and images of divine deliverance were used to stimulate confidence and mobilize solidarity in the hope of a "new exodus." Thematic similarities between Deutero-Isaiah and 1 Peter are abundant.[66] One text which definitely demonstrates the influence of Deutero-Isaiah upon 1 Peter is Isa. 43:20–21, which is adapted by 1 Peter in 2:9.[67] The salvation which "the Lord, your Holy One, the Creator of Israel, your King" (Isa. 43:15) has in store for his suffering servant people (cf. especially Isa. 52: 13–53:12 and 1 Peter 2:21–25) is pictured as a renewed exodus (Isa. 43:16– 20) from another land of *paroikia* (Babylon = Egypt, Isa. 43:14) whereby the distinctive honor, unity and responsibility of the chosen people will be restored: "to give drink to my chosen people, the people whom I formed for myself, that they might declare my mighty saving deeds" (Isa. 43: 21 au.).

In the proclamation and missionary propaganda of the Christian movement this recollection of the divine inversion or reversal of Israel's status was given explicit emphasis. Thus in Paul's address to the Jews and proselytes of Antioch in Pisidia (Acts 13:16–40) we can see the recurrence of all three related factors: Israel's election in its Egyptian *paroikia* constitutes its exaltation. "Men of Israel, and you that fear God, listen. The God of this people Israel *chose* (*exelexato*) our fathers and *exalted* (*hypsōsen*) the people (*ton laon*) in their *paroikia* in the land of Egypt and with an exalted (*hypsēlou*) arm he led them out of it" (13:16–17 au.).

What is it now that is to be surmised from these texts and their bearing upon the issue of the situation and strategy of 1 Peter? The traditional constellation of the ideas of strangerhood, election, covenant and holiness has long been recognized. Our interest here is neither in a recapitulation of a "history of common ideas" nor in the establishment of possible or certain literary dependencies. It is rather the link between these ideas and a common social situation which I wish to stress. Common to the texts with which 1 Peter shows affinity is a social context characterized by the geographical displacement, organizational disintegration and suffering of the people of God. In such repeated situations in the long course of Israel's undulating history, recourse to the images of a divine election and sanctification provided the conceptual means for explaining and enforcing the separate existence and communal responsibilities of a people perennially in *paroikia*. Accommodation to, or amalgamation with, the ways of the Gentiles and failure in the maintenance of social discipline and exclusive religious allegiance were equivalent to a loss of elective prestige and holiness and a rupture of the covenantal relationship with the sole determining power over life and death, Yahweh. Divine election granted and required exclusive social as well as religious "otherness." In this sense election-ideology and *paroikia*-existence are social as well as religious correlates.

It comes as no surprise then that Christian *paroikoi* such as the senders and recipients of 1 Peter should find social as well as religious relevance in the notion of their election and holiness. An experience of social estrangement similar to that experienced by God's people of old has encouraged the author(s) of this letter to turn to the sacred words once formulated in and under similar conditions (Exodus 19, Leviticus 19, Isaiah 43). The choice of these particular texts has been prompted by the *function* which their use might serve in the present, analogous to their function in the past. Here, as in similar previous social contexts, people seeking union with God are reminded of their divine election and holiness, and their extraordinary status and favor with God, as a reaffirmation of their distinctive communal identity and a stimulus to their external separateness and their internal cohesion.

The subject of the role and function of election in the biblical tradition deserves a fresh comprehensive investigation from a sociological-exegetical perspective. Older, more theme-oriented studies need to be evaluated and developed in the light of recent tradition- and redaction-analyses. This, along with a more decisive sociological approach, will facilitate a more precise determination of the social locus, interests and function of election ideologies. The relation of the LXX choice of *eklektos* as a translation for some twenty Hebrew terms to the situation of the third century B.C.E. Alexandrian Jewish community also deserves consideration. The inter-testamental apocalyptic literature and the sociopolitical movements here represented (especially, e.g., in 1 Enoch and Qumran) would likewise be particularly fertile fields for study.[68] The pertinence of election for determining the social setting of both christological traditions (e.g., Luke 9:35; 23:35) and ecclesial communities (e.g., Mark 13:20–27/Matt. 24:22–31; John 6:70; 13:18; 15:16, 19) also might be examined. Such a study ought to be informed by the abundant comparative anthropological and sociological studies of the role and function which the idea of election plays in the ideology of sectarian movements. Perhaps the brief observations made here concerning the motivation and function of the election idea in 1 Peter might serve as impetus for such a larger, more encompassing undertaking.

In 1 Peter specifically the stress on the divine election of Christians serves several related purposes. First, it serves to reassure these strangers and aliens in Asia Minor society of the honor and prestige which is theirs through membership in the Christian community. United, through faith, with Jesus Christ, the "elect" of God, they have a share in his eliteness and exaltation (2:4–10; 3:21–22). God has chosen them (1:1–2) and will continue to exalt those who are humble (5:5–7). Furthermore, their divine election and holiness distinguish them from unbelievers and make the continued separation from Gentiles imperative. Participation in this elect community of God is solely through faith in Jesus Christ. Status here is gained not through blood ties nor by meeting social prerequisites; it is available to all classes and races of mankind as a divine gift. This new criterion of election thus distinguishes Christians from Jews who also claim this special status with God. Insofar as they reject Jesus as the Christ, according to 1 Peter (2:4, 6–8), they forfeit their election. Their disobedience of the word concerning Jesus Christ ranks them now among the Gentiles, those beyond the boundaries of the true people of God. By attributing divine election and other honorific predicates of ancient Israel (2:9) to the Christian sect, the author(s) of 1 Peter have thereby attempted to disenfranchise the Jews of their peculiar "claim to fame." The sect, it is implied, is now the exclusive representative of the chosen people of God, the sole community where the prophetic hopes of Israel are fulfilled.[69]

In response to the suffering of the Christians, this emphasis upon their election consoles and reassures the readers of their divine support, blessing and ultimate vindication. It thereby provides a psychological basis and motivation for the admonitions to obedient and distinctive behavior. Their common election as well as their common experience of social estrangement (1:1–2; 5:12–14), furthermore, is a point which the senders of the letter use to affirm their bond with the recipients. Finally, as these last passages also reveal, through the theme of election two different aspects of the Christian community are shown to be related; namely, their *paroikos* condition in society, on the one hand, and their constitution as the distinctive *oikos* of God, on the other. The fact of being chosen by God qualifies both their situation in society (1:1; 2:11) and their union with God (2:4–10).

In addition to an assertion of the divine election of the addressees, 1 Peter contains other means as well for elevating the self-esteem of its audience and affirming Christian distinctiveness. What the letter proposes is that the apparent bane of Christian experience in society is actually a blessing in disguise. This perspective has already been discussed in connection with the issue of conflict. On the one hand, conflict threatens the well-being and stability of the community. On the other hand, conflict ratifies the distinction between Christians and Gentiles. In similar fashion, the "vice" of zealousness, considered so inimical to the desire for moderation, equilibrium and order in a hellenistic Roman society and thus a cause to defame the Christians as religious "fanatics," becomes in 1 Peter a virtue used to console those committed to doing good (3:13). The opprobrious label "Christian" with its insulting overtone becomes an epithet which brings blessing rather than shame for those who share the sufferings of the Christ and thereby receive the gift of God's Spirit (4:12–16). Slaves who conform to the example of their suffering Lord (2:18–25) are within the Christian community no longer regarded as subhuman members of the species but exalted as paradigms for all Christians to emulate. Along these same lines, humility is transformed from a minus to a plus. In the popular estimation, humility was a detestable position to assume, unworthy of true men. For the Christian community, however, this form of "degradation" was not only essential to Christian harmony; it was in fact demanded by God (3:8; 5:5b-7).

For the Christian community, in other words, there exists a different standard of values, namely the will of God and the exemplary obedience of Jesus Christ, which distinguishes it from outside society. In the estimation of the Gentiles the Christians amount only to a motley collection of lowly aliens, ignoble slaves, religious fanatics and "Christ-lackeys" obsessed with self-humiliation. Within the family of God, however, and in God's estimation, Christians enjoy a new status which can only be retained by avoiding conformity to the degrading social norms of the Gentiles. The addressees are not encouraged to imagine that their situation *in society* is other than it really is. They are, however, reminded that *within their own community* a different situation prevails. 1 Peter is not offering its readers a theological recipe for escaping their social situation but rather a rationale for continued social engagement. Over against the futile world of the Gentiles the Christians constitute an alternative and superior form of social and religious organization.

This fact is important for assessing the role which the stress on the *paroikia* condition of the addressees played in the strategy of 1 Peter. The failure to see that the letter is encouraging its readers *to remain* aliens rather than suggesting that they *have become* aliens in a metaphorical religious sense has resulted in serious misconceptions of the letter as a whole.

A Pilgrim Theology?

In the opening chapter of this study evidence for the linguistic meaning and use of *paroikos(oi)* and its related terms (*paroikia, parepidēmos*) was examined. The conclusion drawn was that in 1 Pet. 1:1, 17 and 2:11 these terms identify the addressees as actual (legally and socially defined) "resident aliens" and "visiting strangers" living in the four provinces of Asia Minor named in 1:1. Various reasons were given for rejecting the conventional theory, reflected not only in the commentaries but also in several biblical translations, that these passages and their terms express a "pilgrim theology" according to which the addressees were to think of themselves as pilgrims on earth yet on the way to their heavenly abode. In order to clarify the letter's actual perspective on Christian social estrangement, it will be useful to evaluate three recent studies bearing on this subject.

Victor Paul Furnish supplies a current example of the spiritual-sans-social perspective taken by many commentators on the "pilgrim motif" in 1 Peter. "The phrase 'elect sojourners of the dispersion' [1:1]," he notes, "introduces a major and pervasive conception in I Peter."[70] He then mistakenly assumes, however, that "Christians are the elect of God *and thus only temporarily resident in this present world*"[71] (emphasis added). Neither textual evidence nor logic supports such an assumption. The Greek text of 1 Peter never qualifies the terms for "dispersion" or "strangers" or "resident aliens" with the phrase "in this present world" (as biblical translations sometimes imply). Furthermore, as Furnish himself recognizes, "since the Babylonian exile Jews living outside Palestine had thought of themselves as 'sojourners,' temporary residents only, whose true home was elsewhere. The term 'diaspora,' of course, came to be used of the entirety of 'dispersed' Judaism, scattered throughout *the Gentile world*"[72] (emphasis added). That "true home" (i.e., Eretz Israel, the Holy Land) and the lands of the dispersion were material plots of contrasted soil and culture and nowhere else but in this present world. The distinction implied by "diaspora," as by "visitor" and "resident alien," was geographical, cultural and religious, not metaphysical.

The fact that 1 Peter is addressed to predominantly Gentile converts leads Furnish to seek a "specifically Christian meaning" for diaspora sojourning which he finds in the concepts of election and eschatology.[73] But these concepts with their obvious Old Testament roots are neither uniquely Christian nor evidence of a cosmological earth/heaven dichotomy in 1 Peter. The reference in 1:4 to "an inheritance which is imperishable, undefiled, and unfading, kept in heaven for you" is only an apparent exception. Here, as throughout 1 Peter, the determining eschatology is not spatial but temporal. The new divine inheritance of the dispersed Christians symbolizes their socioreligious distance from old Israel and implies the superiority of sect over parent.[74]

To see the "earthly pilgrimage theme" as not only "an essential part of [1 Peter's] message" but also "a fundamental aspect of the Christian view of the life of faith"[75] is not only to misconstrue the focus of 1 Peter but also to exaggerate the accent on this theme in the New Testament. To be sure, this theme and an accompanying earth/heaven contrast is central to the Epistle to the Hebrews; yet despite certain terminological similarities and the problem of suffering common to both documents, the cosmology, soteriology, Christology, ecclesiology and thought world of Hebrews are too distinct from that of 1 Peter to support the hypothesis of theological affinity.[76]

The addressees of 1 Peter were *paroikoi* by virtue of their social condition, not by virtue of their "heavenly home." The alternative to this marginal social condition of which 1 Peter speaks is not an ephemeral "heaven is our home" form of consolation but the new home and social family to which the Christians belong here and now; namely, the *oikos tou theou*. This home and the communal experience of salvation which it signifies are not "beyond time and history,"[77] but are already at hand in the community which is "in Christ" (3:16; 5:10, 14). The orientation of 1 Peter is indeed eschatological, that is, it encourages a lively hope in the complete realization of salvation yet awaiting the faithful (1:5, 9, 13; 2:12; 4:5, 7, 17–18; 5:1, 10). At the same time, the achievement of that future reward (5:4) is everywhere linked to, and dependent upon, the believers' maintenance of the bonds of their brotherhood here and now.

Around the same time that Furnish's study appeared, Max-Alain Chevallier had just published an article on the condition and vocation of the Christians in diaspora[78] according to 1 Peter and Christian Wolff presented a study of the Christian and the world in 1 Peter.[79] Both of these studies give more satisfactory attention to the question of the social condition of the addressees. In the end, however, they run aground on the same false assumption underlying Furnish's interpretation. Like Furnish and others, Chevallier and Wolff infer from 1 Peter that the addressees *have become* strangers by becoming Christians, that it was first their conversion which qualified them as aliens. Thus Wolff maintains: "Precisely as God's elect are they strangers . . . first through his being a Christian does the Christian become a stranger."[80] Chevallier in similar fashion looks not to the possibility that the addressees were in fact *paroikoi* or strangers in society long before their adherence to the Christian sect. Instead the situation is reversed: the addressees were called aliens because they were elected by God[81] and intended as "a sign of the eschatological times: the salvation offered to the nations."[82]

Such an approach, however, turns things on their head and mistakes social fact for theological interpretation. Both Chevallier and Wolff correctly recognize that 1 Peter focuses upon, and seeks to provide a positive interpretation of, the estrangement of Christians from their society. However, both assume that the terms "strangers" and "resident aliens" were meant only metaphorically and that they indicated not the actual social condition of the addressees but rather the manner in which they were advised by 1 Peter to think of themselves. As Israel lived in the diaspora as strangers and aliens, so now do the eschatological people of God.[83] Here we must ask whether ideas, what Wolff calls the "concept of strangerhood,"[84] are not taking precedence over social reality. There is no question that in 1 Peter the Christian community is interpreted as the eschatological people of God and heir of all the honors which once characterized Israel of old. There *is* question as to which terms in 1 Peter constitute honorific predicates of Israel now ascribed to the Christian community and which terms describe the actual social condition of the addressees. Despite the fact that *paroikos* (*paroikia, parepidēmos*) occur in the LXX, there is no reason to include them among the special epithets for the covenant people of God. There, as well as in the inscriptions and literature of the hellenistic Roman world, these terms depict people who lived as actual strangers and as legally and socially defined resident aliens in their social environments. The same holds true for their meaning and use in 1 Peter.

1 Peter was directed to actual strangers and resident aliens who had become Christians. Their new religious affiliation was not the cause of their position in society though it did add to their difficulties in relating to their

neighbors. It is precisely this combination of factors which best explains the disillusionment which the converts felt. Attempting to improve their social lot through membership in the community which the Christian movement offered, they experienced instead only further social aggravation. Now they were demeaned not only as social strangers and aliens but for being "Christ-lackeys" as well.

In response to this predicament the author(s) of 1 Peter wrote that, although they are indeed estranged from their society religiously now as well as socially, their salvation is nevertheless assured. Those who bear the name of Christ are elect as he was elect; they are the children of God, his family, his special people. Assured of God's protecting hand, they have cause to endure. Their God will vindicate them. They are strangers and yet they are "elected" strangers who now have a place of belonging "in Christ." As they are the elect of God, so their condition of estrangement in society may be seen as analogous to that of the people of God who once lived in diaspora (1:1). Dispersion could be seen now, as it was once before,[85] not only as a sign of divine judgment but also as God's spreading of his seed among the nations.

"Election," "diaspora," "people of God" and the like—these are the traditional theological terms of 1 Peter's response, not *paroikos, paroikia* and *parepidēmos.* To adopt the attractive distinction made by Chevallier, the latter describe the "condition" of the addressees and the former, their "vocation." In 1 Peter the addressees were not being told that they had been made strangers by God's election but that they could find strength *to remain* strangers in the conviction of their divine election. By interpreting their condition in society as a divine vocation, however, 1 Peter suggests that social marginality and estrangement can be regarded by the Christians as not merely something tolerable but even desirable. Like conflict, estrangement can also have a positive effect. Maintenance of social distance could be one of the chief means by which the coherence of group values was preserved and at the same time a means by which the unique qualities of the Christian sect were made clear and appealing to potential recruits.[86]

GROUP CONSCIOUSNESS, SOLIDARITY AND COHESION

Stress upon the distinctiveness and status of the Christian addressees also involved an emphasis upon their *collective* identity. The fact that the

Christians together constituted one collective enterprise becomes in turn the basis for specific exhortation regarding their internal cohesion.

For the harassed Christian movement in Asia Minor to survive and grow, isolated pockets of believers throughout the provinces required a sense of the ties which bound them in a common cause. If Christians were to resist external pressures and be mutually supportive, a high degree of group consciousness was essential. One means employed by 1 Peter for the "raising of group consciousness," to borrow a contemporary expression, was the stress upon the community into which the believers had been gathered. The prominence of the collective terms and images used to depict the addressees is one of the most distinguishing features of 1 Peter. The readers are characterized collectively as a "Spirit-filled house(hold)" (2:5) or "the house(hold) of God" (4:17), an "elect race" (2:9), a "royal residence" (2:9 [see pp. 165–166]), a "holy body of priests" (2:9), a "holy nation" (2:9), a "people for (God's own) possession" (2:9), a "brotherhood" (2:17; 5:9), and "the flock of God" (5:2, cf. 2:25). These collective terms state explicitly what other metaphors for the act of salvation and its community-creating effect imply: God's activity of building (2:5; 5:10), sanctifying (1:2, 14–16, 22), electing (1:1; 5:13), fathering (1:3, 23; 2:2; cf. 1:17) or (pro-)creating (4:17; cf. 2:13) and gathering (2:25).

All these collective terms, Spörri has observed, "depict the community as a cohesive unity, an intimate association of people of similar origin, with similar experience and self-consciousness, similar heritage and service" (au.).[87] Customarily these collective terms are cited by exegetes to illustrate the extraordinary place which ecclesiology occupies in the letter. I myself have stressed their importance for the interpretation of the rare term *hierateuma* (2:5, 9) in particular.[88] But why is it that ecclesiology and an emphasis upon Christian collectivity play such a significant role in 1 Peter? Establishing the fact is not yet equivalent to determining its intended social effect. Spörri misses the mark in wanting to regard these images as abstract elements of a theological *"Gemeindegedanke."* In his view the community is a flock, a people, "independent of the number, place, time, the individual components and particular conditions which gave these elements concrete and historical shape" (au.).[89] Such a premise, however, is arbitrary and sociologically unjustifiable. Spörri isolates the *idea* of community from the very social reality which gives this idea its sociological urgency and psychological cogency.

133

To the contrary, Christians were reminded of their collective identity because Christianity from the outset envisaged salvation not merely as an individual but primarily as a collective experience which involved the formation of a new and distinctive social structure. Reception of the good news, as the Gospels, Acts and the Pauline literature testify, was a socially infectious and group-building experience. The new social as well as religious bonds brought about by the public proclamation of the gospel were the concrete manifestations of its social conception of the kingdom of God which Jesus was believed to have inaugurated.[90] When this new social as well as religious community was challenged or threatened by outside pressures calling for conformity, as in the case of the Petrine situation, resistance to such forces was imperative. A place of belonging, mutual acceptance and security could only be preserved through a heightened sense of involvement in a communal enterprise. At the same time, membership in this community brought with it social and moral obligations for the development and support of social as well as religious unity. It is this combination of factors which may be seen to have determined the stress upon the *communal* identity of the Christian believers.

Christianity was in competition with other groups which also vied for people's allegiance. The practical concerns for recruitment, member maintenance and social support must be kept in mind. The universal, egalitarian, and socially determined form of communal salvation which these collective terms implied characterized Christianity as an attractive alternative to the options presented by Judaism, the collegia, the mystery cults and the theoretical place of belonging which inclusion in a universal Roman *patria* was supposed to have offered. These symbols of communal identity and communal care effectively expressed the aspirations and values of the Christian sect. They aided in the propaganda of member recruitment and group maintenance. They served in the mobilization of internal cohesion and resistance to external opposition.

This interest in promoting group consciousness and solidarity also accounts for the expansive elaboration on the identity and unity of the believers in 1 Pet. 2:4-10. The location of this passage in its literary context as well as the nature of its content signal the central importance of this text within the letter. It is the culmination of an introductory affirmation of the identity, dignity and commonality of the Christian believers (1:3-2:10). It likewise establishes the basis and premise for the following exhortation to concerted action (2:11-5:11).

It is unified with its preceding context by the golden thread running through the entire first segment of I P[eter]: the bond between the faithful community and her glorified Lord. And as a statement on the election, corporateness and holiness of the believing community, it points both backward to the holiness paraenesis in 1:13 ff. and the birth-growth theme of 1:22 ff., and forward to the social exhortation of 2:11 ff. Here in 2:4–10 the injunction to a holy life, brotherly love, growth in the word and witness to the world receives its most detailed support.[91]

A common faith, according to this passage, is "the tie that binds." Through faith believers are united with Jesus Christ and with each other. Through faith (2:6, 7)[92] believers share in his experience of both suffering and rejection at the hands of men[93] and exaltation and vindication by the hand of God (2:4).[94] As he is the elect stone of God (2:4), so are they (2:5, 9).[95] As he has been made alive ("living stone," 2:4) by God, so they too are "living stones" (2:5).[96] Dignity and honor belong to them both (*entimos,* 2:4; *timē,* 2:7).[97] Jesus Christ is the mediator of their bond with God, their communal salvation (cf. 1:3, 19–31; 2:21–25; 3:18–22; 4:1, 13), glorification[98] and their common service (2:5). Elsewhere the formula "in Christ" (3:16; 5:10, 14) circumscribes this union with God, with the Lord and with each other.

At the same time that faith unites, it also divides those who accept Jesus Christ from those who reject him (2:4, 7), those who obey the word from those who disobey (2:8; cf. 3:1; 4:17). Faith marks the religious line of demarcation between "us" and "them," the believers and the Gentiles, the righteous and the sinners (4:18). Here we note once again the double function of the religious language of the letter. Like "election," "holiness," etc., "faith" is presented as a basis of both the union of the faithful and their distinction from the Gentiles. Solidarity with God, with the Christ and with one another in faith implies, according to 1 Peter, maintenance of social distance. The Christian sect is to pursue a course which leads not to consolidation with outsiders but to independent coexistence.

Solidarity is encouraged, furthermore, not only through the use of collective symbols of group identity but also through a means which is a special characteristic of this letter within the New Testament literature. This is the relatively frequent use of so-called syn- composites or terms which include the prefix "co-" or "sym-." There are eight such constructions in the letter: *mē syschēmatizomenoi* ("do not *con*form," 1:14), *synoikountes* ("*co*habit," 3:7), *synklēronomois* ("*co*heirs," 3:7), *sympatheis* ("be *sym*pathetic," 3:8), *syntrexontōn* (lit.: "run together *with*"; "join *with*," 4:4), *symbainontos* (lit.: "going, coming *with*"; "coming upon," 4:12), *sympresbyteros* ("*co*presbyter," 5:1) and *syneklektē* ("*co*elect," 5:13). Of these eight terms, four (*synoikein, sympathes, sympresbyteros* and *syneklektos*) occur nowhere else in the New Testament; for all but one (*synoikein*) of these four terms there is no pre-Christian evidence. The choice of these unusual terms is obviously part of a particular strategy. This strategy, as our investigation indicates, involves a calculated emphasis upon attitudes and actions which foster social cohesion.

In instructions to members of the household, husbands are told to *co-habit,* live together, with their wives as partners and not as masters. For in the Christian household of God wives are equal *coheirs* of the grace of life (3:7). All members of the household, moreover, are to be *sympathetic* as they are to be "of one mind," "lovers of their brothers" (and sisters) in faith, "compassionate," and "humble" (3:8). These syn- or co- terms, in other words, are employed to encourage the equality, unity and mutual care which should prevail in the Christian community. Like the reference to the coelect (sister)[99] in Babylon (5:13), they also denote the peculiar dignity which Christians enjoy.

In 1:14 and 4:4, on the other hand, these composite forms are used to describe the bonds with Gentiles which the believers are to terminate. Obedient, holy children of God (1:15–16) must not *conform* any longer to the "selfish desires" (*epithymiais*, 1:14; cf. 2:11; 4:2) and inherited social mores of pre-Christian existence (1:18). Redemption is liberation from "the Gentile connection." When these converts did make a break with the past and conformed to the will of God rather than to the desires of the Gentiles (4:2–3), the Gentiles were alienated (*xenizontai*, 4:4; RSV: "surprised") by the fact that their former cohorts no longer conformed or "plunged with (them) in the same stream of debauchery" (BAGD). The recurrence of the alienation-consolidation theme in 4:12 suggests perhaps an intentional pun, in fact. In 4:4 Gentiles were estranged by Christian non-conformity. In 4:12 Christians are advised not to be similarly estranged (*mē xenizesthe*) by the experience of the fiery test (of faith) "as though something strange (*hōs xenou*) were 'con*tacting*' you" (au.). In reality the test of faith affords them "*com*munion" (*koinōneite*) with the sufferings of Christ. The composite terms thus are used to reinforce the social distinctiveness as well as the unity of the Christian sect.[100]

Finally there is the New Testament *hapax legomenon* in 5:1, *sympres-byteros*. Later on in our study[101] we shall consider the reasons for regarding 1 Peter as the product not merely of an individual, the apostle Peter, but of a Petrine group which was writing in Peter's name. In 5:1, however, the impression given is that the chief figure of this group is speaking.

In 5:1 three characterizations of the chief figure of this group are given, one of which is that he is a "copresbyter." Just as this term is unique in the New Testament, so Simon Peter is nowhere else referred to as a presbyter. His preeminent title is that of "apostle" and this is the manner in which he is identified in the letter's salutation: "Peter, an apostle of Jesus Christ." In Christian terminology and perspective the term *apostle* implies special privilege and more authority than does the traditional designation *elder*. What then accounts for the peculiar choice of the term *copresbyter* here?[102] The answer lies in the fact that here also we have another example of the letter's strategy. The point of 5:1 is to underline not so much Peter's authority as his *solidarity* with the presbyters and the flock of God (5:1–5). The first clause of 5:1, "Therefore the presbyters among you I a copresbyter exhort" (au.), declares the parity between the leading figure of the Petrine community and the Christian leaders in Asia Minor. The second and third clauses, "a witness to the sufferings of the Christ" and "the sharer (*koinōnos*) in the glory about to be revealed" (au.), affirm the experiences which Peter and the recipients of the letter have in common. They too shared (*koinōneite*) in the sufferings of the Christ (4:13; cf. 1:10–12) and through their bearing of his name gave witness (4:16). They too would surely participate in the glory to be revealed (1:7, 11, 21; 4:13, 14; 5:4, 10). The term "copresbyter" establishes the basis for a sympathetic as well as authoritative exhortation of presbyters in 5: 2–4. The further characteristics named in 5:1 are an immediate echo of the Christian experiences described in the preceding passage 4:12–19. The persuasive force of the exhortation here as elsewhere in the letter derives not from the titular authority of its chief sender but from the common experience and hope which both senders and recipients shared.

The authors of 1 Peter have employed and perhaps coined composite terms to express the mutuality and commonality which characterize not only the sect in Asia Minor but also the worldwide Christian communion. Its authors were intent on assuring their fellow Christians in Asia Minor that the latter did not stand alone. Lest we overlook the wood for the trees, we should keep in mind that the very composition and dispatch of 1 Peter itself were a demonstration of such concern. The genre of this document has been the subject of extensive debate.[103] Yet what more apposite form of communication might the authors have chosen for an expression of personal bonds and solidarity between two separated groups of the Christian movement than that of the letter? Theories that 1 Peter represents, in the main, a baptismal homily or liturgy, or the epistolary expansion or adaptation thereof, have failed to produce their analogies or motive for such a hybrid form. On the other hand, it bears all the features of a genuine letter in which extensive use has been made of liturgical, catechetical and parenetic tradition. Despite its encyclical address, the contents of this letter indicate the efforts which were made to affirm the bonds between senders and recipients. In addition to the ties discussed in connection with 5:1, the commencement and close of the letter deserve attention. In the salutation and conclusion which frame the entire letter the similarity of the social estrangement and yet divine favor of both recipients and senders is expressed. The Christians who were writing from "Babylon" (i.e., that notorious place where God's people were once dispersed, most likely a metaphorical reference to Rome)[104] had much in common, and could well sympathize, with fellow Christians in the diaspora of Asia Minor. At the same time both groups belonged to the one elect community described in 2.4–10. As the addressees of the letter were elect (1:1), so at least one among the senders is described as the "coelect." As we shall also note below, the household of God to which all the recipients belong embraces also Silvanus, "the faithful *brother*" (5:12) and Mark, the *"son"* (5:13).

The extent of the personal link between senders and recipients is uncertain. Reference to Peter, Silvanus and Mark by name suggests that these persons were known to, and respected by, the addressees. These persons personalized the group from which the letter emanated, its Palestinian Christian roots and its universal missionary vision. The absence of reference to specific individuals among the addressees may be due to the encyclical nature of the letter in which the singling out of individuals would have been inappropriate and the listing of all names, impractical. The encyclical form of the letter is consonant with and serves as a vehicle for emphasizing the common experience and unity of "your brotherhood throughout the world" (5:9). In addressing Christians collectively rather than individually, the authors imply that, despite geographical separation, Christians throughout the Mediterranean world comprise a unitary movement. Wherever they find themselves, all those who have been reborn through the gospel are children of one single brotherhood or family of God.

Finally, this concern for Christian solidarity and cohesion is amply evident in the explicit exhortations of the letter. The predominantly hortatory style and tone of 1 Peter are noted by all commentators. This brief letter contains no less than fifty-one imperatival exhortations. As I have noted elsewhere,[105] the imperatives generally follow, and are based upon, preceding indicative statements and then are substantiated by further subsequent indicative statements drawn from sacred Scripture or Christian tradition. Injunctions regarding the maintenance of internal cohesion generally follow passages which first declare that unity as a divinely established reality. The unity of the community is to be preserved because this is the gift of God and the will of God. Thus the "therefore" of 1:13 which introduces the exhortation concerning separation from former patterns of behavior and union with the holy God (1:13–21) follows as a consequence of the embracing reality of salvation declared in 1:3–12. The injunction to "unhypocritical brotherly love" follows as a logical result of purification and obedience (1:22). Likewise in 2:1 the readers are to desist from every kind of evil and guile, hypocrisy, envy and slander that would impair the experience of the *philadelphia* previously encouraged in 1:22. Or to cite one last extensive example, at a major juncture of the letter through the use of the household code the addressees are exhorted to concretize in action (2:11–5:11) the identity, dignity and unity which they have been given as the elect and holy people of God, the household of faith (1:3–2:10).

Solidarity is to be gained and nurtured through an unceasing love of the brotherhood (1:22; 2:17; 3:8; 4:8); it is signified liturgically with the kiss of love (5:14). Toward such an end subordination is also enjoined. In this *leitmotif* of the household code (2:13, 18; 3:1, 5; 5:5b; cf. 3:22) the accent falls not on the prepositional suffix "sub-" (*hypo-*) but on the verbal stem "ordinate" (*tassō*). The stress is not on submission or subjection but on *order*.[106] Concern for order need not imply that the addressees were engaged in revolutionary activities or that they sought disengagement from the institutional orders of society.[107] Order within the sect was imperative if external pressures for social conformity were to be resisted. Again the social needs and organizational cohesion of the sect must be kept in mind.[108]

Although order is a common *topos* of a conventional household ethical tradition,[109] its stress in 1 Peter is also not in itself evidence of a conformity ethic.[110] To the contrary, the household code has been appropriated in order to depict in familiar terms a form of social and religious communion, a family or a brotherhood, united and motivated by a distinctively different set of loyalties and motives. The Christian community is a household brought into being by God the Father. The motivation for its internal order is required obedience to the will of God. Christian social cohesion has divine sanction. To be subordinate to "every human institution" (2:13), even to those outside the household (imperial officials [2:14–17], nonbelieving masters [2:18–20] or husbands [3:1–6]) is to "do the good"[111] which God, and not merely the state or social convention, requires. The sole criterion for these actions, including "acting conscientiously,"[112] "being obedient,"[113] "leading a good life,"[114] is "the will of God,"[115] the *paterfamilias* of the household. Obedient subordination to the will of God, even and especially under adverse conditions (slander, harsh and unjust treatment, religious divisions within marriage, and perhaps domineering leaders), also entails solidarity with the suffering Lord.[116] Subordination to God and union with the Lord who was also subordinate to the divine will,[117] however, do not imply a policy of integration with external social structures. Christian free men who act in accord with civil law do so because they are "slaves of God" (2:16). Even the state, as a *human* institution or the result of the creative activity of God (*ktisis* can mean both, 2:13), is subordinate to God the creator and judge (4:17–19; cf. *ktistē;* 4:6). To the extent that it enforces what is consonant with God's will (i.e., maintaining justice, 2:14), it may be obeyed without compromise of the distinctive ethic of the family of God. However, Christians are to maintain a clear distinction between respect for the emperor and reverence for God (2:17). The same internal solidarity and external distinction are enjoined in 4:1–2. As Goppelt has noted,[118] 1 Peter encourages a Christian style of behavior which is at the same time in keeping with institutional rules and civil justice and yet not in conformity to bourgeois morality since its norm is a good conscience before God which governs all who are "in Christ" (3:16).

In the passage 4:12–19 this same subtle distinction is present. As we have already observed, the text is permeated with contrasts between those righteous believers united with God and Christ, on the one hand, and the "disobedient," the "impious and the sinner," on the other. The controlling collective image is that of the "household of God" (4:17). The behavior that is commended (vv. 12–14, 16) or condemned (v. 15) is conduct which is compatible or incompatible with membership in this particular household. The criterion for evaluating such behavior is not Roman law or local civic conventions but preeminently the higher law of God by which the members of God's household were bound. The murderer, the thief and the evildoer (4:15) fall under the condemnation of God as well as that of society. Such actions are inconsistent with being a Christian and holding membership in God's household (v. 17).

From this perspective the inclusion and force of the fourth term among the offenses listed in 4:15 becomes clear. *Allotriepiskopos* is another of the New Testament *hapax legomena* in 1 Peter whose meaning is most difficult to assess.[119] The fact that this is the first recorded use of the term in the Greek language[120] suggests that it was coined by the authors of 1 Peter· and that its meaning is determined by its context. The elements of which the word is composed indicate that it designates one who "supervises" or "oversees" (-*episkopos*) "those or that which are/is different or alien" (*allotri-*). When we keep in mind that in Greek the opposite of the adjective *allotrios* is *oikeios* ("of the same household," "those who belong to us")[121] the relation of this term to the governing idea of the household in 4:12–19 becomes evident. Together with the other terms of 4:15 it describes a type of person who acts contrary to the norm, and transgresses the boundaries, of the household of God. Such a person is one who meddles or interferes in the affairs of others to whom he does not belong. In the context of 1 Peter these "others" are the impious and the sinners (4:18) outside the household of God who disobey the gospel of God (4:17). Thus the believers and perhaps particularly their leaders who are described in 5:2 as "exercising oversight" (*episkopountes*) are not to attempt to extend such oversight to the business and affairs of the Gentiles.

To be sure, the meddling of foreigners in things which did not concern them was offensive to the outsiders as well, even though not on a level with murder or theft. Thus Cicero (*De officiis* 1.125) comments:

> As for the foreigner or the resident alien, it is his duty to attend strictly to his own concerns, not to pry into other people's business, and under no condition to meddle in the politics of a country not his own.

From the perspective of the Christian sect, nevertheless, such meddling would do more harm than to provide grounds for further Gentile resentment. It would also obscure the boundary line between sect and society and allow the possibility of reciprocal internal "contamination." As the letter had already made clear, the holiness and purity of the Christian community had to be maintained through severance of social ties. Nonconformity also involves noninterference. God will see to the judgment of the Gentiles (4:6, 17–18). In the meantime Christians are to get their own house in order. Meddling in the affairs of outsiders is, like murder, theft or evildoing, incompatible with the holy way of life demanded of the elect and holy people of God.

The types of behavior proscribed in 4:15 may in fact have been offenses of which non-Christian society thought the Christians were guilty. From the perspective of 1 Peter, however, the point is that such behavior is to be eschewed because it is contrary to *God's* will.[122] Christians are regulated by a norm which embraces and yet transcends civil justice. They are to distinguish carefully the "intentions of the Gentiles" from "the will of God" (4:2–3). They are to be subordinate to human institutions "for the Lord's sake" (2:13). Their holiness and innocence might be lost on society but it is conformity with God's gospel (4:17) and his will (4:19) which ultimately effects their salvation.

If fidelity to the gospel and will of God and the endurance of unjust suffering distinguish the Christian from the Gentile, they are also an important bond which unites the faithful. Suffering "as a Christian" forges solidarity with the suffering Christ (4:13), with God who is glorified by such a name (4:16), and with the worldwide suffering brotherhood (5:9). As the sense and original force of the opprobrious label "Christian" ("Christ-lackeys") are transformed into a sign of unity and blessing, so by the same principle of inversion the "problem" of suffering is transformed into an occasion of joy (4:13; cf. 1:6, 8). Or to put it another way, suffering, positively interpreted, is used as a rationale for reinforcing distinctive status with God and group cohesion. In continuity with an earlier Jewish and Christian tradition[123] which emphasized "joy in suffering," Christian suffering is here hailed as a sign of the end time, of the vindication of the righteous and of their union with God. In the passages 1:6–9, 3:13–17 and 4:12–19 the innocent suffering of the addressees is put in the following perspective.

1. The suffering of God's righteous one is a sign of the end time, of the imminence of the day of judgment.[124]

2. In this final period suffering is an occasion for the *testing* of the purity and steadfastness of faith (1:6–7; 4:12). The willingness to suffer for innocent conduct demonstrates on whose side one stands; it tests allegiance to either God or the godless Gentiles (4:2–3; cf. 2:17).

3. Suffering for "doing good," for obedience to the will of God, will be rewarded by God with "praise, glory and honor" (1:7; cf. 2:7; 3:7; 5:1, 4, 10).

4. Such suffering unites one with the innocent suffering Christ (2:21; 3:18; 4:1, 12–13; 5:1).

5. Thus righteous suffering is a blessing and an opportunity to "keep the Christ (as) Lord holy in your hearts" (3:14–15).

6. Suffering in communion with the suffering Christ and the righteous bearing of his name are a sure sign that "the glory and the Spirit of God rest upon you" (4:13–14).

7. Through suffering "as a Christian" the believer "gives glory to God" (4:16).

8. Righteous suffering effects union not only with God and the Christ but also with the worldwide brotherhood (5:9).

9. Thus the suffering of Christians is not an occasion for grief and despair but for "inexpressible and exalted joy" (1:8; cf. 4:13).

Such an interpretation is hardly a trivialization or "spiritualization" of the actuality of suffering. The deleterious effect of suffering upon the stability of the community is confronted squarely. Attempts at avoiding suffering through conformity to social standards and renewal of old associations had to be resisted. Therefore 1 Peter repeatedly stresses that suffering for obedience to God is a hallmark of Christian uniqueness, a unifying and purifying experience for those who remain faithful. Suffering, according to 1 Peter, is not to be avoided, therefore, but to be embraced as a sign that the fullness of salvation is at hand.

This perspective on suffering and its function of reinforcing distinctiveness, solidarity and commitment are generally missed when the theory of an "official Roman persecution" is introduced. The theory is not only unnecessary for understanding the content of 1 Peter; it also contributes to a distortion of its actual strategy. The term *Christian,* suffering "for the name," and the defense (*apologia*)[125] which believers are called to make "of the hope within" them (3:15) in no way require the premise of Roman sanctioned persecution to make sense; nor, as we have seen, do the offenses condemned in 4:15. The terms *peirasmos(oi)* (1:6; 4:12) and *pyrōsis* (4:12), furthermore, do not denote "persecution" but serve to clarify suffering as a "test" and a "purification" of faith.[126] These terms are part of a conventional theological vocabulary and set of images used to explain and justify adverse experiences of the religious community as moments of cosmic conflict and divine testing. In the New Testament and earlier Jewish tradition, as Karl Georg Kuhn has shown, *peirasmos* refers to the final eschatological conflict and judgment (Rev. 3:10) or the constant peril of the believer living in this world.[127] Similar to the conceptual world of Qumran, the use of *peirasmos* is associated with the idea "of two conflicting powers in the world, God and Satan [cf. 1 Pet. 5:6–11], light and darkness [cf. 2:9], righteous behavior and sinful activity [cf. 4:18]." Constant exposure to the attacks of Satan involves "constant vulnerability to the satanic temptation to sin and thereby to *defection from the faith*."[128] On the other hand, when associated with the themes and images of divine judgment, fire (*pyr, pyrōsis*) and examination (*dokimazein* and paronyms), *peirasmos* also denotes a divine testing of God's elect.[129] In 1 Peter both theological senses are evident. Consistant with the general apocalyptic-eschatological tenor of the document, *peirasmos* and *pyrōsis* depict an aspect of the final divine judgment commencing now with the house of God (4:12–17),[130] an instance of the attack of the devil (5:8–9), and a signal of the final separation of the righteous from the sinners (4:18). At the same time sorrow and suffering are presented as "various kinds of tests (trials)" by which the faith of the believers is tested and refined, like gold in fire, so that ultimately "the genuineness" (*to dokimion,* "probity," "tested quality") of their faith "may redound to praise and glory and honor at the revelation of Jesus Christ" (1:6–7). In 4:12 this same combination of testing-by-fire imagery recurs. "Do not be surprised by the fiery heat present among you (in the form of suffering) which comes upon you (from God) as a test (of faith)" (au.).[131] Although the believers suffer at the hands of estranged former associates (4:4), they are not estranged from Christ. To the contrary, such fiery testing is the opportunity to share the sufferings of the Christ and therefore even joy, both now and at the final revelation of his glory (4:13). Both interpretations serve dual social ends. The distinction between insiders and outsiders is affirmed and the solidarity of those being tested is stressed.

When the attempt is made to reconcile the date of 1 Peter with a period of supposed Roman persecution (the fire in Rome and Christian crimes under Nero? the Domitianic reign of terror? the Pontic affair under Pliny?), the social circumstances of 1 Peter as well as the nature of its response are misconstrued. The problems which suffering raised for the existence of the sect are overlooked and 1 Peter is read as advice for reducing suffering instead of as a confirmation of suffering.

1 Pet. 4:7–11 provides a final example of *actions* which are stressed in 1 Peter for the purpose of encouraging group solidarity. This section is not part of a traditional domestic code parenesis.[132] In 1 Peter this pattern of moral instruction has been broken up (2:13–3:7[12]; 5:2–5) and used to frame the exhortation from 2:13 to 5:5. In this way the interposed material (3:13–4:19; 5:1) receives a domestic orientation. As in the case of 4:12–19, 4:7–11 contains notable elements which presume and affirm the domestic features of the Christian sect.

The initial statement that "the end of all things is at hand" (4:7a) lends special eschatological urgency to the exhortations which follow. Prayer (4:7b) is an expression not only of the union of worshipers with God but also, as 3:7 indicates, of the bond between the worshipers themselves. Therefore "sobriety" and "vigilance" are necessary to maintain cohesion internally just as they are requisite for resisting the adversary externally (note the balanced formulations of 4:7 and 5:8). In the following three injunctions concerning love (4:8), hospitality (4:9) and service (4:10–11) the threefold qualifications of *eis heautous* (v. 8), *eis allēlous* (v. 9) and *eis heautous* (v. 10) ("for, toward one another") stress the reciprocity and mutuality of such actions. The unfailing demonstration of love for each other is a "paramount" (*pro pantōn*) necessity because it is such love which binds together the brotherhood (1:22; 3:8; 5:14). Between "brotherly love" (*philadelphia*, 1:22) and "hospitality" (*philoxenia*, 4:9) there is a social as well as a linguistic relationship.[133] Like love, hospitality forges social bonds. In fact it has been asserted that "hospitality was the chief bond which brought the churches a sense of unity."[134] Selwyn echoes this sentiment and points out how early Christian hospitality was a household-to-household enterprise. The concern here is for the "ordinary social life in the Christian communities, where constant intercourse and meeting were essential to preserve the Church's cohesion and distinctive witness, and where the Christians' households, in default of church buildings, were the local units of the Church's worship (Rom. xvi.5, I Cor. xvi.19, Col.

iv.15)."[135] Thus this injuction, like the content of the household code, calls for a practical demonstration of the familial integrity of the community. Hospitality was, as von Harnack and many others have noted,[136] a *conditio sine qua non* of the mission and expansion of the early church. If dependency on the hospitality of others was essential for the growth of the Christian movement in the relatively confined area of Galilee (see, e.g., Matt. 10:10–15/Mark 6:7–13/Luke 9:1–6), then all the more so was it essential for the consolidation of the widely dispersed addressees of Asia Minor.

The addition of the qualification "without grumbling" (4:9) suggests that such hospitality could become an undesirable burden, especially economically.[137] Abuses or refusal of this means of mutual practical aid and support were not unknown in the early Christian period.[138] It is uncertain whether or not the authors knew of actual reluctance in the matter of hospitality among the readers. From their perspective, nevertheless, its voluntary practice was clearly essential.

The following verses show that as *philadelphia* is related to *philoxenia* so *philoxenia* is tied to *oikonomia* ("domestic order"). Verses 10–11 stress the egalitarian distribution of the gifts of grace (*charismata*), their divine origin (*charis tou theou*) and goal (*hina en pasin doxazētai ho theos dia Iēsou Christou*) and their contribution to the service of the household *oikonomia*. "Hospitality is a divine *charisma* of the believers to be faithfully used."[139] This is part of the responsibility of household management entrusted to the Christians as "good household stewards (*oikonomoi*) of God's varied grace" (v. 10 au.). The social implications of the relation between fraternity, hospitality and household management was stressed over one hundred years ago in a classic study by Edwin Hatch, *The Organization of the Early Christian Churches*.[140] The "internal economy of the Christian communities" made hospitality not simply a *desideratum* but a duty. In addition to the poor, the outcasts, the dispossessed, the imprisoned and the widows and orphans who had to be cared for, there were, according to Hatch,

> the strangers who passed in a constant stream through the cities of all the great routes of commerce in both East and West. Every one of those strangers who bore the Christian name had therein a claim to hospitality. For Christianity was, and grew because it was, a great fraternity. The name "brother," by which a Jew addressed his fellow-Jew, came to be the

ordinary designation by which a Christian addressed his fellow-Christian. It vividly expressed a real fact. For driven out from city to city by persecution, or wandering from country to country an outcast or a refugee, a Christian found, wherever he went, in the community of his fellow-Christians a welcome and hospitality.[141]

Hatch went on to note not only practical but also organizational implications:

> The practice of hospitality was enjoined as the common virtue of all Christians: in the New Testament itself stress is laid upon it by St. Paul, St. Peter, and St. John. But it was a special virtue of the *episkopos*. It was for him not so much a merit as a duty. Travelling brethren, no less than the poor of his own community, were entitled to a share in his distribution of the Church funds.[142]

The specific function which the designation *episkopos* denoted in the Christian communities was, according to Hatch, the same as in other contemporary organizations; namely, that of the administration of funds. Thus "his functions were chiefly known by names which were relative to his administration—oikonomia, diakonia."[143] Although Hatch did not allude in this context to 1 Peter, the occurrences of similar terminology in 4:10-11 (*diakonein, oikonomoi*) could suggest that here reference was being made to the responsibilities of community leaders in particular. Moreover the differentiation of *lalein* and *diakonein* in v. 11 could indicate the differing tasks of preachers-teachers and deacons. Selwyn, however, is probably correct in rejecting this possibility.

> Comparison with Rom. xii and with I Cor. xii indicates that St. Peter is reflecting here a very primitive differentiation of function in the Church, such as meets us in Acts vi rather than in the Pauline Epistles . . . St. Peter lets the organized work of the Church fall into two simple categories, those of teaching and of practical ministry.[144]

In addition to this rudimentary division of common labor, there is no certain evidence that by the time of 1 Peter the terms *diakonein* (*diakonia, diakonos*), *lalein* or *oikonomos* had become technical terms reserved for church leaders.[145] For words addressed to the leaders in particular we must turn to the parenesis of 1 Peter 5:1-5a. In 4:10-11, on the other hand, as in the distributive terms *hekastos, eis heautous, poikiles* and the indeterminate *tis* ("if anyone speaks, serves") indicate, it is all the Christians together (as in 3:8 and 5:5b) who are described as "good[146] household stewards of God's varied grace." Theirs is one concerted effort made possible by the Master of the household (v. 11) to serve the spiritual and practical needs of the family. In that family some might be *oiketai* (2:18) but all, as equal recipients of grace, are *oikonomoi*. That which accounts for the use of *oikonomos* here is not the possibility that the tasks of the leaders are being singled out but the fact that the conduct of the entire *oikos* membership is being summarized. Once again emphasis is laid upon the identification and responsibility of the Christian community as *oikos tou theou*.

All together the exhortations of this passage[147] to vigilance, love, hospitality and household service indicate concrete practical ways in which the sect is to demonstrate and foster its solidarity and cohesion.[148] The possibility as well as the purpose for such communal activity is the community's bond with God. From God come the words and strength, to him ultimately is the glory: *ad maiorem Dei gloriam!*

SUMMARY

This concludes our survey of the socioreligious strategy of 1 Peter in general. In summary, the comparative use of a sect typology has enabled us to construct a more concrete picture of the problems that the addressees encountered and of the particular ways in which the letter was designed to help its recipients confront these issues. In general terms the letter offered consolation and encouragement to suffering Christians who lived on the fringes of the political and social world of Asia Minor. More specifically, the strategy of its authors was to counteract the demoralizing and disintegrating impact which such social tension and suffering had upon the Christian sect by reassuring its members of their distinctive communal identity, reminding them of the importance of maintaining discipline and cohesion *within* the brotherhood as well as separation from Gentile influences *without,* and by providing them with a sustaining and motivating rationale for continued faith and commitment.

Christian/Gentile conflict, like the suffering which ensued, was beneficial and not simply detrimental to the Christian cause. Conflict clarified group boundaries and confirmed differences. It also prompted internal Christian cohesion. By continuing to counter the charges, rather than to conform to the standards, of the non-Christians, the believers could give effective testimony to the hope that was within them and by their unrelenting good conduct eventually win over their detractors. Thus the maintenance of socioreligious distinctiveness was stressed as a prerequisite for effective missionary witness. Perdurance in their *paroikia* condition was essential. Images of rebirth, holiness, ransom and warfare, as well as numerous contrasts between proper and improper conduct, present and former allegiances, were employed to support the injunctions to Christian/Gentile separation.

At the same time these images and epithets of socioreligious distinctiveness, and particularly the stress upon the election of the believers, were designed to underline their extraordinary status as the elect and holy people of God and thus to foster their self-esteem over against the demeaning slander of their opponents. The expropriation, and not simply the sharing, of the honorific titles and prestige of Israel ratified the separation of messianic sect from its parent body. The superiority of the sect over its parent was affirmed through stress upon the living hope, incorruptible inheritance and announcement of salvation which were received by Christians alone. By calling attention to the inversion of values which characterized the Christian brotherhood, 1 Peter gave assurance to slaves, women and others of low social rank that "in Christ" all believers were equal recipients of the grace of God. Bearing the name of Christ, religious zeal and humility were transvaluated from being marks of social scorn to occasions of divine blessing.

Solidarity *between* Christian senders and recipients of 1 Peter was promoted by the composition and dispatch of the letter itself as well as by the common manner in which the condition and vocation of both were described. Both groups were elect strangers living in diaspora. Presbyters in Asia Minor had their counterpart in the copresbyter in "Babylon." Both groups formed parts of one family of God. Suffering for innocent conduct was likewise a mark of Christian solidarity with the suffering Christ as well as with fellow sufferers. Solidarity *among* the Christians of Asia Minor was encouraged not only through the collective terms which were used to express their unity and raise their group consciousness but also through direct appeal for brotherly love, hospitality, mutual service and the kind of conduct which insures group cohesion.

At several points in this general survey it has become clear how central a role the concept of the community as the household of God played in the response of 1 Peter. Having examined the *paroikia* situation of the addressees and the response of 1 Peter in general, we are now in a position to return to the observation which served as a point of departure for our study. In 1 Peter the addressees are described as both *paroikoi* and the *oikos* of God. Inasmuch as these terms refer to contrasting modes of social existence, viz., estrangement and at-homeness, in what sense are they applicable to one and the same community? To pursue this question we now turn to a full examination of the role and function which the model of the household assumes in the response of 1 Peter.

NOTES

1. For the implications of the term see Max Weber, *The Sociology of Religion,* trans. Ephraim Fischoff (Boston: Beacon, 1964), pp. 95–117.

2. For the religious as well as social aspects of this dimension of sectarian life see Harvé Carrier, *The Sociology of Religious Belonging,* trans. Arthur J. Arrieri in cooperation with the author (New York: Herder and Herder, 1965).

3. On the goals and levels of the process of legitimation in general see Peter Berger and Thomas Luckmann, *The Social Construction of Reality: A Treatise in the Sociology of Knowledge* (Garden City, N.Y.: Doubleday, 1967), pp. 92–128.

4. Bryan R. Wilson, "An Analysis of Sect Development," *American Sociological Review* 24 (1959): 3–15.

5. Ibid., p. 8.

6. Ibid.

7. Ibid., p. 10.

8. Ibid., pp. 10–11.

9. Ibid., pp. 12–13. Carrier (*Sociology of Religious Belonging,* pp. 208–27) also points out how the self-image and perceived status of a sect or religious group can either aid or impede social cohesion. "Is the group represented to the members' consciousness as a unified, expanding, accepted community, or rather as a rejected, retrogressive, sociologically amorphous group? If the group is represented as having a high status, cohesion between the members becomes more closely knit. It begins to wane in a group which is accorded inferior status or in a group which disappoints the 'expectations' of its members" (pp. 209–210).

10. Wilson, "Sect Development," p. 13.

11. Ibid.

12. Ibid,, p. 12.

13. Ibid., p. 11.

14. Edward Shils, "The Concept and Function of Ideology," in the *International Encyclopedia of the Social Sciences* (New York: Macmillan and Free Press, 1968), 7: 66–75; quotation from p. 70.

15. Ibid., p. 72.

16. Theophil Spörri, *Der Gemeindegedanke im ersten Petrusbrief: Ein Beitrag zur Struktur des urchristlichen Kirchenbegriffs* Neutestamentliche Forschungen, 2. Reihe; *Untersuchungen zum Kirchenproblem des Urchristentums,* 2. Heft (Gütersloh: C. Bertelsmann, 1925); see esp. pp. 184–246.

17. Ibid., p. 245.

18. Ibid.

19. Ibid., pp. 251–61.

20. Ibid., p. 251: "Rationale Betrachtung, welche in ihr ein durch ein Vertragsverhältnis hergestelltes, aus Nützlichkeitsgrunden, gemeinsamen Bedürfnissen und Interessen hervorgegangenes gesellschaftliches Gebilde sähe, steht ganz ausserhalb des Gesichtskreises."

21. Ibid., pp. 259–260.

22. Ibid., pp. 253–58.

23. Ibid., p. 258.

24. David L. Balch, *"Let Wives Be Submissive . . . " The Origin, Form and Apologetic Function of the Household Duty Code (Haustafel) in I Peter* (Ann Arbor, Mich.: University Microfilms International, 1976).

25. Ibid., pp. 220–30, 247–50. In regard to 2:12 he concludes that "there is no reference to the conversion of the pagans . . . but rather to a 'doxology of judgment' " which will occur on the day of visitation (p. 229).

26. In any case Balch is forced to concede concerning 3:1–2 that the behavior of the wives has a missionary as well as an apologetic aim: "Here it is hoped that . . . the chaste conduct of the wives will convert the husbands" (ibid., p. 250; cf. also pp. 261, 267).

27. Ibid., Introductory Abstract, p. 3.

28. Ibid., p. 230.

29. L. Goppelt, *Der erste Petrusbrief,* KEK 12/1. ed. Ferdinand Hahn, 1 aufl. (Göttingen: Vandenhoeck und Ruprecht, 1978), pp. 40–42, 56–64; see also L. Goppelt, "Die Verantwortung der Christen in der Gesellschaft nach dem 1. Petrusbrief," in *Theologie des Neuen Testaments,* ed. Jürgen Roloff, 2. Teil, *Vielfalt und Einheit des apostolischen Christuszeugnisses* (Göttingen: Vandenhoeck und Ruprecht, 1976), pp. 490–508; further, Karl Phillips, *Kirche*

in der Gesellschaft nach dem ersten Petrusbrief (Gütersloh: Gütersloher Verlagshaus—Gerd Mohn, 1971); and Norbert Brox, "Situation und Sprache der Minderheit im ersten Petrusbrief," *Kairos* 19 (1977): 1–13. The present study was conceived independent of these works and differs not infrequently on several exegetical or sociological points. On the question concerning the social perspective according to which 1 Peter is best understood, however, we seem to be in basic agreement.

30. Georg Simmel, *Conflict,* trans. Kurt H. Wolff (Glencoe, Ill.: Free Press, 1955).

31. Lewis Coser, *The Functions of Social Conflict* (New York: Free Press, 1956).

32. Theodore Caplow, *Sociology,* 2. ed. (Englewood Cliffs, N.J.: Prentice-Hall, 1975), pp. 279–80. On social conflict in general see pp. 275–95.

33. Coser, *Social Conflict,* p. 38.

34. Adolf von Harnack, *The Mission and Expansion of Christianity in the First Three Centuries,* trans. and ed. James Moffatt; 2 vols. (New York: Harper & Row, 1962 [reprint of 1908 ed.]), 1:59.

35. Ibid., p. 95.

36. Carrier, *Sociology of Religious Belonging,* p. 218.

37. Coser, *Social Conflict,* p. 106.

38. Ibid., p. 90.

39. On "Ideology and Conflict" see ibid., pp. 111–19.

40. See particularly Abraham Shalit, "A Clash of Ideologies: Palestine under the Seleucids and Romans," in *The Crucible of Christianity: Judaism, Hellenism and the Historical Background to the Christian Faith,* ed. Arnold Toynbee (New York: World and London: Thames and Hudson, 1969), pp. 47–76 but also passim.

41. On the effect of a sense of "good conscience" on the radicality of commitment see Coser, *Social Conflict,* pp. 112–13.

42. Ibid., p. 114.

43. Ibid., p. 115.

44. Ibid., p. 116.

45. Ibid., p. 121; see pp. 121–37.

46. Ibid., pp. 122–23.

47. J. G. Gager (*Kingdom and Community: The Social World of Early Christianity* [Englewood Cliffs, N.J.: Prentice-Hall, 1975], pp. 79–88) also finds Coser's work useful for analyzing two phenomena of the period later than 1 Peter; namely, "the positive function of heresy" and the significance of the Christian apologies for the self-image of Christians themselves.

48. See 2:24; 4:5, 6; also 1:19–21; 3:10, 18 and the adjective "living" (*zōn*)

in 1:3, 23; 2:4, 5. For a traditiohistorical examination of the theme of rebirth and its association with baptism in the early Christian literature see Kazuhito Shimada, *"The Formulary Material in First Peter: A Study According to the Method of Traditionsgeschichte"* (Ann Arbor, Mich.: University Microfilms International, 1966), pp. 159–82. On the theological (but not sociological) significance of the rebirth theme in 1 Peter, see Samuel Parsons, "We Have Been Born Anew: The New Birth of the Christian in the First Epistle of St. Peter (I Petr. 1:3, 23)" (Doctoral diss. St. Thomas Aquinas Pontifical University, Rome, 1978).

49. See *hagios,* 1:15 twice, 16; 2:5, 9; 3:5; *hagiasmos,* 1:2; *hagiazō,* 3:15.

50. See *eklektos,* 1:1; 2:4, 6, 9 and *syneklektē,* 5:13.

51. See *hagnizō,* 1:22 and *amōmos, aspilos,* 1:19.

52. See *kaleō,* 1:15; 2:9, 21; 3:9; 5:10.

53. In addition to death/life, rebirth (see above, n. 48) see: "formerly/now" (1:14–15; 2:10, 25; 4:2–3); perishable/imperishable (inheritance, 1:4; see 1:23; cf. "unfading crown," 5:4; also perishing flesh/abiding word of the Lord, 1:24–25); reproach/blessing (4:14; cf. 3:14); evil(doers)/good(doers) (2:11–12, 16: 3:9, 11, 17; 4:15–16); flesh/spirit (3:18; 4:1, 6); human desires/will of God (4:2; cf. 2:11; 4:1); rejecting men/accepting God (2:4); devil, lion/brotherhood, God (5:8–11; cf. 2:17). For a list of the negative/positive antitheses in 1 Peter see also J. H. Elliott, *The Elect and the Holy: An Exegetical Examination of 1 Peter 2:4–10 and the Phrase* Basileion Hierateuma, *NovT Supplements* 12 (Leiden: E. J. Brill, 1966), p. 35, n. 2 and add 1:24/25; 2:1/2; 2:4bα/β; 2:7aα/β.

54. Ernst Bammel ("The Commands in I Peter II.17," *NTS* 11 [1965]: 279–81) attributes this chiasmus to an earlier Haustafel which "the author of the epistle has adapted to his own purposes" (p. 281).

55. For the most recent treatments of this passage and its underlying traditions see Klyne R. Snodgrass, "I Peter II. 1–10: Its Formation and Literary Affinities," *NTS* 24 (1977): 97–106 and Max-Alain Chevallier, "Israël et l'Eglise selon la première Epître de Pierre," in *Paganisme, Judaïsme, Christianisme: Influences et affrontements dans le monde antique,* Marcel Simon FS (Paris: E. de Boccard, 1978), pp. 117–25. In this passage the latter author sees an affirmation of "the continuity of the people of God" (p. 125). Its bearing upon the question of the relation of Christianity to Judaism must be spelled out a bit more clearly than Chevallier has done. Not only does this passage imply that in view of faith in Jesus Christ Judaism's "privileges are annulled" (p. 127); it also indicates that, through the expropriation of Judaism's distinctive honors, the Christian community saw itself as Judaism's superior replacement.

56. Ramsay MacMullen, *Roman Social Relations 50* B.C. *to* A.D. *284* (New

Haven: Yale University Press, 1974) pp. 57–87; quotation from p. 62.

57. Ibid., p. 61.

58. On the status of unenfranchised groups in the provinces and their struggles with the citizenry MacMullen notes: "At Tarsus in the second century, the rights of one group came into question—'a group of no small size, outside the constitution, so to speak, whom some people call "linen-workers" and are irritated by them and consider them a useless rabble and the cause of uproar and disorder' [Dio Chrysostom, *Orat.* 34. 21–23]. Though for the most part native-born and admitted to the assembly, they were yet 'reviled and viewed as aliens.' " Parallel situations existed elsewhere as, for instance, in Alexandria (the weavers) and in the city of Messene in Greece (ibid., pp. 59–60). The similarity with the Christian *paroikoi* is striking.

59. Ibid., pp. 118, 215.

60. Ibid., p. 222.

61. I am applying here the observations of Charles Y. Glock in his comments on "Images of 'God,' Images of Man, and the Organization of Social Life," *Journal for the Scientific Study of Religion* 11 (1972): 1–15. I see the image of divine election as analogous to Glock's reference to "imagery about 'God' and man." "The organization of social life is importantly related to prevailing imagery about 'god' and imagery about man. Such imagery contributes to shaping the form of social organization and to rationalizing it, and it becomes crucial to the maintenance of social solidarity and stability" (ibid., pp. 3–4).

62. Wilson, "Sect Development," p. 13.

63. In my *The Elect and the Holy* I considered only the literary and theological aspects of the citation and interpretation of these Old Testament texts in 1 Peter. Their sociological function, however, must also be examined.

64. The social function of the covenant in guaranteeing security has been noted by George E. Mendenhall ("Toward a Biography of God: Religion and Politics as Reciprocals," in *The Tenth Generation: The Origins of the Biblical Tradition* [Baltimore: The Johns Hopkins University Press, 1973], pp. 198–214). "In early biblical law, the security of persons is first of all a function of the covenantal relationship, though it would be difficult to find it specifically stated. This is implied in the concept of a holy people, for holiness is always most closely connected with the concept of the property of God. [Mendenhall cites Jer. 2:3–4; however, the point is equally demonstrated by Exod. 19:5–6 and 1 Pet. 2:9–10.] In practice, then, it meant that the value of a person was not a function of his particular role in society. It furnished everyone with a basis for self-respect, a self-evaluation which seems to be necessary for personal freedom and integrity. Most closely related to this is the nature of obligation, which is not merely a function of status within a political community, but an

obligation permanently binding upon the person no matter what his immediate social context might be, and no matter with whom he is dealing" (p. 207).

65. Although not explicitly cited in 1 Peter, Deuteronomy is generally recognized as close in time and outlook to Deutero-Isaiah, which is quoted. For specific affinities concerning the election theme see Elliott, *The Elect and the Holy*, p. 40, n. 2.

66. Compare, e.g., on exile (1 Peter: *paroikia*): Isa. 45:13; 49:21; 52:4; on election: 41:8–9, 24; 42:1; 43:10; 44:1, 2; 45:4, 49:7; covenant: 42:6; 49:8; 54: 10; 55:3; righteousness and justice: 41:1, 4, 6; 42:21; 43:9; 45:8, 13, 21–24; holiness (God = "the Holy One"): 40:25; 41:14, 16, 20; 43:3, 14, 15; 45:11; 47: 4; 48:17; 54:5; salvation as redemption: 43:1, 3–4, 14; 44:6, 23–24; 47:4; 48:17, 20; 49:26; 50:2; 51:10–11; 52:3, 9; salvation as a renewed exodus event: 43:16– 21; 49:9–11; 55:12–13; salvation as a (re)building: 44:28; 45:13; 54:11–12; affliction: 51:21; 54:11; joy: 42:11; 49:13; 51:3, 11; 52:8; 55:12; God as king: 43: 15; 52:7; "called by my name": 43:1, 7; 44:5; 45:4; 48:1–2; glory, glorification: 40:5; 41:16; 42:8, 12; 43:7; 44:23; 46:13; 48:11; 49:3, 7; 55:5; God as rock (cf. Jesus Christ, 1 Peter): 44:8 51:1; sheep-shepherd: 40:11; 44:28; 53:6; Babylon as locus: 43:14; 47:1–15; 48:14, 20; consolation: 40:1–2, 11; 49:13; 51:12; 52:9. See also Elliott, *The Elect and the Holy*, p. 39, n. 4 and p. 41, n. 3.

In fact, the headings which Bernard A. Anderson (*Understanding the Old Testament*, 3. ed. [Englewood Cliffs, N.J.: Prentice-Hall, 1975], ch. 14, pp. 437–70) uses to describe Deutero-Isaiah could be equally applied to 1 Peter: 1. Gospel; 2. Creator-Redeemer; 3. Light to the Nations; 4. Servant of the Lord; 5. Victory through Suffering; 6. Servant-Messiah. For a further consideration of the similarities between Deutero-Isaiah and 1 Peter see F. W. Danker, "Brief Study," *Concordia Theological Monthly* 38 (1967): 658–59 and id., "I Peter 1: 24–2:17—A Consolatory Pericope," *ZNW* 58 (1967): 93–102. On the response of Deutero-Isaiah to the situation of the exile see P. R. Ackroyd, *Exile and Restoration: A Study of Hebrew Thought of the Sixth Century* B.C. (Philadelphia: Westminster Press, 1968), esp. pp. 118–137.

67. 1 Pet. 2:9 is the only NT instance where the phrase *genos eklekton* occurs and where *genos* is applied to Christians (for Jews see Gal. 1:14; Phil. 3:5; 2 Cor. 11:26; Acts 7:19). Isa. 43:20 and Esther 8:13 contain the only LXX occurrences of the phrase, both reflecting the situation of diaspora. With the sense of "family" (see Friedrich Büchsel, *"Genos," TDNT* 1 [1964/1935]: 684–85) *genos* joins other terms in 1 Peter (e.g., *oikos, adelphotēs*) in expressing the familial or household nature of the Christian community.

68. For recent attention to the subjects of election and covenant in this literature see E. P. Sanders, *Paul and Palestinian Judaism: A Comparison of Patterns of Religion* (Philadelphia: Fortress Press and London: SCM, 1977); the

Tannaitic literature, pp. 84–107; Dead Sea Scrolls, pp. 240–70; Sirach, pp. 329–33; 1 Enoch, pp. 361–62; Jubilees, pp. 362–64; Ps. Sol., pp. 389–90; 4 Ezra, pp. 409–10. Sanders also notes the sectarian function of a stress on election in order to reinforce distinctiveness and to reverse internal status standards.

69. On other sects of Judaism and the tactic of expropriation and appropriation of positive and negative nomenclature, see Peter Richardson, *Israel in the Apostolic Church,* SNTS MS 10; (Cambridge: University Press, 1969), Appendix C, "The Sects of Judaism and 'True Israel,' " pp. 217–28; on 1 Peter see pp. 171–75.

Inasmuch as the Christian faithful now constitute the people of God, those outside this community can be designated by the same term which once identified those outside the community of Israel: "Gentiles"; cf. similar usage in 1 Cor. 5:1; 12:2; 1 Thess. 4:5; 3 John 7; and K. L. Schmidt on *"Ethnos in the NT,"* *TDNT* 2 (1964/1935): 369–72, esp. p. 371. Christians appropriated both the honorific epithets and the discriminating terminology of Israel.

70. V. P. Furnish, "Elect Sojourners in Christ: An Approach to the Theology of I Peter," *Perkins Journal* 28 (1975): 1–11; quotation from p. 3. See also his notes on 1 Peter in the Oxford Study Edition of The New English Bible with the Apocrypha, ed. Samuel Sandmel (New York: Oxford University Press, 1976), pp. 294–98 of the New Testament section.

71. Ibid.

72. Ibid.

73. Ibid., pp. 3–4.

74. In 1:3–5 three results of Christian rebirth are mentioned: possession of a living hope (v. 3); of an incorruptible, inviolable and imperishable inheritance (v. 4); and divine protection for the apprehension of salvation through faith (v. 5). The living hope of Christians is linked with their faith in the "living stone" (2:4) whom the Jews and other unbelievers have rejected (2:4, 6–8). The Christian inheritance is contrasted to the fate of the Jewish inheritance, the Holy Land. The salvation manifested in the resurrection of Jesus (1:3), symbolized in baptism (3:21) and soon to be fully realized by the believers (1:9; 2:2; 4:18), is contrasted with that which was sought but not experienced by the Jewish prophets (1:10–12). The underlying contrasts are temporal (then/now) and socioreligious (Jews/Christians), not spatial.

75. Furnish, "Elect Sojourners," p. 4 with reference to Matt. 6:19–21; Rom. 12:1–2; Phil. 3:20; Eph. 2:19–21; Heb. 13:14.

76. The contrast between earth and heaven, shadow and reality, so basic to Hebrews (3:1; 4:14–16; 7:26; 8:1, 4–5; 9:11–12, 23; 10:1; 12:26 [18–29]; 13:14) is not found in 1 Peter. Whereas Hebrews proposes a soteriological-ecclesiological movement from earth to heaven (the terrestrial people of God follow-

ing the pioneering High Priest now enthroned in heaven, e.g., 1:3–4; 3:1; 4:1, 11, 14–16; 6:20; 10:19–22; 12:2, 18–29), 1 Peter anticipates as the final movement of God's saving act the appearance in present time (and presumably in present space) of the exalted Christ (1:5, 7, 13; 4:13; 5:1, 4). The eschatological perspective of 1 Peter is apocalyptic, not Platonic-Philonic. The goal of the people of God, according to 1 Peter, is not a "heavenly rest" as in Hebrews, but a universal glorification of God by the time of the final earthly visitation (2:12). For further points of contrast between Hebrews and 1 Peter see Elliott, *The Elect and the Holy,* pp. 170–72. On Hebrews see William G. Johnsson, "The Pilgrimage Motif in the Book of Hebrews," *JBL* 97 (1978): 239–51.

77. Furnish, "Elect Sojourners," p. 4.

78. M.-A. Chevallier, "Condition et vocation des Chrétiens en diaspora. Remarques exégétiques sur la 1ʳᵉ Epître de Pierre," *RSR* 48 (1974): 387–98.

79. C. Wolff, "Christ und Welt im 1. Petrusbrief," *TLZ* 100 (1975): 334–42.

80. Ibid., cols. 334 and 338, respectively.

81. Chevallier, "Condition," p. 395.

82. Ibid., p. 396.

83. Ibid., pp. 395–96; Wolff, "Christ und Welt," cols. 333–34.

84. Wolff, "Christ und Welt," col. 334 and passim.

85. See K. L. Schmidt, "Diaspora," *TDNT* 2 (1964/1935): 100.

86. Wolff ("Christ und Welt," cols. 339, 342) sees this latter goal as one of the concerns of 1 Peter but fails to show how it is correlated with the encouragement that Christians regard themselves as strangers. His theory regarding a second concern of 1 Peter raises still further problems. 1 Peter, in Wolff's view, was aimed at correcting a false understanding of Christian freedom which had led to the withdrawal of Christians from society (ibid., cols. 340, 341). If this were the case, then the author (singular for Wolff) would be undermining his own intention by encouraging their socioreligious distance. In fact, however, exactly the opposite was the situation. The addressees were tempted to conform to, rather than to retreat from, the social mores and institutions of their environment. Through stress upon their estrangement, as upon their election, 1 Peter encouraged the Christians to remain distinct.

87. Spörri, *Gemeindegedanke,* p. 38.

88. Elliott, *The Elect and the Holy,* pp 166–69, 196–98.

89. Spörri, *Gemeindegedanke,* p. 39.

90. This is the chief point which I understand Gager and Theissen to be making and attempting to analyze sociologically.

91. Elliott, *The Elect and the Holy,* p. 119.

92. See further 1:5, 7, 8, 9, 21; 5:9.

93. See further 2:21; 3:17–18; 4:1, 12; cf. 2:23 and 4:19.

94. See further 3:18–22; 4:6, 19.

95. See further 1:1; 5:13.

96. See further 1:3, 23; 2:2; also *zōopoiētheis,* 3:18.

97. See further 1:7, 19; 3:7.

98. See further 1:7, 8, 11, 21; 2:12; 4:11, 13, 14, 16; 5:1, 4, 10.

99. For this interpretation see below, chapter 5.

100. For similar accumulation of syn- composite terms which perhaps served a similar purpose see e.g., 4 Macc. 13:1–14:10 (together with *adelphotēs, philadelphia*) and Ign. *Pol.* 6:1 (*synkopiate allēlois, synathleite, syntrechete, sympaschete, synkoimasthe, synegeisesthe hōs theou oikonomoi kai paredroi kai hypēretai*).

101. See below, chapter 5.

102. Modesty has been proposed as a motive (Hans Windisch and Herbert Preisker, *Die Katholischen Briefe, Handbuch zum Neuen Testament* 15; 3. ed. [Tübingen: J. C. B. Mohr, 1951], on 5:1) but without explanation of the need or intended social effect of such modesty. Günther Bornkamm (*"Presbys"* etc., *TDNT* 6 [1968/1959]: 666) is closer to the truth when he states: "It is true that the apostle is here setting himself alongside the presbyters with emphatic modesty. It is also true, however, that he is setting them alongside himself."

103. For the pertinent literature and arguments for the epistolary genre of 1 Peter see Elliott, *The Elect and the Holy,* pp. 12–13, n. 3 and Elliott, "The Rehabilitation of an Exegetical Step-child: 1 Peter in Recent Research," *JBL* 95 (1976) pp. 248–49; also William J. Dalton, *Christ's Proclamation to the Spirits: A Study of 1 Peter 3:18–4:6, Analecta Biblica* 23 (Rome: Pontifical Biblical Institute, 1965), pp. 62–71 and Goppelt, *Der erste Petrusbrief,* pp. 37–47.

104. See below, chapter 5, pp. 271–283, esp. p. 281–283 and n. 15.

105. Elliott, *The Elect and the Holy,* pp. 200 (and nn. 2, 3) and 201 (and n. 1).

106. So Goppelt, "Prinzipien neutestamentlicher Sozialethik nach dem 1. Petrusbrief," in *Neues Testament und Geschichte,* O. Cullmann FS, ed. H. Baltensweiler and B. Reicke (Zürich: Theologischer Verlag and Tübingen: J. C. B. Mohr, 1972), pp. 285–96; quotation from p. 289.

107. Disengagement is the problem according to Goppelt (ibid.) and Chevallier ("Condition et vocation," p. 393, n. 14, following Goppelt).

108. Goppelt does not see this as problematic in 1 Peter and his observations in general are motivated by the desire to discover in this letter principles for contemporary Christian social action (ibid., pp. 285, 296). Overlooking the specific needs of the first century Christian sectarian movement he concludes: "So setzt die neutestamentliche Sozialethik mit der Weisung ein: Stellt euch in die jeweils für euch gegebenen sozialen Ordnungen hinein und verhaltet euch ihren

Spielregeln gemäss" (p. 290). But this is an oversimplification of the situation reflected in 1 Peter and a misreading of the letter's response.

109. See Goppelt, ibid., pp. 289–90 and also his *Der erste Petrusbrief,* pp. 163–79 (Exkurs: Die Ständetafeltradition).

110. Goppelt ("Prinzipien," pp. 290–93) concludes that the principle of social integration (of Christians in society) could lead to "boundless conformism." This is avoided in 1 Peter, he maintains, through an emphasis on "a responsible, critical attitude" toward social institutions. While the criteria for such an attitude are characteristic of 1 Peter (conscience, will of God the creator, union with the Lord), the stance of a "critique from within" is not. Such a stance would not describe the situation or the possibility of a minor religious sect. The sect must remain equal if not superior in its morality but also socially distant.

111. See 2:14, 15, 18, 20; 3:6, 10, 11, 13, 17, 21; 4:19.

112. *Dia syneidēsin theou,* 2:19; that is, with knowledge informed by, and action in accord with, the will of God. Cf. also 3:16, 21.

113. See 1:14, 22; contrast 2:8; 3:20; 4:17.

114. *Anastrophē:* 1:15, 18; 2:12; 3:1, 2, 16; cf. 1:17.

115. See 2:15; 3:17; 4:2, 19.

116. See 2:21; 3:18; 4:1, 12–19; cf. also the similarity between 3:9a ("not returning evil for evil or reviling for reviling," au.) and 2:23a ("who when reviled did not revile in return," au.).

117. Christ "entrusted himself to the one who judges justly" (i.e., to God), 2:23.The passive *hypotagentōn* in the credal formulation of 3:22 implies the ultimate agency of God and the subordination of the Christ; cf., 1 Cor. 15:27–28; Eph. 1:22; Heb. 1:13; 2:5–9. Likewise *Iēsou Christou* in 1:2 is to be taken as the subjective genitive of *hypakoēn kai rantismon haimatos*: "elected . . . for the obedience and the sprinkling of blood which Jesus Christ has accomplished" (1 Pet. 1:2 au.). *Dia ton kyrion* in 2:13 may also be understood in this sense. "Be subordinate . . . because of (the subordination of) the Lord" (au.). This would be consonant with the intention of 2:21–24 as an exemplification of 2:20 and 3:17–18.

118. Goppelt, *Der erste Petrusbrief,* p. 233 (on. 2:13–16), a more subtle distinction than the earlier view criticized in the preceding notes.

119. For discussion of the problems and other proposed interpretations see, inter alia, Spörri, *Gemeindegedanke,* p. 71 and n. 1; H. W. Beyer, *"Allotri(o)-episkopos,"* TDNT 2 (1964/1935): 620–22; Ceslas Spicq, *Les Epîtres de Saint Pierre* (Paris: Gabalda, 1966), pp. 157–59; Balch, *"Let Wives Be Submissive,"* pp. 217–20; most recently, J. B. Bauer, "Aut maleficus aut alieni speculator (1 Petr. 4,15)," *Biblische Zeitschrift* 22 (1978): 109–15.

120. The formulation of Epictetus (*Disc.* 3.22.97) *ta allotria . . . episkopēi* is the closest Greek parallel. The passages, however, bear no similarity. According to Epictetus, when the Cynic is "overseeing the affairs of men" he is not "meddling in the affairs of others" but supervises the affairs which are "proper to him."

121. See LSJ, s.v. *allotrios* and *oikeios*.

122. On this point see also Walter Cornelius van Unnik, "The Teaching of Good Works in I Peter," *NTS* 1 (1954): 92–110, esp. pp. 101–03 on 4:12–19.

123. For an analysis of the content, origin and function of such a "primitive Christian persecution tradition," see Wolfgang Nauck, "Freude im Leiden: Zum Problem einer urchristlichen Verfolgungstradition," *ZNW* 46 (1955): 68–80. Nauck cites as main New Testament texts: Matt. 5:11–12; Luke 6:22–23; 1. Pet. 1:6; 4:13–14; Jas. 1:2, 12; and for earlier stages of the tradition, *Syr. Baruch* 48:48–50; 52:5–7; 54:16–18; Jth. 8:25–27; 2 Macc. 6:28, 30; 4 Macc. 7:22; 9:29; 11:12; Wisd. of Sol. 3:4–6. Regarding 1 Peter he notes: "No other NT author has depended so heavily upon this existent tradition as has the author of 1 Peter" (p. 80). On "Traces of a Persecution-Form" in 1 Peter see also Selwyn, *The First Epistle of St. Peter,* 2. ed. (London: Macmillan, 1955), pp. 439–58.

124. Note especially the eschatological sense of *to telos* in 1:9; 4:7; cf. 4:17; and the stress upon the imminent revelation of Jesus Christ (1:5, 7, 13; 4:13; 5:1, 4). Cf. also 1:12, 20; 4:5–6, 17.

125. See J. Ramsey Michaels, "Eschatology in I Peter iii.17," *NTS* 13 (1966–1967): 394–401, esp. p. 396 and n. 1.

126. On *peirasmos* see Heinrich Seesemann, *"Peira"* etc., *TDNT* 6 (1968/1959): 23–36, esp. p. 30; for a comparison of *peirasmos* with other NT terms for persecution see E. G. Selwyn, "The Persecutions in I Peter," *SNTS Bulletin* 1 (1950): 39–50. On *pyrōsis* see Friedrich Lang, *"Pyrōsis,"* *TDNT* 6 (1968/1959): 950–51 and the Harvard dissertation of Emilie T. Sander, "PYROSIS and the First Epistle of Peter 4:12" (unavailable to me but summarized in *Harvard Theological Review* 60 [1967]: 501).

127. K. G. Kuhn, *"Peirasmos-hamartia-sarx* im Neuen Testament und die damit zusammenhängenden Vorstellungen," *Zeitschrift für Theologie und Kirche* 49 (1952): 200–22.

128. Ibid., pp. 216–17.

129. See, e.g., Ecclus. 2:1 (1–5); 33:1; Wisd. of Sol. 3:5–6 (the similarity of the entire context of 3:1–10 with 1 Peter is noteworthy), 11:9; Ps. 25[26]:2.

130. Compare *Did.* 16:6; on the eschatological dimension of *pyrōsis* and the verb *pyrousthai* see Michael L. Barré, "To Marry or to Burn: *pyrousthai* in 1 Cor. 7:9," *CBQ* 36 (1974): 193–202.

131. Lang's paraphrase (*"Pyrōsis,"* p. 951).

132. For discussion of this traditional code and its use in 1 Peter see below, chapter 4.

133. See, e.g., Rom. 12:9–10, 13; Heb. 13:1–2 ("Let brotherly love continue. Do not neglect to show hospitality to strangers . . . ").

134. V. H. Kooy, "Hospitality," *IDB* 2 (1962): 654.

135. Selwyn, *First Epistle of St. Peter,* p. 218.

136. Harnack, *Mission,* 1: 181–249. See also D. W. Riddle, "Early Christian Hospitality," *JBL* 57 (1938): 141–53; G. Stählin, "Xenos" etc., *TDNT* 5 (1967/1954): 1–36 and esp. "The Custom of Hospitality," pp. 17–25 (bibliography on pp. 1–2); Abraham J. Malherbe, "The Inhospitality of Diotrephes," in *God's Christ and His People,* Nils Alstrup Dahl FS, ed. Jacob Jervell and Wayne A. Meeks (Oslo: Universitetsforlaget, 1977), pp. 222–31; and D. Hiltbrunner, D. Gorce and H. Wehr, "Gastfreundschaft," *RAC* 8 (1972): 1061–1123. For the NT and related occurrences of *philoxenos* and *philoxenia* see 1 Tim. 3:2; Titus 1:8; 1 Pet. 4:9; *1 Clem.* 12:3; *Herm. Mand* 8:10; *Herm. Sim.* 9:27 and Rom. 12:13; Heb. 13:2; *1 Clem.* 1:2; 10:7; 11:1; 12:1; 35:5, respectively.

137. The economic aspects of this form of *diakonia* (4: 10–11) and its burden recall a similar qualification made by Paul in his gathering of the collection (2 Cor. 9:1) among the Corinthian and Macedonian Christians for the poor in Judea (9:6–15).

138. See, for instance, *Did.* 12–13 and the inhospitality of Diotrephes of which the Elder complains in 3 John; cf. also 2 John 10.

139. G. Stählin, "Xenos," *TDNT* 5 (1967/1954): pp. 1–36; quote is from p. 21.

140. Edwin Hatch, *The Organization of the Early Christian Churches* (Oxford and Cambridge: Rivingtons, 1881).

141. Ibid., pp. 43–44. On the travels and interchange of the early Christians see von Harnack, *Mission,* 1: 369–80; and on the church as family or brotherhood, pp. 405–07.

142. Hatch, *Organization,* pp. 44–45, citing 1 Tim. 3:2; Titus 1:8 and *Herm. Sim.* 9:27.

143. Ibid., p. 41.

144. Selwyn, *The First Epistle of St. Peter,* p. 219.

145. The point is simply that these terms which have already been *applied* to the activity of leaders (see, for instance, the evidence in BAGD, s.v.) are not yet terms *restricted* to the functions of leadership as such (as the evidence in BAGD also shows). If they do not yet denote the *exclusive* tasks of leaders, then their meaning, place and function in 1 Peter must be determined on other

grounds. "Speaking" and "serving" are two fundamental types of communal activity which illustrate the aforementioned *charismata* as well as the praying, loving and hospitality of 4:7–9. For a similar rudimentary "word/deed" distinction see Rom. 15:18; Col. 3:17; 2 Thess. 2:17.

Verse 10 is a characteristic Petrine adaptation of a traditional *topos* on the diversity, divine origin and social function of *charismata*. (For the Pauline versions see Romans 12, 1 Corinthians 12 and Ephesians 4.) In contrast to Paul, the interest of 1 Peter is neither in an enumeration of the several gifts (v. 11 merely generalizes) nor in the typically Pauline interpretative motif of the "body of Christ." In contrast to this image of the church through which the diversity of gifts is given its unity by Paul, 1 Peter implies the image of community as *oikos tou theou*. Accordingly, those who employ their gift to serve one another are described as "household stewards of God's varied grace." The phrase *poikiles charitos theou* is unique to 1 Peter in the NT. For NT occurrences of *oikonomos* see Luke 12:42; 16:1, 3, 8; Rom. 16:23; 1 Cor. 4:1, 2; Gal. 4:2; Titus 1:7; 1 Pet. 4:10.

146. *Kalos* here, as in 2:12 (*anastrophēn . . kalēn, kalōn ergōn*), qualifies the common activity of *all* the addressees.

147. Several factors point to the likelihood that 1 Pet. 4:7–11 was fashioned according to a common Christian pattern of parenetic exhortation. This is indicated by the terse, staccato-like *form* of the imperatives, the *serial listing* of differentiated though related themes, and the *affinity of the content* with the material in other NT texts. In addition to the *topos* of the *charismata* already mentioned (i.e., with 4:10–11 compare Rom. 12:6–8; 1 Cor. 12:4–11; Eph. 4:7, 11–12) compare 4:7a and Rom. 13:11–12; 4:7b and Rom. 12:3, 12; cf. 1 Cor. 16:13; Heb. 13:18 (also Heb. 13:4 and 1 Pet. 3:7) on sobriety and prayer; 4:8 and Rom. 12:9–10; cf. 1 Cor. 13:1–13; 16:14; Heb. 13:1 on love; 4:9 and Rom. 12:13; cf. Heb. 13:2 on hospitality; 4:10–11 and 1 Cor. 16:15; 2 Cor. 9:1–15 on *diakonia* and Heb. 13:7, 17 on *logos tou theou*. Selwyn in his Essay II on the "Inter-relation of 1 Peter and other NT epistles" (*First Epistle of St. Peter*, pp. 365–466) offers convenient tabular comparisons of Greek terminology and themes. However, his conclusion concerning the existence (ca. 50–55 c.e.) and widespread use of a twofold baptismal catechism (pp. 459–61) is an exaggerated systematization of the evidence. In the case of 1 Pet. 4:7–11 and its parallels the most that can be cautiously claimed is the varied employment and adaptation of a common oral pattern of parenetic exhortation. In addition to similarities of form and content, 1 Peter 4 and its parallels also manifest the similar *social function* which this pattern of exhortation was intended to serve: namely, the reinforcement of internal group solidarity. This is clearly the case in Romans 12, 1 Corinthians 12, Ephesians 4, and Hebrews 13 as in 1 Peter 4,

however diversely this concern is developed and structured in the individual documents.

Could the similarity of this subject matter and its function in Romans, Hebrews and 1 Peter suggest still another affinity? Could the common association of these documents with Rome (or Italy) point to the Christian community in Rome as the locality where this concern for Christian love, hospitality and cohesion was particularly evident and fostered? "Your faith," Paul assured the Roman Christians, "is proclaimed in all the world" (Rom. 1:8). Similarly, Ignatius in his letter to the Roman community declares them to be "preeminent in love" (Ign. *Rom.* inscr.). Von Harnack (*Mission*, 1: 485) saw in the traditional love, hospitality and mutual support practiced by the Roman community a predominant cause for its rapid rise to leadership within western Christianity.

If von Harnack's theory is plausible, then we have in the *social* concerns of 1 Peter a heretofore unnoticed bit of evidence for its Roman place of origin. Furthermore, together with Romans, *1 Clement, Hermas* and possibly Hebrews, 1 Peter would then offer important evidence for the sense of social solidarity which characterized the Roman Christian community from its earliest days.

148. Friedrich Schröger ("Die Verfassung der Gemeinde des ersten Petrusbriefes," in *Kirche im Werden: Studien zum Thema Amt und Gemeinde im Neuen Testament*, ed. Josef Hainz [Munich: Ferdinand Schöningh, 1976], pp. 239–52), on the other hand, sees in 4:10–11 in particular a form of organization which the presbyteral model in 5:1–5 is intended to supplant. Assuming that 1:1–4:11 and 4:12–5:11 are different letters of different authors (p. 240), he proposes that in a later period of escalated persecution a letter from Rome encouraged the Christians of Asia Minor to adopt a presbyteral form of organization (5:1–5 within 4:12–5:11) in place of the charismatic structure which they had previously known (4:10–11 within 1:1–4:11). The reason for this was that "survival in this situation was possible only with the tested presbyteral form of ecclesial organization" (p. 245).

The argument, however, is implausible on several grounds. There is much stronger evidence for the integrity of 1 Peter than for its composite character. This includes the link between 5:1–5 and the earlier household pattern in 2:13–3:7 to which Schröger gives no consideration. Nor does the evidence suggest "the escalating persecution" (p. 249) which he imagines. In addition to these and other exegetical and historical problems, there is a flaw in his "sociological" (pp. 245–51) reasoning: centralization of authority is *not* the only answer to the quest for group integration. On this point we recall the analysis of Coser (*Functions of Social Conflict*, p. 91) who has observed that "strong group cohesion as a consequence of outside conflict does not necessarily carry with it the need for centralization." The trend toward ecclesial centralization prompted by *internal* discord (e.g., *1 Clement*) cannot be used, as Schröger attempts to do (pp. 250–51), to explain the situation of 1 Peter where conflict with society is the chief problem. Furthermore, Coser notes: "In sects and similar groups which do not require much differentiation of functions (compare the simple division of tasks in 1 Pet. 4:11 where the division of labor remains on a rudimentary level), internal solidarity can to a large extent fulfill the group-integrating functions which in more differentiated groups are fulfilled by more developed authority structures" (ibid., p. 92). As intense conflict with the larger society promotes "such strong cohesion that each member of the group participates in the exercise of control tasks" (compare the charismatic distribution of responsibilities in 1 Pet. 4:7–11), the sect has "no need for centralization of these tasks in the hands of a few" (ibid., p. 91).

The presbyteral functions mentioned in 5:2–3 can hardly be taken as evidence of a centralization of function and authority. Leadership by presbyters reflects a still traditional and rudimentary division of responsibilities within the household or the Christian community identified as a household. The function of the content of 4:7–11 within the domestic pattern of instruction is to assure the readers that having leaders does not preclude the responsibilities which all members of the household have for serving and supporting one another. Thus 4:7–11 is similar in aim to the injunctions of 3:8–9 and 5:5b which conclude, respectively, the domestic exhortation of 2:18–3:7 and 5:1–5a. In sum, the responsibilities described in 4:7–11 and 5:1–5 are complementary rather than contradictory. The combination of these passages in 1 Peter represents at this stage the coalescence of traditions, development rather than displacement.

*". . . You Are the
Household of the Spirit
. . . the Household of God . . ."*

4

The Significance and Function of the Household within the Strategy of 1 Peter

The preceding analysis has indicated that in 1 Peter the household serves in various ways as a model for describing and motivating the Christian addressees as a whole. In this chapter we shall consider the historical, religious and ideological precedents for such a domestic depiction of human community, the development of this familial image in 1 Peter, and the function which it had within the letter's general strategy.

A socioexegetical analysis of the community as *oikos* in 1 Peter is, for the most part, a venture into *Neuland* or no-man's-land. The ecclesiology of 1 Peter has rarely been studied.[1] A monograph or article directly on *oikos* in 1 Peter has yet to be written.[2] The general tendency of commentators on 1 Peter to assume a predominantly or exclusively cultic meaning for *oikos* in 2:5 and 4:17 has obstructed any curiosity concerning the political, economic and social implications of the term. The need for a comprehensive up-to-date study of *oikos* in the New Testament in general has long been recognized[3] but has yet to be met. Earlier research on *oikos* and its paronyms in early Christianity[4] is of only limited use for our purposes here. It has been concerned mostly with the *concepts* and theological *ideas* articulated by these terms rather than with the social structures, needs and functions which these terms imply or to which they refer.

An earlier exception to this "history of ideas" approach to the role of the *oikos* in early Christianity is the 1939 study of Floyd V. Filson on the significance of the early house churches.[5] Observing that "the New Testament church would be better understood if more attention were paid to the *actual physical conditions* under which the first Christians met and

165

lived,"[6] Filson pointed out at least five ways in which the house church functioned as a vital factor in the early church's development:

> It provided the setting in which the primitive Christians achieved a mental separation from Judaism before the actual open break occurred. It gave added importance to the effort to Christianize family relationships. It explains in part the proneness of the apostolic church to divide. It helps us gain a true understanding of the influential place of families of means in what has sometimes been regarded as a church of the dispossessed. It points us to the situation in which were developed leaders to succeed apostolic workers.[7]

This brief article written some forty years ago was more programmatic than exhaustive. Unfortunately, in the period immediately following, Filson's lead was also more ignored than followed. More recently, however, the practical, social and ideological implications of the Christian community as *oikos* have come under renewed consideration from a variety of starting points.

—The question concerning the Christian practice of *infant baptism,* for example, and the meaning of the so-called *"oikos* formula" in the New Testament baptismal texts ("N.N. and his house")[8] has involved extensive analysis of, and debate over, the composition of Christian as well as non-Christian[9] *oikoi* and *domus.*

—Similar to this question concerning the implied inclusion of infants within the juridical and social limits of the household is the issue regarding the presence, role and status of *slaves.* Recent research on Christian attitudes and practice concerning slavery[10] also has underlined the bearing which the composition and prevailing patriarchal concepts of the household have on this subject.

—Renewed attention to the so-called *"household codes"* of the New Testament likewise continues to raise questions concerning the relation of these schemes of household relationships and duties to the internal as well as external circumstances of the Christian communities.[11]

—The social structure and economic aspects of the household have been treated as significant points of reference for analysis of social stratification and *socioreligious conflict* in the early church.[12]

—Furthermore, studies of *ministry and church order* have begun to consider anew how the organization and authority structures of the house-

hold served as a model and basis for the conception, exercise and legitimation of ecclesial authority and leadership.[13]

—The role of house churches as the *locale of Christian liturgical assembly* in the pre-Constantinian period has been studied.[14]

—Sociohistorical descriptions and analyses of the early Christian *missionary enterprise* have called attention to both the disruption of old and
the creation of new forms of familial relationships.[15]

—The Christian household has also received considerable attention as
the social basis and organizing concept for the development and legitimation of *patterns of social obligation.*[16]

—Finally, in one of the most recent studies on the subject to date,[17]
Abraham J. Malherbe has discussed how issues of *hospitality, social stratification* and *other types of household organization* (the guilds) are related to
the household structure and problems of the early Christian communities.

The wide-ranging practical and conceptual implications of household-
familial organization and imagery and the reciprocality of social and theological factors[18] which become evident in such aforementioned research
confirm the appropriateness, if not the necessity, of exploring the social
meaning and function of the image of the household in 1 Peter where it
seems to have played so major a role.

The function of the communal concept of the household in 1 Peter is to
be established, on the one hand, in conjunction with the general situation
and strategy of the document as outlined above. On the other hand, the
question concerning function implies a prior question concerning the
specific meaning which the term *oikos* has in 1 Peter and its semantic relation to further *oikos* paronyms employed in the letter (viz., *oiketēs,* 2:18;
oikodomeisthai, 2:5; *oikonomos,* 4:10; *paroikia,* 1:17; *paroikos,* 2:11; *synoikein,* 3:7) as well as to the variety of further related familial terms and
images. Attention will be directed first, therefore, to the question of meaning and then we shall turn to the question of function.

Up to this point in our investigation *oikos pneumatikos* (2:5) and *tou
oikou tou theou* (4:17) have been taken provisionally in the sense of
"household of the Spirit" and "household of God," respectively. Now that
we are dealing in this chapter with the subject of *oikos* directly, this provisional assumption of meaning requires closer examination. That the
term *oikos* in 1 Peter has the meaning "household" was one of the conclusions I had reached in my earlier study, *The Elect and the Holy.* This

conclusion was the result primarily of literary, tradition-historical and redactional analysis. The chief indication of the meaning and literary function of *oikos* in 1 Peter was shown to be the important pericope in which it first occurs, namely, 2:4–10. This passage is an intricate construction of tradition and redaction whose aim was to affirm the addressees as the elect and holy covenant people of God. The divine election of Jesus (*lithon eklekton*, 2:4, 6) and of the believing community (*genos eklekton*, 2:9) is the principle point of this passage and the determinative concept for the choice, rewording, arrangement and interpretation of the various traditions combined here. The passage is not based upon a Qumran text or influenced by a notion of the believers as a "neo-Levitical community," despite the common use of Old Testament sources such as Isa. 28:16 and Lev. 19:2.[19] It is neither a comment on "spiritualized" Christian worship and cult, nor an attempt to propound a concept of a general "priesthood of believers." The term *hierateuma* ("priestly community," "body of priests") associated with *oikos pneumatikos* in v. 5 is part of an Old Testament covenantal formula (Exod. 19:6, cited in v. 9) which, in accord with its traditional use and interpretation,[20] has been employed not to describe the community in cultic terms[21]—as interpreters have generally and yet erroneously assumed—but to affirm the elect and holy identity, solidarity and status of the eschatological people of God.[22]

With 2:4–10 seen in this light, the phrase *oikos pneumatikos* in v. 5 is a significant redactional creation with a specific redactional purpose.[23] First, the phrase is part of an editorial introduction and interpretation (vv. 4–5) of the complex of sources quoted in vv. 6–10.[24] Second, *oikos pneumatikos* serves as a conceptual link for the combination of different traditions and images (the "stone" imagery and tradition of vv. 4–5a, 6–8 and the communal election epithets of vv. 4, 5c, 9–10). Thus in v. 5 a transition (albeit imperfect syntactically) is provided from the stone image "you yourselves also as living stones are being built up" via "(you are) a household filled with the Spirit" to the elective image "(you are) a holy priestly community . . . " (au.). Third, *oikos* joins the other collective terms of this passage (*hierateuma, genos, basileion, ethnos, laos*) in expressing and emphasizing the communal, elective and holy character of the believers as the eschatological people of God. Finally, the meaning of *oikos pneumatikos* in this pericope is suggested by the relationship of v. 5 to v. 9 specifically.

Oikos pneumatikos is the author's interpretation of the substantive *basileion* which is part of the Exod. 19:6 text cited in v. 9. In v. 9 *basileion* means "royal residence," or "house of the king." The "house of the (divine) king" in v. 9 is, according to v. 5b, to be understood as the "house (i.e., community) in which the (divine) Spirit resides." Before 1 Peter, Philo of Alexandria, as we shall see presently, interpreted *basileion* in the text of Exod. 19:6 in virtually identical fashion. For 1 Peter, as for Philo, both *basileion* and its *interprementum, oikos,* are designations of the socioreligious community which belongs to God. For both, moreover, *basileion* and *oikos* express the elective and covenantal nature of that union.[25]

Thus within the context of 2:4–10, I concluded, *oikos* was best rendered as "house" or "household." Further evidence within the larger context of 1 Peter coincides with and supports this meaning; viz., the communal or social sense of *tou oikou tou theou* in 4:17, the designation of the believers as "good household stewards of God's varied grace" in 4:10, and the domestic character of the household code (2:13–3:9) which immediately follows the passage 2:4–10.

Since the citation of Exod. 19:6 in 1 Pet. 2:9 and its introductory interpretation in v. 5 are not motivated by any discernible cultic concerns of the author or his audience, it is unlikely that *oikos pneumatikos* here means "spiritual temple." The reasons which I have already given for rejecting this meaning in both 2:5 and 4:17 have not, in my opinion, been convincingly disproved by subsequent studies which maintain the contrary.[26] The weaknesses of such studies lie in the tendency to exaggerate the cultic language of 2:5 over against the theme and purpose of 2:4–10 as a whole, to ignore the absence of cultic interests elsewhere in the document, to fail to inquire regarding the meaning and function of the household concept within the situation and composition of 1 Peter in general, and to overlook the diverse social and political implications which the household had in the cultural milieu of 1 Peter.

In order to determine the meaning and function of *oikos* within 1 Peter, in other words, *social* and sociological as well as literary and redactional factors must be considered. With this observation I am proceeding beyond the point where *The Elect and the Holy* left off. The following consideration of the community as household in the social world of 1 Peter, therefore, is intended to provide supplementary and corroborative evidence for the sense of *oikos* in 1 Peter as well as clues concerning its social and ideological function.

THE SIGNIFICANCE AND FUNCTION OF THE *OIKOS* IN THE GRECO-ROMAN WORLD

For an entrée into that social world we may begin with the striking similarity between the Petrine interpretation of Exod. 19:6 and that of a near contemporary, Philo of Alexandria (fl. 39/40 c.e.). In *De Sobrietate* 66 Philo cites and interprets Exod. 19:6 in conjunction with a commentary on Noah's blessing to his sons Japheth and Shem ("God enlarge Japheth and may He dwell in the tents [*oikois*] of Shem," *De Sobr.* 59, cf. LXX Gen. 9:27). This promise of divine indwelling indeed has been fulfilled, states Philo, in Jacob, Shem's progeny, and the twelve tribes of whom it has been said: "they are God's royal residence and body of priests" (*basileion kai hierateuma theou, De Sobr.* 66).[27] Philo then immediately explains the term *basileion* as the "house" or "dwelling place of (God) the king": "for surely by *basileion* is meant the 'king's house'" (*basileion gar ho basileōs dēpouthen oikos* ...).

In *The Elect and the Holy* I have already discussed this Philonic passage along with *De Abrahamo* 56 where Exod. 19:6 is also cited and their significance for the tradition and redaction of 1 Pet. 2:4–10.[28] For our purposes here the following points are of importance. First, in 1 Peter, as well as in *De Sobr.* 66 and *De Abrah.* 56, the term *basileion* of Exod. 19:6 is treated as a substantive; that is, as a self-subsistent epithet alongside of, rather than modifying, *hierateuma*. Second, in both 1 Peter and *De Sobr.* 66, *basileion* is interpreted as referring to the *oikos* of God the king.[29] Third, for both 1 Peter and Philo, *basileion* and *oikos* designate the special chosen people among whom God or the divine Spirit dwells, the communal house(hold) of the divine king. Fourth, neither 1 Peter nor Philo uses *basileion, oikos,* or the Exod. 19:6 text with which these terms are associated to expatiate on the cultic character or cultic activity of the people of God. Their purpose, rather, is to affirm the fulfillment of God's promises and the peculiar distinctiveness of the people among whom God dwells. Finally, for both 1 Peter and Philo, reference to and interpretation of the Exodus text serve a similar socioreligious function. Both Philo and

1 Peter address audiences in similar sociopolitical and socioreligious situations. Philo was writing for the second-class and discriminated Jewish minority of Alexandria. Likewise, 1 Peter was addressed to disadvantaged Christian *paroikoi* of Asia Minor. For both audiences the covenantal epithets are used to assert (by inversion) their dignity before God, affirm their solidarity and explain their socioreligious distinctiveness. In view of the sociopolitical implications of the *oikos* of the political ruler of Egypt, it is conceivable that this term in particular was intended to bring this communal distinctiveness to expression. Accordingly, for 1 Peter as for Philo, resident aliens of the dispersion are identified as the "house of the divine king" in contradistinction to their belonging to the house of a human ruler.

For a resident of Egypt such as Philo we may assume the knowledge of a long-standing local conception; namely, "that the whole land was the personal possession (*oikos*) of the king." As evidence of earlier Ptolemaic governmental administration shows, and as social historians such as Rostovtzeff have frequently noted,

> The whole of Egypt was the oikos of the king, his private household, which he owned in his character of a living god. Parts of this oikos he might entrust to the management of priests for the maintenance of the worship of the gods, or might bestow on members of his household—generals or other military officers and men, officials, members of his family, or favorites. But the whole of Egypt remained nevertheless his oikos, partly subdivided into smaller and less important oikoi.[31]

"The first man in the state beside the king," Martin Hengel has explained,

> was the *dioikētēs*, under Philadelphus from 261 B.C. the Appolonius . . . from whose sphere the Zeno correspondence derives. He bore responsibility for the entire possession and income of the king, i.e., everything connected with the finances, the economy and the administration of the state. . . . Egypt itself had of old been divided into nomes, and these in turn into toparchies. The smallest administrative unit was the village. The most important officials in any district were the military *stratēgos*, the *oikonomos* for administration of finance and commerce, and a series of further functionaries presumably of equal status. The leading places were exclusively in the hands of the Greeks, but there were also many non-Greeks in the lower ranks of administration.[32]

171

The *oikos* thereby provided the model, the terminology and the ideological framework for the organization of the state as a whole, its smaller parts (e.g., *epoikia,* "villages"), its various types of subjects (e.g., *metoikoi, paroikoi,* "resident aliens"; *katoikoi,* "military colonists"), and its administrative officials (e.g., *dioikētēs,* chief financial officer; *hypoikētēs,* his subordinate supervisor of several nomes; and *oikonomos,* the financial administrator of a nome).

Under the Seleucids and later the Romans this organization of political, economic and social life underwent little change. The Romans "took its main features for granted, and they based on them and adjusted to them their own administrative system, which in truth did not differ much from that of their predecessors, the Ptolemies."[33] Among his *Res Gestae* Augustus recounts with self-satisfied understatement: "I added Egypt to the empire of the Roman people" (*Res Gestae Divi Augusti* 5.24). According to Tacitus (*Hist.* 1.11) this amounted to an incorporation of Egypt into the *domus Caesaris* (*Aegyptum ... domi retinere*).

One way which Jewish and other *paroikoi* had of carving out for themselves a niche in this elaborate political household was to secure for themselves the self-consciousness and the legal rights for existing as a minority *politeuma* within or alongside the major *politeia,* as a distinctive *oikos* within an *oikos.* Another quite different approach was for them to take credit for the origin of the state *oikos.* According to Hengel,

> For Artapanus [a Jewish romance writer of the second century B.C.E.], the ordering of the Egyptian state was so impressive that he derived it from Joseph and Moses. Joseph was the first *dioikētēs* of the whole country (*dioikētēs tēs holēs genesthai chōras*), who introduced the surveying and distribution of the country (cf. Gen. 47:20ff.), set apart the temple land and—like Philadelphus in the Fayum—made much unfertile land arable. Moses' contribution was, among other things, the division into 36 nomes, the irrigation system and the absolute monarchy. Here the "culture-bringer" certainly plays a part; but the alien culture was the model.[34]

In any case it is clear that for Philo, as for his predecessors and contemporaries, household management (*oikonomia*) was a self-evident analogue for political statesmanship. In his treatise on Joseph as exemplar of the *bios politikou* ("the life of the statesman"), Philo explicates this link between household management and statesmanship. Joseph's training for becoming a statesman included not only his role as shepherd (§§ 2–3) but also his subsequent charge over his master's household in Egypt (*sympathēs tēs oikias tēn epimeleian,* § 37). This was in reality, states Philo,

> nature's doing, who was taking steps to procure for him the command of whole cities and a nation and a great country. For the future statesman (*politikon*) needed first to be trained and practised in house management (*tois kat' oikonomian*); for a house is a city compressed into small dimensions, and household management (*oikonomia*) may be called a kind of state management (*politeia*), just as a city too is a great house (*oikos megas*) and statesmanship the household management of the general public. All this shews clearly that the household manager (*oikonomikon*) is identical with the statesman (*politikon*), however much what is under the purview of the two may differ in number and size (§§ 38–39).[35]

Here as elsewhere in Philo's writings,[36] house and household membership/city and citizenship, household management/government are natural and frequent correlates. *Oikia kaisaros,*[37] *oikia Ptolemaiōn,*[38] *oikos Klaudiou*[39] etc. refer not simply to the immediate royal families but also to the political administration and bureaucracy of the Ptolemaic and imperial regimes. The *oikos* rule of Egyptian sovereigns is thus for Philo a significant political reality over against which to compare and contrast the identity, organization and allegiance of the *oikos* of God.[40]

Although the equation of state and *oikos* was especially explicit in Egypt where this centralizing concept conformed so obviously to a centralized political, economic, social and national life, the political connotations of *oikos* were known and even basic to the sociopolitical forms of life in the Mediterranean world as a whole. The Ptolemies of course were not native Egyptians but Greeks who introduced Greek culture, language and hellenistic concepts and forms of political administration to their Egyptian subjects. "The titles of the Ptolemaic administrative officials therefore," Hengel has observed, "often derive from the terminology used in large private estates in Greece. The king 'managed the States as a plain Macedonian or Greek would manage his household.' "[41] Thus we may look to the Greek mainland and other spheres of hellenistic influence for similar sociopolitical dimensions of the *oikos.*

As a basis of and model for Greek social, economic and political life from Homeric times through the advent of Roman rule, the nature and significance of the household have been amply discussed and documented.[42] Historically and sociologically there was a natural affinity between *oikos* and *polis* because of the actual social development from initial household to tribe, confederation, *polis* and state. Aristotle, at the outset of his *Politics* (Book 1) expresses the conventional notion that it is the home, family, *oikos* that political life begins with, emulates and extends.[43] Comprising, in addition to immediate family and residence, also land, property and personnel,[44] the household or estate was also the basic economic unit of production and self-support. Economy (*oikonomia*) was a matter of *oikos*-management.[45] The conditions of household structure and management such as land tenure, wealth, kinship relations, familial status, and freedom were determining factors for social class, status and modes of social interaction. It was thus the *oikos*, as, for instance, Xenophon's treatise *Oeconomicus*[46] reveals and as the additional abundant evidence assembled now by Balch demonstrates, which set the context and the presuppositions for the discussion of moral responsibility and exhortation, that is, "household duties."[47] Where the *oikos* is adopted as a model for political affairs, there domestic duties serve as a paradigm for civic responsibilities.

Ethnically, politically and religiously the *oikos* provided the framework for viewing and distinguishing the native (*oikeios*) from the stranger (*metoikos, paroikos = allotrios*), hence the citizen from the quasi- or non-enfranchised, the coreligionist from the "heathen." From the "synoikism"[48] of the ancient Greek city-states to the umbrella-like *domus* of the Roman imperial bureaucracy, the household remained a socially and psychologically effective element of an ideology designed to express, validate and promote intergroup unity, paternal benevolence and international *pax*.[49]

Although in the course of Rome's history, E. A. Judge has noticed, republican institutions vied with and sought to overcome the traditional autonomy of the household, "The household in its broader sense remained a rival body."[50] Even in the Roman republic there was no diminishment in the sweeping powers of the *pater familias* or in the obligations of household loyalty imposed upon slaves and freedmen alike. Toward the end of the republic, while republicanism waned, the household endured as a viable model of social organization. "This intimacy of this grouping offered a kind of security that an over-extended republic was no longer felt to afford. Its solidarity in turn could therefore be turned to their own account by politically-minded patrons, with the result that political competition in the Roman republic consisted of alignment and realignment within the aristocracy, success going to the combination which commanded the greatest voting strength through its *clientela*."[51] The transition from republic to empire was thus marked by the fact that "the institutions of the republic had been concerted to the aggrandizement of the household community."[52] Although republican officials in theory, the Caesars were in actuality dependent for their authority on the patronage of the republican aristocracy.

Beginning with Augustus, moreover, the emperors could and did exploit these personal forms of alignment on their own behalf in the monopolization of political power. Personal loyalty to the emperor was sought not only from patrons but from all segments of the population in the form of a personal oath of allegiance. Such loyalty had its material rewards, of course, be they imperial posts, imperial favor or imperial bequests for the masses. It also had its price. In extension of and yet competition with the traditional authority of the household, the *patria potestas,* there now emerged a more universal claim to power, namely, the *potestas* of a *"pater patriae."*[53] Loyal subjects would be, henceforth, favored sons and daughters of the "father of the fatherland."

The expression of this household or familial ideology could take various forms and serve various aims. The promotion of subject unity and loyalty was one such purpose. Thus the *Res Gestae* of Augustus not only enumerates the incorporation and consolidation of various peoples into "one big happy Roman family." It also constitutes, according to Judge,

> a manifesto addressed to the public, putting on permanent record the long list of benefits they had received, and the honours they had returned him, and culminating in the act that expressed the essential character of their relation to him, the formal and universal acknowledgement of him as *Pater Patriae.*[54]

"This paternalism reveals the emotional basis upon which the power of the Caesars rested."[55] The use to which such an emotional appeal to political "fatherhood" could be put is illustrated by an address of Augustus to the knights of Rome in 9 c.e.[56] Augustus was intent on encouraging marriage and the rearing of legitimate children. Concluding a rebuke of those who sought the repeal of the law (the Julian law of 18 B.C.E., supplemented by the Papian-Poppaean law of 9 B.C.E.) regarding the unmarried and the childless, Augustus asks:

> How could I call myself a good ruler over you if I should endure seeing you becoming constantly fewer? How could I any longer be rightfully named your father, if you rear no children? Therefore, if you really have a regard for me and have given me this title [*pater patriae*] not out of flattery but as an honor, desire yourselves to become men and fathers. Thus you yourselves share this title and also render me well-named.[57]

Paternity is a matter not simply of obedience but of personal integrity and political allegiance. Fertile fathers share in the prestige of the father of the fatherland.[58]

In life, so in death and for eternity. The Roman "family" is to remember with gratitude the loving deeds of its dearly departed "father." Thus it was that at Augustus' funeral Tiberius sums up his encomium of the emperor's life, achievements and service of the Roman people by reminding a bereaved audience:

> It was for this, therefore, I say, that you naturally made him your head and a father of the people, that you decked him with many marks of esteem and numerous consulships and finally declared him a hero and published him as immortal.[59]

In similar fashion Suetonius recalls the fatherly goodness of Titus, "the delight and darling of the human race." After mention of the dreadful disasters during his reign such as the eruption of Mount Vesuvius, a fire at Rome and a terrible plague, the biographer declares:

> In these many great calamities he showed not merely the concern of an emperor, but even a father's surpassing love (*sed et parentis affectum unicum praestitit*), now offering consolation in edicts, and now lending aid so far as his means allowed.[60]

The panegyric of the younger Pliny addressed to the emperor Trajan, in fact, seems to suggest that in the matter of encomia on imperial fatherhood, literally the sky was the limit! In an expression of gratitude for Trajan's benevolent conferral of the consulship upon him (100 C.E.) Pliny goes so far as to celebrate his beloved emperor as earthly representative of Father Jupiter:

... Here is the picture of the father of our state as I for my part seem to have discerned it both from his speech and from the very manner of its presentation. What weight in his ideas, what unaffected genuineness in his words, what earnestness in his voice, what confirmation in his face, what sincerity in his eyes, bearing, gestures, in short in his whole body! He will always remember his advice to us, and he will know that we are obeying him whenever we make use of the liberty he has given us. ... O care truly that of a *princeps,* and even of a god, to reconcile rival cities, to calm peoples in ferment, less by imperial command than by reason, to impede the injustices of magistrates, to annul everything that ought not have been done, in fine, in the manner of the swiftest star to see all, hear all, and like a divinity, be present and helpful forthwith wherever invoked! Such, I imagine, are the things that the father of the world regulates with a nod when he lets his glance fall upon the earth and deigns to count human destinies among his divine occupations. Henceforth free and released in this area he can attend to the sky alone, since he has sent you to fill his role toward the human race. You fulfill the function, and you are worthy of him who entrusted it to you, since each of your days is devoted to our greatest good, to your greatest glory.[61]

In ideology, so in praxis. Having a pater for a princeps involved having his immediate household for a government. To administer the affairs of state, including the keeping of imperial records, the supervision of coinage and the oversight of the fiscal estates, the early emperors employed a vast array of personal servants, imperial freedmen and slaves. This personal, familial mode of imperial bureaucratic administration was known as the "household of Caesar." "In part," R. H. Barrow has noted in his study on slavery in the empire,

> the civil service was developed from institutions of the Republic; other elements were taken from the economy of the Roman household, and therefore many posts were held by slaves or freedmen. The master of that house was the Emperor; his servants, therefore, were the servants of the Empire, for the house was nothing less than the Empire. But, as the servants of a private household may be divided into those who attend to the near and personal wants of the master and those who have charge of his estates, so the Emperor's servants fall into those who are domestic and those who deal with the affairs of the world in what we should call the departments of the civil service. Yet all are *servi Caesaris,* alike the clerk in the imperial treasury and the valet of the imperial wardrobe.[62]

Supplying the junior personnel of lower departments as well, and directly serving the interests of the emperor in the provinces where senior imperial freedmen (*liberti Augusti*) acted as chief executive officers of the procurators along with other assistant household staff, the arm and aura of the imperial household reached from the capitol to the most distant boundaries of the empire.[63] As Paul's letter to the Philippians attests (Phil. 4:22), the early Christian movement not only came in contact with "Caesar's household," but also counted some of its members among its sympathizers or perhaps even converts.

The actual history of the principate was anything but the harmonious interaction of benevolent father with household servants and subjects. Nevertheless, the idea of a common family, like that of an equally utopic "pax romana," apparently served the interests and aims of *patres* and *patria* alike. For the patricians and proletariat, paternalistic control and social security apparently were agreeable trade-offs. For the masses, whose lack of citizenship, liberty and social acceptance implied the absence of the essential qualifications of even humanity, "a compensation for public disabilities [was afforded] in the mutual society and help of the household."[64] For the "fathers of the fatherland," the *politeia* as *oikos* provided the ideological means for legitimating centralized bureaucratic authority along traditional autocratic lines. Moreover, the established notion of an emperor as father could be used to secure and insure the perpetual memory of a benevolent ruler (however despotic), the filial loyalty and subservience of subjects (however exploited), and even the reluctant obedience of imperial legislation where it was declared that the formula "patriotism = paternity" applied to emperor and empire alike.

To some such as Strabo such paternalism may have seemed a practical necessity. He found it "difficult for the Romans to govern so vast an empire in any other way than by entrusting it to one person—as it were to a father . . . and thus Romans enjoyed peace and prosperity as never before" (*Geography* 6.4.2).

The subtle pressures involved in the promulgation of this paternalistic propaganda were not lost on one as perceptive as Juvenal, however. Comparing Octavian Augustus unfavorably with Cicero, he chided:

> Thus within the walls his [Cicero's] toga won for him as much fame and honor as Octavius gained by battle [in] Leucas [Actium]; as much as Octavius won by his sword wet from constant killing on the plains of Thes-

saly; but then Rome was yet free when she styled Cicero the Parent and Father of his country (*sed Roma parentem, Roma patrem patriae Ciceronem libera dixit*) (*Satire* 8. 243–44).

The organization, programs and ideology of the Augustan reform vividly illustrate how regard for the household could be exploited to serve political ends. This was possible because of the traditional association of *oikos* and state and the universal longing for security, order and a place to call home. Community as *oikos* was a form of social grouping which derived its appeal from the common experience, imagination and hope of all peoples.

Further evidence of the political, economic and social connotations of the *oikos*, more conventional and less pretentious than the aforementioned imperial propaganda, is contained in the *Orations* of Dio Chrysostom and an epistle of Pliny the Younger. Both were residents in Bithynia and were speaking or writing at the beginning of the second century c.e. The language of Dio Chrysostom shows how at this time and place *oikos* and its paronyms continued to shape the political and economic vocabulary of the day. *Dioikēsis*, for instance, was the customary term for "financial administration";[65] and in reference to the administration of an office or of the commonwealth Dio speaks of *archēn . . . dioikēsai* or *dioikein ta koina*.[66] Likewise in addressing the Apameians on the theme of concord, he reminds them that the common political ties between him, the citizens of Prusa, and the Apameians, are those of *synoikoi*.[67]

Pliny, the Roman governor of Bithynia-Pontus, shows the currency of the *oikos* (*domus*) = commonwealth equation. Writing to a certain Plinius Paternus, Pliny the patrician alludes to the representative significance which the household has for his slaves:

> I receive and obey their last requests, as so many authoritative commands, suffering them to dispose of their effects to whom they please; with this single restriction, that they leave them to some of my household (*relinquunt dumtaxat intra domum*), for to persons in their station the household takes the place of city and commonwealth (*nam servis res publica quaedam et quasi civitas domus est*).[68]

This material from Bithynia provides direct information concerning the social milieu of 1 Peter. The traditional implications and expressions of *oikos* organization and economic management still current here at the beginning of the second century can safely be assumed to have been known to the audience of 1 Peter twenty to thirty years earlier, not only in Bithynia but throughout the provinces addressed. Pliny's observation that the household "takes the place of city and commonwelath" is particularly helpful for appreciating how the *oiketai* and other members of the Christian community in 1 Peter could understand and accept a similar rationale for their new distinctive communal identity.

The time-honored and universal recognition of the *oikos* as the basis and model for social forms of communal life also accounts for its psychological significance. "Probably no age," the social historian Samuel Dill has written, "not even our own, ever felt a greater craving for some form of social life wider than the family and narrower than the State."[69] This craving was especially acute among the nonprivileged, dispossessed or displaced persons and groups who of necessity had broken ties with home and homeland and were living as rootless immigrants abroad. Asylum for such strangers and a place of belonging were offered, as mentioned earlier, by the many and varied unofficial associations (*koina, collegia*) dotting the map of the empire. These voluntary associations, to which many *paroikoi* and *parepidēmoi* like those of 1 Peter were attracted,[70] included guilds of artisans, tradespeople and entrepreneurs who had joined together not only in the pursuit of common occupational interests but also for the sake of social solidarity. In spite of the fact that the voluntary character of these associations was "one of the critical steps towards breaking the original family domination of Greek society,"[71] and despite the further fact of their suspected potential threat to Roman order and control of the imperial household,[72] there is evidence that they too embraced the self-designation, *oikos*. Thus, for instance, an inscription from Tomoi on the shore of the Black Sea (ca. 160 C.E.) contains reference to "the house(hold) of the Alexandrians" (*ho oikos tōn Alexandreōn*).[73] Franz Poland takes this and similar inscriptional evidence from the area as references to associations of merchants or guilds of shipowners.[74] Not only did such guild members live and work together in the same house and vicinity[75] and erect houses for occupational and possibly religious purposes;[76] as a logical extension of their proximity and communality, they also considered their guild a household as well. For foreigners such as the Alexandrians living as immigrants abroad this undoubtedly meant no small psychological as well as social solace. Whatever the specific goals of the various associations may have been, whether the pursuit of a certain trade[77] or the procuring of a decent burial (*collegia tenuiorum*),[78] their common object was "the cheerfulness of intercourse, the promotion of fellowship and goodwill, the relief of the dullness of humdrum lives."[79] In the words of Dill, "these colleges became homes for the homeless, a little fatherland or patria for those without a country."[80]

A home for the homeless, an *oikos* for *paroikoi*—how fitting such a description might be for the Christian community as well. However the dissimilarities as well as the similarities between these collegia and Christian social patterns are to be evaluated,[81] and however acute the tensions between them,[82] it is clear that for both types of association the *oikos* provided a meaningful and practical form of social identity and base of communal support. Furthermore it was not only guilds which used the term *oikos* as a designation for the group. A forthcoming study of a hellenistic cult in Lydia (ca. late second to early first century B.C.E.) provides evidence that pagan as well as Christian religious groups also conceived of their communities as constituting a household or family.[83]

The political, social and religious role of the household and family in molding social institutions has hardly gone unobserved by sociologists, including those of ancient history. R. M. MacIver, for instance, writing on "The Family as Government in Miniature," in a collection of essays on *The Imprint of Roman Institutions,*[84] has pointed to the family as the primary socializing and regulative agent of social life, "everywhere the matrix of government." One chief reason for this, he observes, is that

> The family is bound up with all the great crises and transitions of life. It is the focus of the most intimate relationships, those in which the personality of man and of woman is most profoundly expressed and most thoroughly tested. It is the primary agent in the folding of the life-habits and the life-attitudes of human beings. It is the center of the most impressive celebrations and rituals, those associated with marriage, with death, and with the initiation of the child into the beliefs and ways of the community. It is the hearth, the home, the place where old and young must learn to make changing adjustments to their everchanging roles in the life-cycle.[85]

It comes as no surprise, therefore, that in the literature of Israel and early Christianity household and family can be seen not only to have shaped the social institutions of these communities but also to have symbolized their profoundest memories and hopes of communal salvation.

THE SIGNIFICANCE AND FUNCTION OF THE *OIKOS* IN THE OLD AND NEW TESTAMENTS

From the foregoing consideration of the social community as *oikos* in the secular environment of 1 Peter we now turn to its role in the religious tradition with which 1 Peter is most closely bound, namely, that of the Old and New Testaments. The sheer abundance of the occurrences of *oikos/oikia* in the LXX (*oikos*: over 1660 times; *oikia*: over 200 times) and New Testament (*oikos*: 112 times; *oikia*: 94 times), quite apart from the occurrence of their paronyms, requires that our investigation remain focused. What do the social, political and psychological connotations and implications of the *oikos* or household in the secular, and now the biblical, literature suggest concerning the social meaning and function of *oikos* in 1 Peter?

In general it can be said that the denotations and connotations of *oikos* and its paronyms in the biblical material are closely parallel to secular usage. Aside from the specific textual references, the categories of meaning or usage of *oikos* listed in the standard biblical Greek dictionaries match those of their secular Greek counterparts.[86] *Oikos/oikia* designates, variously, a building, dwelling, residence; a room or chamber; a hall or meeting place; a storehouse or treasury; a palace; a building in which a divinity is thought to reside, a temple; a burial chamber or tomb; a household, family or lineage; household goods, substance, estate, inheritance; a reigning house or dynasty; a clan, tribe, tribal confederation, nation or state; and a social, commercial or religious organization or community.

It is hardly possible or necessary here to elaborate on the sundry social, economic, political, ethnic or religious connotations of "house" in the Old Testament.[87] Suffice it to note that *oikos* (and its Hebrew equivalent *bayith*) throughout the strata of the Old Testament tradition serves as a prime expression of communal identity and organization and of social, political and religious solidarity. In religious terms it is this form of Israelite community as "house" with which Yahweh has entered into special relationship. It was to the chosen patriarch Abraham and his *oikos* (Gen.

18:19), called from their father's house (Gen. 12:1) into *paroikia* (Gen. 12:10; 15:13; 17:8 etc.), to whom the promises of divine blessing were given (Gen. 12:1–3; 18:19). It was with the *house of Jacob* that God covenanted at Sinai (Exod. 19:3–8), and it was to the *house of Israel* and the house of Judah that he promised the formation of a new and abiding covenant (Jer. 38[31]:31–34). It was to the one incapable of building God a cultic house, King David, that God promised *a regal house,* a royal lineage and reign which would last forever (2 Sam. 7:8–16).

The household or family as "the basis of all definitions" of Israelite community, together with the historical and psychic, as well as social and religious cohesion which this implies, has been stressed by P. S. Minear.

> The idea of the family "is the basis of all definitions [of social cohesion]. . . . It immediately presents itself whenever the Israelite wants to define a community." . . . The homogeneity of the family, the element of kinship, stems from a psychic bond that discloses the fact that contemporary mutualities actually spring from a common source. "Wherever a man goes, he takes his 'house' with him." . . . His history, in terms of his enacted kinship, derives its true stamp from the character of the family whose history is also enacted in it. Having a common stamp is the same as having a common history and as being one people. If this homogeneity is destroyed, the people is destroyed or it becomes a "nonpeople," which is the same as "to perish." On the other hand, wherever homogeneity appears, whether in evil or in good, there appears also a family, a people. It is clear, then, that the pictures of the family, of the household, and of the people tend to coalesce, since all articulate a flexible sense of kinship, a realistic homogeneity in which the "common stamp" of a contemporary community is understood as its participation in a common tradition, a history understood as the continuing life of a common ancestor. This, stated all too briefly, is the cluster of idioms that permeates the New Testament identifications of the household of God with the house of Israel and David, with the covenantal promises and the faith granted to the fathers.[88]

On the relevance of the Old Testament material on *oikos* for the interpretation of 1 Peter, the following points may be singled out.

1. In the religious tradition with which 1 Peter was most intimately associated, *oikos* designated narrower and wider forms of social, political and religious community. It was an extremely frequent expression of Israel's communal identity and socioreligious solidarity, with God and

with one another. Here religious language was derived from and adapted to social reality. Out of individual households and tribes God was said to have created the house of Israel as father and builder. He was viewed as the *paterfamilias,* constructor and ruler par excellence (Ps. 126[127]:1–5). As he destroys an unfaithful household in his wrath, so he also restores and rebuilds the household anew (Jer. 38[31]:28; 40[33]:7; 49[42]:10; Amos 9:11). The house of Israel and the house of Judah in mutual covenant with God was a prophetic hope for the new age (Jer. 38[31]:31–34). In 1 Peter an ancient expression of that covenantal union (Exod. 19:3–8) has been used to describe the new universal household of faith.

2. In the LXX, the formulation *oikos (tou) theou/kyriou* is used almost exclusively for a sanctuary, shrine (e.g., Gen. 28:19; Judg. 17:5; 18:31) or temple (e.g., 3 Kgdm. [1 Kings] 6:1 ff.; Pss. 22[23]:6; 26[27]:4 and passim). In contrast to the frequent occurrences of this usage (and of *oikos* absolute) in the LXX, the comparatively rare occurrence of *oikos* or *oikos tou theou* in the sense of *temple* in the New Testament marks an important shift in interest and focus. On the one hand this could be due to the perpetuation of the criticism already present in the Old Testament (2 Kgdm. [2 Sam.] 7:5–6; 3 Kgdm. [1 Kings] 8:27; Isa. 66:1) of the notion that man could even build God a dwelling place (see Acts 7:47–50; cf. Rev. 21:22). Or, as in Qumran,[90] it could be the result of the socialization or communalization of temple imagery (e.g., 1 Cor. 3:16–17; 2 Cor. 6:16–17; Eph. 2:19–22) which soon lost its polemical or critical significance once the temple was destroyed. Or it could be due to the interest of Christian groups (represented, e.g., by 1 Peter, Hebrews [3:1–6] and 1 Timothy [3:15]), not in their identification with or polemic against Judaism's temple but in the appropriation of Israel's social identity and fulfillment of its history as the household with whom God has established a final covenantal and familial bond.[91]

3. In the Old Testament, as in 1 Peter, the contrast of the *oikos* and the *paroikia* of Israel was a striking means for depicting the oscillating rhythms of Israel's history. The juxtaposition of *oikos/paroikoi, paroikia* and their paronyms (e.g., *oikodomein, oikein/metoikia, metoikein; apoikia, apoikismos*) and synonymous or related factors (e.g., landedness/landlessness) was used to express the contrasting experiences of having a home or being at home versus losing or being uprooted from home. Such juxtapositions graphically express the alternating patterns of Israel's socioreligious integration, disintegration and reintegration.

At the outset of Israel's hisory the father of the nation, Abraham, called by God from his father's *oikos* to become a *paroikos,* became a harbinger of the fate and challenge of his progeny.[92] At Sinai Yahweh's exclusive claim on the house of Jacob (Exod. 19:3) and the exclusivity of its loyalty, obedience and discipline (Exod. 20:3–17) was based upon the fact that he had liberated them from the Egyptian house of bondage (*oikos douleias,* Exod. 20:2; cf. Deut. 5:6, 7–21). "And you shall remember that you were a slave (*oiketēs*) in the land of Egypt and the Lord your God brought you out . . . " (Deut. 5:15 au.). " . . . [Y]ou were a *paroikos* in this land [Egypt]" (Deut. 23:8 LXX, au.). Apostasy and adulteration of the house of Jacob, on the other hand, will result in the dissolution of the household (Deut. 13:6–18).

And so in the days of Jeremiah it came to pass. "His message to Israel, which thought it was ultimately secure and at home, is the coming ultimate homelessness."[93] As a result of its infidelity, Israel was to lose not only its land but also its social cohesion. "The end of the land," as Walter Brueggemann has noted, "of course means the collapse of all public institutions and all symbolic expressions of well-being and coherence."[94] In the prophet's pronouncements of doom and deliverance addressed to "the house of Jacob and all the families (LXX: *patria*) of the house of Israel" (Jer. 2:4),[95] community-as-*oikos* and land are the points of reference for an announcement of Israel's coming exile (*paroikia, metoikia*),[96] its disintegration and dislocation, and its future reconsolidation. "I have forsaken my house, I have abandoned my heritage" (12:7). "But if you will not heed these words, I swear by myself, says the Lord, that this house [the ruling house of Judah] shall become a desolation" (22:5). But as the Lord of the household "plucks up and breaks down," so he will also "build" anew (1:10; 38[31]:28). "Like these good figs, so I will regard as good the exiles (*apoikisthentas*) from Judah. . . . I will bring them back to this land, I will build them up (*anoikodomēsō*) . . . " (24:5/6). "I will restore the homeless community (*apoikian*) of Israel and I will rebuild them (*oikodomēsō*) as they once were" (40[33]:7 au.). As God once intended it, so one day it shall be. "I thought how I would set you among my sons, and give you a pleasant land, a heritage most beauteous of all nations. And I thought you would call me, My Father, and would not turn from following me" (3:19). "In those days the house of Judah shall join the house of Israel, and together they shall come from the land of the north to the land that I gave your fathers for a heritage" (3:18). In the day of salvation and upbuilding (*oikodomein*), those who were once subjected to homelessness (*apoikia*, 47[40]:1, 7 (v. 8 LXX)) in Babylon (*apoikisthēnai hēmas eis Babylōna,* 50[43]:3) will be restored to their native land and reunited as the *oikos*-family of God (3:18; 16:14–15; 38[31]: 27–28, 38–40; 39[32]: 36–44).

In Ezekiel, Jeremiah's contemporary, a similar contrast of *oikos* conditions is evident. According to Ezekiel, the house of Israel has become a "rebellious house" (*oikos parapikrainōn*).[97] As a result, this rebellious house will lose its home and be deported into the *metoikesia* of exile (Ezek. 12:11; cf. 17:12).

Paroikia existence for Jeremiah, however, implied not only dislocation or disintegration as punishment but also the promise and challenge of a new form of faith and social reconstitution.[98] Even in exile God is with his people. Even in *apoikia* the process of building (*oikodomein*) and reconstitution of the *oikos* can take place (Jer. 36[29]:1–7). It is this sense of *paroikia* which includes the paradoxical possibility of community-as-*oikos* that we find reflected in the social vision of 1 Peter.

4. As a final example of the contribution of the Old Testament toward a clarification of the meaning and function of *oikos* in 1 Peter, reference might once again be made to Exod. 19:6 and its context. It has already been noted than 1 Pet. 2:9 explicitly quotes the covenant formula of Exod. 19:6 (*basileion hierateuma, ethnos hagion*) and that 2:5 introduces this quotation and interprets *basileion* with the phrase *oikos pneumatikos*. The house of the king is, in the Christian *oikonomia*, the house of the Spirit. That *oikos pneumatikos* designates the believers to be a communal house or household rather than a temple in a metaphorical sense is corroborated from another point of view. As eventually in 1 Peter, so originally in Exodus, it is a "house" with whom God makes covenant. It is the "house of Jacob" (*oikos Iakōb,* Exod. 19:3) which is to be "a kingdom of priests and a holy nation" (19:6). This house of Jacob which has been liberated from the house of Pharoah and the "house of bondage" (Exod. 13:3, 14; 20:2) is henceforth to be the sole possession and household domain of God the king (19:4–5). The sense of *oikos* as social, political and religious community has been retained in 1 Peter. However, in 1 Peter's eschatological perspective, the house of Jacob has been supplanted by the house of the Spirit, the household of Christian believers.

In the frequent *New Testament* occurrences of *oikos, oikia* and their many paronyms,[99] the familiar constellation of overlapping social, political, economic and religious connotations is once again evident. The scope of the material again can allow only a selective sampling of the main features and functions of usage.

One example of the semantic variety and versatility of the root *oik-* is contained in the fascinating interplay of meanings and ironies developed in the speech of Stephen (Acts 7:1–53). Here in one single context *oikos* designates: (1) the royal Egyptian household over which Joseph was appointed governor (v. 10);[100] (2) the ethnic or national entity of the "house" of Israel (v. 42) or Jacob (v. 46); (3) the household or home of Moses' father (v. 20); and (4) a temple or man-made dwelling place for God (vv. 47, 49).[101] Multiple meanings facilitate multiple dreadful and graceful ironies. The house of Israel which refused fidelity to God (v. 42) was "dehoused," removed from home (*metoikizein*) by God beyond Babylon (v. 43). Against the false witnesses' charge that Stephen "never ceases to speak words against this holy place (*tou topou tou hagiou*, i.e., the temple) and the law" (6:13), Stephen/Luke directs the prophetic critique of their own tradition (7:48–50, quoting Isa. 66:1). The identity of God and temple, divine domain and house of Israel, is denied. In its place a universal course of the Christian mission is set from Jerusalem to the ends of the earth (cf. 1:8) and from temple to households filled with the Spirit (cf. 8:3; 11:14; 16:31–33; 18:8). Earlier in 7:1–10, through the juxtaposition of *metoikizein* (v. 4), *paroikos* (v. 6) and *oikos* (v. 10), the irony already inherent in the Joseph saga is further elaborated. According to that marvelous economy of divine reversal (cf. Luke 1:46–55; 18:14), the preeminent overseer of the Egyptian royal household (v. 10) was none other than the stranger Joseph, heir of the destiny of the displaced Abraham (vv. 4, 6) whose "posterity would be aliens (*paroikon*) in a land belonging to others" (v. 6).

"House" in the ethnic, national or dynastic sense (house of Israel, of Jacob, of Judah, of David) occurs a dozen times in the New Testament.[102] Occasionally it appears in conjunction with *patria* or *patris* ("one's own people, nation, homeland").[103] Just as *oikos* (*oikia*) is joined with,[104] or a substitute for,[105] *polis*, so *paroikos* and its related terms are used to depict the contrast to full citizen status.[106] In combination with political entities such as a kingdom (e.g., Mark 3:24–25/Luke 11:17) and a city (Matt. 12:25), the household[107] is used to exemplify a "political analysis of the consequences of disunity."[108] "Every kingdom divided against itself is laid waste, and no city or household divided against itself will stand" (Matt. 12:25).

The predominant use of *oikia* and *oikos* in the New Testament, however, is in the narration of the starting point and focal point of the "Jesus movement" (using Theissen's expression[109]) and the subsequent believer/Christian movement. *Oikia* in the literal sense of "house" or "building" denotes the *place* where the ministry of Jesus[110] and the Christian mission[111] originated and developed. *Oikos* denotes a *group of persons,* a household as well as the domicile in which they lived;[112] that is, the *basic social community* to whom the message of salvation was addressed. Households thus constituted the focus, locus and nucleus of the ministry and mission of the Christian movement.

In its various social, economic and religious capacities, the household served the movement as both an opportunity and a model for organization, mobilization and proclamation. Respect for the social and religious solidarity of the family or household manifested the communal consciousness of the new movement. On the practical side it also enhanced the movement's ability to compete with other religions and cults for adherents and immensely facilitated its rapid growth. "Whereas, aside from Judaism, all other oriental religions and the cults with which the new faith competed appealed to the individual precisely apart from his familial bonds and routine activities. Christianity forged its way into secular society through individual household communities as the basic unit of its mission" (au.).[113]

This strategy was undoubtedly influenced and aided by the significance and structure of the household in both Judaism and hellenistic Roman culture. In the diaspora the maintenance of unity and religious integrity of the pious Jewish family was an acute problem. The example of the Jewish housefather served as the criterion for the activities and religious alliances not only of his immediate household including its slaves but also of the proselytes and "godfearers" alike.[114] Thus it was the case among the early Jewish converts to Christianity that the conversion of the head of the household resulted usually in the baptism of the dependents as well. The best known examples include the households of the Roman centurion Cornelius at Caesarea ("a devout man who feared God with all his household," Acts 10:1–2), and of the associates of the apostle Paul: Aquila and

Prisca, Crispus the Corinthian ruler of the synagogue, Lydia of Thyatira, Stephanus of Corinth, Nympha of Laodicea and Archippus.[115] In the regions influenced by hellenistic Roman culture the Christian movement could reckon with the predominant position of the *pater familias,* his vast familial influence as well as his embracing *patria potestas.* "The far-reaching legal, economic and religious independence of the ancient household which resulted from the position of the *pater familias* offered the Christian mission the sole possibility for promoting, however fragmentarily, the unfolding and realization of its message in the midst of a pagan society."[116] The conversion of such domestic units, in turn, meant that households of Christians became the basic social and cultic centers, economic support systems and practical means for the further extension of the Christian movement.

It is hardly coincidental, then, that the household influenced the form of Christian communal organization, its functions of leadership and lines of authority as well as its patterns of relationship and responsibility.[117] Nor is it anything but a conceptual extension of this social reality that, as in 1 Peter, the household was adopted as an all-embracing image of the believing community in its entirety. Thus the early Christians were encouraged to consider their new communal identity and the mutual obligations which this implied as determined by the fact that they were now "members of the household of faith" (*oikeioi tēs pisteōs,* Gal. 6:10). All believers, former Gentiles and Jews alike, were "members of the household of God" (*oikeioi tou theou,* Eph. 2:19). All believing households together constituted the one "household of God" (1 Tim. 3:15; cf. 3:4–5; Heb. 3:6; cf. 10:21; 1 Pet. 2:5; 4:17).

Within the household the roles, relationships and responsibilities of its various members—husbands, wives, parents, children, masters, slaves, the married, the unmarried or widowed, the elder, the younger, the heads of the household and their subordinates—are exemplified through the use of traditional patterns of household conduct, the so-called *Haustafeln* or "household codes,"[118] a point which will be taken up in more detail below. It is also likely that the household structure of authority influenced not only the roles but also the eligibility for leadership in the Christian community, especially at the local level.[119] The heads of the households where the Christians assembled for worship and mutual support, because of their already existent social status and economic resources, were the most obvious persons to assume the responsibilities of material aid, hospitality, and the management of communal programs and resources. So it may be conjectured, for instance, that Aquila and Prisca at Ephesus,[120] Nympha at Laodicea,[121] Archippus (and also Philemon and Apphia?) at Colossae,[122] Phoebe at Cenchreae[123] and Gaius[124] along with Stephanas[125] at Corinth in their hosting of the respective Christian communities shared also in further functions of community leadership.[126] In the case of Stephanas Paul has made this explicitly clear. "Now, brothers, you know that the household of Stephanas was the first fruits [i.e., first converts] in Achaia, and that they have devoted themselves to the service of the saints; I urge you to be subordinate to such people and to every fellow worker and laborer" (1 Cor. 16:15-16 au.).

Paul's comment concerning Stephanas points to a further aspect of the influence of the household upon Christian communal relationships. *Subordination* to those in authority is a characteristic feature of household structure and conduct. Within hellenistic Judaism in particular such subordination was seen as commensurate with the obligations of the Fourth Commandment.[127] As children were subordinate to parents in the natural household—the subordination of the child Jesus to his parents is a classical New Testament instance (Luke 2:51)—so subordination to traditional figures of authority was appropriate in the household of faith.[128] In the Christian perspective, to be sure, subordination and superordination are not prescriptions of the natural or social order; they are both social reflexes of faith in Jesus Christ and obedience to the Divine will which he demonstrated. Thus they are also appropriate expressions of *mutual* humility, care and respect.[129] Such qualifications and modifications of interpersonal roles and relationships, however, proceed from and reflect the fact that "the patriarchal order of the household was indeed the social basis of primitive Christian life."[130]

The description of the Stephanas household as the *first converts* of Achaia suggests still a further possible influence of household conditions; namely, the significance of *seniority*. The Corinthians were to subordinate themselves to Stephanas and his household because these people were, as the first converts, "seniors in the faith." They were elders, as it were, not necessarily in natural age but in Christian experience and service. The term "elder" (*presbyteros*) itself, whether denoting one of advanced years in the household or one with special responsibilities in the social or political community (similar, for instance, to the titles *senator* or *gerōn*), makes the sense of seniority explicit. The two usages, of course, were not mutually exclusive in antiquity. Age conferred status and eligibility for leadership. Leaders in turn could be ascribed the status of "elder" which in other instances was attained by virtue of advanced age. The Christians, like their Jewish and secular contemporaries, spoke of "elders" in both the natural and the titular sense.[131] It is possible, perhaps probable, that when they chose and designated their leaders as "elders" the criterion for this choice was not merely natural age but the length of age as a Christian, seniority in the faith. The term *presbyteros* does not occur in the genuine Pauline letters. However, in 1 Corinthians it is clear that Paul considered Stephanas a senior in fact, if not in title. In the deutero-Pauline letter of 1 Timothy, the young man Timothy is also a senior in the faith. Although young in natural age, Timothy is a leader in the church at Ephesus and is advised to "let no one despise your youth, but set the believers an example in speech and conduct, in love, in faith, in purity" (1 Tim. 4:12). As an early convert (Acts 16:1)[132] and then dedicated co-worker of Paul (Rom. 16:21), he was a senior in faith and service. The same criterion was applied to the selection of an overseer (*episkopos*) over the household of God (1 Tim. 3:1–7): "he must not be a recent convert" (*mē neophyton*, v. 6). Experience in the faith and seniority in service apparently were major standards for the selection of Christian leaders as well as the precondition for subordination within the household of God. It is fitting, then, that in the concluding exhortation of the household of God in 1 Peter, the reciprocal relationship and responsibilities of leaders (*presbyteroi*, 5:1–4) and recent converts (*neōteroi*, v. 5a) are mentioned. As the elders are to be "examples to the flock" (v. 3), so the neophytes in the faith[133] are exhorted to "subordinate yourselves to the elders" (v. 5a au.).

Another more immediately apparent product of household affairs is the Christian interest in the *oikonomos* ("household manager" or "steward") as an example of behavior and responsibility. "Who then is the faithful and wise household steward (*oikonomos*), whom his master will set over his household to give them their portion of food at the proper time? Blessed is that servant (*ho doulos ekeinos*) whom his master, when he comes, will find so doing" (Luke 12:42–43 au.). The conduct of the *oikonomos* was used to typify the ordinary as well as the extraordinary (cf. also Luke 16:1–13) needs of the present eschatological hour, the combination of practical and spiritual urgencies. Christians who all receive extraordinary gifts of divine grace are to use these gifts in the service of the community "as faithful household stewards" (1 Pet. 4:10 au.). The apostle Paul wished, along with Apollos and Cephas (1 Cor. 3:22), to be regarded as "servants (*hypēretas*) of Christ and household stewards (*oikonomous*) of the mysteries of God" (4:1 au.). He knew that as an *oikonomos* he was obliged to be trustworthy (4:2). In Titus 1:5–10 further qualifications for household stewards are set. Those leaders (*presbyteroi, episkopos,* vv. 5, 6) who were to function as stewards in God's household were to possess the qualities which would assure sound household management: blameless character, respect for order, integrity, humility, patience, hospitable, not given to greed, and the like.

It is thus evident that the household had a dominant influence not only on the structure and internal conduct of the early Christian groups but also upon their theological perspectives and socioreligious symbols.[134] The *oikonomia tou theou,* the "management of the household of God," could be used to describe not only the responsibility of Paul and his service to the community (Col. 1:25; cf. 1 Cor. 9:17; Eph. 3:2; 1 Tim. 1:4); this action of domestic administration could also be employed to symbolize God's arrangements for human redemption, the plan and process of divine salvation (Eph. 1:9–10; 3:9–10).[135]

In the parables, household management and other diverse aspects of domestic life (familial relationships, conflicts and reversals of status and class, economic production and crisis, codes of custom and conduct) serve abundantly as analogies for, or contrasts to, life in the kingdom of God. The term *basileia* itself, as Sverre Aalen has shown,[136] connotes not only the "reign" but also the "house" of God as a social and localized reality. In the Gospel of John the notion of "the believer's place in the domestic domain of God" is the household image underlying Jesus' reference to "my Father's house" (14:2).[137] Those who have access to this house are not merely servants of the master; they have been elevated to the status of friends. "You are my friends if you do what I command you. No longer do I call you servants (slaves), for the servant does not know what his master is doing; but I have called you friends, for all that I have heard from my Father I have made known to you" (John 15:14–15). Judge sees in these words a reflection of "the peculiar combination of intimacy and subordination that was characteristic of the institutionalized friendship conferred by the great patrons on trusted clients."[138]

The consequences of divided sociopolitical loyalties in the household as in the kingdom and the city, and the realities of household control (Matt. 12:25–30/Mark 3:23–27/Luke 11:17–23) constitute the rationale of Jesus' (and the Christian community's) self-defense against accusations of Satanic allegiance. The wider context of these verses in Mark's composition (3:20–35) illustrates the central importance which the formation of a new form of household acquires in the ecclesiological perspective of the Markan good news. "House," "household" and "family" function not only as link words for the combination of the separate sayings;[139] more importantly, they are parts of a unifying theme[140] for treating the issues of social division, demonic opposition and faithful obedience to the will of God as factors effecting membership in the household of Jesus.[141]

In Luke-Acts the household is prominently contrasted to the temple, the bankrupt seat of Jewish power and piety,[142] and to the city, the arm of "Caesar's network" and locus of social control. Yann Redalié has commented on these contrasts in connection with his analysis of the social and religious tensions which surfaced in the Pauline mission in Philippi (Acts 16:11–40).[143] In the Philippian episode, he observes, the scene shifts repeatedly from city to household. The scene opens in "Philippi which is the leading city of the district of Macedonia and a Roman colony" (v. 12), moves to the household of Lydia and their conversion (vv. 14–15), and then back to the agora, the slave girl, the charges of sedition and the imprisonment of Paul and Silas (vv. 16–24). From the city prison it leads again to the household of the jailer and their conversion (vv. 25–34), then back to the realm of the magistrates (vv. 35–39) and concludes with a departing visit to the household of Lydia and the consolation of the new family of believers (v. 40). This contrast of scenes, according to Redalié, reflects an underlying conflict of contending interest groups and ideologies. "These men are servants of the Most High God, who proclaim to you the way of salvation" (v. 17); "these men are Jews and they are disturbing our city. They advocate customs which it is not lawful for us Romans to accept or practice" (vv. 20–21). "In the long run," Redalié observes,

> the city is the place of authority, a piece of Caesar's network, a link in the power structure. At the beginning of the Gospel Bethlehem is the city where Joseph must register. In the short run the city is the social area which determines roles: "a woman who had a bad reputation in the city," "the poor of the city" etc. The roles of the woman of ill-repute, the judge, the poor, take shape in relation to the city.

"Oikos," the house, is not exactly the sphere of private life. In the New Testament the house is more of a social place, the social nexus that constitutes a person: the buildings, the goods, property, the family, the wife or husband, the children, the employees, or the servants. The house has a continuity that is inherited: "to be from the 'House of Jacob' or 'of David.'"

In addition to this meaning of house in the stories of conversion (Acts 10:2; 11:14; 16:15–31; 18:8), Acts explicitly shows a contrast between "what is public" and "what is not." Describing the places where the community acts, Luke says in Acts 5:42 and 26:46, "in the temple or at home," or in 20:20, "in public and from house to house." In Jerusalem public life is summed up in the temple, but when Paul is in the Roman world, the city is designated by the term *demosiai* (in the public presence).

Thus it seems that given the Jewish space, too narrow for Christians, and faced with the Roman space of the cities, one element of the strategy that Luke stages is the formation of an "independent" space for the Christian community: the house, place of baptism, catechism and sharing (cf. Acts. 16:30–33).[144]

For the Christians, in other words, the *oikos* constitutes not simply an additional form of social identity and religious allegiance alongside others such as the temple, the synagogue or the city. The Christian *oikos* is rather a decisive alternative according to Luke. Membership in the former involves constant conflict with and critique of the latter.

At the same time, the formation of a new household of faith was seen as a social process through which ancient animosities were overcome and diverse peoples and classes were united through a new order of values. In the new household of God, writes the author of Ephesians (2:11–22), "the dividing wall of hostility" between Gentile and Jew has been abolished. The two are made one not through an enforcement of law and ordinance but through a binding faith in the self-offering act of Christ. Those who were once "alienated from the commonwealth (*politeias*) of Israel and strangers (*xenoi*) to the covenants of promise, having no hope and without God in the world," those who were once "far off" now with those who were "near" have common "access in one Spirit to the Father. So then you are no longer strangers and resident aliens (*xenoi kai paroikoi*) but fellow citizens (*sympolitai*) with the saints and members of the household of God (*oikeioi tou theou*)" (au.). In this text, as in 1 Peter, we can see how several social, political and religious factors associated with the *oikos* are used to concretize a new vision of communal identity and solidarity.[145]

Here in Ephesians, ethnic differentiation, political alienation and human deprivation are familiar social realities used to compare and illustrate the new social dimension of salvation through faith in Christ, the unity of former enemies in the holy household of God.[146]

Membership in the household of God entails an intimate degree of familial relationship. The *oikeioi* of God are the "children" of God, sons and daughters of the divine *pater familias*.[147] Through the new bond of faith they are "sisters" (*adelphai*) and "brothers" (*adelphoi*) of the Lord and in the Lord.[148] Salvation as admission to the family and conferral of new status is described as an act of "adoption to sonship" (*huiothesia*) which was "not only legally but morally liberating, since it guaranteed rights of succession and afforded an unchallengeable security."[149] "But when the time had fully come, God sent forth his Son, born of woman, born under the law, to redeem those who were under the law, so that we might receive adoption as sons. And because you are sons, God has sent the Spirit of his Son into our hearts, crying, 'Abba! Father!' So through God you are no longer a slave but a son, and if a son then an heir" (Gal. 4:4–7; cf. Rom. 8:14–17).[150] The community of the believers is a "brotherhood" (*adelphotēs*, 1 Pet. 2:17; 5:9) whose mutual commitment is demonstrated and whose cohesion is maintained through the practice of "brotherly love" (*philadelphia*).[151]

As did the household institution of adoption, so that of slave manumission also served to illustrate the new freedom and status available in the household of faith.[152] Emancipation from the *potestas* of sin and evil, however, involved subjection to the *potestas* of God. "He has delivered us from the dominion of darkness and transferred us to the kingdom of his beloved Son, in whom we have redemption, the forgiveness of sins" (Col. 1:13–14). " . . . [Y]ou have been set free from sin and have become slaves of God . . . " (Rom. 6:22). Thus the images of slavery and servanthood could continue to describe the bond of dependency, submission and loyalty which existed between the believers and God and within the community.[153] Judge sees in the constant assertion that Christians are the servants of God "the most illuminating adaptation of household terms to theological ideas. . . . "

> These metaphors from slavery suggest how far the institution was appreciated as a means of support for the otherwise unrepresented and helpless. The bond frequently excited feelings not of resentment, but of personal

devotion and loyalty toward the master. Moreover, as with the centurion whose servant "was dear unto him" (Lk. vii. 2), the bond could be the basis of mutual affection.[154]

Common subordination to the will of God made slaves of one and all. "Live as free men, yet without using your freedom as a pretext for evil; but live as slaves of God" (1 Pet. 2:16 au.). This common slave (*doulos*) or servant (*diakonos*) status of *all* believers, leaders and other members of the brotherhood alike, vis-à-vis God, was a characteristic feature of the Christian movement. It was likewise *diakonia,* menial household service, which became a predominant term for describing collectively the various forms of mutual Christian ministration. The humble, unpretentious attitude of the household servant served as the fundamental criterion for a critique of all predilections for prestige and power, "So you also, when you have done all that is commanded of you, say, 'We are unworthy servants; we have only done what was our duty'" (Luke 17:10). In the figure of the servant and his lowly status in the conventional household, the believers saw the main example for the function of the Christ and the Christian in the *oikonomia* of God. The servant provided the paradigm, par excellence, for the inversion of status and values which distinguished the Christians from Gentiles and Jews alike.

> The kings of the Gentiles exercise lordship over them; and those in authority over them are called benefactors. But not so with you; rather let the greatest among you become as the youngest, and the leader as one who serves. For which is greater, one who sits at table, or one who serves? Is it not the one who sits at table? But I am among you as one who serves (Luke 22:25–27; cf. John 13:1–16).
>
> . . . But it shall not be so among you; but whoever would be great among you must be your servant, and whoever would be first among you must be slave of all. For the Son of man also came not to be served but to serve, and to give his life as a ransom for many (Mark 10:43–44/Matt. 20: 26–28).
>
> But you are not to be called rabbi, for you have one teacher and you are all brethren. And call no man your father on earth, for you have one Father, who is in heaven. Neither be called masters, for you have one master, the Christ. He who is greatest among you shall be your servant; whoever exalts himself will be humbled, and whoever humbles himself will be exalted (Matt. 23:8–12).

All this makes it abundantly clear that the significance of the household and the family for the mission, growth, organization and self-understanding of the Christian movement can hardly be overestimated. In the focus upon the household and the community as *oikos* of God we have a striking example of the correlation of social reality and theological reflection, of theory and praxis.

It is in view of this fact, namely, the dominant impact of the household upon the social situation and theological thought of the Christian movement, that the sparing use of *oikos* as a designation for "temple" in the New Testament must be understood and interpreted. The New Testament usage stands in striking contrast to that of the Old Testament (LXX) where *oikos (tou theou, kyriou)* is a frequent and standard designation for the Jerusalem temple. In fact, in only fourteen of the 114 New Testament occurrences of *oikos* does the term clearly refer to a temple or the temple. These fourteen instances, in turn, represent only five distinctively independent traditions and even here the sense of the term is determined in part by the Old Testament passages which are quoted.[155] In the vast majority of its New Testament occurrences (over 90 percent) *oikos* denotes a domicile or a domestic form of community. *To hieron* and *naos* are the conventional terms for "temple" and refer either to the Jewish temple in Jerusalem,[156] the Artemis temple in Ephesus,[157] the heavenly temple visualized in Revelation,[158] or, on four occasions, to the Christian community.[159]

Oikos and its paronyms, on the other hand, although possible terms for describing a temple as a building or its construction,[160] have no *intrinsic* connection with either temple or cult. When in the New Testament the Christian community is portrayed as a household (*oikos, oikeioi*) or a building (*oikodomē, oikodomein*) and the term "temple" is added, it is clear that the latter term represents an *expansion* and *extension* of thought.[161] In 1 Pet. 2:5 where the phrase *oikos pneumatikos* is frequently assumed to mean "spiritual temple," this is obviously *not* the case. The author(s), aside from conforming the language of v. 5d ("to offer spiritual sacrifices acceptable to God through Jesus Christ") to fit the activity of a "body of priests" (*hierateuma*, v. 5c), show(s) no interest throughout the remainder of the document in the idea of the Christians as a holy temple or cultic community. To the contrary, it is the Christian household of God upon which the letter focuses from beginning to end. The question concerning the significance and ramifications of the Christian-Jewish controversy over the Jerusalem temple and the identification of the Christian community as a new, different, or eschatological temple is indeed a crucial one.[162] However, it should not be allowed to obscure the semantic versatility of the term *oikos* or its predominant use in pointing to other domestic and sociopolitical aspects of early Christian life, organization and thought.

The various semantic features of *oikos* and its paronyms in the New Testament also imply a variety of its *functions* in Christian narrative, proclamation and exhortation. Historically, the *oikos* was the fundamental social locus and focus of the Christian movement. This was not simply a matter of record but of practical, psychological, sociological and theological consequence. It was in homes and from homes that the first adherents were sought. It was not merely individuals but entire households who were converted and transformed by the good news of human reconciliation and of the new possibilities of life in community. From a practical point of view it was the conversion of households which made possible the rapid growth, mobility and extension of the Christian mission. The sustenance of itinerant missionaries, the hosting of strangers, the care of the needy, the assembling of worshipers, and the economic self-sufficiency of the movement were all made possible by a growing network of Christian households. For the rootless, the aliens, the deprived and the dispossessed, association in a household offered a psychologically important sense of belonging and an opportunity for social integration. As a socially revered institution with honorable goals and values, this extended Christian family posed no necessary threat to existing political institutions. To the contrary, focus on the familial nature and character of the Christian community enabled the movement to accentuate precisely those virtues of social life which were held in respect by society as a whole.

On the other hand, the conception that the Christian community constituted one all-embracing "household of God" reinforced not only the internal solidarity and communality of the faithful but also their independence and distinctiveness vis-à-vis "outsiders." "But we exhort you, brothers, [to love the brothers] more and more, to aspire to live quietly, to mind your own affairs, and to work with your hands, as we have charged you; so that you may command the respect of outsiders, and be dependent on nobody" (1 Thess. 4:10–12 au.). "Conduct yourselves wisely toward outsiders, making the most of the time" (Col. 4:5).[163] Over against other forms of households the Christian community represented a distinctive contrast, be they the designs and ideology of the imperial household, the *oikoi* of the *collegia,* or the house of Israel. "Those who are supposed to rule over the Gentiles lord it over them, and their great men exercise authority over them. But it shall not be so among you . . . " (Mark 10:42–43). In regard to Judaism in particular the household origin and constitution of the Christian movement figured not only as a contrast to, but also as a critique of, temple hegemony and priestly ideology. The locus of salvation and reconciliation is no longer the temple but the home. The inception and inspiration of the Christian movement, the outpouring of the divine Spirit, occurred not in the temple according to Acts (2:1–42) but in an *oikos* (Acts 2:2). The *oikos* and not the *naos* is henceforth the locus of God's presence and benediction. Moses was but a servant *in* God's house, "but Christ was faithful *over* God's house as a son. And we are his house if we hold fast our confidence and pride in our hope" (Heb. 3:5–6). Its identity as the house of God expressed not merely Christianity's continuity with Israel but, more, its superiority.

In contrast to Judaism and Rome, its households characterized Christianity as a private rather than as a public affair. In contrast to the individualism of the cults, on the other hand, the Christian household offered incorporation into a family, a place for permanent belonging, a supportive circle of brothers and sisters. Such contrasts contributed to Christianity's distinctive social composition and hence to its effectiveness in competing with other groups for new members.

The household constitution and ideology of the Christian movement thus served the purposes of external comparison, contrast, competition and critique as well as internal consolidation. It provided the theoretical model and the practical basis for the articulation and institutionalization of the Christian vision of communal salvation.

This concludes our survey of the communal sense of *oikos* and its various ideological functions in the social and religious milieu of 1 Peter. The *oikos* (household) constituted the basic social structure according to which more extensive political, social and religious organizations were patterned. It provided the conceptual model, the vocabulary, and the pattern of roles, relationships and responsibilities with which integrated social, economic, political and religious life was described. Correlatively it set the standard for defining all those outside the household: the strangers, the aliens, the *paroikoi*. The implication that an entire empire (under the *potestas* of a *pater patriae*), a region (Egypt, Greece), a city (Apameia, Prusa), a *collegium,* or a religious community (Israel, Christianity) constituted a a household, or that a household was the equivalent of a commonwealth (Pliny), was a compelling factor in the achievement of order, concord (*synoikismos*), solidarity and loyalty. On the other hand, the independence of distinct households allowed room for the contrast and critique of one *oikos* over against another.

The communal meaning and use of the *oikos* concept in the social and religious world of 1 Peter, the household formation and ideology of the Christian movement, and the similar traditional use of *oikos* to designate the elect and holy people of God (cf. Philo, *De Sobr.* 66) strengthen the conclusion reached on internal evidence that in 1 Peter *oikos* refers to the elect believers as the "household of God."

The foregoing evidence concerning the social implications and applications of the household concept may serve now as a further guide for determining the *function* of the household theme within the social strategy of 1 Peter.

THE ADDRESSEES OF 1 PETER AS THE
HOUSEHOLD OF GOD

In the proclamation and parenesis of 1 Peter, perhaps more clearly and consistently than in any other New Testament document, the "household of God" functions as a major coordinating ecclesiological symbol. The long-standing and wide-ranging social, political, psychological and religious implications of the *oikos* in both the secular and sacred milieu of 1 Peter made the ecclesiological adaptation of this image for the Christian community possible. The household formations of the early Christian movement, moreover, made this embracing symbol for the Christian community sociologically plausible. Finally, the immediate catalyst which triggered such an identification of the Petrine community was the specific situation and condition of the Petrine audience and their need for some appropriately good news. Struggling as aliens, outsiders and second-class people in a strange and increasingly hostile environment and suffering from the suspicion, slander and resentment of their neighbors, the Christians of Asia Minor, according to 1 Peter, found themselves in a precarious situation. They lacked a sense of their distinctive communal identity, a clear vision of their social solidarity and divine vocation. In the Petrine response to this dilemma the affirmation of the readers as a Christian brotherhood, a household or family of God, played a decisive kerygmatic and hortatory role.

At the heart of the coordination of social situation and sociotheological response lies the correlation of the phenomena denoted by the formulations *paroikos* and *oikos tou theou*. That the household theme in 1 Peter is neither accidental nor incidental, but rather a basic component of the Petrine strategy is evident at several points throughout the letter.

1. This is indicated first by the *prominent use* of *oik-* terminology itself in 1 Peter. *Oikos* is twice used to designate the Christian readers as the "house(hold) of the Spirit" (2:5) or the "house(hold) of God" (4:17). The verb *oikodomeō* is used in the passive voice to describe the divine construction and integration of this house(hold) of faith (2:5). Within the household instructions the slaves are specifically called *household* slaves (*oiketai*, 2:18). The verb *synoikeō*, furthermore, which occurs only here in the entire New Testament, is used to depict the manner in which husbands should "live together" with their wives (3:7). Furthermore, "household stewards" (*oikonomoi*) is the term used to depict the recipients and servants of God's varied grace in 4:10. Finally, in contrast to these features of the household which belongs to God, *paroikos* (2:11) and *paroikia* (1:17) indicate the condition of the Christians within and vis-à-vis society.

2. A comparison with parallel New Testament material indicates that the *choice* of *oik-* terminology in 1 Peter was *deliberate*. This is patently obvious in the case of the New Testament *hapax legomenon synoikein*. Similar exhortation concerning the husband-to-wife relationship in Col. 3:19 and Eph. 5:25 (cf. vv. 28, 33) enjoins husbands to *love* their wives (*agapān*). In 1 Peter an expression more linguistically consistent with the household theme was preferred. In addition, the parallel *syn-* composites *synoikountes* and *synklēronomois* in 3:7 (cf. also the composite *sympatheis* in v. 8) underline the mutuality and solidarity of familial relationships, a theme of vital concern to the author(s). Spouses are to "cohabit as coheirs." Likewise, instruction on the slave-to-owner relationship found elsewhere in the New Testament speaks consistently of *douloi* rather than *oiketai* (Col. 3:22; Eph. 6:5–8; 1 Tim. 6:1; Titus 2:9; cf. Luke 2:29).

Again it may be surmised that in 1 Peter a term more explicitly reflective of household circumstances was preferred. In regard to the household building imagery of 1 Pet. 2:5, 1 Cor. 3:9–17 and Eph. 2:20–22 show the possible affinity between building imagery and the construction of a temple. In contrast to both passages, however, 1 Peter has spoken not of the building of a *naos* but of an *oikos*. Finally, a comparison of 1 Pet. 4:10–11 with other passages which enumerate the variety of charismatic gifts (e.g., Rom. 12:3–8; 1 Cor. 12:4–11, 28–30; Eph. 4:11) reveals that nowhere else but in 1 Peter are the recipients of the charismata described as *"household stewards* of God's varied grace." The Petrine preoccupation with household terminology is clear.

3. In addition to the *oik-* terminology itself, further related expressions and images have been employed to highlight the household and familial character of the community. The believing community is called a "brotherhood" (*adelphotēs*, 2:17; 5:9). Its members are encouraged to be "brother- (and sister-) lovers" (*philadelphoi*, 3:8). Those who have been reborn through the living and abiding word of God are to preserve their new familial solidarity by a "sincere love of the brothers" (*philadelphian anypokriton*, 1:22–23). *Adelphotēs* and *philadelphoi* occur nowhere else in the New Testament.[164] Once again the deliberate employment of unconventional vocabulary illustrates the specific emphasis on the household which is characteristic of the Petrine letter. Familial ties, furthermore, bind the senders as well as the recipients of the letter. Reference is made to Silvanus as "the faithful brother" (*tou pistou adelphou*, 5:12) and to Mark as "my son" (*ho huios mou*, 5:13). Within this context it is also likely that the elliptical phrase *hē en Babylōni syneklektē* implies a greeting from the coelect *sister* (*adelphē*)[165] who is in Babylon. The "kiss of love" (5:14) also, according to Goppelt,[166] is a gesture of brotherhood and familial solidarity.

Believers, moreover, are called *"children."* Faithful and fearless wives in particular are declared to be the spiritual children of Sarah, the mother par excellence of the chosen people (3:6). Male and female believers all together are the children of God *their Father.* To the foreknowledge and mercy of a heavenly Father they owe their election (1:1–2; 2:4–10), their rebirth through, and union with, his Son Jesus Christ (1:3, 21, 23; 2:2–3) and their continued reverence and obedience (1:2, 14–16, 17; 2:17). God is the ultimate *pater familias* of the household of faith. The idea of the fatherhood of God, and hence of the familial bond among those to whom he has given birth, is not far removed from the conception of God as "creator" or "founder." In 1 Pet. 4:19 (au.) the suffering Christians are encouraged to "do good and entrust their lives to a faithful creator" (or founder: *pistō ktistē*). The "household of God" mentioned in 4:17 would then constitute that community of which God was the particular (pro)-creator or founder. His *patria potestas,* so to speak, includes not only the power to procreate a family but also to judge it (1:17; 4:5, 17) and preserve it (5:10). God is the father-founder builder of the household, "the God of all grace who has called you to his eternal glory in Christ [and who] will himself restore, establish and strengthen you" (5:10).

The choice of terms in 4:10–11 also reflects the provenance of the household. Here the members of the community are told to "serve" (*diakountes,* v. 10; cf. also v. 11) one another with the various gifts of grace which they have received. As conventional usage indicates,[167] *diakonein* often denotes *domestic service* in particular, the daily round of household chores and menial tasks. By the time of 1 Peter, of course, *diakonein* and its paronyms could have become traditional terms for Christian ministrations in general. However, the specific identification of the agents of such service as "household stewards" makes the *domestic* dimension of this service here quite explicit. The service thus recommended would be the performance of practical tasks which were essential to the sustenance and growth of the household of faith.

The use or possible coinage of still another New Testament *hapax legomenon, allotriepiskopos,* in 4:16 may also be associated with a conception of the Christian household. As indicated earlier,[168] the term implies a we/they perspective, a distinction between "us" and "the others" (*allotri-*). The "others" are those who are outside the household of God (4:17). Christians, members of the household of God, are bound and judged by the will of God (4:19). If they suffer innocently for behaving as Christians, they glorify God. If, however, they were to disobey the rule of the household and suffer for behaving as Gentiles (as murderers, thieves, evildoers) or as meddlers in Gentile affairs (*allotriepiskopos*), they would betray the distinctive ethos of the household and fall under the condemnation of the ungodly and the sinner (4:18). To meddle in the business of outsiders is to endanger the integrity and cohesion of the household of God.

4. This last observation recalls what has already been mentioned concerning the significance of the *oikos tou theou* (4:17) for the passage 4:12–19 as a whole. Membership in the household of God sharply distinguishes and demarcates the believers from the nonbelievers, the glorious destiny of the former and the divine condemnation of the latter. Membership in the household of God determines the characteristic style and norm of one's behavior, the present suffering one can expect and the future vindication of which one can be sure. To be *outside* the household of God is to be a nonbeliever in the gospel of God (v. 17), an impious sinner (v. 18) who will surely be condemned by God for his rejection of the good news and his hostility to the brotherhood which has been constituted through the proclamation of that gospel (cf. 1:12, 22–25). To be *within* the household of God is to have communion with the Christ and his sufferings (4:13), to be blessed by the presence of the divine Spirit of glory (v. 14), to be obedient to God's will and therefore not to be a murderer, thief, evildoer or meddler in Gentile affairs (vv. 15–16), but rather to be one who bears Christ's name and emulates Christ's obedience, thereby glorifying God (v. 16), and, like the Christ, one who entrusts his life and destiny to the care of a faithful creator, sure of that Father's vindication (vv. 18–19). Thus, membership in the household of God provides here the socio-religious rationale for the distinction of Christian and non-Christian, the consolation of the suffering faithful, their exhortation to continued God-pleasing conduct, and the confirmation of the certainty of their salvation.

Other indications of the importance of the *oikos* concept in 1 Peter are the function of the phrase *oikos pneumatikos* (2:5) within the passage 2:4–10 and the role of the *oiketai* exhortation in 2:18–25. Both passages represent fundamental christological and ecclesiological statements of the letter. Both passages, moreover, reveal traces of redactional activity and emphasis.

5. The function of *oikos pneumatikos* within 2:4–10 has already been discussed at length. "(You are) a *house(hold)* of the Spirit" (au.), on the one hand, completes the image of the bond between the Lord, the living stone (2:4), and his believers, the "living stones" who are being built together by God (v. 5a). On the other hand, *"household of the Spirit"* is also the Petrine interpretation of one of the elective epithets, *basileion,* about to be applied to the believers in vv. 9–10. The semantic versatility

of the word *oikos* (house, household) makes it a useful term for uniting different traditions (vv. 6–8, 9–10) and different metaphors for the people of God. More importantly, in this way the author(s) have established the identity of the elected community as the household of faith. To be a member of the household of the Spirit is to be a member of the elect community with whom God dwells and over whom he reigns. This description of God's special people as the household of the Spirit establishes the basis for the following household exhortations concerning the distinctive conduct of the elected household of God (2:13 ff.).

The association of *oikos* and election which is explicit in 2:4–10 may also be implicit in the other instances where the believers are called "elect." In the salutation the recipients are referred to as the "elect visitors of the dispersion in . . . " (1:1 au.). "Visitor" and "dispersion" connote a condition of homelessness, *paroikia* (cf. 1:17; 2:11), and yet God-relatedness ("dispersion" as a designation for the dispersed *of God*). "Elect," in the light of 2:4–10 on the other hand, implies that though these visitors are without a home within the society of Asia Minor, nevertheless as believers they have been regathered (cf. 2:25) as the chosen household of God. At the conclusion of the letter the author(s) include greetings from the "coelect (Christian sister) in Babylon" (5:13). The parallel with 1:1 is striking. Again, "Babylon," like "dispersion," is a symbol for the present dislocation and homelessness of God's people. And again, "coelect," along with the familial metaphors "brother" (5:12), "sister" (inferred) and "son" (5:13), implies comembership in the elect household of God. The coordinated themes of *oikos* and election and the contrast between the *oikos* of God and their *paroikia* (in society) thus shape the letter from beginning to end.

6. The contribution of 2:18–25 to the household theme becomes evident when several of its noteworthy features are taken into consideration. First, in this exhortation to slaves the use of the term *oiketai* (v. 18) is striking. Occurring only four times in the New Testament,[169] it specifically designates *domestic* slaves, servants within the sphere of the household in contrast to the more general and more frequent term *doulos(-oi)*. Furthermore, apart from 1 Peter, it is never used as a reference to slaves in other New Testament exhortations concerning household duties (cf. Eph. 5:22–6:9; Col. 3:18–4:1; 1 Tim. 2:8–6:2; Titus 2:1–10) where the term *doulos* regularly occurs. Second, the *location* of this address to household slaves

is also striking. In contrast to the sequence of all other New Testament lists where the responsibilities of slaves are mentioned *last,* in 1 Peter they are singled out for *first* consideration.[170] Third, in contrast to the other lists again, although reference is made in 1 Peter to the slaves' owners (*despotai,* v. 18), nothing is said of these owners' reciprocal responsibilities.[171] The focus is directed exclusively to the condition and conduct of the household slaves. Fourth, the extension of the thought of vv. 18–20 through the christological passage of vv. 21–25 is noteworthy. Among the various members of the household addressed in 1 Peter (slaves, wives, husbands, elders, novices), it is only the exhortation to the household servants which is given an extensive christological foundation.

The explanation which best accounts for all these peculiarities is that this passage expresses something which is fundamental and paradigmatic for the *oikos* as a whole. The *choice* of the term *oiketai* rather than the customary *douloi* makes the *household* sphere of the instruction explicit. In Selwyn's words this choice "shews that the author has the life and welfare of the family in mind. He is thinking of slaves not as members of a social class . . . but as members of something more fundamental, i.e., the social *unit* of the *oikos* or home."[172] The term *oiketai* calls attention to the fact that what follows is exhortation and encouragement which concerns the household. Not only is it pertinent, it is also paradigmatic. What is said about the condition and vocation of the household slaves is in several basic respects typical of the condition and vocation of all the household. The exposure of the *oiketai* to harsh as well as kind owners (v. 18) typifies the vulnerability of *all* the *paroikoi* to the hostilities of their Gentile neighbors (2:11–12; 3:13, 16; 4:4, 12, 14, 16; 5:8–9). The possibility of their suffering although innocent (2:19–20) is characteristic of the experience of *all* the believers (1:6; 3:14, 17; 4:1, 13, 16, 19; 5:9–10).[173] As the *oiketai,* so *all* the Christians are to have clear consciences (2:19; 3:16, 21), to be subordinate to (2:13, 18; 3:1; 5:5) and act out of reverence for (1:17; 2:17, 18; 3:2) the will of God and thereby do good (2:14, 15, 20; 3:6, 17; 4:19). The calling of the *oiketai* (2:21) is the calling of *all* (3:9). The divine grace they enjoy (2:19, 20) for their steadfastness is the grace intended for *all* (1:2, 10, 13; 3:7; 4:10; 5:5, 10, 12). Thus the condition and experience, the attitude and the steadfastness, the vocation and the reward of the household slaves are paradigmatic for the household membership as a whole.

This accounts for the fact that it is specifically the household slaves whose conduct is grounded in and motivated by the innocent suffering of the Christ (vv. 21–25). The innocent suffering and steadfastness of the *servants* derive their power and motivation from the vicarious suffering of the *Servant of God*[174] par excellence. As the *oiketai* are exemplary for the household of God in its entirety, so their calling to follow in the footsteps of Christ (2:21) represents the calling of *all*. Thus the exhortation to *all* Christians in 3:13–17 followed by the substantiating christological passage of vv. 18–22 parallels the exhortation of *oiketai* in 2:18–20 followed by the christological passage of vv. 21–25.[175]

The paradigmatic function of the *oiketai* perhaps explains why no attention is given to the responsibilities of owners in this section. The focus is reserved for those alone whose condition and calling most clearly represent the situation and vocation of the entire household of God.

This in turn accounts for the prominent location of this slave parenesis at the *beginning* of the household code. The exhortation and encouragement given in this section underlie and coincide with all that is to follow. The term *oiketai* makes clear that what follows pertains to the *oikos*. Insofar as the *oiketai* are paradigmatic for all the members of the household of faith, all the members are in a certain sense *oiketai,* like *oikonomoi* (4:10), servants of one another. To address these exemplary members of the community first[176] is a most apt way of establishing at the outset the principles and prospects which govern the lives of all the members of the household of God.

This passage obviously plays a significant role in the social strategy of the author(s). Designation of the slaves as household servants underlines the household character of the community to which they belong. Singling out slaves as examples for all the believers demonstrates the new status and respect which such lowly persons might anticipate in the new Christian community. At the same time they illustrate the humility which is desirable of all (cf. 3:8; 5:5–6), particularly of those with possible pretensions toward domination, such as husbands (cf. 3:7) or leaders (5:1–5a).[177] Finally, their vulnerability is a sign of the social vulnerability of all suffering Christians and of the solidarity of the suffering brotherhood with its suffering Lord.

7. As 1 Pet. 2:18–25 illustrates the importance and function of the domestic theme in 1 Peter, so does the larger section of which this passage is

a part; namely, the *household scheme of exhortation* in 1 Pet. 2:13–3:9(12) and 5:1–5. Earlier in this study[178] it was observed that in 1 Peter this scheme provided a means for exemplifying and encouraging behavior which would contribute toward internal group cohesion. Now we are in a position to subject the household *context* as well as the *function* of the Petrine *Haustafel* to closer examination.

The Household Scheme of Exhortation

Recent studies on the New Testament *Haustafeln* including surveys of earlier research[179] show that there is no scholarly consensus on either question. A clearer understanding of the function of the Petrine or any of the individual New Testament *Haustafeln* has been hampered, in part, by a tendency to treat all the New Testament household codes *en bloc* rather than to inquire concerning a specific function of a code within a specific document. In part this lack of clarity is due to a further related factor. A prevailing tendency to regard the *form* of the household codes as *parenetic* (i.e., as general rather than specific exhortation) seems to have made the question concerning function inappropriate or even illegitimate. The question concerning function implies a certain relationship between social situation, authorial intention and conventional understanding. If, however, as is now generally agreed since the early work of Martin Dibelius and his student, Karl Weidinger,[180] the New Testament *Haustafeln* are parenetic in form, and if parenetic tradition is, as Dibelius has also asserted, *general* ethical exhortation unrelated to any specific situation,[181] then what remains to be said concerning any specific function of this material?

According to Dibelius and Weidinger, the New Testament *Haustafeln* represented a later Christian adaptation of Stoic codes of duty. The most that could be conjectured concerning their *Sitz im Leben* was a waning hope in an imminent parousia, a supposed abatement of the "hot breath of the first epoch,"[182] and an eventual Christian need to deal with the issue of ongoing life in the world.[183] The Christian *Haustafeln,* in their estimation, represented a late New Testament stage of Christian adjustment to a bourgeois ethic through an adoption of a conventional *Moral des Alltags.*[184] The exegetical weaknesses and ungrounded assumptions of these generalizations concerning the situation have been pointed out in recent critical treatments. Not only has the factor of the delay of the parousia been overplayed; too little attention has also been given to the differences between Christian and non-Christian parallels as well as to the variations among the New Testament materials. Furthermore, as James Crouch has noted,[185] even Dibelius conceded that such variations of the parenetic tradition imply indications of differing situations and specific needs. This variability and flexibility indicate the oral rather than a supposedly fixed literary catechismal *form* of the household tradition.[186] It also makes the question of the historical *occasion* or *stimulus* of the use of this material and its possible *function* a legitimate, if not a necessary, one. Accordingly, Wolfgang Schrage concludes:

> Thus the household codes are neither an unchangeable topos of New Testament ethics—for instance its immutable, indispensable kernel which would be repeated in stereotypical fashion—nor do they offer an ad-hoc ethic conceived from a singular moment and designed for unique situations. They rather combine traditional with situational affinities, convention with flexibility, and each primitive Christian teacher will have combined both of these features in a different manner.[187]

Prior to this relatively recent acknowledgement of the inseparable link between even parenetic tradition and situation, scholars had already implicitly recognized the unavoidability of the question concerning the occasion and function of the household codes. David Schroeder, for instance, who viewed the New Testament household codes as a unique Christian creation, suggested that they were developed in order to suppress social unrest among Christian wives and slaves who were in danger of drawing false conclusions from the Pauline gospel of the equality of all persons in Christ (Gal. 3:28).[188] More recently Crouch proposed along similar lines that the purpose of the Colossian *Haustafel* in particular was to combat "the excesses created by an overemphasis on the equality created by the Spirit."[189] "The historical context of the *Haustafel*," according to Crouch,

> is the clash between Hellenistic and Jewish forms of religiosity or, more specifically, between enthusiastic and nomistic tendencies in Hellenistic Christianity. The *Haustafel* itself was formulated in nomistic circles to combat what was regarded as the growing danger posed by enthusiastic excesses . . . the standards of the social order were being attacked *en kyriō*.[190]

Schrage, on the other hand, has proposed that the household codes express an "offensive" and not simply a "defensive" Christian position.[191]

Over against a danger of Christian withdrawal from the world, he suggests, the household codes were used to encourage a Christian engagement with the structures of society. According to Schrage, the purpose of the *Haustafeln* was to enjoin Christians to practice their obedience to the Lord "not in a ghettoized sphere isolated from the world . . . not in pure inwardness or solely in a churchly conventicle but also in the social sectors of society."[192]

While such attention to the occasion and function of the household codes represents an important exegetical advance in general, the contribution of these studies toward an understanding of the Petrine *Haustafel* in particular is problematic. This is the case for two main reasons. First, the specific situation, structure and needs of the Petrine audience are either ignored completely or they are inaccurately surmised. Seeing the error of a generalizing and harmonizing treatment of the Christian *Haustafeln* en bloc,[193] Crouch intentionally—and justifiably—concentrates on the Colossian code. Thus his analysis, like that of Schroeder, is restricted to problems involving a Pauline proclamation of freedom and its consequences and an internal Christian conflict between enthusiastic and nomistic circles. The situation of 1 Peter and the conflict between sect and society clearly pose a problem of a different order. Accordingly, a more apposite function of the Petrine household code must be sought.

Second, where 1 Peter *is* included in a discussion of the function of the household codes, disagreement on the details of its historical situation poses a problem for the determination of the code's function. As an illustration we may consider the position of Schrage whose commentary on 1 Peter and article on the *Haustafeln* represent some of the most recent thought on both subjects. A certain incongruity in Schrage's remarks raises doubt as to the accuracy of his analysis. On the one hand, Schrage describes the Petrine situation as one of suffering and stress due to the hostile attitude of the surrounding society. The concern of the author is "that unnecessary confrontations and provocations be avoided in order to avoid giving the Gentiles any excuse for their accusations."[194] Within such a situation of conflict and tension between Christians and society, the social-critical function of the code which Schrage notes[195] makes complete sense. Incongruous, on the other hand, is the observation that "the *Haustafel* of 1 Peter . . . is by no means to be conceived as the result of an antithesis but as an explication of the commanded steadfastness within the daily affairs of the world and its structures" (au.).[196] Equally incongruous with

Schrage's first description of the Petrine situation is the implication that the problem which the household codes combat is one of a Christian ascetic flight from the world.[197] Is the situation one in which the Christians are engaged in conflict with society or one in which they are fleeing from society? Are the Christian addressees inclined toward asceticism or toward assimilation? Is the purpose of the Petrine code to discourage "social withdrawal" or to facilitate social competition and conflict?

One factor which may have contributed to the inconsistencies and inconclusiveness of Schrage's analysis is his lack of attention to the sectarian character of the Petrine audience. As a sect, the Christian community in Asia Minor was struggling to maintain its distinctive identity and group solidarity under adverse social circumstances. Social and cultural assimilation rather than ascetic isolation posed the most imminent danger to its existence and growth. The function of the household parenesis must be seen in relation to these two eminent sectarian needs. On the one hand, the social-critical emphasis of the code which Schrage has noted reinforced the distinctive and separate identity of this group. On the other hand, the household code also provided the means for stressing the social engagement and responsibilities of the Christians *within* the sect, thereby serving to foster group solidarity. Indeed, as Schrage asserted, the household code reminded Christians of the need for social engagement. For a sect, however, it is not engagement with *outsiders* which is necessary or even desirable but rather intensive support and cooperation *within* the group. Furthermore, the social conflict in which the Christians were involved is a certain proof and guarantee of their "engagement" with the structures of society.

A further weakness in Schrage's analysis, and in virtually all earlier analyses, of the household codes is the failure to explore sufficiently the relation between the household codes and the household character of the community in which and for which this traditional material was employed. Two related studies of Karl Heinrich Rengstorf[198] represent an important exception to this general tendency. According to Rengstorf, the chief characteristic of the New Testament *Haustafeln* is "that they comprehend the 'household' in its structural and sociological totality, namely, in house-parents, house-children and house-dependents; that they thus claim to be complete 'household codes'" (au.).[199] In contrast to non-Christian parallels, Rengstorf noted, it is important to see "that the [New Testament] *Haustafeln* concern admonitions which expressly concern the *oikos,* that is, the *familia* and its members" (au.).[200] They thereby reflect an explicit and emphatic Christian interest in the relationships which constitute the fundamental form of human communal life in antiquity and an interest in the regulation of such relationships for the well-being of all members of the Christian community.[201]

The failure of scholarship to appreciate and pursue Rengstorf's observations perhaps is due to a remark regarding the uniqueness of the Christian codes. For Rengstorf the peculiarity of the New Testament *Haustafeln* is marked by the choice and sequence of the subject matter which in its *comprehensiveness* manifested the household dimension of the thus explicitly household codes.[202] This observation concerning the peculiar formation and emphasis of the Christian codes, however, has been mistaken as an assertion of the unique Christian *origin* of these codes. In this formulation of the traditional code as an explicitly *household* code he saw "a genuine Christian creation" (*Schöpfung*).[203] The term *Schöpfung* here is perhaps somewhat unclear and misleading. Having already discussed pre-Christian hellenistic and Jewish versions of the codes,[204] he is clearly not speaking of their unique Christian *origin.* Elsewhere he speaks more precisely of their "early Christian formation" (*urchristliche Prägung*).[205]

Nevertheless, Crouch, for example, dismisses Rengstorf's observations out of hand. Against the notion that the *Haustafeln* represent a concern to regulate the relations among the members of the early Christian *oikos,* Crouch maintains: "In reality, however, our N.T. texts nowhere claim to be *Haus*-Tafeln. The *oikos* concept which Rengstorf finds decisive for our understanding of the origin [!] of the *Haustafeln* is not to be found in any of the *Haustafeln* nor in their immediate context."[206] Crouch not only misconstrues Rengstorf's point concerning the Christian originality of the household codes; he also gives no thought to the possible household implications of the *oikos* vocabulary in Colossians, Ephesians or 1 Timothy.[207] And he completely disregards the contextual association of *oikos* and the household code in 1 Peter.[208]

Schrage, on the other hand, although referring to the household sphere of the codes only in passing, does seem to give this factor implicit acknowledgement.[209] Nonetheless, his reference to the *"Pflichtenreihen"* or *"Pflichtentafeln"* (codes of duty) of the New Testament and his reservations concerning the formulation *"Haustafel"*[210] leave it unclear as to the precise sense in which he considers these *Tafeln* to be *Haus-Tafeln.*

The studies of Crouch and Schrage and the previous literature on the household codes which they have reviewed reveal that important issues concerning the household implications of the codes and their social-theological function still remain unsettled. In comparison with the analyses about to be discussed they represent a phase of research on the household codes whose termination is signaled by the introduction of fresh perspectives.

About the time that I presented an initial draft of the thesis of this book to the annual meeting of the Pacific Coast Section of the Society of Biblical Literature,[211] two studies dealing with related material appeared on the scene. D. L. Balch had just completed his Yale doctoral dissertation on the origin, form and function of the household code of 1 Peter (1974).[212] An article also dealing with the New Testament household codes by Professor Dieter Lührmann of the Kirchliche Hochschule in Bethel, Germany, appeared in the following year, 1975.[213] All three investigations were carried out independently and vary in the scope and nature of the subject matter discussed. Nevertheless, on the matter of a new approach to the household codes and their literary and social context, our independent researches seem to share a surprising—and a welcome—measure of agreement. In contrast to earlier scholarship each of us in his own way has recognized and pursued the evident relationship between the household, household management and the household codes. The evidence which Balch and Lührmann have collected corroborates from another perspective the contention put forward here; namely, that the *oikos* or household constituted for the Christian movement as well as for its environment a chief basis, paradigm and reference point for religious and moral as well as social, political, and economic organization, interaction, and ideology.

The studies of Balch and Lührmann demonstrate in particular the ancient and continuous proximity of the subject matter of the household codes to that concerning political ethics (*politeia*) and household management (*oikonomia*). "In approaching this material," Balch states, "I have found two observations to be of basic importance. ... "

The first was made by Friedrich Wilhelm;[214] it is that the three topoi "concerning the state" (*peri politeias*), "concerning household management" (*peri oikonomias*), and "concerning marriage" (*peri gamou*) were so combined and interrelated that it is difficult to distinguish them clearly.

213

Second, I observe that the second of these topoi is nearly identical with the topos which usually is referred to by its German designation *"Haustafel."*[215]

Similarly, Lührmann has noted that the closest literary affinities to the New Testament *Haustafeln* in form, content and emphasis are not the amorphous Stoic "codes of duty" but "a totally different tradition which can be subsumed under the title *oikonomia* or *ho oeconomicus"* (au.).[216]

Lührmann cites five main textual examples (Xenophon's *Oeconomicus*,[217] the first book of Aristotle's *Politics*,[218] the fragmentary *oikonomia* of Philodemos of Gadara, the selection of Hierocles' *Oikonomikos, peri oikōn*,[219] and Seneca, *Epist.* 94) and assumes that their number could be increased.[220] This is precisely what Balch has done through an extensive survey of material from Plato and Aristotle to hellenistic Judaism and the Roman period.[221] This abundant material, as Balch shows, illustrates the antiquity, continuity and universality of the association between the subject matter "concerning the *politeia"* and that concerning "household management" (*oikonomia*).[222] In Aristotle's fundamental statement (*Politics* 1, 1253a 37) on the component parts of the state (*polis*), household management (*oikonomia*) and the household ("master and slave, husband and wife, father and children") Balch finds "the most important extant parallel to the New Testament *Haustafeln."*[223]

According to both Balch and Lührmann, the New Testament household codes clearly stand within what the latter has called an *"oikonomia* tradition."[224] In describing the differences between this tradition and the Stoic codes of duty, however, Lührmann notes much more clearly than Balch the *household* dimension of this material. It is not simply the standard *triadic schema* (husband-wife, father-children, master-slaves) and the concern with the *reciprocity* of these relationships which, as such, distinguish the household tradition from the Stoic *Pflichtenkataloge*. It is also and especially the fact that these features of the household tradition demonstrate the *household* dimension and focus of the material. "In the *oikonomia*," observes Lührmann, "the concern is for the relationships within a household" (au.).[225] This fundamental feature of the *oikonomia* tradition thus corroborates the accuracy of Rengstorf's observation concerning the specifically household character of the New Testament household codes.[226]

Both Balch and Lührmann agree that the close association of the New

Testament household codes with the *oikonomia* texts and traditions has important implications for the *function* of the household codes in the early church. The difference in the implications which they actually draw is due in no small part to the weight which each puts on the relation of Christian *oikos* and Christian household codes. Although Balch deals directly and extensively with the text and context of 1 Peter, his interpretation of the function of the Petrine *Haustafel*, isolated from any consideration of its relation to the *oikos* thematic of the letter, fails to be convincing. Lührmann's remarks, while briefer and broader, nevertheless provide a more adequate perspective for appreciating the correlated function of both *oikos* and household code in 1 Peter and its situation.

The function of the Petrine household code, Balch maintains, was an apologetic one. As all new and foreign cults before them, including Judaism, the sectarian addressees of 1 Peter were being subjected to stereotypical criticisms of sedition, immorality, and of "reversing" traditional household relationships. Following the example of their slandered predecessors, the Christians responded with a defense of their behavior and of the order of their households, similar to Josephus' apologetic, *Against Apion*. 1 Peter, according to Balch, "is addressed to small sectarian Christian groups whose members live in households and cities which are only partially Christian. Society was hostile toward the new, foreign religious community because it was understood to be disturbing proper rule and harmony in house and state."[227] "So the author," Balch explains,

> exhorts the recipients of his letter to the behavior outlined in the Haustafel with the intention of encouraging conduct which would contradict the slanderers. Such behavior would have been demanded, not only by pagan masters and husbands, but also by the aristocratic Roman "governors" mentioned in I P[et.] 2:14. Christians were instructed to give "a defense to anyone who asks"; in this context this means that Christians would outline their *politeia*—the Haustafel—to outsiders, even to the governor concerned to maintain the Roman *politeia*. The customs of the Christians would not subvert the Roman *politeia,* it would be claimed, despite the fact that Christian slaves and wives refused to worship Roman gods. . . . The Haustafel constituted both part of the Christians' "defense" and part of the praise they hoped for from the governor. Christians were claiming that their habits did not subvert the Roman *politeia*. This helped Christians, as a new and foreign religious group, assimilate to Roman society.[228]

215

Such an explanation, I would suggest, misconstrues the function of the Petrine code in particular and the strategy of 1 Peter in general.

The crux of Balch's argument is the dubitable association which he postulates between 1 Peter and Josephus' *Against Apion.*

> It is centrally important that the word "defense" (*apologia*) in I P[et.] 3:15 has its closest parallel in Josephus *Against Apion* II.147.[229] The "defense" anticipated in I P[et.] 3:15 would include the ethics of the Haustafel, just as Josephus' "defense" involved the presentation of Moses' *politeia* which included "marriage laws" (II.199) and "the law for slaves" (II.215). . . . That Christians would outline their *politeia* to outsiders if asked (I P[et.] 3:15) has its antecedents in Philo, *Hypothetica* 7.14 and Josephus, *Against Apion* II.178, 181.[230]

In point of fact, however, Josephus' treatise and 1 Peter have little *specifically* in common. Of course there is the rather obvious fact that Josephus' apology, a composition from "the beginning of the second century,"[231] can hardly have provided an "antecedent" for the composition of 1 Peter which was completed before the turn of the first century. In form, content and function, however, the documents also differ significantly. According to Balch, *Against Apion* has the form of an "encomium" of the Jewish nation and its *politeia;* as an *apologia* (II.147) it is addressed primarily to *outsiders.* 1 Peter, on the other hand, is a letter of exhortation and encouragement (5:12) addressed solely to Christian *insiders.* The term *apologia* used in 1 Pet. 3:15 describes not the form, content or function of the letter as composed but the kind of response which the addressees *might* offer sometime in the foreseeable future after the reception of the letter. Indeed, allusion might then be made to the harmony of their households. Within its present literary context, however, the Petrine *Haustafel* is used to exhort the household members themselves. The single term *apologia* (*Against Apion* II.147; 1 Pet. 3:15) is hardly sufficient basis for establishing a "close parallel" between the two documents. Nor is the form or content of the Petrine *Haustafel* itself realistically comparable to the extensive expatiation of Josephus. While both touch on the subject matter of household roles, the household code can hardly be considered a full-fledged elaboration of the Christian *politeia* as *Against Apion* is of the Jewish *politeia.* Furthermore, the specific passages of Josephus' work to

216

which Balch refers (II.147, 178, 181, 199, 215) nowhere include the specific characteristics of the Petrine or New Testament household codes; namely, a triadic schema, stress on reciprocity of relationships, and a concern for the integrity of the household.[232] This is due to the fact, I would suggest, that the Petrine *Haustafel* has a *function* which differs from the general reference to the laws concerning marriage or slaves in Josephus' *Against Apion*.

For a determination of the function of the Petrine *Haustafel*, it is not a comparison with Josephus' *Against Apion* but rather a consideration of the situation and strategy of 1 Peter which provides the surest clues. Balch by no means neglects this latter point, but in my opinion he misconstrues the strategy of the Petrine author(s). He refers in passing to the addressees as composing "small sectarian Christian groups,"[233] but pays insufficient attention to the condition and needs of these sectarians. Hence he fails to perceive the nature and strategy of the Petrine response.

Faced with their suffering as a result of unfounded Gentile slander and typical animosity toward foreigners, the Christian sectarians indeed needed to "set the record straight" concerning their respect for law and order, civil and private. The urgent exhortations to separation from Gentile ways (1:14–16; 2:11; 4:2–5) and the variety of emphases upon distinctive group identity and behavior, however, make it clear that something more serious than a clean record or a defensible posture before the nonbelievers was at stake. The existence and growth of the sectarian movement itself were imperiled. Attacks from without were corroding or impeding cohesion within. The Petrine strategy was to avert such forces of social disintegration through a reinforcement of the distinctive identity of the Christian community and of its socioreligious cohesion. Stress upon the household identity of the community and on the importance of its God-pleasing maintenance of familial integrity was a major accent of the Petrine response. If effective, such a strategy could avert the disintegrative dangers of despair, renunciation of the faith, and the return of converts to their previous Jewish or pagan associations.

Balch's interpretation takes only one aspect of this complex social problem into account. In his view "the purpose [of the *Haustafel*] is to reduce tension between society and the church, to stop the slander. Christians must conform to the expectations of Hellenistic society, so that society will cease criticizing the new cult."[234] The mention of harmony which he notes in 1 Pet. 3:8–9[235] is seen as a reminiscence of an "old topos" rather than as a socially conditioned imperative. Thus he underestimates both the critique of society encouraged in the *Haustafel* (2:13–17) as well as the code's purpose of integrating internal community life. The social conformity and assimilation which, in his view,[236] the Petrine *Haustafel* is intended to foster are precisely the dangers which 1 Peter through the household instruction intended to discourage. Had he paid attention to the role of the household code within the comprehensive *oikos* ideology of 1 Peter, perhaps this one-sided conclusion concerning the apologetic function of the *Haustafel* could have been avoided.

In sum, while Balch's study provides much valuable material for a fresh analysis of the function of the New Testament *Haustafeln,* his interpretation of 1 Peter[237] and its household code remains inconclusive. The household instruction of 1 Peter and the stress upon the household/familial character of the Christian community have as their common focus *the internal as well as the external* relations of the addressees.

Lührmann's comments on the internal integrative function of the New Testament household codes in general and their relation to the household formations and ideology of the early church lend this observation added support. Lührmann shows the use of the *Haustafeln* in post-Pauline Christianity to be a continuation of the socioreligious concerns of the earlier Pauline period. Comparing the form and content of the *Haustafeln* with such Pauline passages as Gal. 3:28, 1 Cor. 12:13 and 7:21–24 and the letter to Philemon, he notes that the common point at issue is the stimulus which the new Christian vision of salvation provides for new forms of social community and relationships. That which Christianity offered ancient society with its antiquated and objectionable forms of social differentiation was "new possibilities of identification which become concrete in social community" (au.).[238] The proclamation of a communal rather than an individual salvation grounded in an identification with the crucified Christ served not as a legitimation of social revolution but indeed as a lasting impulse for the creation of new traditions and forms of Christian social life.[239] Among the various possible patterns of communal life, only a few proved viable in the later post-Pauline phases of the Christian movement. Here the issue was not so much a supposedly waning hope in the parousia but, as expressed already in the earlier Pauline texts, how it was possible for an eschatological community to be realized *"under the conditions of this world"* (au.; original emphasis).[240]

One such viable form of community through which both the new identity and integrity of the Christian movement could be established was the household. Already from the beginning of the Christian mission it had provided the social and economic "crystallization point of the new communities and thereby also shaped the social structure of these communities" (au.).[241] Clarification of the new lines of relationship and new modes of responsibility within these Christian households was accomplished through the instruction contained in the household codes. The use of these codes implies neither the sacrifice of an eschatological ethic nor the yearning for conformity. Their aim was rather the promotion and strengthening of the social bonds upon which the life of the Christian movement depended, namely, those of the household.[242] At the same time, the link between this *oikonomia* tradition and political ethics means that the *Haustafeln,* as in 1 Pet. 2:13–17, include "a latent political claim" and facilitate a critique of conventional societal conditions.[243]

The function of the household codes, in Lührmann's view, is to concretize the communal implications of the early Christian proclamation of salvation. The literature in which these codes are found, including 1 Peter, reflects a continuous Christian concern since Paul for establishing the communal identity and integration of the Christian movement. The household and household instruction together provided an indispensable means and model for accomplishing this constructive task amid the destructive forces both inside and outside the Christian body.[244]

In his approach to the situation and structure of the early Christian communities and the function of the household codes in general, Lührmann has arrived at conclusions which concur with and corroborate the observations made in this present study concerning 1 Peter and its domestic code in particular. "Identity" and "integration" appear to both of us to be key terms for describing the social needs of the Christian sectarians and the function of their literature and socioreligious strategies. We further concur on the central role which the household played within the Christian movement. It stimulated the Christian adaptation of traditional household instruction and provided a concept of the entire believing community as the household of God.

Thus, from different starting points Lührmann and I have moved to conclusions similar to those of E. A. Judge. Of the bifocal internal and external social Christian perspective which its household formation and theology represent he writes:[245]

> With regard to the household obligation, the New Testament writers are unanimous: its bonds and conventions must at all costs be maintained. . . . There is of course no mistaking in this [as the case of Philemon suggests] the interest of the patronal class which normally sponsored Christianity to its dependents, but the *primary reason* [emphasis added] no doubt is that the entrenched rights of the household as a religious and social unit offered the Christians the best possible security for their existence as a group. Any weakening here would thus be a potentially devastating blow to their own cohesion, as well as having revolutionary implications from the point of view of the public authorities. . . . It was only within the intimacy of the Christian associations themselves, untrammelled by past history or ulterior objects, that free expression could be given to the principles of fraternity. . . .

On the other hand, Judge points out:

> It could be disastrous if enthusiastic members failed to contain their principles within the privacy of the association, and were led into political indiscretions or offences against the hierarchy of the household. Hence the growing stress on good order and regular leadership within the associations themselves.

Finally, he notes, that it was also in this context "that the tradition of the frank and uninhibited social criticism of Jesus was maintained."

This concludes our survey of the features of 1 Peter that illustrate the major role which the identification and exhortation of the Christian addressees as the household of God play in the letter. We are now in a position to consider the role and socioreligious function of the household theme within the general strategy of 1 Peter.

THE ROLE AND FUNCTION OF THE HOUSEHOLD THEME
IN 1 PETER: A SUMMARY

The deliberation with which *oikos* terminology, imagery and tradition have been selected, arranged and accentuated in 1 Peter indicates the major role which the concept of the household (of God) plays in the *literary and theological integration* of the letter. In 1 Peter, moreover, the ecclesiological image of the believing community as the family of God also has a key *social* significance, a *sociological as well as literary and theological function.*

The symbolization of the people of God as an *oikos* or household is no creation of the author(s) of 1 Peter, however central its role in this document. On the contrary, this concept of community had its roots in the age-old universal importance of the *oikos* in secular as well as religious history. It is from a universal interest in the implications and applications of the household in a great variety of political, economic, social and religious spheres of life that the image of the household of God in 1 Peter derives its socioreligious significance and its emotional power.

In secular society, as the preceding pages have shown, the *oikos* constituted the primary social unit and model for the genesis of broader, more encompassing structures and concepts of communal life. The practical and moral reflections on the management and maintenance of the *oikos,* namely, *oikonomia,* provided a traditional mode for the discussion of the roles, relationships and responsibilities which characterized the governing of life in the larger social arena of the *polis,* namely, its *politeia.* Incorporation within an *oikos,* whether a natural local household or another form of social group which offered the protection and solace of a home, was a universal desire. This was especially true in an age of anxiety, turmoil and dislocation such as that of the hellenistic Roman era. To the countless number of displaced and dispossessed strangers and aliens of this period, membership in an *oikos,* be it in a community of fellow expatriots, fellow immigrants, co-tradesmen or coreligionists, meant the possibility of at least a minimal degree of social security and of a psychological sense of belonging. For these same reasons the offer of a home to the homeless constituted a powerful element in the current political as well as religious missionary propaganda. The propagation of the notion of a new universal *patria* or fatherland to which all subjects of the Roman empire belonged and the declaration of the emperor as *pater patriae* figured significantly in the legitimation of the consolidating efforts of the Caesars, their monopolization of authority and the subordination of their multinational subjects.

Throughout the various stages of Old Testament social history the household also served as a basis of communal self-definitions of the people of God. "House" or "household" designated both the narrower and the broader forms of social, political, ethnic and religious community. The contrast of *oikos* (linked regularly with "the land" and meaning Israel's "home") and *paroikia* (= "homelessness") occurs regularly in the narration of the oscillating history of Israel's bond with or break from the covenant will of its God. The fate of the temple as the house or dwelling place of God among his people was likewise inseparably linked with the fidelity or infidelity of the house of Israel and the house of Judah. Among the prophets the reconsolidation and renovation of the communal house of Israel along with the reconstruction of its house of worship figured centrally in the eschatological expectations concerning life in communion with God.

In the New Testament, *oikos* was still occasionally used to designate a dynastic or ethnic or national entity, such as the house of David or of Israel. Likewise, on occasion, the Jerusalem temple was referred to as the "house of God." With related terminology the believing community was also depicted occasionally as the eschatological temple in which the Spirit of God now dwells. In the predominant number of its occurrences, however, *oikos* with its paronyms was used to describe the social starting point and focal point of the Christian movement. The *oikos* was the household which constituted the focus, locus and socioreligious nucleus of the ministry and mission of the Christian movement. Historically, the movement originated in and owed its growth to the conversion of households or representative members thereof. Economically, the *oikos* and the hospitality it provided were the practical basis of the everyday support, material self-sufficiency, mobility and geographical extension of the Christian missionary enterprise. Where, through individual conversions, old familial ties were ruptured, new fraternal bonds of unity supplanted them—bonds which were inspired by a common faith in Jesus as the Christ and mutual subordination to the will of God as he articulated it in his message and ministry. Socially, the *oikos* provided a practical basis and theoretical model for Christian organization as well as its proclamation and exhortation. The household served as the paradigm for delineating respective roles, relationships and responsibilities within the religious community. The *oikos* suggested familiar as well as familial imagery for depicting both the religious and the social dimensions of life in the kingdom of God. With its wide field of associated terms and images such as fatherhood, childhood, birth, adoption, brotherhood, fraternal love and domestic service, the household supplied powerful social, psychological and theological symbols for depicting the radical and comprehensive nature of Christian conversion and cohesion, the commonality of Christian values and goals, and the distinctive character of communal Christian identity. The use of *oikos* to designate the consolidation of individual Christian households into one all inclusive macrohousehold of God is analogous to the similar expansion of the term *ekklesia*. Both terms, *oikos* and *ekklesia,* originally were employed by Christian missionaries to depict local individual households or public assemblies of believers, respectively. In the eventual expansion and consolidation of the Christian movement both terms also were used subsequently in a comprehensive manner to designate the sum total of Christian *oikoi* and *ekklesiai* as constituting the one universal household or assembly of God.

This concern with social or ecclesial consolidation which is suggested by the presence of the *oikos* imagery of 1 Peter is related, in turn, to the factors which account more immediately for the use and function of the *oikos* terminology and tradition in this letter. More than conventional social and religious associations of *oikos* in the secular and sacred milieu of 1 Peter can be seen to have determined the role and function of the *oikos* material here.

It is possible that the immediate geographical and social environment of the authors and addressees of 1 Peter influenced the choice of ecclesial metaphors. For both Rome[246] and Asia Minor[247] in particular, scholars have occasionally observed, there is evidence to suggest that an early (in the case of Rome) and an enduring (in the case of Asia Minor) form of communal Christian organization was that of the household. If this is so, then it is conceivable, if not likely, that in literature associated with these localities the specific form of household organization has influenced the terminology and imagery used to portray the religious composition and character of the Christian community. This point, however, needs to be examined in more detail[248] before it can shed definitive light on the stimuli of 1 Peter.

The clearest and most direct evidence for the factors that motivated the choice of the household terminology and symbolism of 1 Peter is to be seen in the specific condition and needs of the audience to which the letter is addressed. The foregoing analysis of this point has shown that in the letter of 1 Peter the condition of its addressees is one of geographical dislocation; social, cultural and religious dissociation and estrangement;

political, legal, social and psychological inferiority or marginal social status; and physical and psychological deprivation and vulnerability. Their conversion to the Christian faith had exacerbated their already tenuous social position as *paroikoi*. The exclusivity requirements of their new religious sect, when confronted by the ignorance, suspicion and disdain with which the native population conventionally encountered exotic religions from the East, had led to a further diminishment of their social status and self-esteem. It had led also to sporadic outbreaks of social conflict. Labeled "Christ-lackeys" (*Christianoi*) by the Gentile "insiders" and suffering from having been made the butt of social recrimination, slander, and unjust reproach for supposedly being fanatic and immoral nonconformists, the sectarian "outsiders" were in danger of allowing these external pressures to erode their internal group consciousness, confidence, cohesion and commitment. Suffering was leading to fear and to a diminishment of hope concerning the actuality of their status before God, the solidarity of their bond with one another, and the certainty of their imminent salvation. The serious social consequences of such disillusionment involved the impairment of internal solidarity or its disintegration; Christians were bickering among themselves, reproaching or exploiting each other. In an attempt to avoid suffering they were also succumbing to the external pressures calling for assimilation and social conformity. The potential loss of a distinctive group identity in turn undermined the very basis of the call for conversion. The sacrifice of the peculiarity and communion of the Christian cause which had once attracted the present converts in the first place threatened not only the continuation of the movement's momentum but also any conceivable missionary success among the Gentiles in the near future. In order for this jeopardized religious movement in Asia Minor to survive, let alone flourish and expand, three related factors required attention. The dangerous and deteriorating situation called for: (1) a reassertion of the Christian converts' distinctive communal identity; (2) a reinforcement of their internal group cohesion; and (3) a plausible interpretation of the compatibility of their experience and their expectations, of their social condition and their divine vocation.

1 Peter constitutes a perceptive and sympathetic response to such a complex of socioreligious needs. For this reason it indeed must be appreciated for what it itself claims to be (5:12): namely, a fraternal letter of encouragement and exhortation, consolation and confirmation.

The purpose of the letter is obscured and the detection of its strategy is hindered, however, when its response to these specific needs is not seen. The same is true when the response is not clearly distinguished from the precipitating situation of the addressees. While the foregoing description of the condition and needs of the audience may be deduced from the internal evidence of 1 Peter, other theories concerning the situation of the recipients lack such internal corroborating evidence. There are neither convincing internal nor external data to support the hypothesis, for instance, that the problem to which 1 Peter was a response was an imperially mounted official worldwide persecution of those who bore or admitted to the name "Christian." Such a theory relies upon undemonstrable assumptions concerning the date of 1 Peter, the existence of an official imperial policy regarding the Christians as well as the intensity and extent of its execution, and the hypothetical interpretations of terms such as *apologia* (3:15), *peirasmos* (1:6; 4:12), *pyrōsis* (4:12) and passages such as 4:15–16 or 5:8–9. Nor has a convincing case been made for a situation in which the Asia Minor Christians were "emigrating" from society or withdrawing into quasi-ascetic ghettos. The foregoing analysis has shown that precisely the opposite was most likely the case. The problem was not one of religious asceticism but of cultural assimilation.

Thus the response of 1 Peter cannot be seen as a consolation designed to remind "pilgrims here on earth" of their "home in heaven." Nor is it an admonition that the Asia Minor Christians should avoid giving the courts and the official authorities legitimate grounds for their prosecution. Nor is 1 Peter simply encouraging world-weary believers to remain within the structures and institutions of society. 1 Peter is rather a response to the typical set of problems created by the tension between sectarian particularism and societal pressures for conformity. The language, socioreligious symbolism, and literary accents of the document are best perceived in relation to its literary-social-religious strategy on the whole. This strategy, in turn, involves a deliberate attempt to address the basic issues of sectarian group formation and consolidation: problems concerning distinctive communal identity, social cohesion and the socioreligious conceptual integration of experience and expectations.

Throughout the letter, various and mostly interrelated means were employed for affirming the distinctive communal identity of the Christian movement, for reinforcing its social cohesion, and for clarifying, legitimating and integrating the social condition and divine vocation of the Christian *paroikoi*. The distinctiveness and separateness of the Christian community vis-à-vis the nonbelievers were emphasized through a series of contrasts and antitheses drawn between characteristic modes and norms of pre-Christian (or Gentile) and Christian behavior; through the use of imagery symbolizing the transformative nature of Christian conversion and exclusive union with God; through stress upon, and perhaps even exaggeration of, the prevailing conflict between Christians and Gentiles; through stereotypification of the one common diabolical "enemy" who opposed both the Christians and their God; through explicit exhortations to continued separation; and through reiteration of the distinctive qualities of Christian communion with Jesus Christ: faith, obedience, election and holiness, suffering, hope and vindication.

The distinctiveness of those in union with God through faith in Jesus Christ served as a basis for the distinction made between the status of the Christians in the eyes of society and in the sight of God. From the perspective of society, the Christians were *paroikoi*—strangers, aliens, unrooted transients, dangerous nonconformists. They were despicable fanatics, lowly slaves, "Christ-lackeys," obsequious advocates of humiliation. Within the community embraced by God, however, according to 1 Peter, these marginal people have experienced a transformation of status and dignity. While acknowledging and even emphasizing the inferior social status of the addressees, the author(s) simultaneously stressed the inversion of their position in the Christian brotherhood. Here *paroikos* existence, alienation from society, zeal in doing the good, bearing the name of Christ, servitude and humility were transformed from Gentile-condemned "vices" into the divinely rewarded "virtues" of God's diaspora people.

The passage affirming the election and holiness of God's special people in 1 Pet. 2:4–10 is a particularly graphic illustration of the manner in which sacred Israelite tradition had been appropriated to affirm the continuity and yet the novelty and unique identity and status of the eschatological people of God. Emphasis upon the union of the believers with Jesus Christ, with God, and with each other which here comes to expression is paralleled elsewhere by several other means through which fraternal solidarity is stressed. The genre of the document itself, its letter form, its personal names and its encyclical address express the personal bond which exists, or is desired to exist, between author(s) and recipients. The similarity between the location of both author(s) ("Babylon") and addressees ("diaspora") underlined their common alienated condition. The deliberate use of several extraordinary *syn-* formulations, the stress upon the common experience and suffering and upon the internally cohesive force of conflict, the repeated explicit exhortations to internal harmony, and the use of the household code as a pattern for integrating group roles, relationships, and responsibilities all illustrate related techniques for reinforcing and religiously validating the communal identity and integrity of the Christian movement.

A major feature of this strategy was the identification and exhortation of the Christian community as the household of God. For Christian *paroikoi* demeaned, deprived and dispersed within a strange and alienated society, their identification as the elect and holy household of God was a most effective means for affirming their distinctive communal identity and socioreligious integrity. The image of the *oikos tou theou* served as an eloquent ideological expression of their true condition before God, their self-consciousness and their calling in society.

Oikos, of course, is not the only collective term or image used to describe the Christian community in 1 Peter. 1 Pet. 2:9–10 contains no less than five communal epithets for the believers: elect generation, house of the king, body of priests, holy nation, and people belonging uniquely to God. In addition the addressees are called, collectively, a brotherhood (2:17; 5:9) and the flock of God (5:2). Some of these images, furthermore, recur in different sections of the letter and thereby serve to maintain its general line of thought. Thus, for instance, the present inclusion of the recipients in the people of God (2:9, 10) serves as a contrast to, and basis for, their continued disengagement from their former Gentile associations and patterns of behavior (1:14, 18; 2:11; 4:3). Having the name "the ones shown mercy," like their receiving the name "the people of God" with which it is combined in 2:10, restates the import of 1:3: Christians are reborn because of the great mercy of God. Likewise the identification of the community as a *holy* body of priests (2:5) and a *holy* nation (2:9) links the believers with the sanctifying activity of the Holy Spirit (1:2, 12), the holiness of God (1:15–16), and the purity of the Christ (1:19; cf. 1:2) and provides a rationale for the exhortation to live a holy way of life through the doing of good (3:5, 15). Again, the symbolization of the believers as the flock of God (5:2) is anticipated by the metaphor employed in 2:25 to describe the unifying result of the act of salvation: "For you were straying like sheep, but now have been returned to the shepherd and overseer of your lives" (au.). The sheep-shepherd metaphor is further continued in 5:2 and 5:4 where faithful shepherd-presbyters are promised an unfading crown of glory when the "chief Shepherd" (i.e., the Christ) appears.

This association of the Christ and his followers through the use of a shepherd-sheep image, moreover, is similar to other means we have observed by which the solidarity of believers with their Lord is stressed. His followers bear his very name, even as a label of opprobrium (4:16). As the Christ was rejected by men (2:4) and suffered unjustly (2:21–24 and passim), so also are those who bear his name (2:12, 20 and passim). As the Christ, however, was also raised and vindicated by God (1:3, 21; 3:22), so shall his followers be likewise (2:24; 4:5–6, 17–18). As he is a living stone (2:4), so they are living stones (2:5) filled with a living hope (1:3) because of their reception of the living Word of God (1:23). As he was subordinate to the will of God in the doing of good (2:21–24), so they are to conduct themselves likewise (2:20 and passim). As he is the elect and honored one of God (2:4, 6), so those who believe in him constitute the elect community (2:9; cf. 5:13) to whom honor also belongs (2:7; 3:7). "Because of the Lord" (2:13) the Christians are also to subordinate themselves to the Creator's will; "in Christ" (3:16; 5:10, 14) they find their solidarity. Through a diverse array of images and metaphors, the author(s) have developed a consistent line of thought which affirms, and grounds in the action of God, the distinctive communal identity and solidarity of the Christians with God, Jesus Christ and their fellow believers.

It is, however, the identification and exhortation of the audience as the household of God which served as the most *comprehensive* means of the Petrine strategy for integrating the kerygmatic and parenetic elements of the letter, and even more importantly, its theological and its social points of reference.

It is the image of the addressees as the household or family of God, more than any other collective symbol of 1 Peter, which *coordinates* the various traditional metaphors used in the document to describe the character of the new life, solidarity and salvation of the faithful. The *oikos* of God is the new family into which they have been born through conversion; it is the household where they are united with Jesus Christ and the divine Spirit as the covenant people of God; it is the brotherhood which binds them through the bond of fraternal love and mutual service; and it is the peculiar realm of the children of God and the Father's grace.

Oikos pneumatikos, furthermore, in the centrally important passage of 2:4-10, is a crucial phrase used in the *combination* of independent traditions concerning the Messiah (vv. 6-8) and the messianic community (vv. 9-10). Those who adhere in faith to Christ the elect and living stone have themselves become elect and living stones, a new elect and holy covenant community of God that is a household in which the divine Spirit dwells.

Through the continuation of the household image in the following sections of the letter, the author(s) have created a *logical consistency* between the identity of the addressees and their corresponding responsibilities. Since the believers constitute the household of God, they are to live and behave as the distinctive *oikos tou theou*. Subordination to the will of God is outlined according to the pattern of the household code. Household servants/slaves are singled out as primary exemplars of the reversal of status within the Christian community and the preeminence of servanthood; with them in particular is linked the christological affirmation of innocent suffering. All the members together are encouraged to serve one another as household stewards of God's varied grace. As the household of God they are to break with Gentile ways and to be innocent of Gentile sins. They are to maintain the unity of the brotherhood through steadfast resistance to evil. They can even rejoice when their faithfulness to God's will alone causes suffering, since innocent suffering is a distinguishing mark of their communion with Christ. The vindication which he experienced is the surety for that of the household which bears his name.

The image of the household thus serves as an integrating thematic medium for uniting and giving conceptual consistency to diverse literary and theological elements of the document. Of equal, if not more, importance, however, is the manner in which this portrayal of the addressees as the household of God functions *socially*. From the vantage point of the letter's socioreligious strategy, the identification and exhortation of Asia Minor Christian sectarians as the household of God may be seen as a most effective means for responding to the three major needs of the group as a sect. The affirmation and encouragement of the audience as the household of God were not only powerful ways of reinforcing a sense of the distinctive and prestigious character of their communal identity and for prompting a strengthening of their religious steadfastness and social solidarity; they were also a brilliant means for acknowledging the tension and depicting the correlation between the condition of the sectarians within society and within the believing community. *Paroikoi* they were, and must remain, within society; for within the believing community they constituted the *oikos tou theou*.

The compelling force of *oikos* as a symbol of communal identity and basis of ethos can be traced to a variety of factors: the universal experience of home and family as a fundamental form of social life, hence its regular occurrence in the sacred traditions as a central image of human unification and reunification; its semantic versatility, hence its power to attract and combine various important images of group identity (such as house, home, lineage, building, temple, people, family, brotherhood); its immediate reflection of the practicalities of everyday economic and social necessity (the business of maintaining a home and a place of livelihood), hence its further reflection of the manner in which the Christian communities were actually organized; and its embodiment, at the emotional and the psychological level, of the common memory of and quest for home, companionship and a place of belonging.

As *oikos* symbolizes the bonds which unite, it also implies the factors which divide. Thus the communal image of the household was most germane for describing the situation and experience of the sect. Emphasis upon the brotherhood of the faithful promoted not only internal consolidation but also external contrast. Incorporation in a house or home implies a distinction between inside and outside, between the members within and the nonmembers without. For its continued existence the sect is, and must remain, ever conscious of this distinction and of the necessity of its preservation. *Outside* the home the Christian sectarians lived a threatened and vulnerable existence in hostile Gentile territory. There they were strangers and aliens, suspected, accused, maligned, misunderstood, grieved and caused to suffer unjustly. In outside society, there was no promise of relief or hope for salvation. To the contrary, there the Gentiles were in league with the ancient adversary of God, the devil himself (1 Pet. 5:8), resolutely working toward the sect's demise. Salvation, community, acceptance and love were available only within the household of God, the family of faith. Here alone, through rebirth, faith in Jesus Christ and "infamilialization," did strangers and aliens secure the certainty of lively hope, salvation and inheritance. Here alone were the marginals of society moved to the center of the world's stage. In this family alone did former outcasts become the elect and privileged people of God. Here alone was a community shaped and motivated by fraternal love, mutual respect and humble service. Here alone were people empowered through faith in the suffering Christ to accept innocent suffering and embrace it with rejoicing. For here in this household of God alone was the certainty of salvation and eternal life as a reward to those who were faithful to God's holy will.

As part of the expression of this bipolar perspective, the household code, like other elements of the household theme, was used to promote both the internal solidarity of the sectarian movement and its external distinction from Gentile motives and manners. The scheme of ethical exhortation it provided was not simply that of a code of duties or a table of social positions. In 1 Peter it is clearly a *household* code which was used to elaborate on the roles, relationships and responsibilities of the people embraced in the household of God. Its use in 1 Peter implies neither the adoption of a bourgeois ethic, nor an attack upon incipient asceticism nor an apologetic for the good behavior of Christians loyal to the state. It rather forms a natural part of a household theme whose function is to exemplify and encourage modes of maintaining internal sectarian cohesion and external social contrast. The household code material compares the Christian brotherhood with other households and their management only eventually to contrast them. The Christian household practices subordination "because of the Lord" (1 Pet. 2:13). The *rule of this family,* its criterion of good and evil, is neither a conventional, nor a philosophical, nor a Roman legal standard. It is the *will of God* as obeyed by the suffering servant(s). From all Gentile modes of behavior and sin this household is to distance itself (2:11; 4:2–4, 12–19). To the emperor, as to all people in general, it may show respect. Love, however, is a distinctive mark of the brotherhood; and reverent awe the household reserves for God alone (2:17).

The concept of the household thus serves an integrative literary, theological and sociological function. The identification and exhortation of the Christian communities as the household of God were a most direct, realistic and cogent way of correlating religious rationale and social reality. The most obvious and ingenious example of such correlation is the set of terms used to describe the social condition and divine vocation of the audience and the authors: *paroikoi* and *oikos tou theou.*

231

In the tension between *oikos* and *paroikoi* was reflected the tension between sect and society. In the relation of these terms is affirmed the connection between destructive predicament and creative possibility. The terms *paroikoi* and *oikos* both refer to present social realities: a condition of sectarian life in society and a particular type of fraternal organization.

The terms *paroikoi, parepidēmoi and paroikia* were not used in 1 Peter to construct a theology of an earthly pilgrimage of God's people. They reflect a socioreligious tension, not a cosmological one. They were conventional sociolegal Greek terms for describing the limited status and rights of foreigners in Greco-Roman society. The addressees of 1 Peter lived and were known as aliens before the authors ever wrote to them. It was just this alien status which made the sectarians so suspicious in the eyes of the natives. It was this strangeness of theirs, religious as well as social, which was the cumulative cause of the tension and conflict between the addressees and their pagan neighbors. There are no grounds for imputing a purely "spiritual" sense to these terms or for the assumption that they refer to a Christian's "exile on earth" in contrast to his "home in heaven." Despite the misleading textual additions in the biblical translations of these verses, there is no evidence in the original Greek text of such an implied or intended cosmological contrast. 1 Peter does not state that the addressees *became paroikoi* by becoming Christians but that as Christians they should *remain paroikoi*. The Christian gospel and the Christian community, according to 1 Peter, are a *response* to the predicament of strangerhood.

The terms "diaspora" and "Babylon" are a part of this response. They aid in building the conceptual bridge between social alienation and union with God. As familiar symbolizations of Israel's displacement and estrangement in foreign and hostile territory, they recall the fact that even there the promises and providence of God were not withdrawn. Even among the Gentile dispersion and the idolatries of Babylon God enabled his people to keep alive the hope of reunification and homecoming. For those who saw themselves as the heirs of the covenant of Israel these terms could also be used to suggest the simultaneity of *paroikia* existence and privileged peoplehood. Both terms, moreover, referred to experiences of estrangement which were historical and social in nature, not earthly sojourns of God's celestial people.

The central term, however, in the Petrine response to *paroikia* was *oikos*. Both terms had a social and a present point of reference. Those without a home in society had the possibility of a home in the believing community. The context of the Christians' *paroikia* is said to be not the earth (in contrast to heaven), but the hostile pagan society of Asia Minor. The alternative to this predicament of *paroikia* was not a future home in heaven but a place within the Christian fraternity here and now. This does not mean that the actual tensions and conflicts concomitant with *paroikia* existence were denied or trivialized. Nor does 1 Peter articulate an interim ethic which calls only for steadfastness in the hope of future reward. To the contrary, emphasis is given to the importance of maintaining a stance of strangeness vis-à-vis an unbelieving society. Such a posture is possible in view of the fact that here and now the Christian community constitutes a home for the alienated and the estranged. If, moreover, this community was to endure and grow, then it was essential that its distinctive features be preserved at all costs, even at the cost of conflict and suffering. Only through confrontation with the strangeness and otherness of the Christian way of life would Gentile outsiders perceive and be attracted to the uniqueness of the brotherhood. Christian persistence in *paroikia* was possible, even joy in the face of suffering, for innocent suffering was a sign of union with Christ. Union with Christ, in turn, assured union with God and with all those who constituted the household of faith.

The correlation of *paroikia* and *oikos tou theou* and of the two disparate social realities which they represented constitutes, in a nutshell, the focus of the socioreligious strategy of 1 Peter, the heart of its evangelical message. The chief unsettling and debilitating experience of the addressees was a sense of homelessness in an increasingly hostile environment. In a letter of consolation and confirmation the authors respond by assuring these Asia Minor Christians that in the Christian community all the homeless have a home in the household of God. Christian community and fraternity, however, were not simply religious visions or ideas; they had to be transformed into social realities. The strategy of 1 Peter, therefore, was to motivate the communal self-consciousness and to mobilize the solidarity and steadfastness of the audience by appealing to them as uniquely graced and honored members of the household of God. In this message the household of God functioned as a potent symbol socially, psychologically and religiously, for articulating and integrating the expressions of faith and the experiences of life.

A Periphrastic Outline of 1 Peter

A periphrastic outline of 1 Peter which attempts to reflect the literary structure and composition of the text as closely as possible while also explicating its integrating theme and emphases would read as follows.

1:1-2   Epistolary Salutation: The apostle Peter to the elect homeless believers in the diaspora of Asia Minor.

I.   1:3-2:10   By the mercy of God you strangers in society have become the elect and holy people of God, the household of faith.

   A. 1:3-12   Praise be to God for the distinctive hope in salvation which we have through faith in Jesus Christ!

     1 1:3-5   Through the resurrection of Jesus Christ God the Father has "rebirthed" us for a living hope, an incorruptible inheritance, and a sure salvation in this final age.

     2. 1:6-9   You can rejoice in this fact and await the revelation of this salvation with hope and with a faith tested by suffering.

     3: 1:10-12   The good news of salvation which the prophets sought has been revealed now exclusively to you.

   B. 1:13-21   You, God's holy people, are to lead a distinctive, holy way of life in the hope of the revelation of God's grace.

   C. 1:22-25   As a brotherhood purified through obedience to God, maintain your unity through constant brotherly love; for you have been reborn through a permanent word, namely, the good news of the Lord.

   D. 2:1-3   Therefore avoid all acts of dissension and continue to feed on the milk of the word, namely, the Lord.

   E. 2:4-10   You adhere in faith to the Lord Jesus Christ, the Elect and Holy One of God through whom, by God's mercy, you have become the elect and holy community of God, the household of the Spirit.

II.   2:11-4:11   As strangers and resident aliens in society, through obedience to God preserve the distinctiveness and solidarity of your household of faith to the glory of God.

A. 2:11–12 (Transition) As the elect and holy household of faith (1:3–2:10), live as holy strangers so that through your distinctive style of behavior even hostile outsiders ("Gentiles") might come to glorify God.

B. 2:13–3:12 Be subordinate and respectful to all human authority because of the Lord.

    1. 2:13–17 Be subordinate to civil authority, but love the brotherhood and fear only God.

    2. 2:18–20 Household slaves, be subordinate to your owners by doing good, even if you suffer unjustly.

    3. 2:21–25 You (household slaves) have been called to follow the Christ who, by also suffering unjustly in subordination to the will of God, has made it possible for you to do the same.

    4. 3:1–6 Wives, be subordinate to your husbands by doing good and not fearing them.

    5. 3:7 Husbands, live in household harmony with your wives and respect them as coheirs of the grace of life.

    6. 3:8–12 All members of the household, maintain the unity of the community; you have been called to avoid evil and do good.

C. 3:13–4:11 Distinguish yourselves by the doing of good, even in the face of outsiders' ("Gentiles'") hostility; God vindicates the righteous.

    1. 3:13–17 If you should be caused to suffer by your detractors, let it be only for the doing of good in obedience to God's will.

    2. 3:18–22 Christ, the righteous one, also suffered. His innocent suffering, death and resurrection/exaltation is the basis of your salvation and your vindication.

    3. 4:1–6 Separate yourselves from the sinful outsiders ("Gentiles") who condemn you. God will condemn them and vindicate the faithful.

    4. 4:7–11 Maintain the solidarity of the household of God to the glory of God.

III. 4:12–19 Rejoice in the test which your suffering brings for being distinctive. Suffering for being obedient to the will of God is the distinguishing mark of your union with the Christ and of membership in the household of God.

IV. 5:1–11   Through responsible leadership, subordination, mutual humility and resistance to the opposing forces of evil, maintain the unity of the brotherhood. The God who called you shall surely confirm you.

  A. 5:1–4   Leaders ("elders"), be responsible and not selfish shepherds of the flock of God; when the chief shepherd appears, he will reward you.

  B. 5:5a   Recent converts ("young people"), be subordinate to your leaders.

  C. 5:5b–11   All of you, through mutual humility, subordination to God, and concerted resistance to evil opposition, maintain the unity of the brotherhood. The God who called you shall surely confirm you.

5:12–14   Epistolary Conclusion and greetings from the associates of Peter in Babylon (especially Silvanus his faithful brother, Mark his son, and his coelect sister).

In his essay, "The Homecomer," the social theorist Alfred Schutz has reflected on the profound depth and evocative power of the reality called "home." Home-leaving, homelessness and homecoming from time immemorial have shaped the dramatic substance of man's story and his history. Odysseus is the archetype of Everyman. House and home have figured so centrally in the human experience and its recapitulations because they recall not simply a place or a time but a state and condition of being. "Geographically 'home' means a certain spot on the surface of the earth. Where I happen to be is my 'abode'; where I intend to stay is my 'residence'; where I come from and whither I want to return is my 'home.' "[249] With house and home are linked the existential issues of identity and belonging, personal and collective origin and destiny.

The role which the concept of home and family played in the ideology not only of 1 Peter but also in the subsequent course of Christian history is the subject to which we will turn in the following chapter. Considering 1 Peter in its own time and place, however, we must marvel at the ingenious and sensitive manner in which the Christian gospel has been formulated to meet the predicament of social alienation and estrangement. By focusing on the bipolar experience and symbols of isolation and community, homelessness and home, its authors have not only challenged their own community to be a hope-giving and life-sustaining fellowship amid a world of strangers; they have also given to Christian history a profound concept of religious community and a potent symbol, socially, psychologically and religiously, for integrating the expressions of hope and the experiences of life.

NOTES

1. Fifty years separate the works of Theophil Spörri (*Der Gemeindegedanke im ersten Petrusbrief: Ein Beitrag zur Struktur des urchristlichen Kirchenbegriffs*, Neutestamentliche Forschungen, 2. Reihe; *Untersuchungen zum Kirchenproblem des Urchristentums*, 2. Heft [Gütersloh: C. Bertelsmann, 1925]) and Horst Goldstein (*Paulinische Gemeinde im Ersten Petrusbrief*, Stuttgarter Bibelstudien 80 [Stuttgart: Katholisches Bibelwerk, 1975]).

2. For some limited reflections see, inter alia, E. G. Selwyn, *The First Epistle of St. Peter*, 2. ed. (London: Macmillan, 1955), additional note H: "The 'Spiritual House,' Its Priesthood and Sacrifices in ii. 5–9," pp. 285–98; and J. H. Elliott, *The Elect and the Holy: An Exegetical Examination of 1 Peter 2:4–10 and the Phrase* Basileion Hierateuma, *NovT Supplements* 12 (Leiden: E. J. Brill, 1966), pp. 149–66. Goldstein, to be sure, has often commented on the significance of the *oikos* image in 1 Peter (*Ersten Petrusbrief*, pp. 55, 59, 77–78, 101, 109) and has observed: "Die vom Autor unseres Schreibens bevorzugte Begrifflichkeit ist die des Hauses and des Hausbauens" (p. 55). He fails to explore sufficiently, however, the *social* function of this Petrine characteristic.

3. Otto Michel in his article on *oikos* (completed in 1948) made this point over thirty years ago (*TWNT* [1954]: 122–61; *TDNT* 5 [1967]: 119–59; see esp. *TWNT* 5: 133, n. 42). Karl Heinrich Rengstorf, writing soon after Michel, heartily concurred ("Die neutestamentliche Mahnungen an die Frau, sich dem Manne unterzuordnen," in *Verbum Dei Manet in Aeternam*, Otto Schmitz FS; ed. Werner Foerster [Witten: Luther Verlag, 1953], p. 140, n. 22; id., *Mann und Frau im Urchristentum*, Arbeitsgemeinschaft für Forschung des Landes Nordrhein-Westfalen, Geisteswissenschaften, Heft 12 [Köln/Opladen: Westdeutscher Verlag, 1954], p. 32, n. 62).

4. For the meager literature see Michel, "*Oikos*," p. 122. Philipp Vielhauer (*OIKODOME, Das Bild vom Bau in der Christlichen Literatur bis Clemens*

Alexandrinus [Karlsruhe: Gebr. Tron, 1939]) treats only *oikodomē* and its verbal forms. Josef Pfammater (*Die Kirche als Bau: Eine exegetisch-theologische Studie zur Ekklesiologie der Paulus Briefe,* Analecta Gregoriana, v. 110, sect. B, no. 33 [Rome: Gregorian University, 1960]) treats only the Pauline literature and ignores the political-social implications of *oikos* altogether.

5. Floyd V. Filson, "The Significance of the Early House Churches," *JBL* 58 (1939): 105–112.

6. Ibid., p. 106.

7. Ibid., p. 112.

8. Joachim Jeremias (*Die Kindertaufe in den ersten vier Jahrhunderten* [Göttingen: Vandenhoeck und Ruprecht, 1958]) and Kurt Aland (*Die Säuglingstaufe im Neuen Testament und in der Alten Kirche,* Theologische Existenz Heute NF, 86; 2. aufl. [Munich: Kaiser, 1963]) initiated the debate (see J. H. Elliott, "Infant Baptism: A Review of a Controversy," *Una Sancta* [New York] 21 [1964]: 70–73). Ludger Schenke ("Zur sogenannten 'Oikosformel' im Neuen Testament," *Kairos* 13 [1971]: 226–43) reviews the subsequent extensive literature and provisional conclusions; see esp. Gerhard Delling, "Zur Taufe von 'Häusern' im Urchristentum," *NovT* 7 (1965): 285–311.

9. August Strobel, "Der Begriff des 'Hauses' im griechischen und römischen Privatrecht," *ZNW* 56 (1965): 91–100.

10. For example, Hennecke Gülzow, *Christentum und Sklaverei in den ersten drei Jahrhunderten* (Bonn: Rudolf Habelt Verlag, 1969), esp. pp. 42–46, 52–53; S. Scott Bartchy, *MALLON CHRHSAI: First-Century Slavery and the Interpretation of 1 Corinthians 7:21,* SBL Dissertation Series, 11 (Missoula, Mont.: Scholars Press, 1973), esp. p. 59 and n. 187; and P. Stuhlmacher, *Der Brief an Philemon,* Evangelisch-Katholischer Kommentar zum Neuen Testament (Zürich, Einsiedeln, Köln: Benziger Verlag and Neukirchen-Vluyn: Neukirchener Verlag, 1975), esp. p. 20 and n. 10 (explicitly quoting the above-mentioned article of Filson) and his excursus on "Urchristliche Hausgemeinden" (pp. 70–75, with bibliography, p. 70).

11. For the most recent treatments and reviews of earlier literature see James E. Crouch, *The Origin and Intention of the Colossian Haustafel,* FRLANT 109 (Göttingen: Vandenhoeck und Ruprecht, 1972) and Wolfgang Schrage, "Zur Ethik der neutestamentlichen Haustafeln," *NTS* 21 (1974): 1–22. For the household *oikonomia* as the social context of the household codes see Dieter Lührmann, "Wo man nicht mehr Sklave oder Freier ist: Überlegungen zur Struktur frühchristlicher Gemeinden," in *Wort und Dienst,* Jahrbuch der Kirchlichen Hochschule Bethel NF 13; ed. H. Krämer (1975), pp. 53–82, esp. pp. 75–83, and David L. Balch, *"Let Wives Be Submissive . . . " The Origin, Form and Apologetic Function of the Household Duty Code (Haustafel) in I Peter* (Ann Arbor, Mich.: University Microfilms International, 1976).

12. For example, the studies of G. Theissen, "Soziale Schichtung in der korinthischen Gemeinde: Ein Beitrag zur Soziologie des hellenistichen Christentums," *ZNW* 65 (1974): 232–72; "Die Starken und Schwachen in Korinth: Soziologische Analyse eines theologischen Streites," *EvTh* 35 (1975): 155–72.

13. For example, J. Hainz, *Ekklesia, Strukturen Paulinischer Gemeinde Theologie und Gemeinde-Ordnung*, Münchner Universitäts-Schriften, Katholisch-Theologische Fakultät (Regensburg: F. Pustet, 1972), esp. pp. 345–48; A. Strobel, "Säuglings- und Kindertaufe in der ältesten Kirche," in *Begründung und Gebrauch der heiligen Taufe*, ed. Otto Perels (Berlin: Lutherisches Verlagshaus, 1963), pp. 7–69; see also Theissen, "Legitimation und Lebensunterhalt: Ein Beitrag zur Soziologie urchristlicher Missionäre," *NTS* 21 (1975): 192–221.

14. For example, Willy Rordorf, "Was wissen wir über die christlichen Gottesdiensträume der vorkonstantinischen Zeit?" *ZNW* 55 (1964): 110–28, esp. pp. 111–22.

15. Several of Theissen's works are pertinent here. See especially "Itinerant Radicalism: The Tradition of Jesus Sayings from the Perspective of the Sociology of Literature," trans. A. C. Wire, with abridged notes, in *The Bible and Liberation: Political and Social Hermeneutics*, A *Radical Religion* Reader, ed. Norman K. Gottwald and Antoinette C. Wire (Berkeley: Community for Religious Research and Education, 1976), pp. 84–93; and *Sociology of Early Palestinian Christianity*, trans. John Bowden (Philadelphia: Fortress Press, 1978). See also H. Gülzow, "Soziale Gegebenheiten der altkirchlichen Mission," *in Kirchengeschichte als Missionsgeschichte*, ed. Heinzgünter Frohnes, Hans-Werner Gensichen and Georg Kretschmar; *Die Alte Kirche*, vol. 1, ed. Heinzgünter Frohnes and Uwe W. Knorr (Munich: Chr. Kaiser, 1974), 189–226.

16. Above all, in E. A. Judge's chapter on "The Household Community: Oikonomia" in his book *The Social Pattern of the Christian Groups in the First Century: Some Prolegomena to the Study of New Testament Ideas of Social Obligation* (London: Tyndale, 1960), pp. 30–39; and "The Social Consistency of Christian Groups," pp. 49–61. Paul S. Minear in his survey of *Images of the Church in the New Testament* (Philadelphia: Westminster Press, 1960) also devotes a section to the image of "the household of God" (pp. 165–72).

17. A. J. Malherbe, *Social Aspects of Early Christianity* (Baton Rouge: Louisiana State University Press, 1977).

18. Minear, among others, makes this reciprocity explicit: "Through our whole discussion we have been impelled by the images to rethink the essential structure of the community in terms of such simple constituents as faith and obedience, grace and forgiveness, hospitality and love. We should not overlook this important corollary: because the people of God must be defined in

terms of such qualitative human relationships as are indicated by hospitality and forgiveness, these very relationships must be reconceived in terms of their sociological, ecclesiological, and ontological implications. To give a cup of cold water becomes much more than an instance of private morality; it becomes an event in the creation, edification, and redemption of human community" (*Images,* p. 172).

19. For the discussion of these points see *The Elect and the Holy,* pp. 208–213.

20. On the history of the transmission and interpretation of Exod. 19:6 see *The Elect and the Holy,* pp. 50–128.

21. "To offer spiritual sacrifices (i.e., motivated by the Spirit) acceptable to God through Jesus Christ" (2:5d) is a figurative equivalent here for the "doing of good" (*agathopoiia*) and the "leading of a holy way of life" (*anastrophē*) emphasized throughout 1 Peter (ibid., pp. 174–85). The cultic metaphor was probably used as appropriate for a description of the activity of a priestly community. However, this metaphor is thoroughly *incidental* to the theme and focus of the passage as a whole. In 1 Peter *hierateuma* expresses the holiness and election of the people of God. The redactional qualification of *hierateuma* by *hagion* in 2:5 makes this absolutely clear. Holiness, in turn, is for 1 Peter a concept with social and ethical dimensions, not cultic ones. As a holy community the addressees are at once distinguished from the "unholy" Gentiles externally and obligated internally to maintain this holy bond with the holy God (see 1:14–16) through holy behavior and thereby maintain their internal cohesion. What superficially appears to be cultic is, on closer sociological inspection, socially functional.

The implication of this for the meaning and function of *oikos* in v. 5 is obvious. Although on the basis of general word usage *oikos* could mean "temple," especially in association with *hierateuma* (see, e.g., Selwyn, *First Epistle of St. Peter,* p. 160, 291; more recently, E. Best, *I Peter,* New Century Bible [London: Oliphants, 1971], pp. 101–102), its actual meaning and function must be established not simply on the basis of possible or apparent linguistic or traditional usage but on the grounds of demonstrable redactional and socially functional factors as well.

22. See *The Elect and the Holy,* pp. 141–45.

23. For discussion of the following points see ibid., pp. 16–49, 148–218.

24. Best ("I Peter II 4–10—A Reconsideration," *NovT* [1969]: 270–93) opposes this point by arguing: (1) that the Old Testament language adopted in 1 Peter confirms or advances (rather than introduces) a line of thought; and (2) that 2:9–10, in contrast to v. 5, introduces a new line of thought (esp. pp. 271–75, 277–78, 289). The first objection is too general. In the particular case of

2:4–10, the function of vv. 4–5 is to introduce an indicative statement (the confirmation of which commences in v. 6 [*dioti* . . .]) and its terms obviously derive from the Old Testament texts which are subsequently cited in vv. 6–10. The second objection rests on a false assumption. Assuming that *oikos* in v. 5 means "temple," he correctly notes that *basileion* in v. 9 refers to people. But this suggests to him a discontinuity in the line of thought. If, as I have pointed out, *oikos* and *basileion* both refer to the same object, namely, the people of God, the "discontinuity" of thought is nonexistent. Moreover, that vv. 9–10 "show the continuity between the new and the old Israel" (p. 278) is hardly a new or different line of thought over against v. 5. Rather as *oikos* in v. 5 explicates *basileion* in v. 9, so *hierateuma hagion* and the remainder of v. 5 explicate the meaning of *hierateuma* and the remainder of v. 9. Where a term such as *hierateuma* occurs twice in the same confined pericope and only there in the entire New Testament it is implausible to conclude, without convincing demonstration, that it advances different lines of thought! In both instances it is the distinctiveness and solidarity of the believers which are affirmed.

Best makes a weak case only worse by attributing supposed inconsistency to the intellectual limitations of the author: "Peter's mind as revealed by his letter is not creative; it is therefore [*sic!*] unlikely that he by himself derived from Ex. xix 6 the conception of the priesthood of the church"; he rather adopted it (in 2:5) from the "tradition of the primitive church . . . and then applied Ex. xix 6 to it" (p. 284). Quite apart from the absence of evidence of any such tradition prior to 1 Peter, this kind of reasoning seems rather desperate.

25. In the transmission and interpretation of Exod. 19:6 prior to 1 Peter, this passage is never used to make a statement about the people of God as "temple." From the beginning this covenantal formula was applied to the "house of Jacob" and the "sons of Israel" (Exod. 19:3). For the conjunction of covenant, election and house(hold) also apart from the Exodus formula see also, e.g., Heb. 8:8, 10 (and its source, Jer. 31:31–34) and Heb. 3:1–6; Luke 1:69, 72; esp. the explicitly antitemple interpretation of *oikos* and covenant in Acts 7: 46–50 (reflecting 2 Sam. 7:11–16); according to 1 En. 53:6 the righteous and elect one (the Son of man) shall "cause the house of his congregation to appear."

26. For the earlier discussion on this issue see *The Elect and the Holy*, pp. 148–98. Subsequently some scholars have still preferred to render *oikos* as "temple" and to attribute significance to the "cultic overtones" of the passage, 2:5. Best ("I Peter II 4–10," p. 280 and *I Peter*, pp. 101–102), for example, points to LXX usage (where *oikos* in combination with *oikodomein* denotes the building of the temple), "the many close contacts between I Peter ii 4–10 and

the idea of the new temple of Qumran," and New Testament texts where the church is referred to as the new temple (e.g., 1 Cor. 3:16; Eph. 2:18–22). While such usage is not to be denied, the point is that *oikos* is a term pregnant with various meanings and certainly not always synonymous with *naos,* the proper term for "temple." The precise meaning of such a flexible term can be determined only within its immediate and general literary context, leaving each author sufficient compositional latitude. Within the New Testament *oikos* certainly does designate the faithful community as "house(hold)" rather than "temple" (e.g., Heb. 3:1–6, 1 Tim. 3:15 [cf. 3:5]; cf. also Gal. 6:10, Eph. 2: 19–21 and 1 Tim. 5:8). Within the context of 1 Peter, *oikos* is part of a passage whose primary stress is on the theme of election, not cult. It is related to an exhortation emphasizing household duties, not worship.

R. J. McKelvey (*The New Temple* [Oxford: Oxford University Press, 1969], pp. 124–32) suggests that "It is as the place of worship that I Peter is most interested in the new temple" (p. 131). But this and similar interpretations fail to note that nowhere in the rest of 1 Peter is this supposed interest in worship made explicit. To the contrary, it is not as a "new temple" that the readers are subsequently exhorted, but as members of the divine household. This criticism applies also to the studies of Elisabeth Schüssler-Fiorenza; see her *Priester für Gott,* NTAbh 7 (Münster: Aschendorff, 1972), pp. 94–101 and "Cultic Language in Qumran and in the NT," *CBQ* 38 (1976): 159–77. Fiorenza is the only one among those who have favored the cultic interpretation of *oikos* in 2:5 and 4:17 to have recognized the exegete's obligation to consider the social context and social function of the supposedly cultic interests of 1 Peter. Her interpretation, however, fails to convince. She asserts but fails to demonstrate that temple and cult played an important role in the interaction of the Petrine audience and its social environment. This cannot be demonstrated in fact because temple, priesthood and cult play no central role in 1 Peter. Her theory, like McKelvey's, fails to explain the absence of any concern in 1 Peter with cultic issues as it fails to consider the social ramifications of *oikos* as a designation for the Christian community as the "household of God." For further variations on the cultic theme see Andre Feuillet, "Les 'sacrifices spirituels' du sacerdoce royal des baptisés (1 P 2,5) et leur préparation dans l'Ancien Testament," *La nouvelle revue théologique* 96 (1974): 704–28; Chevallier, "Israël et l'Eglise selon la première Epître de Pierre," in *Paganisme, Judaïsme, Christianisme: Influences et affrontements dans le monde antique,* Marcel Simon FS (Paris: E. de Boccard, 1978), pp. 123–25; Georg Klinzing, *Die Umdeutung des Kultes in der Qumrangemeinde und im Neuen Testament,* SUNT 7 (Göttingen: Vandenhoeck und Ruprecht, 1971), esp. on 1 Peter, pp. 191–96, 216–18, 222–23. Against the notion that in Qumran the temple served as a model for the community see Allan J. McNicol, "The Eschatological Temple in the Qumran Pesher 4QFlorilegium 1:1–7," *Ohio Journal of Religious Stud ies* 5 (1977): 133–41.

Opinions vary concerning the consistency of the meaning of *oikos* in 2:5 and 4:17. Some (e.g., Selwyn, *First Epistle of St. Peter,* pp. 159–60, 226; Michel, *"Oikos," TDNT* 5 [1967/1954]: 127; J. N. D. Kelly, *A Commentary on the Epistles of Peter and of Jude,* Harper's New Testament Commentaries [New York: Harper & Row, 1969], pp. 89, 193; Best, *I Peter,* p. 165) assume the meaning "temple" in both passages. Others (e.g., McKelvey, *New Temple,* pp. 128, 133; Wolfgang Schrage, *Die "Katholischen" Briefe: Die Briefe des Jacobus, Petrus, Johannes und Judas,* 11. aufl., with Horst Balz, *NTD* 10 [Göttingen: Vandenhoeck und Ruprecht, 1973], pp. 82, 112) presuppose an inconsistent usage in 2:5 ("temple") and 4:17 ("household"). I propose that *oikos* in both instances means "household (of God)." It has been suggested that the prophetic notion of the temple's destruction as a sign of the end time lies behind 4:17. But the closest parallel, Ezek. 9:6 (LXX), states that judgment will begin "with my holy ones." The context, 9:3–11, clearly refers to "the guilt of the house of Israel and Judah" and to the punishment of the *people* as well as the defilement of the temple (*naos,* 8:16). *Oikos* here is used in the communal as well as the cultic sense. The context of 1 Pet. 4:17, namely, 4:12–19, requires for *oikos* the sense of *people* (namely, the *Christianoi* in contrast to the impious and sinners) as well.

27. Text according to the edition of L. Cohn and P. Wendland, *Philonis Alexandrini Opera Quae Supersunt,* 1–6 (Berlin: de Gruyter, 1896–1915). *De Sobr.* 66 = C–W 2: 228.

28. *The Elect and the Holy,* pp. 96–101.

29. A further example of the equivalence of *oikos* and *basileion* is provided by the LXX and Theodotion variant readings of Dan. 6:19. The former reads: "Then the king (Darius) returned to his *palace (ta basileia)* . . . " while the latter has: "Then the king departed to his *house (ton oikon)."* See also the parallelism of *basileion* and *oikos theou* in Philo, *De Praemis et Poenis* 123: " . . . in truth the wise man's mind is a *palace* and *house of God."* Philo then continues: "This it is which is declared to possess personally the God who is the God of all. This again is the chosen people (*kai laos exairetos palin houtos*), the people not of particular rulers but of the one and only true ruler, a people holy even as he is holy."

30. M. Hengel, *Judaism and Hellenism: Studies in Their Encounter in Palestine during the Early Hellenistic Period,* 2 vols. (Philadelphia: Fortress Press, 1974) 1: 19.

31. M. Rostovtzeff, *The Social and Economic History of the Hellenistic*

World (SEHHW), 3 vols. (Oxford: Clarendon Press, 1941), 2: 1309; also id., *The Social and Economic History of the Roman Empire (SEHRE)*, 2. ed. rev. by P. M. Fraser (Oxford: Clarendon Press, 1957), 1: 278.

32. Hengel, *Judaism and Hellenism*, 1: 19.

33. Rostovtzeff, *SEHRE*, 1: 273, describing Egypt under Flavian and Antonine rule.

34. Hengel, *Judaism and Hellenism*, 1: 29; see *FGrHist* III C 726 fr. 2,2; 3,4 (Eusebius, *Pr.Ev.* 9,23 and 27).

35. Text and translation according to F. H. Colson, *Philo*, LCL (Cambridge: Harvard University Press, 1959) 6: 160–161.

36. In *De Post.* 52 Philo expresses a general conception of antiquity regarding the relation of the *oikos* and the *polis* and the roots of the latter in the former. The literature is too replete with examples to require illustration. The following texts may illustrate, however, the naturalness and regularity with which the terms and concepts of *oikos, oikodomein* etc. were used in conjunction and comparison with *polis* and related terms or concepts: *De Post.* 49, 50; *De Mig.* 90; *De Cher.* 126; *De Sac.* 124; *Leg. All.* iii. 228; for *politeia/oikonomia*: *De Ebr.* 92; *De Ios.* 38; *Spec. Leg.* iii. 170; *Quod Omn. Prob.* 83; for *politikos/oikonomos*: *De Praem.* 113; for *politikos/oikonomikos*: *De Ebr.* 91, 92; *De Fug.* 36; *De Ios.* 38; for *oikos* in conjunction with *polis, gōra, ethnē, klimata*: *De Mig.* 120; with *patrikos*: *De Mig.* 160; with *patrōos* (opp. *xenē*): *De Som.* i. 256; with *patris, syggeneis, philoi*: *De Praem.* 17. See also the comparison of cities (*astē*) with households (*oikiai*) in *Spec. Leg.* iii. 170.

37. See *In Flacc.* 35; cf. also *oikos Sebastos, In Flacc.* 23, 49, 105.

38. See *De Vita Mos.* ii. 30; cf. *oikia Pharaō, De Mig.* 160.

39. See *Legatio* 33; cf. also ibid. 156, 166, 279. See Michel, *"Oikos,"* TDNT 5: 133, n. 12.

40. For *oikos tou theou* in Philo see *De Cher.* 49, 52; *Quod Deus* 137; *De Plant.* 53; *De Sobr.* 66; *De Praem.* 123; *De Aet.* 112.

41. Hengel, *Judaism and Hellenism*, 1: 19, quoting Rostovtzeff, *SEHRE*, 1: 269.

42. Among the abundant literature see esp. A. W. Van Buren, *"Oikos,"* PW (1937) 2119–2123; M. L. Finley, *The World of Odysseus* (New York: Viking Press, 1954); A. W. Gouldner, *Enter Plato: Classical Greece and the Origins of Social Theory* (New York: Basic Books, 1965); Max Weber, *Essays in Sociology*, ed. H. H. Gerth and C. W. Mills (New York: Oxford University Press, 1946), esp. pp. 236–41; id., *Economy and Society*, 3 vols., ed. Guenther Ross and Claus Wittich (New York: Bedminster, 1968) 3: Index, s.v. "households"; Rostovtzeff, *SEHHW* and *SEHRE*, see indices s.v. "houses," "house-economy," "house-industry" etc.; E. Betti, "Das Wesen des altrömischen

Familienverbandes (Hausgemeinschaft und Agnatengenossenschaft)," *Zeitschrift der Savigny-Stiftung, Rom. Abteilung* 71 (1954): 1–24.

43. At first Aristotle allows a relationship but not a direct analogy between household, village and city-state because of different kinds of authority and rule (*Politica* 1.2.1252a). Later, however, as Colson has pointed out in an appended note to Philo, *De Ios.* 38 (Philo [LCL] 6: 600) Aristotle does admit the analogy for the monarchy (3.10.2; cf. also *Eth. Nic.* 8.14.1162a). This then coincides with the opening of Plato's *Politicus* (esp. 259c) where the similarity of *basilikē, politikē* and *oikonomikē epistemē* ("knowledge, skill") is asserted.

44. See, e.g., Aristotle, *Politica* 1.3.1253b and Delling, "Zur Taufe," pp. 288–90 for further examples. See also J. Marquardt, *Das Privatleben der Römer*, vol. 1, *Die Familie* (Darmstadt: Wissenschaftliche Buchgesellschaft, 1964), pp. 1–2: "Zu einer vollständigen Familie . . . gehört der Hausherr (*pater familias*), die Hausfrau (*mater familias*), die Söhne und Töchter, die Kinder der Haussöhne und die Sklaven, alle vereinigt zu einem geschlossen Ganzen, dessen Oberhaupt, der pater familias, allein *sui iuris* ist, während die anderen Glieder der Familie als *alieno iuri subiecti* der Gewalt des Hausvaters unterworfen sind"; and J. Gaudemet, "Familie I (Familienrecht)," *RAC* 7 (1969): 286–358.

45. On *oikos*-management see Max Weber, *General Economic History*, trans. F. H. Knight (Glencoe, Ill.: The Free Press, 1927), esp. pp. 26–50, 124–131, 146, 162; id., *Economy and Society*, 1: 356–84; Rostovtzeff, *SEHRE* 1: 349–50; J. H. Broek, *Griechische Wirtschaftgeschichte* (Tübingen: J. C. B. Mohr, 1931), esp. pp. 15, 24, 27–29, 38, 46, 69, 284; on "Aristotle and Economic Analysis" see M. I. Finley, *Studies in Ancient Society*, ed. M. I. Finley (London/Boston: Routledge & Kegan Paul, 1974), pp. 26–52; see also M. I. Finley, *The Ancient Economy* (Berkeley/Los Angeles: University of California Press, 1973) and the literature cited in n. 42 above. An instructive sociological analogue is provided by M. C. Yang's study of a 1920s Chinese family in his essay "The Family as a Primary Economic Group," in *Tribal and Peasant Societies*, ed. G. Dalton (Garden City, N. Y.: The Natural History Press, 1967), pp. 333–46.

46. For the religious, social and moral responsibilities of the householder see *Oecon.* 2.5–7; on the proper relations of husbands and wives, 3.10–16, 7.3–43, 8.2–23; on the responsibilities of overseers, *oiketai* etc., 12.1–15.1.

47. Balch, *Wives*, pp. 33–180. Lührmann ("Wo man nicht mehr Sklave oder Freier ist," esp. pp. 76–79) also has seen this connection and like Balch considers it the basis for a correct understanding of the New Testament "household codes."

48. *Synoikism*, according to Weber (*Economy and Society*, 1: 278), designates "the organization of ancient city states with their councils organized on the basis of clans, phratries and phylae" which reflect a "governing authority

(Herrschaftsverbrand) [which] has arisen from the Vergemeinschaftung or Vergesellschaftung of previously autocephalous groups. . . . " In later hellenistic time the appeal to a communal form of *synoikism* is used to assuage the tensions between urban and rural elements. Rostovtzeff (*SEHRE,* 1: 257) notes: "In his well-known speech on *synoikismos* Dio of Prusa [*Or.* 45] gives us a glimpse into the conditions created in the cities by this antagonism between the city and the country. As a liberal and a philosopher, he insists on a *synoikismos* which would unite city and country into one social and economic body. The question was a vital one for many cities of Asia Minor, for instance, the capital of Phrygia, the prosperous Celaenae, which had numerous villages attached to it." On this and the related point of the economic and social standing of the *paroikoi* and *katoikoi* in Asia Minor see also ibid., 2: 654–55, n. 4. See further, T. R. S. Broughton, "Roman Asia Minor," *ESAR* 4 (1938): 640, 697.

49. On the relation of *oikos,* economy and the traditional form of domination see Weber, *Economy and Society* 1: 236–41.

50. Judge, *The Social Pattern,* p. 31.

51. Ibid., p. 32.

52. Ibid.

53. For a study of the nature and significance of the *patria potestas* in Rome's republican period and its cooptation in the imperial age see R. A. Nisbet, "Kinship and Political Power in First Century Rome," in his *Tradition and Revolt: Historical and Sociological Essays* (New York: Random House, 1968), pp. 203–224. Nisbet sees in the *imperium militiae* the significant factor for the diminution of traditional family authority and its aggrandizement by the emperors. The power of the emperor was the power of his legions. Military allegiance was won at the expense of former kinship ties.

54. Judge, *The Social Pattern,* pp. 32–33.

55. Ibid., p. 33.

56. Dio Cassius, *Annals,* 56.1–10.

57. Ibid., 56.9.

48. On the role of the *pater patriae* ideology in the "organization of opinion" for acceptance and support of the principate, see Ronald Syme, *The Roman Revolution* (Oxford: University Press, 1939), pp. 509–24, esp. pp. 519–20; cf. also pp. 459–75.

59. Dio Cassius, *Annals* 56.35–41, esp. 41.

60. Suetonius, *Titus* 8.3.

61. Cited from Naphtali Lewis and Meyer Reinhold, eds., *Roman Civilization, Sourcebook II: The Empire* (New York: Harper & Row, 1966), pp. 99–100. For further references to the political paternity of the emperors see the evidence assembled and translated on pp. 6, 8, 19, 62, 63, 75, 76, 97, 99, 100.

62. R. H. Barrow, *Slavery in the Roman Empire* (New York: Barnes and Noble, 1928; reprinted, 1968), p. 141.

63. On the household of Caesar see also A. N. Sherwin-White, "The Roman Government and the Christian Church," in *The Crucible of Christianity: Judaism, Hellenism and the Historical Background to the Christian Faith,* ed. Arnold Toynbee (New York: World and London: Thames and Hudson, 1969), pp. 141–46, esp. p. 144.

64. Judge, *The Social Pattern,* p. 29.

65. Dio Chrysostom, *Orations* 45.6, 10; cf. 51.7.

66. Ibid., 49.8, 50.10; cf. 49.13: *tēn autou polin . . . dioikein.* In the provinces of Asia Minor following the commencement of Roman rule (133 B.C.E.) *dioikēseis* (= Latin *conventus*) designated communities divided into circuits for juridical purposes: cf. A. H. M. Jones, *The Cities of the Eastern Roman Provinces* (Oxford: Oxford University Press, 1937), p. 61. LSJ renders "assize-districts" (cf. Strabo, *Geography* 13.4.12; Cicero, *Epistulae ad Familiares* 13.53.2, 67.1; *OGIS* 458.65); later (fourth cent. C.E.), a "group of provinces" (CIL 3.352); cf. the ecclesiastical "diocese."

67. Dio Chrysostom, *Orat.* 41.10.

68. Pliny, *Epistles* 8.17.

69. S. Dill, *Roman Society from Nero to Marcus Aurelius* (Cleveland/New York: World Publishing Co., 1964/1911), p. 267.

70. F. Poland, *Geschichte des griechischen Vereinswesens* (Leipzig: B. G. Teubner, 1909), p. 110 and n. 2 (abundant inscriptional data).

71. Judge, *The Social Pattern,* p. 40.

72. R. MacMullen, *Enemies of the Roman Order: Treason, Unrest, and Alienation in the Empire* (Cambridge, Mass.: Harvard University Press, 1966) pp. 173–79, 341–44, 347 n. 24. In regard to the province of Bithynia-Pontus in particular see the classic case of Trajan's attitude toward the proposed formation of a guild of firemen *(collegium fabrorum)* in Pliny, *Epistles* 10.33–34.

73. Poland, *Vereinswesens,* p. 596, E 25.

74. Ibid., p. 114, followed by A. W. Van Buren ("*Oikos,*" pp. 2119–2123, esp. 2123) who notes that this usage dates as far back as 396/395 B.C.E. (cf. *SIG*³ [Dit. Syll.] 921, 1. 33: . . . *ton Dekeleiōn oikon*).

75. R. MacMullen (*Roman Social Relations, 50 B.C. to A.D. 284* (New Haven: Yale University Press, 1974), pp. 132–35) offers an illustrative list of crafts' localities in Rome, Italy and the provinces.

76. David Magie (*Roman Rule in Asia Minor to the End of the Third Century after Christ,* 2 vols. [Princeton: Princeton University Press, 1950], 1: 588, 590; 2: 1448 n. 57) comments on the "house of the ship-builders" in Nicomedia and Amastris in Bithynia (cf. I. G. R. III. 4 *[te]me[n]os kai o[i]kos nauklē [rikos]*) and speculates that it possibly contained "a sanctuary of Vespasian to

whom the building was dedicated." On this text see also Broughton, "Roman Asia Minor," pp. 774, 777 and 844.

77. On the guilds associated with the sheep and wool industry in the province of Asia (Hierapolis, Laodicea, Colossae) as well as with other trades of, e.g., potters, leather workers, bakers, smiths, slave merchants (Thyatira) see Jones, *Cities of the Eastern Roman Provinces,* pp. 73–74 and Broughton, "Roman Asia Minor," pp. 841–49.

78. On the great variety of Greek and Roman associations (*collegia,* corporations etc.) and their diverse interests see, inter alia, W. Liebenam, *Zur Geschichte und Organization des römischen Vereinswesens* (Leipzig: B. G. Teubner, 1890); E. Ziebarth, *Das Griechische Vereinswesens* (Leipzig: S. Hirzel, 1896); Poland, *Vereinswesens;* and esp. the monumental work of J.-P. Waltzing, *Etude historique sur les corporations professionelles chez les Romains* 4 vols. (Louvain, 1895–1900), esp. 3: 24–65 ("Collegia in Asia Minor"). Also see above, Ch. 2, p. 94, n. 40.

79. Dill, *Roman Society,* pp. 266–67.

80. Ibid., p. 271. On the colleges and plebian life see pp. 251–86.

81. The similarity between the Greek and Roman associations and early Christian social formations, in regard to social circumstances, internal composition and organization, purposes and activities, extends well beyond a mutual interest in, or use of, a self-designation such as *oikos.* On the other hand, its sectarian exclusiveness and cohesiveness, demand for conversion, and religious ideology clearly mark Christianity as a *collegium* of quite a different order. The relation of these comparable social institutions warrants a fresh examination along more rigorous sociological lines. For an earlier sociological treatment of the *collegia* see Joachim Wach, *Sociology of Religion* (Chicago: University of Chicago Press, 1971/1944), esp. pp. 237–51. For a recent proposal that "house churches should be examined in light of the relationship between collegia and household communities" see Malherbe, *Social Aspects,* pp. 84–91.

82. See Judge, *The Social Pattern,* pp. 40–48 ("Unofficial Associations: Koinonia").

83. Stephen C. Barton and G. H. R. Horsley, "A Hellenistic Cult Group and the New Testament Churches" (forthcoming). I am grateful to Mr. Barton for furnishing me a copy of this study of the inscription SIG³ 985 prior to its publication.

84. R. M. MacIver, "The Family as Government in Miniature," in *The Imprint of Roman Institutions,* ed. D. W. Savage, *Western Man: An Interdisciplinary Introduction to the History of Western Civilization,* (New York: Holt, Rinehart and Winston, 1971), pp. 7–11. On "The Kinship Basis of Authority and Values: The Roman Aristocratic Family" in general see pp. 1–31.

85. Ibid., p. 7.

86. Compare, e.g., the headings of BAGD, *TWNT* (*TDNT*) with those of LSJ and PW. On the Hebrew equivalent *bayith* see E. Jenni, *"Bayith," THAT* 1: 308–13 and H. A. Hoffner, *"Bayith," TWAT* 1 (1972): 629–38. On *bayith* in the talmudic, midrashic and targumic literature see M. Jastrow, *A Dictionary of the Targumim, the Talmud Babli and Yerushalmi, and the Midrashic Literature* I (New York: Pardes Publishing House, 1950), s.v.

87. On the household family, the royal household and the household as basis and model for the craft guilds see Roland de Vaux, *Ancient Israel, I. Social Institutions* (New York: McGraw-Hill, 1965), pp. 19–23, 76–78, 115–26. See also the literature listed by Hoffner (above note), pp. 629–30 as well as Peter Weigandt ("Zur sogenannten 'Oikosformel'," *NovTest* 6 [1963] 49–74), esp pp. 50–63 and Delling ("Zur Taufe von 'Häusern'"), pp. 286–88.

88. Minear, *Images of the Church*, pp. 166–67, following in part J. Pedersen, *Israel, Its Life and Culture,* 4 vols. (London: Oxford University Press and Copenhagen: Paul Branner, 1946), esp. vol. 1–2: 48–60.

89. For the texts and discussion of this point see *Elliott, The Elect and the Holy,* pp. 157–59.

90. The sectarians of Damascus and Qumran interpreted their community to be constituted by God as "a sure house in Israel" (CD 3:19 [cf. 1 Sam. 2:35; 2 Sam. 7:16; 1 Kings 11:38]), or a "holy of holies for Aaron" (1QS 8:5–8; 9:6). Cf. also the designations "house of Judah" (CD 4:11; 1QpHab. 8:1; 4QpPs^a 2:14) and "house of Torah" (CD 20:11–13).

91. It is not apparent that *oikos* or *oikos* (*tou*) *theou/kyriou* was used in the Old Testament as a *formal* epithet for the people of God. However, the usage of Jeremiah (quoted later in this chapter) and Num. 12:7 deserves notice: "Not so with my servant Moses; he is entrusted with (is faithful over) my whole house (au)." The equation of "house" and Jerusalem (comprising its inhabitants) occurs in the allegory of 1 En. 89:50–67 which is mentioned, in turn, in the Testament of Levi 10:5: "For the house which the Lord shall choose shall be called Jerusalem, as contained in the book of Enoch the righteous." In the Enoch passage the house is Jerusalem and the temple, a tower. In 1 En. 53:6 the association of "house" and community of the righteous is even clearer: "And after this the righteous and elect one shall cause the house of his congregation to appear; henceforth they shall be no more hindered in the name of the Lord of Spirits." Cf. also 38:1. In the Christian literature, *oikos* (*tou theou*) as a designation for the people of God becomes more pronounced. Thus in Hebrews the *oikos* of Num. 12:7 is expressly taken as referring to God's community and then is applied to the Christian believers: "And we are his house if we hold fast our confidence and pride in our hope" (Heb. 3:6). Cf. also

10:21 where, unless *oikos* refers to the heavenly sanctuary (so BAGD, s.v.), it denotes the people of God as the new temple of God.

92. See Gen. 12:1, 10; 15:13; 17:8; 18:19 etc. and, for the significance of this event for the Christian community, Acts 7:2–8; Heb. 11:8–10. The reference to Abraham and Sarah in 1 Pet. 3:5–6 may well have been intended as an example of *oikos* life in a *paroikia* situation.

93. So Walter Brueggemann, *The Land,* Overtures to Biblical Theology (Philadelphia: Fortress Press, 1977), p. 108. Brueggemann particularly stresses the equation of homelessness and landlessness and its political, economic and social implications for Israel's identity and hope.

94. Ibid., p. 114.

95. See also "house of Judah" (Jer. 11:10, 17; 13:11 etc.), "houses of David" (21:12) etc.

96. For *metoikia* see Jer. 9:10 (LXX); 20:4; also *metoikizein* (20:4; 22:12), *metoikesia* (50[43]:5) and *metoikos* (20:3 LXX). The noun *paroikia* does not occur; but see *paroikos* (14:8; 29[49]:18; 30[49]:5) and *paroikein* (6:25 LXX; 27[50]:40; 51[44]:14, 28). See also *apoikia* (18 times), *apoikizein* (10 times), *apoikismos* (26[46]:19; 31[48]:11; 50[43]:11) and *anoikodomein* (1:10; 18:9; 24:6). These terms, along with *oikos* (114 times), *oikia* (18 times) and *oikodomein* (33 times), indicate the basic and pervasive importance of *oikos* terminology and conceptuality for the message of Jeremiah.

97. Note the contrast of *oikos tou Israēl* and *oikos parapikrainōn* in Ezek. 2:3/5, 6, 7; 3:7/9, 17/26, 27; 44:6.

98. See Brueggemann, *The Land,* pp. 122–29.

99. Xavier Jacques (*List of New Testament Words Sharing Common Elements* [Rome: Biblical Institute Press, 1969], p. 79) lists, besides *oikia,* 36 other paronyms of *oikos.*

100. See Gen. 41:40.

101. The temple built by Solomon (Acts 7:47) and the prophetic critique of such temple-building (v. 49, quoting Isa. 66:1).

102. See Matt. 10:6; 15:24; Luke 1:27, 33, 69; 2:4; Acts 2:36; 7:42, 46; Heb. 8:8 (twice), 10.

103. See Matt. 13:54–57/Mark 6:1–4; Luke 2:4.

104. See Matt. 10:14; 12:25; also Acts 20:20 *(dēmosia kai kat' oikous).*

105. "Behold, your house is forsaken" is Jesus' lament over the city of Jerusalem (Matt. 23:37–38/Luke 13:34–35). The possible influence of the prophecy of Jeremiah (cf. Jer. 22:1, 2, 4, 5, 8) would suggest that the destruction encompasses the ruling house(s), inhabitants and city all together. In retrospect of the destruction of 70 c.e. this lament would indeed be applicable to the entirety of Jerusalem, the temple, the city and its inhabitants. For the use of *oikos*

terminology to describe the task of a municipal administrator, see Paul's reference to "Erastus, the city treasurer" (*oikonomos tou poleōs,* Rom. 16:23). Note also Heb. 8:11 which implies that every member of the future house of Israel and Judah (8:8, 10) will be a fellow citizen (*politēs*) and fellow brother (*adelphos*).

106. See the contrast between Abraham's living by faith as a resident alien (*parōkesen*) in the land of promise, as in a foreign land (Heb. 11:9) and his looking forward to "the city which has foundations, whose builder and maker is God" (v. 10). With a similar contrast the author continues (vv. 13–16): "These [Abel, Enoch, Noah, Abraham, Sarah and their descendants] all died in faith, not having received what was promised, but having seen it and greeted it from afar, and having acknowledged that they were strangers and exiles (*xenoi kai parepidēmoi*) on the earth. For people who speak thus make it clear that they are seeking a homeland (*patrida*). If they had been thinking of that land from which they had gone out, they would have had opportunity to return. But as it is, they desire a better country, that is, a heavenly one. Therefore God is not ashamed to be called their God, for he has prepared for them a city (*polin*)."

As already pointed out, while the contrast between *paroikia* existence and its alternative, viz., rest in the city (Hebrews) or life in the *oikos* (1 Peter), reflects the rift seen by both authors between the Christian community and its social environment, the responses to this condition proposed by the authors vary considerably. 1 Peter speaks of a counter- or compensatory community here and now; Hebrews, on the other hand, shifts the focus and the goal from life vis-à-vis an earthly city to life in a heavenly abode.

Thus 1 Peter is closer to the perspective of Ephesians where the contrast of citizenship and noncitizenship, strangerhood and household membership, is used to describe the former alienation of Gentiles and Jews which has since been eliminated through their unification in the household of faith here and now in the present social order (Eph. 2:11–21, esp. vv. 12 and 19).

107. *Oikos* in Luke 11:17, *oikia* in the parallels of Mark 3:25 and Matt 12:25.

108. So Robert M. Grant, *Augustus to Constantine* (New York: Harper & Row, 1970), p. 55, noting that the images and interests of early Christian organization were politically influenced and motivated.

108. Theissen, *Sociology.*

110. E.g., the house of Simon and Andrew (Mark 1:29), of Levi (Mark 2:15), of the Syrophoenician woman (Mark 7:24), of Simon the leper (Mark 14:3), of the Pharisee (Luke 7:37), and of Martha and Mary (Luke 10:38).

111. E.g., the house of Judas in Damascus (Acts 9:11, 17), of Simon the tanner in Joppa (Acts 10:6, 17, 32; 11:11), of Mary in Jerusalem (Acts 12:12),

of the Philippian jailer (Acts 16:32), of Jason in Thessalonica (Acts 17:5), and of the Corinthian Titius Justus (Acts 18:7).

112. For *oikos* = household members see, e.g., Luke 10:5; 11:17; 12:52–53; 16:27; 19:9; Acts 10:2; 11:14; 16:15, 31; 18:8; Rom. 16:5; 1 Cor. 1:16; 16:19; 1 Tim. 3:4, 5, 12; 5:4; 2 Tim. 1:16; 4:19; Titus 1:11; Heb. 11:7. For *oikos* in the sense of "home" see, e.g., Mark 2:1, 11; 3:20. The distinction, however, between *oikia* (= building) and *oikos* (= household) was not rigid. See, e.g., the variants in Mark 7:24/30, Luke 7:36/37; Mark 5:38 and Luke 8:41/Matt. 9:23; *oikia* = family or household in Mark 6:4; John 4:53; 1 Cor. 16:15; Phil. 4:22 (household of Caesar); *oikos* = building in Luke 7:10, 36; Matt. 12:44/ Luke 11:24; Acts 16:31–34.

113. Gülzow, "Soziale Gegebenheiten," p. 198.

114. On the house synagogues of the Jews in the diaspora see Martin Hengel, "Die Synagogeninschrift von Stobi," *ZNW* 57 (1966): 145–83, esp. p. 161; and on these house synagogues as a model for Christian groups see Stuhlmacher, *Der Brief an Philemon*, pp. 70–75 ("Exkurs: Urchristliche Hausgemeinden"), esp. pp. 72–73.

115. See 1 Cor. 16:19; Rom. 16:5; 1 Cor. 1:14; Acts 18:8; Rom. 16:23; Acts 16:15, 40; 1 Cor. 1:16; 16:15; Col. 4:15; Philem. 2; Col. 4:17. See also the conversion of the official of Capharnaum and his household (John 4:46–53) and that of the Philippian jailer and his household (Acts 16:31–34).

116. Gülzow, "Soziale Gegebenheiten," p. 199.

117. See Hainz, *Ekklesia*, pp. 345–48.

118. See Eph. 5:22–6:9; Col. 3:18–4:1; 1 Tim. 2:8–15; 3:1–15; 5:1–22; 6:1–2; Titus 2:1–10; 3:1–2; 1 Pet. 2:18–3:9(12); 5:1–5; also *1 Clem.* 1:3; 21:6–9; *Pol. Phil.* 4:1–6:3.

119. So Filson, "Early House Churches," pp. 111–12 and Hainz (*Ekklesia*, p. 346) who sees the function of these household heads/leaders corresponding to that of the *proistamenoi* of Thessalonica (1 Thess. 5:12) or the *episkopoi* of Philippi (Phil. 1:1) and included among the *kybernēseis* ("administrational capabilities, capacities") in 1 Cor. 12:28.

120. 1 Cor. 16:19: " . . . Aquila and Prisca, together with the church [meeting] in their house . . . "; cf. also Rom. 16:3.

121. Col. 4:15: "Give my greetings to the brothers at Laodicea, and to Nympha and the church [meeting] in her house (au)."

122. Philem. 2: " . . . to Philemon our beloved fellow worker and Apphia our sister and Archippus our fellow soldier, and the church [meeting] in your [sing.] house."

123. Rom. 16:1–2: "I commend to you our sister Phoebe, a deaconess of the church at Cenchreae, . . . for she has been a helper [*prostatis*, lit. "patron"] of many and of myself as well."

124. Rom. 16:23: "Gaius who is host to me and to the whole church, greets you." Cf. also 1 Cor. 1:14.

125. 1 Cor. 16:15–16.

126. This fact is further signaled by the qualifications which Paul regularly gives to his associate leaders and co-workers such as "fellow worker" (Philemon; for Stephanus see 1 Cor. 16:16; for Prisca and Aquila see Rom. 16:3), "fellow soldier" (Archippus), "deacon" (Phoebe; for Stephanus see *diakonia,* 1 Cor. 16:15); cf. E. E. Ellis, "Paul and His Co-workers," *NTS* 17 (1971): 437–52. If a further observation of Ellis is correct, then "brother" and "sister" were used not simply as general terms for fellow members of the family of faith but also specifically of its leaders, thus here of the "brothers" in Laodicea and of the "sisters" Apphia and Phoebe.

127. See E. Kamlah, *"Hypotassesthai* in den neutestamentlichen 'Haustafeln'," in *Verborum Veritas,* Gustav Stählin FS, ed. O. Böcher and K. Haacker (Wuppertal: Theologischer Verlag—Rolf Brockhaus, 1970), pp. 237–43; on this point, esp. p. 238, n. 2 with reference to Philo, *Decal.* 165–67; *Spec. Leg.* 2: 226–33.

128. See, e.g., 1 Cor. 14:32; 1 Pet. 5:5; 1 Thess. 5:12; Heb. 13:17 (cf. v. 7).

129. So Kamlah, *"Hypotassesthai,"* pp. 241–43, in regard to all occasions for subordination. This is especially clear in 1 Peter where subordination to government officials, masters, husbands (2:13–3:7), and leaders (5:5a) is immediately followed by an exhortation to general mutual humility (3:8; 5:5b–6).

130. Ibid., p. 240.

131. See Günther Bornkamm, *"Presbys"* etc., *TDNT* 6 (1968/1959): 651–83 and L. Coenen, "Presbyter," *TBLNT* 3 (1972): 1003–1010.

132. See also Acts 21:16 where it is noted that the house at which Paul and his companions stayed in Caesarea belonged to Mnason of Cyprus, "an early disciple" (*archaiō mathētē*).

133. For a more extended discussion of *neoteros* in this sense and of the related New Testament material see J. H. Elliott, "Ministry and Church Order in the NT: A Tradition-Historical Analysis (1 Pet 5,1–5 and plls.)," *CBQ* 32 (1970): 367–91.

134. See John Reumann, " 'Stewards of God'—Pre-Christian Religious Application of OIKONOMOS in Greek," *JBL* 77 (1958): 339–49; Wilfred Tooley, "Stewards of God: An Examination of the Terms OIKONOMOS and OIKONOMIA in the New Testament," *Scottish Journal of Theology* 19 (1966): 74–86; and for hellenistic usage, Peter Landvogt, *Epigraphische Untersuchungen über den OIKONOMOS: Ein Beitrag zum hellenistischen Beamtenwesen* (Strassbourg: M. Dumont Schauberg, 1908).

135. See John Reumann, "OIKONOMIA = 'Covenant': Terms for Heilsgeschichte in Early Christian Usage," *NovT* 3 (1959): 282–99.

136. S. Aalen, " 'Reign' and 'House' in the Kingdom of God in the Gospels," *NTS* 8 (1962): 215–40.

137. See R. Gundry, " 'In My Father's House Are Many *Monai*' (John 14: 2)," *ZNW* 58 (1967): 68–72.

138. Judge, *The Social Pattern*, p. 38.

139. In Mark 3:20–35, vv. 20–21 and vv. 31–35 (*oikos* in the former = the family of Jesus explicitly in the latter) frame the verse units 22–26 (*oikia* = household), 27 (*oikia* = house) and 28–30. Through this elaborate form of composition the author has compared and contrasted those who stand with Jesus and those who oppose him, those who are actually in alliance with Beelzebul and those in alliance with God. For a detailed structural analysis of this passage see Jan Lambrecht, *Marcus Interpretator* (Brussels/Utrecht: Desclée de Brouwer, 1969), pp. 13–97; see also id., "The Relatives of Jesus in Mark," *NovT* 17 (1974): 241–58.

140. *Oikos* and *oikia* figure significantly throughout the Gospel of Mark. The house is the locus of exclusive instruction (9:28–29, 33–50; 10:10–16) for those "insiders" to whom the mystery of the kingdom has been given (4:11). In the concluding apocalyptic discourse vigilance in the household serves as a simile for apprehension of the coming kingdom (13:33–37). Discipleship of Jesus involves the disruption of old familial alliances (cf. 6:1–6; 10:29–30; 13:12–13, 15–17) as well as the construction of new familial bonds (3:35; 10: 10–16).

141. Theissen, in his fascinating analysis of the social shape and ethos of the earliest Jesus movement (see esp. his "Itinerant Radicalism" and *Sociology*), has stressed its radical renunciation of home, family, possessions and protection. What now requires closer attention is the manner in which this radical tradition of homelessness was interpreted by the movement after 70 c.e. and especially in the diaspora. What role in particular did the *oikos* play not simply in "tempering" early Christian radicalism ("Itinerant Radicalism," p. 91) but in suggesting equally authentic social expression of the message of Jesus?

142. On this point see Henri Mottu, "The Pharisee and the Tax Collector: Sartian Notions as Applied to the Reading of Scripture," *Union Seminary Quarterly Review* 29 (1974): 195–213.

143. Y. Redalié, "Conversion or Liberation? Notes on Acts 16:11–40," in *The Bible and Liberation: Political and Social Hermeneutics,* ed. A. C. Wire and N. Gottwald (Berkeley: Community for Religious Research and Education, 1976), pp. 102–108.

144. Ibid., p. 105.

145. When this *constellation* of social, political and religious factors is overlooked and the image of "temple" (*naos*, v. 21) is assumed to dominate the

passage, the *social* novelty and significance of the community which the author affirms are obscured, if not lost. Thus E. Schüssler-Fiorenza ("Cultic Language in Qumran," pp. 159–77, esp. p. 173), who focuses only on the cultic imagery, concludes: "The Gentiles are no longer strangers and foreigners who are excluded from the holy temple of the endtime. Instead they have full members of the temple community." The sociopolitical terms "stranger" and "foreigner" refer, however, to the former estrangement of the Gentiles from the *politeia* of Israel and its national covenantal promises (v. 12). This former political, social and religious alienation is contrasted to their now being *sympolitai* ("co-citizens") and *oikeioi* (equal "household members," v. 19). Jews and Gentiles now constitute not merely a figurative "temple" (which is only one of several corporate images alongside household, building and plantation) but an actual social community in which old ethnic, political and social barriers no longer exist.

146. The similarities between Eph. 2:11–22 and 1 Pet. 2:4–10 should not obscure the differences which indicate independent composition and not literary dependence. The issue requires separate treatment. Only some of the most obvious points can be mentioned here. (1) In Ephesians *only Gentiles* are said to have been *paroikoi previously;* in 1 Peter *all the believers are paroikoi presently.* (2) In Ephesians the point of reference for estrangement is the former relation of Gentile to Jew; in 1 Peter it is the present relation of believers in contrast to their social environment. (3) In Ephesians the household is used to address the *internal* issue of Gentile-Jewish Christian harmony and equality within the church; 1 Peter stresses the *oikos* character of the community in order to deal with *external* pressures as well. (4) In Eph. 2:20–22 several building images (*epoikodomeisthai, themelion, akrogoniaios, oikodomē, synoikomeisthai, katoikterion*) are extended by the explicit inclusion of the term *naos* and are used to accentuate the unity and growth of the community "built upon the foundation of the apostles and prophets, Christ Jesus himself being the chief cornerstone." In 1 Peter both *naos* and interest in apostolic authority (cf. also Eph. 3:4–6 and 4:11–16) are absent. Instead, "stone" tradition (1 Pet. 2:4, 5, 6–8) has been combined with honorific predicates of the people of God (vv. 9–10, having no parallel in Ephesians) in order to express the elect and holy nature of the household of the Spirit. While the social implications of *oikos* terminology are useful to both Ephesians and 1 Peter, their differences in literary composition and theological focus indicate the independent and, in my opinion, later composition of Ephesians. Whatever the judgment concerning relative dating, it is advisable to avoid an interpretation of the *oikos* of 1 Peter by the *naos* of Ephesians.

147. The theological elaboration of the child (son, daughter)/Father (God)

relationship and the various related images of (pro-)creation, (re)birth, filial obedience etc. are too well-known to require enumeration. In Galatians, the underlying concept of the household is evident, for instance, in the identity of the children of God (3:23–4:7) with the "household of faith" in 6:10. In Hebrews, note the juxtaposition of 2:10–18 and 3:1–6. For the integration of household and familial imagery in 1 Peter, see below. For a recent treatment of the use of the "father image" in the New Testament see Robert Hamerton-Kelly, *God the Father: Theology and Patriarchy in the Teaching of Jesus*, Overtures to Biblical Theology (Philadelphia: Fortress Press, 1979).

148. *Adelphos* and *adelphē*, in Christian as in Jewish and secular usage, designated those bound not only by ties of blood or kinship but also by close association and common commitment. See H. von Soden, *"Adelphos"* etc., *TDNT* 1 (1964/1933): 144–46; W. Günther, "Bruder *(adelphos)*," *TBLNT* 1 (1972): 146–49. Believers in Jesus Christ as Son of God or Lord became his siblings and beneficiaries (cf., e.g., Rom. 8:9–17, 29–30; Gal. 3:26–27; Heb. 2:10–18; Mark 3:33–35; Matt. 23:8–9; 25:40; John 1:12–13). They are "brothers (or sisters) in the Lord" (Phil. 1:14; for further passages see BAGD s.v. *adelphos*). See further Karl Herman Schelkle, "Bruder," *RAC* 2 (1954): 631–40; Adolf von Harnack, *The Mission and Expansion of Christianity in the First Three Centuries*, trans. and ed. James Moffatt; 2 vols. (New York: Harper & Row, 1962 [reprint of 1908 ed.]), 1: 405–07; and below, p. 258, n. 165.

149. Judge, *The Social Pattern*, p. 38.

150. Texts such as these show that it was in baptismal tradition that the fatherhood-sonship-family constellation of ideas was especially stressed. It is quite possible, then, that it was missionary propaganda and prebaptismal instruction through which the Christian adherents were first introduced to the idea of the community as a spiritual family or household. The actual baptism of households was certainly an appropriate occasion to discuss the *paternitas* and *potestas* of God, the sonship of Jesus and the familial character and domestic responsibilities characteristic of this distinctive form of religious association.

151. For *philadelphia* see Rom. 12:10; 1 Thess. 4:9; Heb. 13:1; 1 Pet. 1:22; 2 Pet. 1:7; for *philadelphos*, 1 Pet. 3:8.

152. See, e.g., Rom. 6:1–14; 8:23; Eph. 4:30; Col. 1:14; 1 Pet. 1:18–19; Mark 10:45; and the slave/freedman language of 1 Cor. 7:22.

153. The Christian adoption, for instance, of the terms *doulos* and *diakonos* as self-designations is extraordinarily frequent in the New Testament (see BAGD s.v.). The composite term *syndoulos* ("coslave") expresses the *bond* of slavery which unites the believers (Col. 1:7; 4:7) and serves as a virtual synonym for "brother" (Col. 4:7; Rev. 6:11; 19:10; 22:9). See also David Daube, *Studies in Biblical Law* (Cambridge: University Press, 1947), for a detailed

study of "change of masters" language in the Old Testament with reference to its New Testament implications.

154. Judge, *The Social Pattern*, p. 38.

155. See (1) Matt. 12:4/Mark 2:26/Luke 6:4; (2) Matt. 21:13/Mark 11:17/ Luke 19:46 (all quoting Isa. 56:7); cf. John 2:16 and 2:17 quoting Ps. 68(69): 9; (3) Luke 11:51; (4) Acts 7:47 (narrating 1 Kings 6:1, 14); cf. the critique in 7:49 (quoting Isa. 66:1–2); (5) Matt. 23:38 where *oikos* probably includes city and people as well as the temple.

156. *To hieron,* 70/71 times (cf. John 8:2); *naos,* 18 times (*naos* = Jesus' body, John 2:21).

157. *To hieron* (Acts 19:27), *naoi* (Acts 17:24; 19:24).

158. *Naos,* 14 times, in addition to Rev. 21:22 where it is said that in the new Jerusalem there shall be no temple "for its temple is the Lord God the Almighty and the Lamb."

159. *Naos* is used in all instances: 1 Cor. 3:16–17; 6:19; 2 Cor. 6:16; Eph. 2:21.

160. For the use of *oikos* in this sense, see the texts mentioned in n. 155 above. For *naos* as the object of *oikodomein* see, e.g., Matt. 26:61/Mark 14:58; Matt. 27:40/Mark 15:29; John 2:20.

161. Thus in 1 Corinthians 3, to the portrayal of the Corinthians as the "planting" (*geōrgion*) and "building" (*oikodomē*) of God (vv. 9–15) is added a different yet related image of the community as the holy temple of God in which God's Spirit dwells (vv. 16–17). The image of the community as the product of Paul's apostolic "foundation-laying" activity (i.e., the proclamation of the gospel) and the divine judgment of this activity is expanded by the metaphor of the believers as a temple filled with God's presence and secure in his protection. Similarly in 2 Corinthians 6, a statement on the incompatibility of righteousness/iniquity, light/darkness, Christ/Belial, believer/unbeliever, the temple of God and idols (vv. 14–16a) is extended by the words "For we are the temple of the living God" (v. 16b), which thought is then expanded through allusion to a catena of Old Testament passages (vv. 16c–18: Lev. 26:12; Isa. 52:11; Ezek. 20:34; 2 Sam. 7:14). In Ephesians, as already noted, the unification of former Jews and Gentiles in the household of God (2:11–19) is a point expanded by the addition of the images of construction, foundation and temple (vv. 20–22) in order to express the basis, cause of integration, and holy (divine) character of the new community.

162. See G. Schrenk, *"Hieros," TDNT* 3 (1965/1938): 221–47, esp. pp. 242–47; O. Michel, *"Naos," TDNT* 4 (1967/1942): 880–90; and more recently, F. W. Young, "Temple Cult and Law in Early Christianity," *NTS* 10 (1973): 325–38.

163. For the distinction of "insiders/outsiders" see also Mark 4:11 (cf. 3:20–

35); 1 Cor. 5:12–13; 10:32–33; 1 Thess. 4:11–12; 1 Tim. 3:7; Rev. 22:15. Cf. also Matt. 8:12; 22:13; 25:30.

164. For *philadelphia* see Rom. 12:10; 1 Thess. 4:9; Heb. 13:1; 2 Pet. 1:7 (twice). In the LXX it is only in the Maccabean literature that these terms occur: see *adelphotēs,* 1 Macc. 12:10, 17; 4 Macc. 9:23; 10:3, 15; 13:19, 27; *philadelphia* only in 4 Macc. 13:23, 26 and 14:1; and *philadelphos* in 2 Macc. 15:14; 4 Macc. 13:21; 15:10. For a stress upon brotherhood (*adelphotēs*), brotherly love (*philadelphia*) and solidarity (*syn-* composites) as a bulwark against outside opposition see 4 Macc. 13:1–14:7.

165. For *adelphē* used of a Christian "sister" (in the faith) see also Rom. 16:1; 1 Cor. 7:15; 9:5; 1 Tim. 5:2; Philem. 2; Jas. 2:15; 2 John 13 (*adelphēs ...eklektēs*). See above, p. 225, and n. 148.

166. Goppelt, *Der Erste Petrusbrief,* KEK 12/1, ed. Ferdinand Hahn, 1. aufl. (Göttingen: Vanderhoeck und Ruprecht, 1978), p. 354, n. 44.

167. See, e.g., Mark 1:29–31; Luke 10:38–42; 12:35–38; 17:7–10; 22:27; John 12:1–3. 1 Cor. 16:15 and 2 Tim. 1:16–18 speak not simply of service *in* the household but of service *by* entire households (of Stephanas and Onesiphorus, respectively).

168. See above, p. 252, n. 119.

169. See Luke 16:13; Acts 10:7; Rom. 14:4 in addition to 1 Pet. 2:18.

170. Ludwig Radermacher ("Der erste Petrusbrief und Silvanus," *ZNW* 25 [1926]: 287–99) noted this unusual aspect of the passage and considered it "psychologisch interessant" (p. 290).

171. 1 Tim. 6:1–2 is another exception, although here the masters are mentioned indirectly as possibly being fellow believers.

172. Selwyn, *First Epistle of St. Peter.* p. 175.

173. Among the specific household members addressed (slaves, wives, husbands, elders, novices), innocent suffering is mentioned only in connection with the *oiketai.*

174. The christological tradition of 1 Pet. 2:21–25 echoes the terminology and thematic of the fourth servant song of Deutero-Isaiah, 52:13–53:12; cf. esp. the verbal affinities in v. 22 (Isa. 53:9), v. 24 (53:11) and v. 25 (53:5, 6). *Oiketēs* does not occur in the LXX version of this Isaianic passage but it is closely related to the two terms which are used: *pais* in 52:13 and *douleuonta* in 53:11. Underlying both these terms, as well as all occurrences of *oiketēs* in the LXX, is the same Hebrew term, namely, *'ebed.*

The stimulus and function of a specific servant Christology here in 1 Peter are determined by the specific condition of the addressees. The innocent suffering of the Christian servants was a problem to which the innocent suffering of Jesus Christ, described in the language of the Isaianic servant of God, was designed to supply a justification and a point of comparison. As the Christ suffered, though innocent, so they also who bear his name (cf. 1 Pet. 4:12–16). As they are but humble servants, so also was he.

On the earlier association of the Isaianic suffering servant passages with a Jewish sectarian document and circle see Julian Morgenstern, "The Suffering Servant—A New Solution," *Vetus Testamentum* 11 (1961): 292–320, 406–31, esp. pp. 428–31. Morgenstern locates this sect in the vicinity of Dor or Galilee. "This assumption would account in altogether likely manner for the obvious currency of our drama and of the tradition and doctrine which it recorded among the Galilean sectaries, as Jesus and his followers undoubtedly were, some four centuries or more after its composition" (p. 430).

175. As far as the *theological* tradition and transmission of a suffering servant of God Christology are concerned, Oscar Cullmann (*The Christology of the New Testament*, trans. S. C. Guthrie and C. A. M. Hall, rev. ed. [Philadelphia: Westminster Press, 1959], pp. 51–82) has ventured the hypothesis that an *Ebed Yawheh* Christology may well have been a characteristic of the apostle Peter and the Petrine circle. Of the four New Testament instances where Jesus is explicitly called the *pais* (of God), two such designations occur within a speech attributed to Peter (Acts 3:13; cf. Isa. 52:13; Acts 3:26) and two others in a situation where the witness of Peter is prominent (Acts 4:27, 30). 1 Peter, quite apart from the question of its authenticity, would reflect, like Acts, the common knowledge of a Petrine preference for a suffering servant of God Christology; cf. Cullmann, esp. pp. 73–75.

176. The preceding parenesis of 2:13–17 applies to all the recipients. 1 Pet. 2:18–25 introduces the first specific group *within* the household of God to be addressed.

177. In Deuteronomy, the fact that Israel itself was once an *oiketēs* in the land of Egypt (5:15) and was liberated from the "house of bondage" (*oikou douleias,* 6:12) is used as a motivation for keeping the commandments of God (6:21, 16:12) and for showing humane treatment to fellow Hebrew slaves (15: 12–15) as well as other defenseless persons such as the resident alien, the orphans and the widows (24:17–22).

178. See above, pp. 239–254.

179. J. E. Crouch, *Colossian Haustafel;* W. Schrage, "Haustafeln"; D. Lührmann, "Wo man nicht mehr Sklave oder Freier ist"; D. L. Balch, *"Let Wives Be Submissive . . . ".* For surveys of previous literature see Crouch, pp. 9–36; Lührmann, pp. 71–76; Balch, pp. 8–27. See above, p. 238, n. 11.

180. M. Dibelius, *An die Kolosser, Epheser, an Philemon,* HNT 3, 2 (Tübingen: J. C. B. Mohr, 1913), esp. the excursus following Col. 4:1; K. Weidinger, *Die Haustafeln: Ein Stück urchristlicher Paränese,* Untersuchungen zum Neuen Testament 14 (Leipzig: J. C. Hinrichs 1928).

181. Martin Dibelius, *Die Formgeschichte des Evangeliums,* 5. aufl. (Tübin-

gen: J. C. B. Mohr, 1966), p. 239: "Die Regeln und Weisungen sind nicht für bestimmte Gemeinden und konkrete Fälle formuliert, sondern für die allgemeinen Bedürfnisse der ältesten Christenheit. Sie haben nicht *aktuelle,* sondern *usuelle* Bedeutung."

182. Weidinger, *Haustafeln,* p. 52.

183. Dibelius, *Kolosser,* p. 48; *Formgeschichte,* p. 241.

184. Weidinger, *Haustafeln,* pp. 11–12.

185. Crouch, *Colossian Haustafel,* pp. 120–21. See also Schrage, "Haustafeln," p. 4, n. 1.

186. For a critique of the theory that the household codes formed part of an early Christian catechism, see Crouch, ibid., pp. 13–18.

187. Schrage, "Haustafeln," pp. 3–4.

188. D. Schroeder, "Die Haustafeln des Neuen Testaments: Ihre Herkunft und ihr theologischer Sinn" (Doctoral diss., Hamburg, 1959).

189. Crouch, *Colossian Haustafel,* p. 141; cf. pp. 120–45.

190. Ibid., p. 157.

191. Schrage, "Haustafeln," p. 5.

192. Ibid., p. 22.

193. Crouch, *Colossian Haustafel,* pp. 32, 155. This means, however, that whatever conclusions are drawn concerning the situation and function of the Colossian code they cannot summarily be applied to any of the other New Testament *Haustafeln.* Each New Testament code requires its own specific analysis.

194. Schrage, "Der erste Petrusbrief," in "Die 'Katholischon' Briefe," p. 61.

195. Schrage, "Haustafeln," pp. 10–11; cf. also *Der erste Petrusbrief,* pp. 87–90 and id., *Die Christen und der Staat nach dem Neuen Testament* (Gütersloh: Gütersloher Verlagshaus—Gerd Mohn, 1971), pp. 63–68 (on 1 Peter 2). L. Goppelt ("Prinzipien neutestamentlicher Sozialethik nach dem 1. Petrusbrief," in *Neues Testament und Geschichte,* O. Cullmann FS, ed. H. Baltensweiler and B. Reicke [Zürich: Theologischer Verlag and Tübingen: J. C. B. Mohr, 1972], pp. 285–96; *Der erste Petrusbrief,* esp. "Exkurs: Die Standetafeltradition," pp. 163–79) presents a similar position.

196. Schrage, "Haustafeln," p. 6, n. 3.

197. Ibid., p. 22.

198. Karl H. Rengstorf, "Mahnungen," pp. 131–45; id. *Mann und Frau,* pp. 7–52. (See above, p. 237, n. 3.)

199. Rengstorf, *Mann und Frau,* p. 25; cf. "Mahnungen," p. 134.

200. Rengstorf, "Mahnungen," pp. 136–37.

201. Rengstorf, *Mann und Frau,* p. 24: "Ihr Sinn ist, die mit dem 'Hause,' d.h. mit der jeweils im gleichen Hause lebenden Gemeinschaft, der Familie als

der Grundform menschliches Zusammenlebens im Altertum gegebenen Beziehungen auch im christlichen Bereich zu aller Beteiligten Wohle christlich zu ordnen."

202. Rengstorf, "Mahnungen," p. 136; cf. *Mann und Frau*, p. 25.

203. Rengstorf, "Mahnungen," p. 136.

204. Ibid., p. 134.

205. Rengstorf, *Mann und Frau*, p. 28. Schrage ("Haustafeln," p. 6, n. 3) notices this also.

206. Crouch, *Colossian Haustafel*, p. 104; cf. pp. 24–26.

207. The last of these texts he dismisses with the remark that "The *oikos theou* in I Tim. 3:15 reflects a later interest of the Haustafel schema after it had been adapted to the concerns of an emerging church order" (ibid., p. 104, n. 12).

208. Crouch's failure to consider these points is all the more regrettable in view of the evidence which he himself cited earlier in his own work. Thus, within the Stoic tradition he noted a certain "tendency to treat the members of the family as a unit" among those texts which show a departure from the traditional Stoic treatment of duties (ibid., pp. 71–72). Likewise he observed within hellenistic Judaism an abundance of evidence for "practical advice concerning the relationship among members of the family" (ibid., pp. 74–83). In fact, concerning the text which he considers to be "the closest parallel to the pattern of the Colossian *Haustafel* which we have observed" (ibid., p. 107), namely, the Philonic fragment *De Hypothetica* 7.14, he has appropriately remarked that "it was the duty of the head of the house to instruct the members of the family in the Law, and Philo summarizes this duty in the form of a *Haustafel*" (ibid., p. 82). The text of *De Hypothetica* 7.14 reads: "The husband seems to be competent to transmit the laws to his wife, the father to the children, the master to his slaves." Unfortunately, Crouch failed to pursue the implications of the household dimension of the household codes for the Christian household instruction and its *oikos* context as well.

209. See Schrage, "Haustafeln," pp. 6, 12 (with approving reference to Rengstorf), and 13.

210. Ibid., p. 2. To his objection that the circle of duties extends beyond the limits of the natural household and, as in 1 Pet. 2:13–17, embraces civic responsibilities as well, two things must be said. First, the *oikos* and the *polis* are long associated social entities; responsibilities in the former realm naturally recall or suggest responsibilities in the latter. Second, according to 1 Peter in particular, while the Christian community as *oikos* of God is advised of its civic responsibilities, it is also reminded of its familial distinctiveness and of its subordination for the sake of the will of God alone. Toward the emperor and all

men they may show "honor," but "reverence" is due to God alone and "love" is reserved for the members of the household, the brotherhood (2:17). Even in regard to the state, the *oikos* character of the Christian community provides the basic point of reference.

211. "Sociological Exegesis mit Textprobe: The Church as *Oikos*," April 18, 1975.

212. I am grateful to Mr. Balch for calling my attention to his work at the 1976 general meeting of the Society of Biblical Literature in St. Louis, Mo. A 1976 copy of his dissertation is available at University Microfilms International, Ann Arbor, Michigan and London, England.

213. I am also indebted to Prof. Lührmann for sending me a copy of his study as a result of our conversation at the 1977 annual meeting of the Studiorum Novi Testamenti Societas in Tübingen, Germany.

214. Friedrich Wilhelm, "Die Oeconomica der Neupythagoreer Bryson, Kallikratidas, Periktione, Phintys," *Rheinisches Museum für Philologie* 70 (1915): 163–64, 222.

215. Balch, *Wives*, p. 27.

216. Lührmann, "Wo man nicht mehr Sklave oder Freier ist," p. 76. As another related *Stichwort*, Lührmann (ibid., n. 84) mentions *oikon (di)oikein* (Xenophon, *Oeconomicus* 11.10; Dio Chrysostom, *Orat.* 69.2).

217. Concerning the influence of this text on both economic and moral thought up until the modern era see the comment of the economic historian M. I. Finley ("Aristotle and Economic Analysis," pp. 26–52, esp. p. 48): "However, neither speculation about the origins of trade nor doubts about market ethics led to the elevation of 'the economy' (which cannot be translated into Greek) to independent status as a subject of discussion or study. . . . The model that survived and was imitated was Xenophon's *Oeconomicus*, a manual covering all the human relations between husband and wife, between master and slaves, between householder and his lands and goods. It was not from *Hausvaterliteratur* [such as this] that modern economic thinking and writing arose in the late eighteenth century, but from the radical discovery that there were 'laws' of circulation, of market exchange, of value and prices. . . . "

218. Lührmann ("Wo man nicht mehr Sklave oder Freier ist," p. 78) also includes the three books of the *Oikonomika* attributed to Aristotle and based upon his and Xenophon's earlier works.

219. For an extensive discussion of the context and content of this material see Balch, *Wives*, pp. 9–15.

220. Lührmann, "Wo man nicht mehr Sklave oder Freier ist," pp. 76, 77–79.

221. Balch, *Wives*, pp. 33–114.

222. For Balch's summary of this material see ibid., pp. 112–14.

223. Ibid., p. 49.

224. Lührmann, "Wo man nicht mehr Sklave oder Freier ist," pp. 79, 76–79.

225. Ibid., p. 79.

226. For Lührmann's reference to Rengstorf see ibid., p. 74.

227. Balch, *Wives,* Abstract, p. 3.

228. Ibid., pp. 264–65.

229. The content and function of the Josephus text is discussed by Balch, ibid., pp. 134–80.

230. Ibid., p. 213.

231. H. St. J. Thackerey's introductory comment on the *Contra Apionem* in his LCL edition and translation of *Josephus, The Life, Against Apion,* vol. 1 (Cambridge, Mass.: Harvard University Press, 1961), p. xiii.

232. Balch (*Wives,* pp. 236–37) maintains that only one (wives-husbands) of the three traditional *pairs* is contained in 1 Peter (3:1–7) and that only this one is concerned with reciprocity. While the element of reciprocity is absent in 2:18–20 (only slaves are addressed), it is stressed in the final pair which Balch ignores; namely, the elders-novices instruction of 5:1–5. This latter passage is a variation of the pair "parents-children" and represents the accommodation of the household instruction to the organization of the wider Christian community.

233. Ibid., Abstract, p. 3.

234. Ibid., p. 230.

235. Ibid., pp. 230–36.

236. Ibid., pp. 214, 235, 265.

237. His criticism of my earlier remarks (*The Elect and the Holy,* pp. 179–80 and elsewhere) concerning the "missionary" thrust of 1 Pet. 2:4–10 in particular, however, is well-taken (*Wives,* pp. 220–27). This present study should make clear my revised and present assessment of the function of this passage. In regard to the relation of 2:4–10, 4:7–11 and 5:1–5 (cf. *The Elect and the Holy,* pp. 192–96) it now appears to me that: (1) while all three passages focus on the internal cohesion of the community, 2:4–10 establishes the theological *basis* for such cohesion and 4:7–11 and 5:1–5 elaborate on the *functions* which foster such cohesion. (2) 2:4–10 as a whole expresses the distinction of the community, the basis of its separate and exalted status. Within this context the idea of an "outer-directed mission" now appears to me a bit overdrawn. (3) All three passages reveal a common concern with the *oikos* of God, its origin and nature (2:4–10), its activities (4:7–11) and its order (5:1–5). (4) Whereas 4:7–11 and 5:1–5 address particular practical aspects of communal behavior, 2:4–10 explicates the general theoretical framework for the letter as a whole.

238. Lührmann, "Wo man nicht mehr Sklave oder Freier ist," p. 67.

239. Ibid., pp. 69–70.

240. Ibid., pp. 70–71.

241. Ibid., p. 70.

242. Ibid., pp. 81–82.

243. Ibid., pp. 79–80.

244. Ibid., pp. 82–83.

245. Judge, *The Social Pattern*, pp. 75–76.

246. Nils A. Dahl, *Das Volk Gottes: Eine Untersuchung zum Kirchenbe-wusst-sein des Urchristentums* (Darmstadt: Wissenschaftliche Buchgesellschaft, 1963), pp. 202–03.

247. Sherman E. Johnson, "Asia Minor and Early Christianity," in *Christianity, Judaism, and other Greco-Roman Cults,* Morton Smith FS, ed. Jacob Neusner; *Part Two: Early Christianity;* (Leiden: E. J. Brill, 1975), p. 105, following the theory of Georg Kretschmar, "Christliches Passa im 2. Jahrhundert und die Ausbildung der christlichen Theologie," *RSR* 60 (1972): 287–323, esp. pp. 298–303.

248. As evidence that the Christians of Rome conceived of themselves as a *brotherhood* rather than as an *ekklesia,* Dahl pointed to Paul's Letter to the Romans and the Gospel of Mark. In the latter, the term *ekklesia* is noticeably absent. Jesus forms a community of disciples but he does not build a church. (In addition, it may be noted that the predominant Markan communal image is that of the *oikos* of God, cf. 3:21–35.) As in 1 Peter, *ekklesia* is *not* used as a designation of the Christians in Rome in Romans 1–15, contrary to customary Pauline usage. In Romans 16 the term designates only Christian communities in places other than Rome. Accordingly, Dahl suggests that in Rome the "saints" (Rom. 1:7; 16:2) or the "brothers" (Rom. 1:13; 16:14 etc.; Acts 28:14–15) formed not a single *ekklesia* but, like the Jewish synagogues of Rome, several smaller brotherhood communities.

To this evidence perhaps could be added occasional *oikos-* or familial-related imagery in other documents associated with Rome such as *1 Clement* and Hermas (e.g., *adelphotēs, 1 Clem.* 2:4; *Herm. Man.* 8; *philadelphia, 1 Clem.* 47:5; 48:1; the household code material in *1 Clem.* 1:3; 21:6–9, 38:1–2; the designation "brother" or "sister" (22 times in *1 Clement*]; or the explicit designation of the Christian community as the *oikos tou theou* in *Herm. Sim.* 9.13.9 and 9.14.2). Likewise attention could be drawn to the recurrent references to the "household" of Hermas (*Vis.* 1.1.9, 1.3.1, 3.1.6 and passim) as paradigmatic for the revelation and instruction intended for all the Christian households of Rome. See the household groups suggested by Rom. 16:3–16 according to E. A. Judge and G. S. R. Thomas ("The Origin of the Church at Rome: A New Solution," *Reformed Theological Review* 25 [1966]: 81–94, esp. p. 91), followed by F. F. Bruce, *New Testament History* (Garden City, N.Y.: Doubleday, 1972), pp. 393–414. On the archeological evidence for house churches in Rome in the second and third centuries c.e., see Joan M. Petersen, "House-Churches in Rome," *Vigiliae Christianae* 23 (1969): 264–72.

Taken on the whole, however, the evidence at best allows rather than demonstrates that the household constituted the basic form of organization among the Christians in Rome. By the time of *1 Clement* (1:3) and Ignatius (Ign. *Rom. inscr.*) the term *ekklesia* was used to designate the Roman Christian community as a whole and in no Roman document other than 1 Peter did the household serve as a predominant image for the totality of the believing community.

The early Christian literature associated with Asia Minor, on the other hand, provides much clearer and more abundant evidence of Christian household organization and *oikos*-based theological symbolism. For one thing, there are several explicit references to Christian households and household worship assemblies. In addition to generalized and unlocalized statements such as Acts 20:20; 1 Tim. 3:4, 12; 5:4; and Titus 1:11, there is specific evidence for Christian households in Ephesus (1 Cor. 16:19; 2 Tim. 1:16–18; 4:19), Troas (Acts 20:7–12), Colossae (Philem. 2), Laodicea (Col. 4:15) and Smyrna (Ign. *Smyrn.* 13:1–2; Ign. *Pol.* 8:2), for example. Such household organization provided the model for, and hence is also reflected in, the symbolization of the believing community as a household of God (1 Tim. 3:4–5, 15; 1 Pet. 2:5; 4:17) and object of the divine *oikonomia* (Eph. 1:10; 3:2, 9; Col. 1:25; 1 Tim. 1:4; Ign. *Eph.* 6:1; 18:2; 20:1). It is in this Asia Minor literature in particular that such terms as *oikeioi* and *oikonomoi* are used to depict the Christians (Gal. 6:10; Eph. 2:19; cf. 1. Tim. 5:8; 1 Pet. 4:10) or their leaders (Titus 1:7; cf. Ign. *Eph.* 6:1). Here in the Pastorals, as in 1 Peter, we find the *oikos* to be the chief ecclesiological symbol and the household code the major pattern for outlining communal roles, responsibilities and relationships (cf. also Eph. 5:22–6:9; Col. 3:18–4:1; Ign. *Pol.* 4:1–6:2; Polyc. *Phil.* 4:1–6:3; 1 John 2:12–14). Here, likewise, familial terms abound for describing the Christian brotherhood ("brother": 1 Tim. 4:6; 5:1; 6:2; 2 Tim. 4:21; Philem. 1, 7, 16, 20; 2 Pet. 1:10; 3:15; 1 John 2:9 and passim; 3 John 3, 5, 10; Rev. 1:9; 6:11; 12:10; 19:10; 22:9; Ign. *Eph.* 10:3; 16:1; Ign. *Smyrn.* 12:1 13:1; Ign. *Pol.* 5:1; "sister": 1 Tim. 5:2; Philem. 2; 2 John 13; spiritual "child" or "children": Gal. 3:21–4:7, 19, 28; Eph. 5:8; 1 Tim. 1:2, 18; 2 Tim. 1:2; 2:1; Titus 1:4; Philem. 10; 1 John 3:1, 2, 10; 5:2; 2 John 1, 4, 13; 3 John 4 etc.). If, as Hans von Campenhausen suggests (*Ecclesiastical Authority and Spiritual Power in the Church of the First Three Centuries,* trans. J. A. Baker [Stanford: Stanford University Press, 1969], pp. 76–123 on "The System of Elders and the Beginnings of Official Authority"), it is appropriate to think of the Christian presbyters as "fathers" since "this word [father] best conveys the emotional overtones of the concept of 'elder'" (p. 76, n. 1; p. 162, n. 73), then the presbyterial forms of organization typical of both the Roman and the Asia Minor Christian communities (on this see below, p. 503 n. 31) would also be consonant with, if not evidence of, the influence of the household.

As evidence of the perdurance of the household structure of Christianity in Asia Minor and its *oikos* ecclesiology in post-New Testament times, Kretschmar ("Christliches Passa") has pointed to the Passover liturgical tradition characteristic of Asia Minor Christianity. This tradition which preserves the heritage of an old Jewish Palestinian "family ethic" reflects the central importance of the family and the household as the locus of worship and focus of solidarity. Maintenance of such familial unity, he suggests, was an essential means for counteracting the ascetic demands of itinerant charismatics. Thus, as Johnson ("Asia Minor") also agrees, the household pattern of Christian organization and theological symbolization contributed significantly toward the theological as well as the social consolidation of the Christian movement in Asia Minor.

249. Alfred Schutz, "The Homecomer," in *Collected Papers,* vol. 2, *Studies in Social Theory,* ed. A. Brodersen, Phaenomenologica 15 (The Hague: Martinus Nijhoff, 1964), pp. 106–17; quotation from p. 117. On the correlative theme of strangerhood see a further study in this collection, "The Stranger: An Essay in Social Psychology," ibid., pp. 91–105.

1 Peter—Its Group Interests and Ideology*

Our investigation, up to this point, has focused upon the available evidence and perspectives for interpreting the letter of 1 Peter, the situation to which it was addressed, and the content and strategy which constitute its response. An examination which purports to be a sociological exegesis, however, has one final, if albeit difficult, question to consider: namely, the ideological implications of the document under consideration.

BEYOND THEOLOGY TO IDEOLOGY

In referring to the "ideological implications" of a document I am speaking of more than its ideational or "theological" content or constellation of "religious" ideas. A sociological exegesis is not complete until it has explored the manner in which the "comprehensive patterns of cognitive and moral beliefs about man, society and the universe in relation to man and society"[1] contained and advanced in a given document are intended to *function* in the social order, the collective needs and interests they represent, and the way they exemplify the intersection of ideas, ideals, and social action. Thus attention to a document's ideological implications includes, but embraces more than, the conventional concern for the "theology

---

* Some of the material in this chapter appears under the title "Peter, Silvanus and Mark in 1 Peter and Acts: Sociological-Exegetical Perspectives on a Petrine Group in Rome" in *Wort in der Zeit,* Neutestamentliche Studien, Festgabe für Karl Heinrich Rengstorf zum 75 Geburtstag, ed. Wilfrid Haubeck and Michael Bachmann (Leiden: E. J. Brill, 1980), pp. 250–267.

of document X" or the theological roots and perspectives of X's author(s) or X's position on the "trajectory" of theological developments. Whereas the "theology" of a given author or document usually implies, or can be taken to imply, a conceptual framework which is separable or even isolated from the social matrix within which and for which it was formulated, the matter of a document's "ideological" character does not allow such a separation. In fact, it presumes the opposite; namely, an interrelation and inseparability of social and religious frames of reference, meaning and function.

The issue of ideology in general, as is universally recognized, is a notoriously complex problem with a history which cannot be rehearsed at this point.[2] Nothing close to a semblance of consensus prevails concerning the concept and function of ideology, the dynamics involved in the conflict of contending ideologies, or the nature of its relation to religious or theological phenomena in particular. Nevertheless, analyses of biblical social history have spoken of respective ideologies evident in the biblical literature and rightly so.[3] All social and socioreligious movements, including the literature which they produce, involve implicit or explicit ideological perspectives and strategies. For present purposes I am using the term "ideology" to refer not to the Marxian concept of false consciousness or the dominant ideas of the dominant class(es) or to the Mannheimian notion of unrealized situationally transcendent ideas (unactualized utopian visions) but to the more neutral conception of "an integrated system of beliefs, assumptions and values, not necessarily true or false, which reflects the needs and interests of a group or class at a particular time in history."[4]

This integrated system proceeds from the need to understand, to interpret to self and others, to justify, and to control one's place in the world. Ideologies are shaped by specific views of reality shared by groups—specific perspectives on the world, society and man, and on the limitations and potentialities of human existence. Such perspectives are conditioned by the experiences and hopes which unite individuals into collectivities ready and willing to take concerted action in order to achieve commonly shared values and goals. Inasmuch as all religious groupings and movements have specific collective needs, interests and objectives which they seek to relate to ultimate sacred[5] norms and principles—in Christianity, to the will and action of God as revealed in Jesus Christ—all religious movements, including early Christianity, develop ideological positions and perspectives.

Ideologies are distinguishable from other patterns of beliefs such as "outlooks, creeds, systems and movements of thought and programs"[6] by their high degree of explicitness of formulation over a very wide range of objects with which they deal; by their authoritative and explicit promulgation; by their relatively high systematization or integration around one or a few preeminent values such as salvation, equality or ethnic purity; by their insistence on their distinctiveness from, and unconnectedness with, the outlooks, creeds and other ideologies existing in the same society; by their resistance to innovations in their beliefs; by the highly affective overtones that accompany their acceptance and promulgation; by the demand for total consensus and complete individual subservience on the part of adherents; and by the presence of a corporate collective form that is regarded as the mode of organization of the adherents which is appropriate for maintaining discipline among those already committed and for winning over others. "Because ideologies are modes of consciousness, containing the criteria for interpreting social reality, they help define as well as legitimate collective needs and interests. Hence there is continuous interaction between ideology and material forces of history."[7]

Sociological exegesis has the task of examining and explaining such ideology as it is reflected and can be detected in the biblical literature. In regard to our study of 1 Peter in particular this task involves the literary, theological and sociological analysis not only of the integration of religious beliefs, traditions, values, norms and goals present in the document but also of the collective needs and interests of author(s) and audience and of the function which this integration of ideas was intended to have in the immediate social context of the letter's composer(s) and recipients. Eventually, as the scope of investigation broadens from a sociological-exegetical to a sociological-historical analysis and moves from the immediate to the wider fields of social interaction, the perspective must become diachronic as well as synchronic. Attention would then be given to the import and impact which the document and the ideology it represents have had *within* the theological, historical and social developments of early Christianity. Finally we would seek to trace its impact upon subsequent phases of the Christian movement in its interaction with the social forces of the empire as a whole. This would bring us in the post-New Testament centuries to the explicit clash in ideologies which their history records.

Pursuit of these latter sociological-historical issues would lead us well beyond the exegetical limits of this present study. Therefore on this point

I shall offer but a few concluding observations intended to highlight some ideological links between 1 Peter and the subsequent course of Christian history. Initially, however, I wish to focus on the immediate context of 1 Peter, the function of its ideology and the interests of those among whom the letter originated.

THE PETRINE CIRCLE BEHIND 1 PETER

One major feature of the ideological implications of 1 Peter has already been described and summarized in the preceding chapters. In the face of hostile external pressures which threatened the cohesion and viability of the Christian household communities in Asia Minor, 1 Peter was designed, through an identification and exhortation of the suffering Christians as constituting one unified brotherhood of faith and family or household of God, to promote the distinctive collective identity and self-esteem of the addressees, as well as their internal cohesion and their continued commitment to the values and ideals of the Christian movement. In respect to the literary construction of the letter as well as to its coordination of theological symbolism and social reality, the idea of the community as the *oikos tou theou* functioned as the chief integrative concept of 1 Peter.

To explore further ideological implications of the letter it is now necessary to consider not only the intersection of ideas and social action but also the matter of the needs and self-interests of those propounding such ideological formulations. Thus we are led to ask: which person, or more realistically which collectivity of persons, produced this document and out of which group interests was the letter composed and transmitted to the Christians of Asia Minor?

This brings us, albeit from a new perspective, to the old contested issue of the authorship of 1 Peter. At present the only agreement among scholars on this question appears to be the agreement to disagree.[8] Indeed, 1 Peter is a notorious New Testament example of a document whose question of authorship is inseparably related to a wide range of disputed questions such as the letter's genre, destination, historical and social situation, place and date of composition, the traditions it incorporates, its literary style, its proximity to other New Testament writings (especially of Paul and the Pauline circle), its suggested affinities with the epistles and era of Pliny the Younger, the position of the Roman empire toward Christianity at the time of its composition, the function of pseudonymity within the early Christian literature, and of course its theological message. As the history of interpretation of 1 Peter demonstrates, exegetical positions taken on one or more of these issues have determined opinion and generated assumptions concerning the document's authorship.

My own research, including the points treated in the present study, leads me to the conclusion that the cumulative evidence pertaining to the issue of authorship puts its composition by the apostle Peter into serious doubt. J. A. T. Robinson, it must be recognized, has made a recent and valiant attempt to salvage its authenticity. He has argued for its apostolic composition in the year 65 c.e. chiefly because he sees in the letter a reflection of the situation in Rome around the time of the Neronian persecution.[9] In my opinion, however, the content and strategy of the letter point to a date subsequent to the apostle's death chiefly on the basis of its reflection of the situation of the Christian movement in Asia Minor in the following two decades.[10]

On the other hand, while the pseudonymity of the letter is supported by perhaps a majority of current scholars, there is little consensus among these exegetes in regard to the purpose of its composition and the function of its ascription to Peter.[11] Those who attribute 1 Peter to a Paulinist in particular, an anonymous author of the Pauline circle, tend to equate the use of common tradition with literary dependency, to confuse the addressees of 1 Peter with a supposed exclusively Pauline mission field, and, in general, to underestimate and fail to account for the distinctions between 1 Peter and the Pauline (and deutero-Pauline) literature. This is to say nothing, of course, of the difficulty of accounting for the ascription to Peter of a document purportedly representative of Paul.[12] That 1 Peter is the product of some kind of *Unionspolitik* is, as Norbert Brox has recently objected,[13] a speculation too far removed from the evidence to deserve serious consideration. Our foregoing study rather further corroborates the view that the literary composition, historical situation, theological perspective and socioreligious strategy of 1 Peter place it within a broad stream rather than an exclusive Pauline current of early Christian tradition.[14]

A particular weakness of the Paulinist theory is the apparent inability or unwillingness of its supporters to conceive of an *independent* Petrine mission and an independent Petrine group with independent interests in and contacts with the Christians of Asia Minor. Hypotheses of pseudonymity, on the other hand, which propose other named (Silvanus, Aristion) or unnamed *individuals,* fail to explore the possibility that behind the letter stands a *group* rather than a single individual.

In order to approach the issue of authorship anew and at the same time to advance toward an understanding of the interests which motivated the composition of 1 Peter, I propose the following as a possibility worthy of further consideration. It is conceivable, if not most likely, that 1 Peter originated from a *Petrine group* in Rome[15] which included persons named Silvanus and Mark and an unnamed Christian "sister" (5:12–13) and was sent in the name of the martyred apostle Peter, with whom this group had been most intimately associated, to the suffering Christian household communities of Asia Minor. The origin of 1 Peter within a Petrine *group* makes the question concerning the individual who did the actual writing of secondary importance (as, for instance, in the letter to the Romans which was actually written by one of Paul's associates, namely, Tertius; see Rom. 16:22). The letter would be authentically Petrine in the sense that it conveys the traditions known to, and the ideas, theology and social outlook once held by, the apostle Peter and then shared, preserved and developed by the group who reckoned him as their spiritual leader.

The idea that 1 Peter is to be linked with a Petrine group or circle is not novel, although it has been mentioned, for the most part, only in passing and without elaboration.[16] It is, moreover, plausible on both sociological and exegetical grounds. First of all, this theory accords with the dynamics of a social and religious movement. The experiences, thoughts, visions and actions of one person only become socially relevant and effective when they are shared by a group or groups of sympathizers. The "Jesus movement," to use Theissen's phrase, became a movement only as others responded to Jesus' invitation to discipleship and joined the cause. This movement, in turn, became a Christian movement beyond the boundaries of Palestine only through the formation of new collectivities, the establishment of household communities, and the development of team missions and group ministries. Although there is more New Testament evidence for the existence and collective activities of a Pauline group, there is no reason to doubt, and every practical reason to assume, that other missionaries and leaders such as Simon Peter, John and James also had their group of associates, co-workers, aides and supporters. Itinerant missions as well as local ministries and interprovincial communication must have been from the outset group enterprises.[17]

The existence of a Petrine group was inevitable from a social and practical point of view. There is also, however, the record of the New Testament that Peter did not live or act alone. In addition to (1) his regular place among "the twelve,"[18] mention is also made of (2) his associations with smaller groups: "Peter and those with him";[19] Peter, James and John of Zebedee,[20] and Andrew;[21] Peter and John;[22] Peter and James (of Zebedee);[23] Peter (Cephas), James (brother of the Lord) and John;[24] Peter and the brothers of the Lord;[25] and Peter and the household of Mary (including John Mark).[26] These groupings may reflect not only familial (Andrew) or local associations (Galilee, Jerusalem, Antioch, Corinth?) but also teams of ministry, groups of leaders and circles of support.

Third, the existence of a Petrine group is suggested in 1 Peter itself where the salutation from Peter is linked with the reference to Silvanus and the greetings of "the coelect (sister) in Babylon" and "Mark, my son" (5:12–13). The combined reference to these names may indicate not only the partial composition of a Petrine group in Rome;[27] it may also be an important clue concerning the interests of this group which prompted the composition of 1 Peter.

Four members of the Petrine group in Rome are mentioned; three are explicitly named. There are several questions which these names raise. To which persons do these names refer? Why have precisely these names been selected for mention? What is the relation of these names to the content of the letter and its strategy? What might they suggest concerning the interests of the group to which they belong? The following points deserve consideration.

The person under whose name the letter was chiefly written was "Peter, an apostle of Jesus Christ" (1:1) who, it may be assumed from the lack of further descriptive evidence (aside from 5:1), was known by reputation, if not by personal encounter, to the Asia Minor addressees.[28] He was the recognized leader of the group which composed 1 Peter, the one to whom the other members of the group were attracted and whose theological and social outlook and interests they shared. 1 Peter is first and foremost the evangelical and social witness of the apostle Peter after whose suffering and martyrdom in Rome and in whose name the Petrine community then has written to the suffering Christians of Asia Minor.

Greetings were also sent from "Mark, my son" (5:13). The traditional epithet "son" or "child," as Leonhard Goppelt has noted,[29] depicted Mark as Peter's spiritual child and disciple. This description, like the qualifications "Silvanus, the faithful *brother*" (5:12) and the "the coelect (*sister*)" (5:13), accorded with the image of a Roman community composing part of the larger family of God to which the addressees also belonged. The terms, as well as the greetings as such,[30] thus underlined the solidarity of the Christian communion. Accordingly, Silvanus also was portrayed as the *"faithful* brother"—to Peter ("as I consider him," 5:12) and to the Lord. Thus the Petrine group of Rome was of one heart and mind just as the addressees are encouraged to be.

What would these names have signified to the addressees? What impression was their mention intended to have and how might this effect have been related to the thrust of the letter as a whole? These questions move beyond the narrower issue of authorship, per se, to that of the relationship of senders and recipients. Furthermore they imply that the content and strategy of the document itself are the surest controls for determining the reasons for the choice of these names and the possibilities of their function.

One function of the names, as already mentioned, was to personalize the letter and its message. As one would expect of a personal communique such as a letter, greetings from specifically named individuals presume, establish or promote a personal bond between senders and recipients. Furthermore, the names authorized the content of the message and gave it weight. Precisely how the names lent import and credibility to the letter, however, depended upon the precise identity of the persons referred to. While the identity of Peter is clear, who were Silvanus and Mark? Can other New Testament data shed light on this issue?

Peter in 1:1 is clearly the apostle, one of the earliest followers and emissaries of Jesus, eminent witness to, if not of, the Lord's suffering (5:1) and resurrection (1:11, 21 etc.), and evangelical spokesman of the earliest post-Easter believing community (Acts 1:15–26; 2:1–42 etc.). That some of the addressees were present at that first Jerusalem Pentecost and heard or became acquainted with Peter personally, or that some of the addressees learned about Peter from those who were there, is quite possible. Acts 2:9 records the presence at this Pentecost of, among others, "residents of Cappadocia, Pontus and Asia, Phrygia and Pamphilia." The only other New

Testament reference to representatives from Pontus and Cappadocia occurs in 1 Pet. 1:1 (except for the information that Aquila was a native of Pontus, Acts 18:2). Whether, of course, Peter ever had missionized within the provinces mentioned in 1 Pet. 1:1 is a notoriously moot point. In any event, the apostle was a leading representative of the Palestinian community and of the diaspora mission and certainly one of whom they would have heard (also in Galatia, cf. Galatians 1–2) and known to be of preeminent importance in the Christian movement.

While such importance lends weight to the import of the letter, it is not his apostolic preeminence as such but rather his *fellowship* with the addressees which the letter stresses. It is his *koinonia* (cf. 4:13 and 5:1) with the recipients in suffering, steadfastness and hope (Peter's experience in 5:1 mirroring that of the addressees in 4:12–19) which most commends these words of exhortation and encouragement to the readers. Furthermore, in this same verse (5:1) Peter is represented as addressing the leaders-elders not as superior apostle but as "fellow elder." The traditional form of household authority ("elder") was chosen and expanded ("co-") to express the common bond of those charged with the responsibilities of leadership. The term *sympresbyteros* is a reflection of the presbyterial (and traditional) form of organization and authority characteristic of both Roman and Asia Minor Christian communities.[31]

The function of the Petrine signature thus admirably conforms to the content and strategy of the letter as a whole: (1) it identifies the one within the Roman community to whom its contents and theology most owe their origin and inspiration; (2) it accounts for the broad range of traditions which were known and used by a wide-ranging missionary and his associates; (3) it establishes and enhances the personal bond between this Roman Petrine community and their Asia Minor brethren; and (4) it authenticates an encouragement to distinctive self-consciousness, steadfastness and solidarity by rooting the message in the personal experience and faith of its chief author and source of inspiration. If, as seems likely, the letter was written after the apostle's death, it becomes for its recipients as for its actual authors an expression of the Petrine gospel, his vision of and hope for the Christian movement.

This brings us to Silvanus and Mark. Are these simply two otherwise unidentifiable members of the Petrine circle in Rome? If so, then nothing more can be added to what has already been said concerning the function of their mention in 1 Peter. If, on the other hand, they are the same Silvanus (or Silas) and (John) Mark of whom the New Testament speaks elsewhere, their explicit mention in 1 Peter takes on certain added significance. The majority of scholars find the latter alternative more plausible. Here is one point at least where we concur with the majority opinion. If this Silvanus and Mark were those natives of Jerusalem who subsequently had a share in the movement's Asia Minor and Aegean mission, and who now compose part of the Petrine group in Rome, then their names too lent weight, credibility and force to the message of 1 Peter.

The first we learn of John Mark in the account of Acts is of his home in Jerusalem and of his possible association there with Peter. According to Acts 12:12–17, upon his escape from prison (12:1–11) Peter "went to the house of Mary, the mother of John whose other name was Mark" (12:12). While Mark at this moment, according to Luke, was in Antioch with Barnabus and Paul (cf. 11:30) and only returned to Jerusalem (12:25) after Peter's departure "to another place" (12:17), Peter's flight to Mark's household indicates an obvious close association of the two. Thereafter Mark joined Barnabus and Paul on the so-called first missionary journey but only as far as Perga in Pamphilia (13:13). From there he returned to and presumably remained in Jerusalem (13:13, cf. 15:37). Rejected by Paul as a companion for a subsequent mission on the grounds of his desertion at Pamphilia, Mark was the cause of the split between Barnabus and Paul and was taken by Barnabus to Cyprus (15:37–39). The following verse, 15:40, suggests that Mark and Silas (Silvanus) were there together since Paul immediately "chose Silas and departed." Subsequent references to a Mark (whether the same Mark is not certain) suggest a possible rapprochement between him and Paul and, depending on the place of composition of the documents (Col. 4:10; Philem. 24; 2 Tim. 4:11), allow for his possible later presence in Colossae, Ephesus or Rome.

For our purposes that which is noteworthy about this New Testament evidence on Mark is: (1) the limited certain contact and strained relationship between Mark and Paul; (2) the minimal certain contact of Mark with the Christians of the areas named in 1 Pet. 1:1; (3) Mark's favorable association with Peter; (4) his earliest ties with the Jerusalem church, probably including Silvanus (Silas) as well as Peter; and (5) his later involvement and ministry in some phase of the diaspora mission.

Several of these features recur in the New Testament evidence pertaining to the person referred to variously as "Silvanus" or "Silas."[32] While no explicit statement attests the fact that Silvanus and Peter knew each other and were associates once in Jerusalem as well as later in Rome, the account of Acts seems to imply the former. Furthermore, while Silvanus had a much more positive and intimate association with Paul than did Mark, this fact cannot be used to assert that Paul alone shaped Silvanus' theology or monopolized his activities. The reference to Silvanus in 1 Peter, just as little as the mention of Mark, in no way "proves" the letter to have been a product of the Pauline school. Likewise, the collaboration of Silvanus with Paul on the so-called second missionary journey in no way requires or proves the conclusion that 1 Peter, because of its reference to Silvanus, is a Paulinist letter addressed to exclusively Pauline communities or territories.

Aside from 1 Pet. 5:12 and Acts 15, the New Testament references to Silvanus concern only his activities and whereabouts on the second missionary journey of Paul (Acts 15:40–18:22; cf. 2 Cor. 1:19; 1 Thess. 1:1; 2 Thess. 1:1). On this journey the two missionaries, soon joined by Timothy (Acts 16:1–3), visited or passed through the territories/provinces or cities of Phrygia and Galatia (Acts 16:6) and Troas (16:8) in Asia Minor before sailing to the shores of Europe (Macedonia). According to the account in Acts (16:6–7) they specifically did *not* enter or proclaim the word of God in Asia and Bithynia. Luke underlines this point (and accounts for it theologically) by explaining that their attempt to enter these provinces was "forbidden by the Holy Spirit" (16:6). "The Spirit of Jesus did not allow them" (16:7). Furthermore, no mention whatsoever is made of any contact with the province of Cappadocia. Thus in three of the four/five provinces addressed in 1 Peter neither Paul nor Silvanus, according to Paul's own words or the record of Acts, ever set foot. That 1 Pet. 1:1 continues to be used as a proof of the Pauline interest of 1 Peter and the Pauline territories of its destination simply defies comprehension! This is quite aside from the fact that Gal. 2:7–9 (Peter's gospel to the Jews, Paul's to the Gentiles—according to Paul's version!) can hardly be understood on geographical terms or taken as an actual agreement on missionary strategy. As one author has recently put it, "whether it is understood geographically or ethnographically it seems to be impractical and unrealistic."[33] Neither Galatia nor Asia [34] (the other two provinces mentioned in 1 Pet. 1:1), quite apart from Pontus, Cappadocia and Bithynia, can be considered *exclusively* Pauline mission territory. An explanation for the motivation of the mention of Silvanus in 1 Peter must seek a reason other than his being a representative of Paul and a link with Pauline communities.

This reason may be found in examining the evidence of Acts 15 and the role of Silvanus in, and his associations with, the Jerusalem church. The last thing we learn of Silvanus in Acts prior to his association with Peter and Mark in Rome is his arrival with Timothy and their rejoining Paul in Corinth (18:5). His intermediate whereabouts, activities and associations are unknown. The first thing, however, which Acts relates about him provides important information on his role and reputation and thus may shed light on his significance in 1 Peter.

Silvanus (Silas), according to Acts 15, and Judas Barsabbas were prophets (v. 32), men who had risked their lives for the sake of the Lord (v. 26) and "leading men among the brethren" (v. 22) who had gathered in Jerusalem to discuss and debate the strategy, composition and future of the Christian movement particularly in regard to the conversion of the Gentiles.[35] At the conclusion of the meeting Judas and Silas were sent as personal emissaries of "the apostles and the elders, with the whole church" (v. 22) at Jerusalem to Antioch with a letter addressed to "the brethren who are of the Gentiles in Antioch and Syria and Cilicia" (v. 23). There, in the company of Paul and Barnabas (vv. 22, 35), they delivered the letter, described the events of the meeting, the conclusions reached and the content of the letter "by word of mouth" (v. 27). They "exhorted the brethren with many words and strengthened them" (v. 32). The outcome was joyful and peaceful. "And after they had spent some time, they were sent off in peace by the brethren to those who had sent them" (v. 33).

This event as described by Luke is hardly devoid of characteristically Lukan features. The chapter, in fact, has been seen as "a watershed in the book of Acts . . . a, if not the, turning point of the whole narrative."[36] Nevertheless there is no compelling reason for doubting its historical basis or the significance of the meeting itself for the future of the worldwide Christian movement. At a crucial point in its history the Christian brotherhood expressed and received an affirmation of the impartiality of God's grace and salvation by faith which, in line with the prophetic words, became a cornerstone of the movement's solidarity and universal appeal. And in this event, as Luke would say, Silvanus played no small role. Furthermore, as subsequent indication of his unifying role, this leading man among the brothers in Jerusalem collaborated with Paul on a mission to the diaspora (Acts 15:40).

For our present purposes several points are important. (1) At this important meeting two of the people we have been discussing, Peter and Silvanus, played key roles. (2) This is the only instance other than 1 Peter where Peter, Silvanus and Mark (implicitly)[37] occur together. Their common roots are in the community and traditions of the Jerusalem brotherhood, and in Rome they have joined forces once again. This would account for the presence of Palestinian tradition in 1 Peter.[38] This tradition would constitute a vital link then between the Christians of Palestine, Rome, and Asia Minor. (3) In 1 Peter, as in Acts 15, Silvanus is designated as the bearer of a letter. In fact, the terminology of 1 Pet. 5:12 and Acts 15:22–23 is remarkably similar and supports the theory that in 1 Pet. 5:12 *dia Silouanou . . . egrapsa* also refers to the *emissarial* rather than the secretarial function of Silvanus.[39] (4) There is also a marked similarity between the general import and intention of 1 Peter and the decisions of the Jerusalem meeting and between the letter and the speech of Peter in particular.[40] 1 Peter, like the Jerusalem council, is concerned with the universality and unification of the Christian movement. (5) While all three, Peter, Silvanus and Mark, are linked with the Palestinian church, the first two in particular represent the ecumenical and coalescing forces of the Christian movement. In 1 Peter, therefore, they may be taken to represent and authenticate to the Asia Minor addressees what they stood for earlier in Jerusalem: the universal dimension of God's grace, the furtherance of a community open to believers of all races, and the unity of believers in one common brotherhood.

Even if all three names be conceded to have been part of the fiction of pseudepigraphy—a large concession for which there is no convincing evidence nor necessity—the significance of the names for the addressees would remain. The careers and reputations of the three persons mentioned are linked with the origins, crucial developments and decisions, and widest outreach of the worldwide Christian movement. Their association in Jerusalem as well as later in Rome attests the personal cohesion and cooperation of which their letter speaks. Their activities in east and west and points in between and now in 1 Peter their concern for the movement in Asia Minor confirm the universal ethnic and geographical dimensions of the universal grace of which they write. And their own experience of suffering, especially that of the martyred Peter, gives personal witness and authority to the message of comfort and hope which they send to their suffering fellow believers. In a word, these three eminent members of the Petrine circle in Rome have already attested with their own lives what they now ask of others in writing.

THE SELF-INTERESTS OF THE
PETRINE CIRCLE IN ROME

To inquire into the self-interests of this Roman Petrine group is a most difficult, perhaps some would say hopeless, undertaking. Difficulties notwithstanding, I offer the following thoughts for consideration. The strategy of 1 Peter and the reputations of the persons associated with it indicate a vital interest in the solidarity and growth of the Christian movement, its unified resistance to external pressures for conformity and its social and religious consolidation.[41] In 1 Peter the social and religious bond between the Christians of Rome and those of Asia Minor is affirmed through reference to commonly known persons, commonly shared kerygmatic, liturgical, catechetical and parenetic traditions, common experiences of suffering and estrangement, common enjoyment of dignity and hope, and common membership in the household of God. Thus, through 1 Peter the Petrine community is promoting and acting as a stimulus for the distinctive identity and unity of the Christian brotherhood throughout the world.

What self-interests may have been behind such goals? The answer may lie in the desire of this group to stabilize and enhance its position in Rome as well as its influence and authority within the Christian movement abroad.

1 Peter reveals an interest of the Roman Christians in having their Asia Minor confreres know of their personal concern for the latter's situation. This creates a bond of fellowship and builds a bridge of support which can be traveled in both directions. Roman emperors and governors were not the only ones with interests in the provinces; so were the Christians of Rome. Whether material sustenance accompanied the moral support which they sent we do not know. In any case the letter itself and the personal presence of their representative, Silvanus, would forge a bond upon

which the Roman Christians could count if and when it was required in the future.

Such a communique would also extend the influence of the Roman group abroad. In turn, such influence abroad could enhance the stability and prominence of the Petrine group in Rome. This would have been of particular importance if the deaths of the two leading figures Peter and Paul had occasioned any problems over organization and leadership among the believers at the capitol. The Petrine group would have been intact and its leadership capabilities recognized, at least by the Christians abroad.

Whatever respect for the authority of the Roman community might be won in Asia Minor could also have an effect on the influence and reputation of this group elsewhere. On the one hand, traces of the Roman community's ecumenical concern can be seen shortly after 1 Peter in the letter of *1 Clement* to the church of Corinth as well as in Hermas' communication of his visions "to the cities abroad" (*Vis.* 2.4.3). On the other hand, Ignatius already attests to the fact of the reputation and admiration of the Roman Christians as far east as Syrian Antioch. "You have never envied anyone; you have taught others" (Ign. *Rom.* 3:1). In even more effusive terms he hails them at the outset of his letter as having "the presidency in the country of the land of the Romans, worthy of God, worthy of honour, worthy of blessing, worthy of praise, worthy of success, worthy of its holiness, and preeminent in love, named after Christ, named after the Father . . . united in flesh and spirit in every one of his [God's] commandments, filled with the grace of God without wavering and filtered clear of every foreign stain . . . " (Inscription, LCL translation).

It would be unlikely for a group at the political, economic and cultural hub of power and influence not to derive benefits from its location and not to take advantage of its position and capabilities in the furtherance of personal as well as movement-wide causes. The advantageous position of the Roman Christians would make it an ideal center for the congregation of the "faithful from everywhere" (Irenaeus, *Adv. Haer.* 3.3.2), the coalescence of traditions, the convergence and distribution of information, and contact with diversely separated areas abroad.

By virtue of its geographical location and its early role in Christian history the Roman community quickly attained an eminent (though not yet preeminent) position in the Christian movement. Not only did the Roman

Christians use this position to influence other wings of the movement; their prestige and influence were also enhanced by the respect which was shown them by Christians abroad. 1 Peter is the first existing document of the attempt of the Christians in Rome to extend their influence and establish a bridge between the movement in Rome and its counterpart in Asia Minor. This bridge was to be traveled many times in both directions in the subsequent course of the movement's history.[42] Although the Petrine community may only have dreamed but never dared to hope, eventually all ecclesiastical roads also led to Rome.

The interests of the Petrine group in Rome were to strengthen the religious commitment and unify the harassed groups of Christians in Asia Minor with the possibility in view that such consolidation abroad would redound to the benefit of its most energetic proponents in Rome. To that end it dispatched a letter in the name of its most notable leader, Peter, to be delivered by Silvanus (among others), the contents of which reflected an ecclesiology and an ideology of the entire Christian movement as constituting in society a distinctive household of God. Such an ideology was destined, and most likely designed, to serve not only the interest of the Christians at Rome but also the successful course of Christianity at large.

THE IDEOLOGY OF 1 PETER IN THE SUBSEQUENT CLASH
OF CHRISTIAN AND NON-CHRISTIAN IDEOLOGIES

This brings us to the second of our points concerning the ideology of 1 Peter: namely, its role in and contribution toward the clash of Christian and non-Christian ideologies. The impact of 1 Peter and of the ideology it represents is to be viewed in relation to at least two aspects of Christian social history. On the one hand there is the question of its relation to other ideological perspectives and pursuits *within* the early Christian movement and to its place within the growing stream of tradition associated with the apostle Peter. This issue is too complex to be taken up in the present study. It may suffice to say that the figure of Peter, Petrine tradition, and the ideology of ecclesiastical solidarity and social engagement played a central role in the consolidation of the Christian movement and its struggle with factionalism and heresy in the decades and centuries following the composition of 1 Peter. What Shirley Jackson Case has described as the focus of

Christianity's attention following the death of Paul certainly describes a subject to which 1 Peter has made an initial and substantive contribution:

> Perhaps it would not be too bold to describe the characteristic developments within Christianity for nearly a century after the time of Paul as dominated primarily by an interest in working out in one form or another means of control that would render its position in society more attractive, stable, and permanent, that would prevent disintegration of the new movement through the explosion of forces from within, and that would give it more complete mastery over its own developing social life, both within the separate groups and throughout Christendom as a whole.[43]

The household ideology of 1 Peter provided a model for internal sectarian integration and a concept for linking the symbols of the communal dimension of faith (brotherhood, family of God) with the experience of alienated (*paroikoi, paroikia* in society) and collective (household communities) social existence.

On the other hand, this household ideology served as the conceptual medium for both the comparison and contrast of Christian community with other forms of social groupings (collegia, cults, and its parent body, Judaism). Over against the latter it provided the means for asserting Christianity's continuity with (through appropriation of) the religious traditions of Israel while at the same time maintaining the superiority and finality of the new people of God. The community, intimacy of relationship and discipline which Christian fraternity symbolized also enabled it to compete effectively with other groups seeking adherents and allegiance. The institution of the family, representing as it did time-honored relationships, roles, responsibilities, values and loyalties, served the competitive interests of empire and Christian sect alike. Each found the concept of an all-embracing family of nations, tribes, tongues and people (cf. Rev. 14:6) a compelling model for the illustration of the universal integration of peoples which it sought. Each could use this image of the "megafamily" to legitimate incursions into the rights of existing kinship groups. And each could appeal to the paternal implications of organizational leadership: the emperor as *pater patriae* and the Christian elders as legitimate father figures or representatives of God the Father. For the Christian movement the household ideology provided a plausible social as well as religious rationale for the encouragement of Christian resistance to alien social pressures and even for the critique of imperial paternalistic pretensions.

The social impact of an ecclesiastical household ideology extended beyond the period of 1 Peter, moreover. Among the various reasons proposed for the eventual ascendancy of Christianity within the empire, three frequently recur. And all three reflect features of the character of Christianity which we have found accentuated in 1 Peter. According to some scholars such as Ernest Cadman Colwell, it was Christianity's *distinctiveness* which most accounts for not only the tribulations of the movement but also its final triumph. "It was not only the existence in Christianity of disturbing elements, peculiar practices, and peculiar beliefs but the more general matter of Christianity's conception of itself as distinctive that led to opposition."[44] Following an explicit reference to 1 Pet. 2:9–10, Colwell notes:

> The concept of the third race, of the Christians as a new and distinct grouping of mankind, was the basic cause of the popular opposition in the first few centuries; it was also the victory that overcame the world. The Christians were a self-conscious brotherhood, the ecumenical brotherhood from the days of Paul on. . . . Within this brotherhood the poor man found recognition, affection, insurance for his wife and children, decent burial, victory over sin, and the assurance of immortality. Before there was canon, creed or priesthood the brothers found their relationship strongly based on their common devotion to the Lord Jesus through whose activities all these benefits were mediated to them. By claiming to be a new race they aroused the hatred of the masses; by living as members of this third race they won over the masses. This is the paradox of the first and greatest triumph of the church.[45]

To this stance of distinctiveness W. H. C. Frend would add another feature of Christianity reminiscent of 1 Peter which accounted for its persecution but also its victory: the readiness and willingness of the Christians to suffer. In contrast to the conformist and individualistically oriented Gnostics, "the future lay with the Church of the Martyrs."[46] It was those who were willing to suffer for their faith to whom "the other great Christian virtues in the eyes of the people, alms-giving and charity" belonged (Ign. *Smyrn.* 6:2).[47] It was the suffering of the martyrs which led not only to the consolidation of the church and its eventual clash with Rome but also to its ultimate victory.

A third factor given to account for the triumph of Christianity also recalls the concerns stressed in 1 Peter. This factor is what Gager has described as

> the radical sense of Christian community—open to all, insistent on absolute and exclusive loyalty, and concerned for every aspect of the believer's life. From the very beginning, the one distinctive gift of Christianity was this sense of community. Whether one speaks of "an age of anxiety" or "the crisis of the towns," Christian congregations provided a unique opportunity for masses of people to discover a sense of security and self-respect.[48]

Christianity, according to Arthur Darby Nock, was a movement which sustained a call to conversion with a community of care.

> The success of Christianity is the success of an institution which united the sacramentalism and the philosophy of its time. It satisfied the inquiring turn of mind, the desire for the escape from Fate, the desire for security in the hereafter; like Stoicism, it gave a way of life and made man at home in the universe, but unlike Stoicism it did this for the ignorant as well as for the lettered. It satisfied also social needs and it secured men against loneliness. Its way was not easy; it made uncompromising demands on those who would enter and would continue to live in the brotherhood, but to those who did not fail it offered an equally uncompromising assurance.[49]

In each of these features of Christianity and in their sum echo the early notes of 1 Peter. But perhaps it is one further feature which most graphically suggests the lasting contribution of 1 Peter and its ideology to the success of Christianity in its conflict with and victory within society. This is is accentuation of the specifically familial and household character of the Christian community. The sociologist Robert A. Nisbet, in discussing the relation of Christianity to the subject of "community and conflict in Western thought," has identified Christianity's redefinition and restructuring of kinship ties and values as one of the most important aspects of its conflict with and contribution to ancient society.[50] Nisbet does not refer to 1 Peter directly; nevertheless, the relevance of his observation to our foregoing interpretation of the document as well as to the subsequent impact of the household ideology it represents can best be appreciated by quoting him at length.

> Among all the other social and psychological conflicts in first and second-century Rome is the struggle between Christianity, first as a sect, then as

a church, and those forms of traditional belief and membership that militated against Christian efforts. We are accustomed to think of this conflict as largely one between Christianity and the emperor, one of our favorite images of this conflict in legend being Christians thrown to the lions in the Colosseum. And we should never doubt that conflict between Christianity and the Roman state did indeed exist, often becoming very intense, with executions, tortures, and public spectacles of humiliation occasionally taking place. . . .

Even so, we are obliged to look to still another style of conflict in order to explain a great deal that from at least the late first century on has been fundamental in Christian belief and practice. Here I refer to a conflict of values and allegiance at a level well below that of politics but in many ways far more intensive and penetrating far more deeply into the psychological aspects of Christian proselytism, a conflict rarely thought of in the usual history of Christianity: that between Christianity and the Roman family.[51]

To illustrate this conflict Nisbet cites "three very important passages from the New Testament Gospel," Matt. 10:34–39, Mark 3:31–35, and Luke 14:25–26 to demonstrate the role which the new *oikos* of Jesus played in the formation and self-consciousness of early Christianity.[52] Whether these words, he then continues, reflect the context of Roman Judaea during Jesus' own lifetime or some other part of the Roman empire later, "the practical import is the same. Plainly, the words register sharp conflict between the religious community and the values of kinship."[53]

To the question of why the formation of a new household continued to figure so centrally in the Christian movement and its social ascendancy, Nisbet offers a threefold answer. First, it was an expression of Christianity's "intensely communal character."

Christianity was no mere pattern of beliefs spread among multitudes of people. It took form as primitive community: community in the hard sense of small groups of persons who often lived together, who sometimes pooled their property, and whose bounden responsibility it was to look out for one another in this world.[54]

Second, it was a strategic response to the social condition in which people found themselves and the kind of society in which they lived.

This society was deeply disorganized by the impact of war, depression, and the *uprooting* [emphasis added] of membership in ancient structures . . .

ages of perceived disorganization and dislocation are almost invariably rich in efforts to achieve forms of community through religious, as well as political[55] and social, channels. Rome during the first century A.D. was fertile soil indeed for the proliferation of religious cults which could offer their communicants not merely hope of a better world after this life but also *some kind of communal release from alienation and insecurity in this life.*[56] Christianity, most especially its primitive first-century form, was almost ideally equipped to *respond to such alienation and insecurity;*[57] for its message, its "good news," was precisely that of communal refuge.[58]

Third, disorganized as Roman society may have been, there was "yet one structure at least which continued to command a great deal of allegiance" and hence "a formidable barrier to acceptance of Christianity's tenets." "This was the historic and still powerful family, organized on the basis of the *patria potestas.*"[59] So long as this religious as well as social institution remained unchallenged, "just so long did its very structure act to mediate, even to interfere with, the proselytizing efforts of the missionaries of Christ."

The specific Christian strategy

> was thus a vital and almost obvious one: to denigrate so far as possible the historic and still deeply rooted kinship tie and to offer the community of Christ as itself the only real and true form of kinship. Thus we have, in the passages I chose from the New Testament (and there are others beside these which make the same point), the stress placed by Jesus on the insubstantiality and unreality of the kinship relation, even and especially his own relation to mother, father, brothers, and sisters; and thus, too, his transcending emphasis at one and the same time on the family character of Christianity.[60]

Christianity, Nisbet goes on to note, addressed a great deal of its message to women. To succeed in disengaging these women in particular from their family ties, as with all prospective converts in general,

> it was necessary at one and the same time to denigrate the family and to proffer Christianity itself as a family—the highest of all types of family.[61]

This issue of kinship, according to Nisbet, continued as a basis of conflict and definition of Christian community long after Christianity had become the official religion of the empire.[62] But we may break off here.

That which Nisbet has stressed from a sociological perspective coincides with and only further confirms what we have observed from an exegetical perspective: namely, the essential role which the household or family played in the origin and development of the Christian movement. In its competition with, critique of, and conflict with other forms of social allegiance the Christian movement regarded the household and the family as the indispensable basis and model for its social organization, ideological struggle and evangelical message.

If this focus on the family is to be taken along with the other features which have been mentioned (namely, Christianity's distinctiveness, its solidarity in suffering, and its social cohesion), as the chief characteristics contributing toward the ultimate success of Christianity, then at one and the same time they measure the profound contribution of 1 Peter and its household ideology to the course of Christian history. For in this one document all four of these features of Christianity's response to society are given an integrated accentuation. In its message the strangers, the rootless, the homeless of any age can take comfort: in the community of the faithful the stranger is no longer an isolated alien but a brother or sister. For the *paroikoi* of society there is a possibility of life and communion in the *oikos tou theou*, a home for the homeless.

NOTES

1. From Edward Shils, "The Concept and Function of Ideology," in the *International Encyclopedia of the Social Sciences,* vol. 7 (New York: Macmillan and the Free Press, 1969), pp. 66–75; quotation from p. 66.

2. For an instructive historical review see George Lichtheim, "The Concept of Ideology," in *The Concept of Ideology and Other Essays* (New York: Random House, 1967), pp. 3–46.

3. See, e.g., Abraham Shalit, "A Clash of Ideologies: Palestine under the Seleucids and Romans," in *The Crucible of Christianity: Judaism, Hellenism and the Historical Background to the Christian Faith,* ed. Arnold Toynbee (New York: World and London: Thames and Hudson, 1969), pp. 47–76; Patrick D. Miller, Jr., "Faith and Ideology in the Old Testament," in *Magnalia Dei: The Mighty Acts of God,* G. Ernest Wright FS; ed. Frank Moore Cross et al: (Garden City, N.Y.: Doubleday, 1976), pp. 464–70; and John G. Gager, *Kingdom and Community: The Social World of Early Christianity* (Engle-

wood Cliffs, N.J.: Prentice-Hall, 1975) pp. 82–83. The implications of this concern with the interrelation of religion and ideology on the part of exegetes and social historians, however, deserve a thorough discussion.

4. Following David Brion Davis, *The Problem of Slavery in the Age of Revolution 1770–1823* (Ithaca/London: Cornell University Press, 1975), p. 14. Davis (p. 350, n. 7), in turn, like Gager (p. 5, n. 14 and passim) notes indebtedness to Peter L. Berger and Thomas Luckmann, *The Social Construction of Reality: A Treatise in the Sociology of Knowledge* (Garden City, N.Y.: Doubleday, 1967); on ideology see pp. 6, 9–10, 12, 14, 123–25, 127–28, 180.

5. So Shils, "Ideology," p. 68.

6. Ibid., pp. 66–67.

7. Davis, *The Problem of Slavery*, p. 14.

8. Compare, e.g., the literature cited and the discussion offered by Werner Georg Kümmel (*Introduction to the New Testament*, trans. Howard Clark Kee, rev. English ed. [Nashville: Abingdon, 1975], §28, pp. 416–25) and Donald Guthrie (*New Testament Introduction*, 3. rev. ed. [Downers Grove, Ill.: InterVarsity Press, 1970], pp. 771–813. See also John H. Elliott, "The Rehabilitation of an Exegetical Step-Child: 1 Peter in Recent Research," *JBL* 95 (1976): 243–54.

9. J. A. T. Robinson, *Redating the New Testament* (London: SCM Press, 1976), pp. 140–69.

10. For arguments similar to my own see Leonhard Goppelt, *Der erste Petrusbrief*, KEK 12/1; ed. Ferdinand Hahn; 1 aufl.; (Göttingen: Vandenhoeck und Ruprecht, 1978), pp. 27–30, 56–70.

11. See, most recently, Norbert Brox, "Zur pseudepigraphischen Rahmung des ersten Petrusbriefes," *Biblische Zeitschrift* 19 (1975): 78–96. On the subject of pseudepigraphy in general and related literature see especially W. Speyer, *Fälschung im heidnischen und christlichen Altertum,* Handbuch der Altertumswissenschaft I/2 (Munich: C. H. Beck'sche Verlagsbuchhandlung, 1971) and the collection of essays in *Pseudepigraphie in der heidnischen und jüdisch-christlichen Antike,* ed. Norbert Brox, Wege der Forschung 484 (Darmstadt: Wissenschaftliche Buchgesellschaft, 1977).

12. Brox's ("Pseudepigraphischen Rahmung") variation on the Pauline hypothesis is itself no more than a counsel of despair. He asserts without further ado that the names of Peter, Silvanus and Mark all belong to the "pseudepigraphic framework" of 1 Peter which was composed by "a writer who (without necessarily having known it) stood within an expressly Pauline colored tradition [and] disguised his Pauline colored theology and diction as the utterance of Peter" (p. 95, au.). The reason for this curious and surprising choice

of authors (for a supposedly Pauline document), he suggests, is that it comes from Rome (= "Babylon") which serves as "a bridge to the name Peter" (p. 96). He then concludes with an even more curious set of alternatives. "Since the author actually or fictionally wrote from Rome, he wrote under the apostolic authority of the name which through history was associated with Rome. Or: since he wanted to effectively style his composition of warning and encouragement with the name Peter, he situated it in Rome" (p. 96, au.). As Brox himself admits, such alternatives certainly do leave us "in the dark"—not only regarding the authorship of 1 Peter but concerning other implicated issues as well.

13. Norbert Brox, "Situation und Sprache der Minderheit im ersten Petrusbrief," *Kairos* 19 (1977): 1–13, esp. pp. 1–4 (including the literature pertaining to the "Unionsthese" [stemming from the Tübinger Schule] according to which 1 Peter, inter alia, represents an "unionistische Tendenz" of the early church)

14. See also Goppelt, *Der erste Petrusbrief,* pp. 47–56 and, earlier, the analysis of K. Shimada, *The Formulary Material in First Peter: A Study According to the Method of Traditionsgeschichte* (Ann Arbor, Mich.: Xerox University Microfilms, 1966). Even Horst Goldstein (*Paulinische Gemeinde im Ersten Petrusbrief,* Stuttgarter Bibelstudien 80 [Stuttgart: Katholische Bibelwerk, 1975]) who erroneously assumes 1 Peter to have been written to a "Pauline community" in Asia Minor, like Goppelt frequently notes the literary and theological features *peculiar* to 1 Peter; cf. pp. 25–33, 79–86, 99–103, 104–13.

15. The reasons (of varying degree of weight) which have been given for Rome as the most likely place of origin include the following: (1) the attestation of Papias and Clement of Alexandria (*Hypotyposes,* Book 6) in Eusebius, *H.E.* 2.15.2, cf. 3.39.15; (2) the association of Peter with Rome as the place of his last activity and death in the early Christian tradition; (3) the traditional association of Mark with Peter and thus Rome (although it is possible that this association was suggested by or based on a verse of 1 Peter itself, 5:13); (4) the similarities between 1 Peter and Romans, 1 Peter and *1 Clement,* which may be taken as reflections of tradition common to the Roman community; (5) the ecclesiological model of the household in 1 Peter as a reflection of the brotherhood form of organization in Rome; (6) the stress on mutual service, love, and hospitality in 1 Peter which were characteristics for which the Roman community was particularly renowned by the time of Ignatius (Ign. *Rom.* inscr.); (7) indications in 1 Peter of the situation in Rome around the time of the Neronian anti-Christian action; (8) the term "Babylon" taken as a symbolization of Rome as the capital of an idolatrous empire forcing its subjects into

conformity; (9) Rome would be a plausible point of origin of an encyclical letter addressed to Asia Minor, especially if the sequences of provincial names in 1 Pet: 1:1 suggested the landing point (Pontus, for one coming by ship from the west) and route of the letter-bearer; and (10) Rome, as the location, destination, and meeting place of so many early Christians, would be an obvious place for the coalescence of the variety of geographical and theological traditions represented in 1 Peter.

16. See, e.g., Eduard Lohse, "Paränese und Kerygma im 1. Petrusbrief," *ZNW* 45 (1954): 68–89, esp. pp. 83–85; Ernest Best, *1 Peter,* New Century Bible (London: Oliphants, 1971), pp. 59–65; J. H. Elliott, "The Rehabilitation of an Exegetical Stepchild: 1 Peter in Recent Research," *JBL* 95 (1976) pp. 246–48; Goppelt, *Der erste Petrusbrief,* pp. 30–37, 66–70, 345–55. Lohse and Goppelt speak of a Roman community; Best, more specifically of a "Petrine school" (ibid., p. 63). Since the term "school" might suggest an association of teachers, students and writers similar to the schools of the rabbis or the Greek philosophers, I prefer the more neutral term "circle" or Petrine "group." For a brief but welcome consideration of the phenomenon of groups within early Christianity, see Klaus Berger, *Exegese des Neuen Testaments: Neue Wege vom Text zur Auslegung* (Heidelberg: Quelle & Meyer, 1977), pp. 226–34.

17. On the "collective subject" rather than the "individual subject" as the moving force of history, including Christian history, see K. Messelken, "Zur Durchsetzung des Christentums in der Spätantike: Strukturell-funktionale Analyse eines historischen Gegenstandes," *Kölner Zeitschrift für Soziologie und Sozialpsychologie* 29 (1977): 261–94, esp. pp. 262–63. The point is an especially important one to be made among theologians and exegetes who are still viewing the New Testament according to the (individual) theology of its (individual) *Hauptfiguren.*

18. See the Gospels-Acts lists of the twelve (Matt. 10:1–4/Mark 3:13–19/Luke 6:12–16), the eleven (Acts 1:13), or the seven of John 21:2.

19. See Mark 1:36; also Luke 8:45 (variant reading), 9:32 (Peter "and those with him" refers to John and James, 9:28); Mark 16 (Conclusio brevior: " . . . to those associated with Peter"—the eleven? a larger or smaller group?); cf. Acts 13:13 ("those associated with Paul" referring to at least Barnabas and John Mark, cf. 13:2–5); cf. also Ign. *Smyrn.* 3:2 (referring to the resurrection appearance of Jesus "to those with Peter").

20. See Mark 5:37/Luke 8:51; Mark 9:2/Matt. 17:1/Luke 9:28; Mark 14:33/Matt. 26:37; Luke 5:10.

21. See Mark 1:16–20/Matt. 4:18–22; Mark 1:29; 13:3; Acts 1:13. For Peter and Andrew see John 1:40–42, 44; cf. 6:8.

22. See Luke 22:8; Acts 3:1, 3, 4, 11; 4:13, 19; 8:14. For the association of Peter "and another disciple (whom Jesus loved)" see John 18:15; 20:2, 3, 4; 21:15–23.

23. See Acts 12:1–3 (execution of James and arrest of Peter in Jerusalem by Herod Agrippa I).

24. See Gal. 2:9; cf. 1:18–19 (Cephas and James only); cf. also Acts 12:17 (report of Peter's prison escape "to James and the brothers") and Acts 15.

25. See 1 Cor. 9:5 and Acts 1:13–14; 12:17; ch. 15; Gal. 1:18–19; 2:9, 11–12; cf. Mark16:7 with Matt. 28:10 and John 20:17. Robinson (*Redating the New Testament,* p. 197) cites this data to ask whether the similarities between 2 Peter and Jude do not also suggest a personal association of Peter and Jude, the Lord's brother (or "brother of James," Jude 1).

26. See Acts 12:12–17.

27. George La Piana, in a classic essay, "Foreign Groups in Rome during the First Centuries of the Empire" (*HTR* 20 [1927]: 183–403) has described the existence, composition and activities of various distinctive groups in Rome around the time of the composition of 1 Peter. Jews also were among these groups and while the evidence indicates a community-wide coordination of decisions and activities, it fails to show the existence of any central officer (such as an ethnarch). Different groups of Jews had come from different parts of the Mediterranean world, lived in different parts of the city, practiced different trades, had their separate synagogues and so forth. On this analogy, the closest one for the early Christians in Rome, it is probable that the Christians were organized in smaller, quasi-independent groups also. One such group, independent of a Pauline group (but by no means necessarily at odds with it!) would have been the Petrine circle. As 1 Peter indicates, this group had specifically named members, an acknowledged leader and a distinctive theological, ecclesiological and social point of view.

28. For a survey of the New Testament material on the person, career and tradition associated with Simon Peter see R. E. Brown et al., *Peter in the New Testament: A Collaborative Assessment by Protestant and Roman Catholic Scholars* (Minneapolis: Augsburg and Paramus, N. J.: Paulist Press, 1973); see further the literature cited in Elliott, "1 Peter in Recent Research," p. 253, n. 58; and most recently Goppelt, *Der erste Petrusbrief,* pp. 30–37.

29. Goppelt, *Der erste Petrusbrief,* pp. 352-53 and n. 37. He also takes *hē en Babylōni syneklektē* (5:13) as a reference to the Roman community as a whole, "die mitauserwählte (Gemeinde) in Babylon" (pp. 345, 350–51) and finds the expansion *ekklēsia* in several of the Mss (‭א‬ ps vg sy^p) appropriate (*sachgemäss*). While the preferred original ellipsis (the more difficult reading "clarified" by later scribes) allows this interpretation, "sister" is a more preferable

inference. *Ekklēsia* occurs nowhere else in the document whereas "sister" fits naturally with the qualifications of Silvanus ("brother") and Mark ("son") and the designation of all the believers as brothers and sisters of one spiritual family. In either case, however, the familial character of both authors and addressees is clearly accentuated.

30. So also Goppelt, ibid., p. 345.

31. On the presbyterial form of organization in both Rome and Asia Minor see Carl Andresen, *Die Kirchen der alten Christenheit, Die Religionen der Menschheit,* ed. Christel Matthias Schröder; vol. 29, 1/2 (Stuttgart: Kohlhammer, 1971), esp. pp. 50–67; id., *Geschichte des Christentums,* vol. 1. *Von den Anfängen bis zur Hochscholastik,* Theologische Wissenschaft, vol. 6 (Stuttgart: Kohlhammer, 1975), esp. pp. 6–8; Gerd Lüdemann, "Zur Geschichte des ältesten Christentums in Rom. I. Valentin und Marcion; II. Ptolemäus und Justin," *ZNW* 70 (1979); 86–114, esp. p. 104 and n. 52. On Asia Minor see also Leonhard Goppelt, *Christentum und Judentum im ersten und zweiten Jahrhundert: Ein Aufriss der Urgeschichte der Kirche,* Beiträge zur Forderung christlicher Theologie, 2. Reihe, Band 55 (Gütersloh: C. Bertelsmann, 1954), pp. 263–67.

32. Although it cannot be asserted categorically, the coincidence of the available evidence strongly favors the identification of Silvanus with Silas, as almost all commentators concur.

33. S. G. Wilson, *The Gentiles and the Gentile Mission in Luke-Acts,* SNTS Monograph Series, 23 (Cambridge: Cambridge University Press, 1973), p. 185. For further discussion of this point see pp. 182–87.

34. Paul of course did eventually work in this province, also according to Luke; cf. Acts 18:19 and 19:22–20:38.

35. It is not necessary to enter into a discussion of the details and exegetical problems associated with this meeting and its varying accounts. For a recent appraisal (also of the earlier literature) see the work of Wilson, *The Gentiles and the Gentile Mission,* pp. 178–95.

36. Ibid., pp. 192–93.

37. According to Acts 13:13 Mark may be assumed to have been in Jerusalem at this time.

38. On the Palestinian tradition incorporated in 1 Peter see Lohse, *Paränese und Kerygma,* passim; and Goppelt, *Der erste Petrusbrief,* pp. 53–56, 67–68, 348 and passim. Goppelt states that the diversity of traditions in 1 Peter corresponds to the career and contacts of Silvanus (pp. 68, 348); but this could equally be true of all three persons named in 1 Peter.

39. For the use of *dia* plus name (genitive) to designate a letter's emissary see also Ign. *Rom.* 10:1 (*dia Ephesiōn;* N.B.: plural!); Ign. *Phil.* 11:2 and

Smyrn. 12:1 (*dia Bourrou*); cf. also Pol. *Phil* 14:1 (*per Crescentum*) and a papyrus letter (41 c.e.) in G. Milligan, *Selections from the Greek Papyri* (Cambridge: University Press, 1910), p. 39. The evidence is still indecisive, although Brox ("Pseudepigraphischen Rahmung," pp. 84–90) argues a stronger case for the emissarial alternative than Goppelt (*Der erste Petrusbrief*, p. 347) does for the activity of Silvanus as author. The existence of a "specific Silas-tradition" (Brox, ibid., p. 89), however, is neither a demonstrable nor necessary postulate. Silvanus-Silas, like Peter and presumably Mark, could have been known by his general reputation communicated by word of mouth. Intergroup oral communication and gossip accounts far more reasonably for the exchange of information in the early church than does the assumed existence of countless literary or quasi-formal "traditions."

40. Compare, e.g., (1) Peter's address of the *adelphoi* (Acts 15:7) with the dominant brotherhood image of 1 Peter; (2) God's action of election (Acts 15:7 and 1 Pet. 1:1; 2:4–10; 5:13); (3) *Peter's* proclamation of the gospel to the Gentiles and their coming to faith (Acts 15:7, 8–11; also 10:1–11:18; 1 Pet. 1:14; 2:10; 4:3 and passim on faith); (4) the Gentiles' reception of the Holy Spirit (Acts 15:8; 1 Pet. 1:2, 10–12; 4:14); (5) the impartiality of God (Acts 15:9; 1 Pet. 1:17); (6) faith as a purification of heart (Acts 15:9; 1 Pet. 1:18–19, 22–23; cf. 1:2); (7) salvation as the gift of grace (Acts 15:11; 1 Pet. 1:2, 10, 13 and passim) and object of faith (Acts 15:11; 1 Pet. 1:3–5, 10–12; 2:2; 3:21); (8) the equal status of Jewish and Gentile believers (Acts 15:8, 9, 11; 1 Pet. 2:4–10); (9) the cohesion and solidarity of the Christian movement which Peter supports in both Acts 15 and 1 Peter.

41. I wish to stress *social* as well as religious consolidation. Theological "heresy" is not an issue dealt with in 1 Peter. If *theological* consensus between Pauline and Petrine groups had been the aim of the letter, the author failed miserably in making that clear. Not only is Paul never mentioned (cf., e.g., 2 Pet. 3:15), as would have been expected of an *Unionsdokument;* the peculiar themes of Pauline theology (justification by faith alone, *freedom* from the law, etc.) are never treated or attempted to be *reconciled* with Petrine characteristics. The greatest weakness of this view of the purpose of 1 Peter, however, is its reduction of all problems to theological ones and thus its blindness to the social situation to which 1 Peter is addressed and the social strategy which it has developed.

42. For an enumeration of early contacts see Adolf von Harnack, *The Mission and Expansion of Christianity in the First Three Centuries,* trans. and ed. James Moffatt, 2 vols. (New York: Harper & Row, 1962 [reprint of 1908 ed.]), 1: 369–76.

43. S. J. Case, *The Social Origins of Christianity* (Chicago: University of

Chicago Press, 1923), pp. 162–63. For Case's observations on "The Consolidation of the Christian Movement" see pp. 161–207.

44. E. C. Colwell, "Popular Reactions against Christianity in the Roman Empire," in *Environmental Factors in Christian History,* Shirley Jackson Case FS, ed. John Thomas McNeill, M. Spinka, H. R. Willoughby (Chicago: University of Chicago Press, 1939; New York: Kennikat Press, 1970), pp. 53–71; quotation from p. 57. Colwell describes this conviction of distinctiveness as "inherited from Judaism" (p. 57). Christianity, however, "inherited" from Judaism not simply an idea of distinctiveness but also an experience of social alienation and hostile pagan reaction to which the affirmation of its distinctiveness was a response as well as a cause.

45. Ibid., p. 71.

46. W. H. C. Frend, "The Gnostic Sects and the Roman Empire," *Journal of Ecclesiastical History* 5 (1954): 25–37; quotation from p. 36.

47. Ibid.

48. Gager, Kingdom and Community, p. 140.

49. Arthur Darby Nock, *Conversion: The Old and the New in Religion from Alexander the Great to Augustine of Hippo* (New York: Oxford University Press, 1961 [1933]), pp. 210–11.

50. R. A. Nisbet, *The Social Philosophers: Community and Conflict in Western Thought* (New York: Thomas Y. Cromwell, 1973), pp. 174–81.

51. Ibid., pp. 175–76.

52. Ibid., p. 176.

53. Ibid.

54. Ibid., p. 177

55. Nisbet sees the imperial exploitation of *patria potestas* functioning in this way; see also pp. 35–43 on "The Augustan Revolution: 27 B.C."

56. Emphasis added.

57. Emphasis added.

58. Ibid., p. 177.

59. Ibid., pp. 177–78.

60. Ibid., p. 178.

61. Ibid.

62. Ibid., pp. 179–81.

Indexes

OLD TESTAMENT

APOCRYPHA AND PSEUDEPIGRAPHA

JEWISH HELLENISTIC LITERATURE

NEW TESTAMENT

EARLY CHRISTIAN LITERATURE

GREEK AND ROMAN LITERATURE

INSCRIPTIONS

MODERN AUTHORS